The Conformist Rebellion

The Conformist Rebellion

Marxist Critiques of the Contemporary Left

Edited by
Elena Louisa Lange and Joshua
Pickett-Depaolis

ROWMAN & LITTLEFIELD
Lanham • Boulder • New York • London

Published by Rowman & Littlefield
An imprint of The Rowman & Littlefield Publishing Group, Inc.
4501 Forbes Boulevard, Suite 200, Lanham, Maryland 20706
www.rowman.com
86-90 Paul Street, London EC2A 4NE

Selection and editorial matter © Elena Louisa Lange and Joshua Pickett-Depaolis, 2022
Copyright in individual chapters is held by the respective chapter authors.

All rights reserved. No part of this book may be reproduced in any form or by any electronic or mechanical means, including information storage and retrieval systems, without written permission from the publisher, except by a reviewer who may quote passages in a review.

British Library Cataloguing in Publication Information Available

Library of Congress Cataloging-in-Publication Data

Names: Lange, Elena Louisa editor. | Pickett-Depaolis, Joshua, 1988- editor.
Title: The conformist rebellion : Marxism, social movements, and the political left / edited by Elena Louisa Lange and Joshua Pickett-Depaolis.
Description: Lanham : Rowman & Littlefield, [2022] | Includes bibliographical references and index.
Identifiers: LCCN 2021060859 (print) | LCCN 2021060860 (ebook) | ISBN 9781538160152 (cloth) | ISBN 9781538160176 (paperback) | ISBN 9781538160169 (ebook)
Subjects: LCSH: Communism. | Right and left (Political science) | Capitalism.
Classification: LCC HX45 .C657 2022 (print) | LCC HX45 (ebook) | DDC 335.43—dc23/eng/20211230
LC record available at https://lccn.loc.gov/2021060859
LC ebook record available at https://lccn.loc.gov/2021060860

To Juno and Felix *(Elena Louisa Lange)*
To the undefeated in defeat *(Joshua Pickett-Depaolis)*

***

There are only two parties: those who want to conserve the current social order and those who do not want to conserve it. Everything else is nothing but a sham, a mask.
Auguste Blanqui, 1869[1]

The almost insoluble task is to not let oneself be made stupid by the power of others, nor by one's own powerlessness.
Theodor W. Adorno, 1951[2]

Without people, we don't stand the slightest chance of survival.
Thomas Bernhard, 1985[3]

NOTES

1. In Philippe Le Goff, *Auguste Blanqui and the Politics of Popular Empowerment* (London/New York: Bloomsbury, 2020), 73.
2. Theodor W. Adorno, *Minima Moralia. Reflexionen aus dem beschädigten Leben* (Frankfurt: Suhrkamp, 2003 [1951]), 63. Own translation.
3. Thomas Bernhard, *Alte Meister. Komödie* (Frankfurt: Suhrkamp, 1988 [1985]), 291. Own translation.

Contents

List of Illustrations ix

Introduction: The Conformist Rebellion of the Contemporary Left xi
Elena Louisa Lange and Joshua Pickett-Depaolis

PART I: FROM CLASS TO COMMUNITY—RACE, GENDER, AND CROSS-CLASS STRUGGLES 1

1 Antidiscrimination and the End of Marxism: The Roots of Contemporary Politics in Cold War Theory and Culture 3
Todd Cronan

2 The Dubious Wonder of Identity 25
Robert Pfaller

3 The Meaning of "Gender" in Current Debates of the Left: A Discussion between Elena Louisa Lange, Joshua Pickett-Depaolis, and Jane Clare Jones 43
Elena Louisa Lange, Joshua Pickett-Depaolis, and Jane Clare Jones

4 Mourning and Melancholia: The Millennial Left between New Left and Old Left 59
Anton Jäger

5 The Poverty of Immediacy: A Critique of the Communization Current 73
Joshua Pickett-Depaolis

PART II: THE CULTURE OF THE CONFORMIST REBELLION—CULTURE WARS, IDENTITY POLITICS, AND ART   95

6   Popular Sovereignty, Left Liberalism, and the Brexit Culture Wars   97
George Hoare

7   Dictatorship Contra Critique   113
Samir Gandesha

8   Cultural Representation: The Backlash against Woke Aesthetics as *Anti*-politics   129
Maren Thom

9   On What Art Is Not: Or Art as a Left-Wing Hobby   147
Haseeb Ahmed

PART III: ECLIPSE OF EMANCIPATION—CONFRONTING STREAMS IN THE ACADEMIC AND ACTIVIST LEFT TODAY   173

10   Racial Capitalism and Social Form   175
Nick Nesbitt

11   Is Postcolonial-Theory's Ethical Turn a Political Dead End?   201
Nivedita Majumdar

12   Growth and the Appropriation of Nature: Left-Wing Misanthropy, the Rise of Authoritarianism, and the Pro-Capitalist Character of Environmental Discourse   217
Austin Williams

13   Outside(r) Fetishisms: Pathologies of Displaced Critique   237
Raji C. Steineck

Bibliography   251

Index   277

Author Biographies   289

List of Illustrations

Figure 9.1 Detail: "Muqarnas" in "The Common Sense" 165
Figure 9.2 "Ummah HQ" 166

Introduction

The Conformist Rebellion of the Contemporary Left

Elena Louisa Lange and Joshua Pickett-Depaolis

This book aims to revive the Marxist tradition of social critique. Not "social critique" as an academic discipline to be put on a pedestal alongside disciplines like "social history" or "political philosophy," performed in liberal arts colleges, and published in peer-reviewed academic journals, or as a methodological orientation in the "positive sciences," but social critique as *Gesellschaftskritik*, as a practice of thought that views capitalist relations of production as a *totality*.

But what does *social critique* as a *critique of totality* mean today? How can capitalism's self-sustenance be explained on the basis of the complex apparatuses of political domination which serve it? And what exactly should become its object in a time of "post-" or even "*anti*-politics,"[1] when the established neoliberal order transitions to a new period of managed stagnation? Is social critique really exhausted with the rise of a now ubiquitous "progressive" social consciousness that critically addresses nationalism, racism, sexism, homophobia, transphobia, poverty in the global south, climate change, and the lackluster handling of the COVID-19 pandemic?[2] That capitalism isn't healthy, beneficial, or good seems to have become a consensus across a wide spectrum of the educated middle class, when this insight was previously limited to the "lived experience" of retail workers, agricultural day laborers, Amazon MTurk Human Intelligence taskers, and everyone else barely living off the "fruits" of their labor.

The great preoccupation of social critique in the Marxist tradition has always been its relation to the political left. This implies a preoccupation with the repeated integration of the workers' movement as a stabilizing factor within bourgeois society. Today, however, with the temporary defeat of the workers' movement, bourgeois society as the left's traditional object of *critique* has been obscured by the overwhelming dominance of a left no longer grounded in workers' struggles but grounded in middle-class paternalism. With the rise of managerial elites, experts that play their part in social engineering, and the death of politics proper—and with it, the death of the politician, replaced by social media pundits grabbing for likes and retweets in an infinite mirroring of popularity rates reflecting programmatic emptiness—this left not only acquiesces in but actively *contributes* to the self-abolition of politics proper and with it, *social emancipation* itself. It does so by merely paying lip service to, instead of consciously identifying, the core problem of the social relation that constitutes capital: *class*. It is this basic social relation that the proliferation of ever narrower cross-class interest groups, issued in convoluted acronyms,[3] catchy abbreviations, or neologisms,[4] and based on subjective consciousness of oppression, does its best to conceal.

If the self-imposed task of this volume is to view capitalism as a totality, that is, as a historically specific form of social production, and not merely as an institutionally or politically positioned entity, then the question of the relation between capitalism (a historically specific economic form-determination based on the exploitation of wage labor) and the left (an ideological position within the confines of the nation-state and its supranational articulations) is paramount to also understanding its self-sustenance, its ideological reproduction, and even its enhancement. Because "the left"—or what claims this title in the absence of an independent workers' movement—is no longer the political adversary of the social forces that reproduce and enhance "capitalist realism" and the neoliberal management it hinges on, it is often its foremost accomplice. And sometimes, it is even its beneficiary.

The thematization of this problem is the topic of this edited volume. It is the first of its kind to address the ideological, theoretical, and practical dilemmas of the contemporary academic and activist left from a decisively Marxist standpoint in the form of an edited collection. In line with this problematic, we aim to present the left with a long-overdue critical and theoretical confrontation with the myriad ways it has tended to *accommodate* itself to neoliberal ideology, and sometimes even functioned as its main *producer*, rather than fundamentally *opposing* it. By diagnosing today's most severe and devastating predicament as the increasing preemptive resistance to the independent articulation of worker interests, and the de facto abolition of class struggle, this volume assembles thirteen interventions by Marxist critics, philosophers, social historians, literary and political theorists, and cultural critics who aim to formulate opposition to the accommodation to the state project of capital performed by the left, and its disjunction from a politics in the interests of the working class.

This volume argues that the left has abandoned the project of the abolition of the capitalist relations of production. It has thus abandoned the abolition of the concrete form of specifically capitalist domination, namely *exploitation*, and replaced it with moralistic concerns about sexism, racism, ableism, homophobia, transphobia, Islamophobia, and so on, as forms of *discrimination* or *oppression, but within* the capitalist order. This shift in the discursive reality of the left, from the abolition of wage labor, and hence *capitalism itself*, to the abolition of discrimination *within capitalism*—leaving capitalist relations of production, that is, the relation between capital and labor intact—is not only not radical but shrouded in accommodation to the hegemonic ideology of capital. And while the neoliberal order seems to crumble and yet carries on—"everything is prolonging its existence by denying that it exists," as G. K. Chesterton put it[5]—it is unsurprisingly the educated class which is most committed to capital's utopia of technocracy without political antagonism. The professional middle-class cadres of the liberal center-left have become the "last standard bearers of the neoliberal package," as Hochuli/Hoare/Cunliffe have recently emphasized.[6]

We view the present "rebellion" of the left, occurring in the context of the managed stagnation, increasing mass immiseration and continued atomization of the working class, following the crisis of capitalist valorization in the "financial crash" of 2008, not as a rebellion against the liberal status quo that both produces and obscures the dubious victory of capital but as a *conformist rebellion*—a rebellion of the middle strata who function as shock troops of capitalist command over labor. As soon as the ensnarement of this progressivism with a bourgeois face and bourgeois aims[7] is pointed out by critics, however, moral condemnation and silencing is encouraged, and the critic's motivation is depicted as a direct expression of "bigotry"[8] or "fascism."[9] Accordingly, these movements often guard against criticism through the invocation of a constant state of emergency, whether this be defined as the ubiquitous "fascist creep" or an equally alarming "climate crisis," but certainly not the immiseration of the global workforce, based on specific class interests.[10] And yet, can there be said to exist an intellectual-historical trajectory that helps to understand the current domination of the toothless insurgency the left presents today?

One of the major political and cultural shifts of recent decades is the rise of new and myriad forms of identity politics. They correspond to a new "trinity formula" in the leftist analysis of capitalism—race, class, and gender.[11] Following this schema, major currents in the contemporary Left have moved away from the problematization of capital as a relation. Not only do most leftist theorists and activists conform to the neoliberal discursive structures of "gender/queer/race theory," of which "intersectional theory" remains the best-selling brand, they also reduce the analytical categories of class and the dynamic of capitalist accumulation to a subcategory of personal forms of domination. This shift, we believe, has a historical and theoretical predecessor in the New Left and the international student movement of the 1960s.

Its idiosyncratic reading of Marx's economy-critical work, prompted by an increasing incapacity to adequately address the problem of impersonal domination which constitutes capital as a relation, allowed for a misidentification of the law of value as transhistorical and neglected the significance of its monetary dimension. Much of the left has therefore been unable to overcome the naturalisms, or, in Marx's idiom, the *fetishisms* of bourgeois political economy, and adequately grasp the basic dynamic of capitalist domination, the reproduction of the wage relation, and hence the worldwide articulation of impersonal capitalist supremacy. Radicals increasingly focused on more "concrete" and "personal" forms of power—napalm bombings and warfare, colonialism, the patriarchy, racial segregation—and thereby obscured the constitutive dynamic of modern society, regressing to a pre-Marxist critique of "injustice." Seeing the latter as the main engine of capitalist relations allowed for a convenient suppression of the question of impersonal power— a more unsettling matter. The result was a striking inability to organize an adequate response to the challenge of capital as a social relation, a failure which still impacts us today.

The positivist approach to capitalist relations of production taken by today's left has largely capitulated to an understanding of capital not as a totality but rather as an "assemblage" of "individual" sets of oppression that can be addressed as "parts of a whole feeding into each other," and in which every social relation counts as equally significant. This is reflected in the regressive trend toward identity, that is, cultural, ethnic, or "gendered" communalism, the fetishization of which has not only stifled Marx's critique of capital as a critique of *class society* but brought us a fantastic new repertoire of ever new forms of horizontal oppression, as is manifest in terms like "microaggression,"[12] the administered call for "diversity," and a whole dictionary of terms reacting to specific cultural sensitivities that serve the neoliberal need to atomize individuals based on their real or imagined identities.[13] The left's moralistic and epistemologically flawed logic is based on oppression's alleged *ubiquity*, thereby *obscuring* the particular insight of Marx's critique: the problem of unequal exchange between capital and labor on the basis of the formal validity of equivalent exchange. It is *wage labor* that comprises the historically specific essence of capitalist *exploitation*. Exploitation through wage labor is the sine qua non of the *general and universal* social mediation under the rule of value. To view "oppression" as central to today's social challenges thereby contributes to their mystification.

But here lies an important terminological, and therefore factual, *failed distinction* in leftist theorizing today—the distinction between oppression and exploitation. Their difference, as crucial as it is to theorizing structures of domination, is almost everywhere disregarded or conflated. While in feudal societies rents in labor, means of subsistence, and money depend on direct personal oppression to consolidate an "exploitative" praxis, exploitation in its full sense necessitates the *wage form*. Its economic specificity consists in its appearance as *paid labor*, that is, as something that represents the monetary equivalent to the *whole working day*—and not just its "necessary" part. What therefore appears as equal exchange—in line with "freedom" and "equality" as the signifiers of liberal bourgeois society—is, in fact, unequal exchange. The whole allure of bourgeois society consists in the fact that inequality *appears as* equality, unfreedom *as* freedom—as "equal market participation."

Oppression, on the other hand, is less specific. It demands the existence of one (or many) personal oppressor(s) and the oppressed, be they economically or otherwise defined. Because, for example, slaves do not receive a wage for their labor, they are victims of oppression—but not of exploitation. There is nothing more "taken away" from them than apparent to oppressors and oppressed: in most cases, some would say, their humanity. And yet, it is precisely because slaves are deprived of their humanity that they are not exploited, for they cannot even enter a "free and equal contract" with their employer—they are not even treated *as though they were* equals. In pre-capitalist class societies, relations of personal domination and oppression were inextricable from the specific forms of extraction of surplus from the immediate producers, which defined the dynamic of these societies. Under capitalism, on the other hand, although oppression may politically facilitate the maximum extraction of the surplus, the relation itself is defined by formal freedom and equality. The critique of oppression and the demand for equality is not a Marxist critique of bourgeois society but a liberal or Jacobin aspiration for its full realization.

By relocating its "area of intervention" away from exploitation toward individually and morally motivated forms of the critique of oppression, thus discarding Marx's analysis, the contemporary left internalizes a methodology which neoliberalism itself has propagated to erode worker resistance worldwide.[14] The contrast between the Marxian emancipatory project and its caricature in the progressive left today has never been more glaring than now, a time in which capital no longer seems to confront a political barrier.

To understand this predicament, in the following we shall identify a central logical and systematic flaw within the leftist discursive framework—a flaw whose *function* Marx had already identified in the bourgeois economists. We call this operative flaw in the contemporary left the "Trinity Formula" of "race, class, and gender." How it *produces*, rather than deconstructs, the mystification of the capital relation (the relation between capital and wage labor) shall be elaborated next. To show how the Trinity Formula of "race, class, and gender" is implemented and activated in the theoretical production of the left, we will, first, briefly discuss some symptomatic arguments for that tendency in some representative theorizations of the academic and activist left today.

Second, within that tendency, we shall highlight the more specific and yet decisive role of intersectionality as a weapon against universal emancipation on the basis of class politics, which functions to stifle critique and solidarity through an omnipresent moral blackmail. Third, we will summarize the contributions included in this volume, which, while different in specific interest and scope, present both a panorama and critique of a left which is compelled to vacillate between the one-sided affirmation and negation of bourgeois society and its mystified self-image. This systematic critique, we argue, is the precondition to confront the left with its shortcomings and resuscitate the centrality of the *overcoming* of bourgeois society.

THE TRINITY FORMULA AND SO-CALLED CLASS REDUCTIONISM

Building on that broader intent, the return to the critique of political economy itself, and therefore the conscious abandonment of its culturalist distortions, is key. The "Trinity Formula" of race, class, and gender, implying a "conceptual autonomy" of race and gender and allegedly "widening" the "narrow lens" of class, not only functions to mystify the wage relation itself. Its *function* in the twenty-first century is strikingly similar to the function of the "Trinity Formula" in eighteenth- and nineteenth-century classical bourgeois economy (the "three sources of revenue" in Adam Smith's terminology): namely, to obscure the wage relation as the central mechanism of capitalist society.

According to Smith, the wealth of a nation is composed of and yields the revenues paid by labor (wages), capital (profit), and land (rent): "Wages, profit, and rent, are the three original sources of all revenue as well as of all exchangeable value. All other revenue is ultimately derived from some one or other of these."[15] Smith's conceptualization of "natural price," resolving into the price of labor, capital, and land (i.e., wages, profit, and rent), has given the foundation to the (Sayian) theory of the "factors of production"—the "Trinity Formula" in Marx's dictum—which no longer sees human labor as the sole source of value.

The groundwork to refute the first supposition, namely that labor "yields" wages, has been provided by Marx in *Capital* Volume I[16] and elaborated in Volume II: for labor, as the sole source of value, does not only reproduce the value of the commodity labor power, it produces the total value of the whole annual product of circulating commodities, including the money value, which turns the surplus product into profit, a profit "that costs the capitalist class nothing."[17] Marx's critique of Smith and Ricardo's distorted view, which limits labor to yielding wages, and not capitalist profit as well—the latter being labor's primary function in capitalist societies—forms the basis for demystifying the fetishistic illusion that it is *only one among many forms* of social wealth. For Marx, abstract human labor is the only source of wealth in its specifically capitalist form. In his critique of Smith's Trinity Formula, adapted by Ricardo and later vulgar economists as predecessors of neoclassical marginalism, Marx impressively demonstrates how the notion of capital yielding profit (including interest and profit of enterprise), and the notion of land yielding rent, is a fetishism based on the naturalization of the social form specific to capital, in which social production is stripped of its particular form as the exploitation of wage labor. Marx's critique of the theory of the "three sources of revenue" precisely demonstrates its *heteronomy*, a heteronomy that serves to obscure the real source of profit. He comments that "the ostensible sources of the wealth annually available belong to completely disparate spheres and have not the slightest analogy with one another. Their mutual relationship is like that of lawyer's fees, beetroot and music."[18] But the conceptual muddling of these "completely disparate spheres," culminating in an apologia for capitalist social relations—as though capitalists and landowners contributed to social wealth as workers did (and in equal parts at that!)—originated in their "bourgeois consciousness," which was unable to clearly identify the sources of profits, interest, and rent as forms of value. It therefore mystified the source of value in the exploitation of wage labor.

We argue that the mystification of the relation between wage labor and capital performed by the bourgeois political economists is reproduced in the theoretical writings of the left today. In systematizing our approach, we identify this mystification as the hegemonic trend in the contemporary left. This is not only obvious from the elaborations of Marxism-feminism, especially its "Social Reproduction Theory"-variant[19] and the exponents of "racial capitalism," such as Cedric Robinson,[20] Robin Kelley, Olúfémi O. Táíwò and Liam Kofi Bright, Charlie Post, Nikhil Pal Singh, and others. The problem goes deeper and does not concern a particular misunderstanding—it is grounded in a resentment against Marx's entire mode of social analysis: the primacy of the class relation.

Nowhere is this clearer than in the alleged "refutations" of so-called class reductionism. As Ashley Bohrer, author of *Marxism and Intersectionality: Race, Gender, Class and Sexuality Under Contemporary Capitalism* and an apt representative of contemporary leftism deeply in conflict with Marx's critique, says, "Class reductionist Marxism isn't compatible with intersectionality just as liberal reform-oriented intersectionality isn't compatible with revolutionary social reproduction Marxism."[21] The faux radicalism of this view is grounded in an empiricist resentment against the abstraction required to identify the capital relation itself as a *problem*. Bohrer continues,

But the actual historical arrangement of capitalism isn't like that—it's vast, varied, and uneven. Capitalism is variable and changeable, it's plastic and responsive to various conditions. I think sometimes when we attempt to whittle away all of that diversity and complexity in order to have the most "elegant" theory or one most easily digested in a sound-bite, we lose many of the ways that capitalism is and has always been a differentiated system.[22]

Class is not the defining social form of capitalism as a historical society and therefore the condition for it to become an object of critique but simply one among many superficially apparent "facts," says the Marxist scholar today.

Asad Haider's rejection of class reductionism, as formulated following the exclusion of political scientist Adolph Reed Jr. from a DSA-hosted event in June 2020 for "ignoring race," is—at first sight—more substantial. In his appeal for a de facto primacy of cross-class democratic struggles, Haider argues that both the "'class-' and the 'race reductionism'" argument "go nowhere," for they underestimate the power of positive change both worker and anti-racist struggles have produced. He further stresses that, just as official anti-racism may serve elite interests, workerism, that is, "the demands and struggles of essential workers," may not be incompatible with capitalism.[23] This analogy, however, is inaccurate: the latter threatens profit margins and hence extended reproduction of capital. Its inherent dynamic points toward the overcoming of capital. Worker struggle can only be rendered compatible with capital through the sacrifice of workers' interests. Anti-racism, however, is by definition the struggle for equal treatment *within* the relation of exploitation. However much it might destabilize historically contingent relations of oppression, it can only assist in the naturalization of the wage relation itself. In a society already defined by democratic equality and the universality of free wage labor, such as the United States, anti-racism becomes a politics of lip service, symbolism, empty gestures, and bribery of elite brokers. In that sense, while "establishment Democrats . . . taking a knee" does indeed indicate that "significant social changes have taken place," as Haider argues, these "social changes" occur on the level of the ideology of the exploiting class and of a redistribution of resources and opportunities to elements of the middle class subject to racial oppression. The quantitative balance (let alone qualitative content) of the relation between the exploiting class and the exploited does not change *in the slightest*. To avoid revealing to itself the class interests it serves in the name of the universal, anti-racism is compelled to regress to idealism. Accordingly, while Haider appeals to scrutiny regarding the "underlying property relations of capitalism," a materialist (and worthwhile) claim, he cannot implement the same for "race." The materialist analysis, which presumably Haider, a good Althusserian, considers crucial, becomes vague when "racial capitalism" (a term he is quick to denounce) or "race" enters view. When Reed, according to Haider, posits "class politics as a self-sufficient alternative to anti-racism, it flattens the real contradictions and challenges of class organisation." But what does the "flattening"—another term for "reducing"—consist in, and how can it be avoided? What are the "real contradictions and challenges" to class organization—which, according to Haider, cannot be addressed by a rigorous working-class internationalism that finds its objective base in the shared position of workers as workers within capitalist production relations? Haider cannot answer this and remains in the tautological realm of explaining the "social construction" of race by "race" being a social construction. As Haider, arguing that "material relations" cause racial discrimination at the level of ideology, says, "However, this conscious prejudice [racism] isn't the cause, but the effect of the material relations which secrete ideology." But if these "material relations" are not produced by the capital relation, which class politics—and class politics alone—could address, they must be produced by racism. Racism, however, is never the *motive* for exploitation—surplus value is.

How, then, does Haider explain "race"? "Race" is ultimately understood as a construct *based on* material disparities—but it does not itself *have* a material reality. "Race," according to Haider, is an "ideology." But even if we grant that "race" has a material basis, can the "racism-tautology" be avoided if we replace the biological with a "socially constructed" view of "race"? In other words, if "race" is just a social construct, then why insist on its material and social *objectivity*? The problem seems to be that he and other "social constructivists" are ready to reject a biological (or even "cultural") use of "race" but invite the same ontologizations through the back door when they insist on its "material objectivity," no matter how "socially constructed" it is. Accordingly, the talk of "race" as "ideology" becomes disingenuous, because Haider—who would not call "class" an ideology—contrary to his claim treats race as though it were *objectively given*.

Yet, despite the fallacies, tautologies, and lack of methodological grounding of this approach, the hypostatization of a trinity of race (and gender) *separate from and equal to* class, just like the Trinity Formula of classical political economy, successfully contributes to the mystification of class in the current debate.

Rejecting the racialism implied in Haider's argument, however, does not mean that Reed Jr.'s insistence of a "Myth of Class Reductionism" is more to the point, even if his statement may be empirically true. That is, while it may be correct to assert that "no reputable voices on the left seriously argue that racism, sexism, homophobia, and xenophobia are not attitudes and ideologies that persist and cause harm,"[24] the challenge exists elsewhere. The challenge of "class reductionism," and with it, the widespread resentment against "economism," the alleged "narrowing down" of capitalism's "complex logic," and the often-heard "reduction of the manifold aspects of human life to questions of economic survival," exists on an entirely different level of debate: it consists in comprehending the *reduction* of human lives under capitalist relations of production to their *class position*. Moneyed wage dependency is not a "hypothesis" in the mind of a theorist (Marx included!) but a *real abstraction*. In the words of Frankfurt School theorist Alfred Schmidt, "The one-sidedness idealistically lamented as 'economism' . . . is an abstraction not performed by the theorist, but by social reality."[25] "Class reductionism" is a different name for the reduction of human lives to their *monetary* value. It is practically demonstrated in the fact that the majority of people on the planet in their daily lives *depend on a monetary wage to exist*. Wage laborers depend on *quantified time*—a wage socially reproduced under laws of competition—of which the direct expression is *money*.

It is indeed remarkable how little wage and money dependency as structuring the very possibilities of participation in social life is put in question in the "critical" writings of the left today.

USE VALUE FETISHISM AND "NEORACIALISM"

This disregard for the problem of monetary wage dependency in people's daily lives is eminent in another prominent academic Marxist, Jason W. Moore. His *Capitalism in the Web of Life* (2015) and his ensuing edited volume *Anthropocene or Capitalocene?* (2016) are both equally reluctant to address the systematic foundation of the capital relation. "Drawing on environmentalist, feminist, and Marxist thought,"[26] as his publisher declares, and rushing to broaden the "race, class, gender"–trinity to include "sexuality" and the "nation," Moore dutifully obeys the current paradigm of leftist discourse. His theoretical interest lies in uncovering the "Capitalocene's" impact on global life and how "cheap nature" has been put to work for the benefit of capital. Within it, Humanity and Nature (Moore uses capital letters to emphasize their ideological nature) play a significant role: "Backed by imperial power and capitalist rationality, it mobilized the unpaid work and energy of humans—especially women, especially the enslaved—in service to transforming landscapes with a singular purpose: the endless accumulation of capital."[27] But caution is recommended where Moore speaks of "unpaid labor" —for at no point does it even occur to him *that wage labor is also unpaid labor* for the greater part of the working day. He conceptually limits "unpaid labor" to the labor of women, "the enslaved," and the "labor" of nature, which not only introduces the naturalization of labor and the anthropomorphizing of nature—the classic criteria for what Marx calls the fetishism of bourgeois relations of production—but thus presents an argument burdened with an array of faulty premises, of which his reifying and fetishistic approach to "women," "the enslaved," and "nature"—a fetishism that ironically reproduces the "Eurocentrism" Moore understands his work as an intervention against—may be the most egregious. The tacit premise of Moore's theorizing lies in elevating the status of the "concrete" against the "abstract," the "immediate" against mediation, the "individual" against the universal, the "natural" against the socially processed, "women" against men, and "non-Whites" against White "Humanity." All of these oppositions ironically presuppose a morally charged dualism of good/desirable and bad/undesirable that both facilitates and lends an "aura" to categorizations based on trivial logic. In Marxist critical theory and in Marx himself,[28] this procedure is known as the fetishism or apotheosis of *use value against value*, which has become a pervasive symptom of so much academic writing on the left today, including Moore's. This dualistic implication of use value against value, implying a moral supremacy of the former over the latter, misrecognizes the *really existing abstraction* that the law of value imposes on all social relations under capital. It therefore disregards the fact that the question of "value" as an *economic form-determination* completely transcends the moralistic dualisms implied by the "more desirable" framework of use value. The hypostatizations of use value against value also contradict Moore's own rejection of the "Cartesian dualism" (subject/object, mind/matter) allegedly responsible for nature's subordination to (White, heterosexual, male) Humanity: Moore himself constantly implies, although he is not aware of it, dualistic schemes.[29] His partiality to irrationalism and his schism between method and analysis notwithstanding, Moore's intervention culminates in a romantic and morally charged idealism that puts the exploitation of "cheap nature" of women's labor, slave labor, nature's labor at its center and thus not only has nothing to do with Marx's analysis but perverts its critical aims to the point of unrecognizability: for Moore, capitalism is an economic system that essentially relies on all kinds of social relations—"inequality, commodification, imperialism, patriarchy," as Moore puts it,[30] *except wage labor*. Because he, though he is by no means alone in his error,[31] does not grasp the capital relation as constituted by the wage relation—he vaguely refers to a "cash nexus" whose fundamental significance entirely escapes him—he sneers at money as the defining feature of capitalist socialization: "Most people—and most scholars—still think about capitalism as matter of 'economics.' Markets, prices, money, and all that is not necessarily the most exciting thing to think about," he laconically asserts.[32] This implies the disavowal of wage dependency as the *really existing* reduction of humans to their class position within the capital relation. Just how capital *becomes capital*, and as such, an object of social cognition, is completely outside of Moore's theoretical scope. One of Marx's contemporaries, the vulgar economist Frédéric Bastiat (1801–1850) had a similar contempt for understanding the centrality of the wage as a form of value, which prompted Marx to comment,

> One can therefore conclude from this what an F. Bastiat understands of the essence of capitalist production when he declares the wage system to be a formality, external to capitalist production and irrelevant to it, and makes the discovery "that it is not the form of the remuneration which creates this dependence for him (for the worker)."[33]

In his "On Race, Violence, and So-Called Primitive Accumulation" (2016), Nikhil Pal Singh exhibits a similar disinterestedness in the capital relation based on wage labor and conflates race with class *verbatim*:

> In no period has racial domination not been woven into the management of capitalist society. . . . Exploitation and the constitution of an objective order of market dependency, not direct racial violence and domination, are thought to be [*sic*] continuously reproductive of capitalist relations of production. But if land, labor, and money are fictitious commodities that comprise foundations of capitalism, they also constitute what Patrick Wolfe has called the "elementary structures" of race.[34]

Unfortunately, because the race/class-coincidence can as little be demonstrated as the coincidence of beetroot and music, Singh, like other exponents of the neoracialist view of capitalism, cannot prove his claim. Hence, arguments in this line of thought—though we must mention the literature in the field of Marxism-feminism and "gendered exploitation" with it—always remain on the level of an *assertion*: "[Racial] capitalism is retained as an integral part of capitalism's ongoing expansion"; " the reproduction of capitalism daily hides the social character of necessary gendered exploitation."[35] But as soon as we ask "how?," the evidence is missing.[36] Assertions appealing to the moral conscience of the reader function as stand-ins for the actual analysis. They take place within an idealist horizon of a litany of forms of oppression that demonstratively withdraw from the terrain of the capital relation.

INTERSECTIONALITY'S REJECTION OF SOLIDARITY

Unlike the elaborated theoretical interventions mentioned earlier, but nonetheless representative of much theorizing on the left today, the contribution of the Combahee River Collective's (CRC) "Black Feminist Statement," an early manifesto for identity politics, what in Kimberlé Williams Crenshaw's work (1991)[37] became the theory of "intersectionality," and its reappraisal in the work of Keeanga-Yamahtta Taylor (2016 and 2017),[38] strikes one as a particularly crude example of racial paternalism in the guise of social justice. The CRC, founded in 1974 by Black lesbian and straight women, was "committed to struggling against racial, sexual, heterosexual, and class oppression" and saw its "particular task" in the "development of integrated analysis and practice based upon the fact that major systems of oppression are interlocking."[39] Central to the CRC's claims is the focus on the "multilayered texture of black women's lives," which already signifies a departure from socioeconomic analysis toward "inwardness" and prefigures the neoliberal logic of self-care. In Taylor's words, elucidating the work of the CRC, "Black women's experiences cannot be reduced to either race or gender, but have to be understood on their own terms,"[40] a claim she counterfactually insists "is not a concession to 'political correctness' or 'identity politics.'" Hardening the evidence for cognitive dissonance in Taylor's argument, this statement is followed by the plea to "validate the particular experiences of Black women in our society while also measuring exactly the levels of oppression, inequality, and exploitation experienced in African-American communities."[41]

Again, for Taylor, this has allegedly nothing to do with "identity politics." But, *what else but an exact expression of identity politics* such an "exact measure" of "levels of oppression" that allegedly validates "the particular experiences of Black women" would be, remains in the dark.

The CRC statement narrates the members' disillusionment with conventional liberation movements in the 1960s and 1970s—civil rights, Black nationalism, and Black Panthers—as a rejection of solidarity with other groups based on their *identity*. Solidarity with White women is allegedly impossible because of their racism, and solidarity with Black and White men impossible because of their sexism[42]—although in a later passage, the authors resort to a rhetorical move where race trumps sex, so that Black men can be made "allies" based on the color of their skin, while White men and women are signified by the "negative solidarity" of being "racial oppressors."[43] Surprisingly, between passages of glaring racial essentialism and chauvinism of this kind, one can find a small nod to the "socialist" project:

> We are socialists because we believe the work must be organized for the collective benefit of those who do the work and create the products and not for the profit of the bosses. Material resources must be equally distributed among those who create these resources,

only to be followed by a strong disclaimer: "We are not convinced, however, that a socialist revolution that is not also a feminist and antiracist revolution will guarantee our liberation."⁴⁴ But it is clear from the structure of the CRC's argument that not despite but, rather, *because of* its nod to "class oppression," the authors have a concept of neither capital nor class. "Class" is simply understood as a mode of *discrimination*. In the CRC's statement, there is not a word on relations of production, on the relation between capital and labor as inherently contradictory, and hence, not a word about exploitation. In fact, a theory where exploitation is no longer thematic, where the enabling mechanism of specifically capitalist relations of production falls out of the picture, where the clear identification of the structure of domination and power is rejected, lends itself to acquiescence with social reality as it is. From the CRC statement, as well as Taylor's 2017 reappraisal, there emerges a deep agreement with capitalist relations of production *as they are*. There is not the slightest interest in fundamentally questioning property relations. Their intervention is limited to modes of discrimination *within the capitalist social order*. This is also reflected in the CRC's relation to Marx: for their agreement with Marx's theory is conditioned on the premise that it "must be extended further . . . to understand our specific economic situation as black women"—when this "extension" is never arrived at, because the CRC's project, as well as the project of "intersectionality," is inherently *anti*-Marxist. In addition, unlike the neoracialist insistence on the "unitary" structure of class exploitation and racial oppression, the CRC and its acolytes simply strip the notion of class of any economic content. Class becomes a mode of *oppression* or *discrimination*, like gender or race. It is retained in the framework of "classism," the only form of "class oppression" the CRC knows. It views membership in the proletariat as an identity that should be respected and viewed with appropriate decorum. It is, after all, about "empowerment." Accordingly, the contradiction between capital and labor is falsely reproduced in the more "tangible," "immediate," and "concrete" dissonances between Black and White people, women, and men. The tone of the statement, unaware of the false dichotomies it reproduces, suggests pseudo-concreteness, while at the same time remaining defensive and vague. This is spectacularly illustrated in the passages that refer to the project of "consciousness-raising" as a political strategy, which resists any materialist logic.⁴⁵

As Mike Macnair emphasizes with regard to the shared logic of the People's Front policy of the 1934 Seventh Congress of the Comintern, the CPUSA in the 1930s–1960s, and the CRC, the aim of all three is twofold: to undermine solidarity—a solidarity with workers-qua-workers, which their strategy "renders impossible"⁴⁶—and to obscure domination. Macnair observes in an apt characterization of the left's conformist rebellion, summed up in its most strikingly regressive manifestation of intersectionality, [intersectionalism] can be called the "highest stage" of western Stalinism because it carries the popular-frontist project to the point of erasing the significance of the *ruling* class as a class; it also becomes a justification not merely for *party* self-censorship, but for *generalised* censorship regimes in the names of "no platforming," "safe spaces," and so on; and it logically implies the actual liquidation of any independent workers' or communist party into liberalism (as happened in Britain and Italy in the 1990s); so that by fully adopting intersectionalism, Stalinism disappears as such into a (more repressive) form of liberalism.[47]

In leftist identity politics and intersectionality theory, the mystification of the capital relation is complete.

THE FALSE CONTRADICTION BETWEEN THE REJECTION AND THE AFFIRMATION OF BOURGEOIS EMANCIPATION

If the postmodern identitarian iteration of the Trinity Formula forms the most obvious and pervasive manifestation of the conformist rebellion of leftism, which this collection takes as its object of critique, the phenomenon itself has deeper roots. The premise for the almost universal acceptance of the Trinity Formula is an intellectual culture of empiricism, positivism, and even vitalist irrationality,[48] which prides itself in taking appearance for essence. This intellectual culture undergirds not only the technocratic jargon of the left liberal elite but also the "healthy common sense," to which its populist nemesis appeals.

Since the physical destruction of both critical Marxist *theorists* and critical Marxist *theory*, engineered by the Stalinist reaction of the 1930s, and with redoubled intensity in the aftermath of 1989, the historically determined totality of capital has been free to naturalize itself. Even the substantive modification of the balance of power within the wage relation in favor of labor has faded into the mists of utopia. The abolition of the relation itself now appears as an esoteric fantasy. The critique of the historically specific form of the social totality and the elucidation of its irreducible, yet unfulfilled, emancipatory potential has become the preserve of marginal sects and isolated critics.

In such an environment, where the monetary form of social mediation appears as definitionally equivalent to the socialization of labor itself, the dissatisfied are left with two options: either to demand that the society of universal exchange conform to its own mystified self-image and salute the accelerating or already accomplished decomposition of archaic forms of oppression as the *telos* of freedom itself or to mourn the socialization of labor as the loss of primitive immediacy. Marx already identified this sterile alternative as that between liberalism and romanticism.[49] In the absence of a critique of capitalism as a *totality*, which sees the universality of the exchange relation as the necessary basis of a universal community that remains qualitatively distinct from the former,[50] intellectual engagement is left to drift helplessly between these complementary and mutually reinforcing poles.

It is this dynamic which forms the constitutive internal contradiction of the conformist rebellion taken in the broadest terms. If the neoliberal left inclines to the first with its aspiration toward a borderless world of atomized individuals who find a freedom without security in limitless fluidity, its "postliberal"[51] conservative and reactionary critics seek refuge from the ravages of the global market in the comforting arms of the second. Meanwhile, on the furthest fringes of contemporary thought, those who recoil in horror from the social totality constituted by exchange value indulge in nightmarish fantasies of a rupture in the socialization of labor in general and a return to primitive barbarism.[52]

If at the origins of modern bourgeois society Hegel confidently asserted that reality was rational,[53] intellectuals in the period of its decline either celebrate or denounce its superficial appearance. In either case, physical constants are equated to historically mutable social forms, and a comprehension of the *total dynamic* of the social whole is rejected in favor of an empirical catalogue of "facts." These facts, however, more resemble the jumble of occurrences assembled by medieval chroniclers than the systematic understanding of the logic of the process—a logic which today would be stigmatized as "dogmatic" or "mystical" from the standpoint of the prevailing empiricist approach. The postmodern rendition of the Trinity Formula is only one of many symptoms of a comprehensive regression in the capacity of the present to understand the historical process.

LIBERATION FROM OPPRESSION AS THE HORIZON OF PETTY BOURGEOIS DEMOCRACY

If at the end of the nineteenth-century Engels could repeatedly observe to Bernstein (much to the distress of the latter) that "we are not democrats,"[54] and at the same time enthusiastically support every forward advance of bourgeois democracy[55] as a step toward its own abolition,[56] today's left is incapable of such dialectical thought-praxis. For the partisans of the Trinity Formula, from the most blandly technocratic policy wonks to the most nihilistic connoisseurs of riot tourism, every social ill is first and foremost to be blamed on sexism, racism, fascism, patriarchy, colonialism, in short, everything other than the normal operations of the bourgeois democratic regime of abstract equality.

In their drive to avoid the real contradictions of the present, they erase the incredible social progress of recent times. Unlike our forebears of a century ago, we live in a world where national self-determination and equality under the law are taken as global norms. The long arc of national liberation struggles from Indo-China to Zimbabwe played a crucial role in this unprecedented historical advance, which had its basis in the global spread of capitalist relations of production.

Today we deal with the results of a century of struggle against colonialism and racial discrimination. And what are they? Unfettered capitalism and the most ruthless possible exploitation and repression of the working class.[57] This would have come as no surprise to Marx or Lenin, who enthusiastically supported democracy and national liberation precisely because they provided the framework for the furthest possible development of capitalist exploitation and, by extension, of the possibility of its overthrow. For the contemporary left however, which has long forgotten the communist critique of universal democracy as the political expression of the universalization of the commodity form, such an outcome is incomprehensible.

As a result, we find ourselves in a topsy-turvy world, where a nominally Marxist left stigmatizes the critique of democracy as "reactionary." At the same time, the real movement of history has transformed democracy itself from the preeminent banner of struggle against absolutism and colonialism into the main bulwark of reaction. If yesterday democracy and self-determination were indispensable battering rams against the divine right of kings and the White man's burden, today they stand exposed as the perennial rallying cry of a new absolutism come into its own. This is the impersonal absolutism of capital, which liberates the citizen as an individual by enslaving her insofar as she belongs to a class.[58]

An illustrative example of the willful blindness of the identitarian left to the actuality of democracy is the identification of police violence and mass incarceration directed against the working class in the United States as primarily a legacy of chattel slavery.[59] In reality, both a professional police and large-scale incarceration were absent from the semifeudal backwardness of the slave states.[60] The modern professional police emerged first of all from the need to discipline free wage labor[61] and has remained a characteristic component of the democratic state ever since. The victims of police sadism so relentlessly instrumentalized in recent American political discourse are killed not by any anomalous legacy of personal domination[62] but by the normal operations of the modern regime of democratic equality. It is a regime in which, as Marx observed, the worker as a *human person* is objectively worthless.[63]

In our epoch, the most barbaric acts of plunder from the breakup of Yugoslavia to the invasion of Iraq are always justified with reference to democracy and self-determination, which forms the indispensable juridical-ideological packaging[64] for the most refined and flexible forms of the exploitation of labor power. The long twilight of capitalist stagnation is a morbid festival of democracy, freedom, and the rights of man. Those who are still loyal to reason and Enlightenment need democratic freedom like "light and air,"[65] precisely to freely critique the democratic order itself.

OUTLINE OF THE VOLUME

The above should illustrate our position in the current moment, while at the same time situating the program and aims of the present volume. Although the contributors and indeed the authors of this introduction reserve many disagreements on the way forward, they find unity in recognizing the necessity for a ruthless criticism of the present: a task whose abdication by the self-styled critical intelligentsia is the common target of the texts which this volume assembles.

Part I, "From Class to Community—Race, Gender, and Cross-Class Struggles," carries out a critical engagement with the shift from a discourse of universal emancipation premised in worker centrality toward a "communitarian sensibility." The latter, we believe, oscillates between a liberal critique of discrimination and regressive fantasies of destruction, perceived as liberation. Todd Cronan's chapter "Antidiscrimination and the End of Marxism—the Roots of Contemporary Politics in Cold War Theory and Culture" (chapter 1) situates the roots of contemporary liberal identity politics in Cold War liberal anti-communism, both in its theoretical and cultural artifacts. Philosopher Robert Pfaller's "The Dubious Wonder of Identity" (chapter 2) interrogates how the subjective insecurities generated by the realization of the very regime of economic equality provide the raw material for today's "gender trouble." In chapter 3, our discussion with feminist philosopher Jane Clare Jones further engages with the dynamics at the root of contemporary conflicts over gender and sexuality and the limitations of feminist and trans politics. The two closing chapters of this section, chapters 4 and 5, reflect, first, on the unresolved contradictions of a millennial left not quite able to renew class politics in an era of atomization in Anton Jäger's "Mourning and Melancholia—The Millennial Left between New Left and Old Left" (chapter 4) and, second, on the communization current as an artful effort to evade the same problem in Joshua Pickett-Depaolis's contribution "The Poverty of Immediacy—a Critique of the Communization Current" (chapter 5).

Part II, "The Culture of the Conformist Rebellion—Culture Wars, Identity Politics, and Art," examines how the turn away from the working class as historical subject has impacted cultural expression, from academia and art to the framing of political debate. Chapter 6, "Popular Sovereignty, Left Liberalism, and the Brexit Culture Wars," has George Hoare documenting how left liberalism sees the workers as not only victims of discrimination but a "dangerous class," whose failures to capitulate to technocratic management puts popular sovereignty into question. In "Dictatorship Contra Critique" (chapter 7), Samir Gandesha, using examples from recent debates in the art world, investigates the contradictions of a left liberal anti-fascism which in its hostility to critical reason comes to increasingly mirror what it aspires to oppose. Film critic Maren Thom's investigation "Cultural Representation— the Backlash against Woke Aesthetics as *Anti*-politics" explores the reduction of the critique of popular culture to the demand for representation, and the artist Haseeb Ahmed reflects on the impact of the left's increasing disinterestedness in the problem of (artistic and political) freedom on art and art's possibilities (chapter 9: "On What Art Is Not, or: Art as a Left-Wing Hobby").

Part III, "Eclipse of Emancipation—Confronting Streams in the Left Today," explores how the retreat from class has restricted the capacity for a critical understanding of the social whole by removing its necessary starting point. In chapter 10, Nick Nesbitt subjects both Anglophone and Francophone critiques of racial slavery to a Marxist interrogation, which elucidates their empiricist and idealist limitations ("Racial Capitalism and Social Form"). In her chapter, "Is Postcolonial Theory's Ethical Turn a Political Dead End?" (chapter 11), Nivedita Majumdar examines how postcolonial theory has detached Gramsci's concept of subalternity from its structural framework and reduced it to a subjective individualism in the process. The last two chapters, chapters 12 and 13, deal with another leftist preoccupation: the environment and revolutionism in the time of regression and counterrevolution. In his "Growth and the Appropriation of Nature: Left-Wing Misanthropy, the Rise of Authoritarianism, and the Pro-Capitalist Character of Environmental Discourse" (chapter 12), Austin Williams investigates how middle-class green politics functions as a managerial modality of capitalist stagnation. And in the final chapter of this section and the volume as a whole, "Outside(r) Fetishisms: Pathologies of Displaced Critique," Raji C. Steineck examines how the loss of faith in the transformation of capital from *within* has resulted in regressive hopes of a "liberation" from *without*.

In a moment where the crisis tendency of capital is accentuated by the impact of the COVID-19 pandemic upon systematically underfunded health care systems and the intensified biopolitical police control of society imposed in response, the need for a "party of extreme opposition,"[66] which premises its political strategy in a rigorous critique of capital, is more urgent than ever.

While the center-left celebrates the tepid "Keynesian moment" embodied in the stimulus policies of the Biden administration,[67] we confront a global tendency toward a further intensification of exploitation[68] and restriction of democratic rights.[69] Indeed, the former is best understood as a bare minimum attempt to preempt the emergence of any resistance to the latter from a working class, which remains in the thrall of historic levels of demoralization and disorganization.

Today we confront an overwhelming consternation in the "progressive" part of society. It is no longer able to differentiate between the realization of bourgeois democracy and the overcoming of the same.[70] It is equally unable or unwilling to differentiate between its own class interests and those of the workers it claims, more or less convincingly, to defend. Hence it takes the midpoint for the final goal and comes to prefer the prospect of a plunge into the void to the completion of the project, which began with the revolutions of the eighteenth century. Evading this stasis means rearming ourselves with the critique of political economy, which clarifies the real governing dynamic of modern society and in the process reveals the means to overcome the unresolved problem it poses. With this volume, we hope to open a wide-ranging discussion on how best to accomplish this in the most pressing areas of inquiry.

NOTES

1. See Hochuli/Hoare/Cunliffe 2021.
2. An illustrative example of the left's technocratic paternalist critique of public health policy during the COVID-19 pandemic is the Zero COVID-19 initiatives in the UK, Germany, Canada, and other places. See https://zero-covid.org/language/en/.
3. As for acronyms, for example, POC, BIPOC, BIMPOC, QTIBIPOC, QTIBIMPOC, BAME, LBGTQAI2S+, and FLINTQ, they have been recently established. An easy guide to the newest forms of the categorization of humans can be found here: https://www.lib.sfu.ca/about/branches-depts/slc/writing/inclusive-antiracist-writing/glossary-terms.
4. For example, cis, trans, genderqueer, chestfeeding, nonbinary, able-bodied, and neurodiversity, see also https://www.lib.sfu.ca/about/branches-depts/slc/writing/inclusive-antiracist-writing/glossary-terms.
5. G. K. Chesterton 1927, 139.
6. Hochuli/Hoare/Cunliffe 2021, p. 17.
7. The global outcry in the wake of the killing of George Floyd has led not only to massive protests on the streets but to hundreds of think pieces in the liberal media for whom the rekindled focus on "systemic racism" was a very welcome distraction from the COVID-19 disaster's economic impact and the plight of Amazon and other "essential workers." See https://twitter.com/ZachG932/status/1267507175011819520. *The Washington Post* is owned by Amazon chief executive Jeff Bezos.

8. As the authors of *The End of the End of History* emphasize, there are three contradictions in the current left liberal perception: (1) "recent political history is *just one fucking thing after another*" (emphasis in original) (Brexit, Trump), seen as a continuing force of "wreckage after wreckage" imposed from the outside, so that "[allegations] of foreign interference—normally ridiculed as paranoia, when voiced by say, Serbians or Venezuelans . . .—have become an accepted explanation for political events in the United States, the most powerful country on Earth" (Hochuli/Hoare/Cunliffe 2021, 67); (2) the glaring contradiction between the serious diagnosis of "fascism" (embodied in Trump) and the childish and "ironic" means chosen to resist it ("pussy hats"), which expresses a refusal to take politics seriously (ibid., 72); and (3) the liberal emphasis of "moderation, collegiality, principles over partisanship" that nostalgic viewers of the TV series *The West Wing* found missing in Trump, while the same moderate liberals called Brexit voters "racist," "selfish," or, almost poetically, "frightened, parochial lizard brain[s]" (Hochuli/Hoare/Cunliffe 2021, 72).

9. For an analysis in the wider context of the left's submission to bourgeois hegemonic liberalism against the background of COVID-19 authoritarianism and the George Floyd protests of 2020, see Lange and Depaolis-Pickett, 2020.

10. See the contribution by Austin Williams in this volume.

11. The *history* of the ideology of the trinity of "race, class, and gender" in the left is explicated by Mike Macnair (Macnair 2018, 551).

12. Ibram X. Kendi rejects the term "microagression" in favor of (racial) "abuse": "I do not use 'microaggression' anymore. I detest the post-racial platform that supported its sudden popularity. I detest its component parts—'micro' and 'aggression.' A persistent daily low hum of racist abuse is not minor. I use the term 'abuse' because aggression is not as exacting a term. Abuse accurately describes the action and its effects on people: distress, anger, worry, depression, anxiety, pain, fatigue, and suicide" (Kendi 2019, 49). As with every phenomenon designating all-encompassing character ("everything is ideology," "everything is racist," "everything is gendered," and "God is everything"), it loses its significance, because there is nothing to differentiate it against. Yet, Kendi continues in this vein: "There is no such thing as a nonracist or race-neutral policy. Every policy in every institution in every community in every nation is producing or sustaining either racial inequity or equity between racial groups" (Kendi 2019, 20); "The heartbeat of racism . . . is beating within us" (ibid., 12). The apolitical, ahistorical, and asocial character of his guidebook to antiracism becomes clear with his insistence that we can be anti-racist by *confessing our sins*: "The heartbeat of racism is denial, and the heartbeat of antiracism is confession" (ibid., 240). The openly religious imposition of his "project" notwithstanding—the analytical value of this book is in joining the church of anti-racism—Kendi's racialist view of society and individuals is representative for what Campbell/Manning have termed "Victimhood Culture" (see Campbell/Manning 2018).

13. See Meghan Daum's *The Problem with Everything* (2019).

14. To mention one example, Gary S. Becker's seminal *The Economics of Discrimination* (1957) was funded by the University of Chicago's Department of Economics. It is a product of "Chicago Boys"-style political economy. See Macnair 2018, 555.

15. Smith 1846 [1776], p. 24.
16. See Marx 1976, pp. 677-81.
17. "If the capitalist class casts a certain sum of money into circulation in the shape of revenue, it appears as if it paid an equivalent for this part of the total annual product, and that this has thereby ceased to represent surplus value. But the surplus product in which the surplus-value is represented costs the capitalist class nothing. As a class, it possesses it and enjoys it free of charge, and the monetary circulation cannot alter this in any way. The change that this brings about simply consists in the fact that each capitalist, instead of consuming his own surplus product in kind, for which in most cases it would not be suitable, withdraws commodities of all kinds from the total stock to the amount of the surplus value that he appropriated, and appropriates these. . . . If the capitalist not only withdraws surplus value from the commodity market in the form of commodities for his consumption fund, but at the same time the money with which he buys these commodities flows back to him, he has evidently withdrawn the commodities without an equivalent. They cost him nothing, even though he pays for them with money" (Marx 1978, p. 550).
18. Marx 1981, p. 953.
19. For a discussion of its most representative authors and a critical analysis of their arguments, see Lange 2021a.
20. See Nick Nesbitt's contribution in this volume.
21. https://salvage.zone/online-exclusive/marxism-and-intersectionality-an-interview-with-ashley-bohrer/.
22. Ibid.
23. See https://asadhaider.substack.com/p/class-cancelled.
24. Reed Jr., Adolph, 'The Myth of Class Reductionism', *The New Republic*, September 25th, 2019.
25. Schmidt 1968, 33.
26. https://www.versobooks.com/books/1924-capitalism-in-the-web-of-life.
27. Moore 2016, 79.
28. See Hafner 1993, as well as the reader *Society and Cognition. Contributions to a Materialist Epistemological and Social Critique* (Behrens 1993 (ed.)). For the theoretical underpinning in the exchange process of commodities, see Marx 1976, 156 and 163-4, furthermore his critique of Condillac in Marx 1976, 261 ff., and his reference to crisis, ibid., 236: "Profane commodities can no longer replace [money]. The use-value of commodities becomes valueless, and their value vanishes in the face of their own form of value." One can say that Marx's whole project is aimed at deconstructing the semblance of use value as the site of economic manifestations. For a discussion of the fetishism of use value within Marx's Critique of Political Economy, see Lange 2021b.
29. "In highlighting Cartesian dualism as a key source of the problem . . . we are seeking to make sense of three great thought-procedures that have shaped the modern world: (1) the imposition of 'an ontological status upon entities (substances) as opposed to relationships . . .' (2) the centrality of a 'logic of either/or (rather than both/and)'; and (3) the 'idea of a purposive control over nature through applied science'" (Moore 2016, 88).

30. Moore 2016, 82.

31. See Robinson 1983, Singh 2016, Táíwò and Bright 2020, and Post 2020. For a response to Post, see https://beefheart.substack.com/p/toward-division. Accessed July 12, 2021.

32. Moore 2016, 85. He continues, "What if, instead of thinking capitalism = economics, we asked if 'capitalism' was about something much more profound?" (ibid.). His "much more profound" analysis—"capitalism as a new way of organizing nature, and therefore a new way of organizing the relations between work, reproduction, and the conditions of life"—however presents nothing that economics does not also address, especially if taken to mean the study of the (capitalist) economy. The alleged "profoundness" only suggests an auratic realm beyond the wage relation that serves Moore's idealism.

33. Marx 1994 (1861–4), 414.

34. Singh 2016, 31.

35. Gonzalez 2013.

36. This is why Táíwò and Bright circumvent the challenges posed by Michael Walzer's critique: early English or contemporary Chinese wage labor does not rely on "racial" distinctions, nor does Eastern European agricultural wage-slave labor in Germany, to name a few examples. The fact that the "Black slaves in the American South" "raised and harvested" the cotton that the workers in Manchester in 1844 processed, as Walzer concedes, does not render the Manchester workers less exploited. Racial distinctions in global production, both then and now, are nonsensical. See Walzer 2020.

37. Kimberlé W. Crenshaw, 'Mapping the Margins: Intersectionality, Identity Politics, and Violence against Women of Color', in *Stanford Law Review*, Vol. 43, No. 6 (Jul., 1991), 1241-1299.

38. K. Yamahtta-Taylor, *From #BlackLivesMatter to Black Liberation*, Haymarket 2016 and K. Yamahtta-Taylor, *How We Get Free: Black Feminism and the Combahee River Collective*, Haymarket 2017.

39. Combahee River Collective 2019 (1977).

40. Taylor 2019.

41. Ibid.

42. "It was our experience and disillusionment within these liberation movements, as well as experience on the periphery of the white male left, that led to the need to develop a politics that was antiracist, unlike those of white women, and antisexist, unlike those of black and white men" (Combahee River Collective 2019 [1977]).

43. "Although we are feminists and lesbians, we feel solidarity with progressive black men and do not advocate the fractionalization that white women who are separatists demand. Our situation as black people necessitates that we have solidarity around the fact of race, which white women of course do not need to have with white men, unless it is their negative solidarity as racial oppressors" (ibid.).

44. Ibid.

45. The soft Maoist origins of this political strategy have been pointed out by Macnair 2018, 552.

46. Macnair 2018, 548.

47. Macnair 2018, 543 (emphases in original).

48. For an insightful critique of the comprehensive decadence of bourgeois thought which has only become more so in the decades since its first publication, see Georg Lukacs, *The Destruction of Reason*, 1980.

49. "It is as ridiculous to yearn for a return to that original fullness as it is to believe that with this complete emptiness history has come to a standstill" (Marx 1973, 162).

50. In the ancient community, the function of production was the reproduction of a given type of individual bounded by fixed personal relations of domination and servitude. In the community of capital, the function of reproduction of individuals is the reproduction of capital. The potential future community once again proceeds from the reproduction of individuals as its aim. But this individual is a universal individual produced by the generalization of exchange value.

51. https://unherd.com/2019/11/a-post-liberal-reading-list/. Accessed July 12, 2021.

52. For a representative "left" articulation of such a perspective see Astarian and Dauvé 2015. For the right, Linkola 2009 and Donovan 2016 are typical. There is no doubt that the postmodern subject finds it easier to imagine the end of civilization than the end of capitalism.

53. Hegel 1991, 20.

54. Bernstein to Kautsky, February 20, 1898. Cited in Waldenburg 1980, 144.

55. "If one thing is certain it is that our party and the working class can only come to power under the form of a democratic republic. This is even the specific form for the dictatorship of the proletariat, as the Great French Revolution has already shown" (Engels 1990 [1891], 227).

56. As he observed of Republican France, the best thing about universal suffrage is that "it indicates with the most perfect accuracy the day when a call to armed revolution has to be made." Engels to Lafargue, November 12, 1892, included in Engels 2010 (1892), 29.

57. More than twenty years after the "peaceful" transition from White minority rule, South Africa remains one of the most unequal societies in the world (see Dessus & Hanusch 2018). In the neighboring countries of Southern Africa which experienced more comprehensive anti-colonial revolutions the story is much the same. This outcome is no surprise to those who understand the class content of the project of national emancipation. Only a noteworthy lack of intellectual dexterity is capable of equating such an understanding with opposition to the authentically emancipatory gains of the national liberation struggles.

58. "The constant renewal of this relation of *sale and purchase* only mediates the permanence of the specific relation of dependence, giving it the deceptive *semblance* of a transaction, a contract, between *commodity owners* who have equal rights and confront each other equally freely. This *initial* relation now appears as itself an immanent moment of the domination, produced in capitalist production, of objective labour over living labour" (Marx 1994 [1861-1864], 465) (emphases in original).

59. For a typical example, take the statement by Black Lives Matter leader Alicia Garza, in her preface to the 2016 edited collection *Who Do You Serve, Who Do You*

Protect?, that "[modern]-day policing locates its origins in the slave economy, which helped build the wealth and the industrialized economy of this nation and of other nations around the world." Garza in Schenwar, Macaré, Price (ed.), 2016, vii. Such statements are simply false.

60. Indeed, not only was the prison population of the slave South as little as *one-tenth* that of the North convicts, it was almost exclusively free Whites (McLennan 2009, 65). The prison is an actuality of modern freedom, not a legacy of archaic systems of bondage.

61. For a classic treatment of the conditions leading to the necessity (for the propertied) of modern professionalized policing, see Colquhoun 1797. It leaves little doubt that this institution found its essential logic not in any system of bonded labor but in the swelling mass of free proletarians, which not long afterward Hegel was to characterize as a "dangerous evil" (Hegel 1973, 322).

62. The common equation between contemporary police murders and mob lynchings under Jim Crow further facilitates this ideological operation. Bureaucratically legitimized killings by agents of the modern state in a society defined by the enforcement of equality under the law have no simple continuity with the crude personal violence of the semifeudal and caste-divided past.

63. "As a free wage-worker, he [the worker] has *no value*; it is rather his power of disposing of his labour, effected by exchange with him, which has value. It is not he who stands towards the capitalist as exchange value, but the capitalist towards him. His *valuelessness* and *devaluation* is the presupposition of capital and the precondition of *free* labour in general" (Marx 1973) (emphases in original). It is perhaps noteworthy that the rap-metal group Body Count came closer to this basic truth with their 2017 track "No Lives Matter" than most of the allegedly erudite academics who peddle racial hysteria.

64. On the judicial metaphysics of freedom and equality as the bourgeois secularization of theological mystification, see Engels and Kautsky 1977.

65. Kautsky 1903, 82.

66. Lenin 1962 (1905), 76.

67. https://foreignpolicy.com/2021/03/05/bidens-stimulus-is-the-dawn-of-a-new-economic-era/. Accessed July 12, 2021.

68. See ILO 2021 for a summary of the impact of the "Corona Crisis" on labor.

69. https://findings2020.monitor.civicus.org/rating-changes.html. Accessed July 12, 2021.

70. For the *qualitative* distinction between the two, see Lenin 1972, 66.

Part I

FROM CLASS TO COMMUNITY—RACE, GENDER, AND CROSS-CLASS STRUGGLES

Chapter 1

Antidiscrimination and the End of Marxism

The Roots of Contemporary Politics in Cold War Theory and Culture

Todd Cronan

FROM PROLETARIAT TO JEW: THE FRANKFURT SCHOOL, C. 1940

On August 5, 1940, a few weeks after the fall of France, Theodor W. Adorno who lived in New York City at that time, wrote to Max Horkheimer expressing his increasing concern about the state of the Jews in Europe. "I cannot stop thinking about the fate of the Jews," he tells Horkheimer. If everything he had written up to that point had focused on the plight of the proletariat, political circumstances had induced him to change his mind. "It often seems to me that everything that we used to see from the point of view of the proletariat has been concentrated today with frightful force upon the Jews," Adorno writes.[1] This moment marks an essential turn in the attitude of the Frankfurt School toward the question of class struggle, as the Jew replaces the proletariat as the ones who "are now at the opposite pole to the concentration of power."[2] Rolf Tiedemann grasps the centrality of this point for Adorno's thinking: "These lines ... provide us with a key to Adorno's thinking from 1940 on."[3]

This "turn" in Adorno's thinking—from the proletariat, a class position, to the Jew, the subject of discrimination—was in fact long prepared in the earlier writings of the Frankfurt School. At least since the late 1920s, Horkheimer had broadcast his discontent with the changing character of the working class. Horkheimer's "Impotence of the Working Class," an essay published in his first book, *Dämmerung (Twilight)*, a 1934 collection of essays, considers the current state of the "reserve army," a class position described by Marx in part 7, chapter 25, of *Capital*. The reserve army of unemployed workers plays a central role in the life of the employed worker as they are manipulated by owners to exert pressure on employees. The reserve army function as a standing threat to employees, signaling the capacity of the owner to replace the worker at a moment's notice, a capacity that is exploited by the owner to suppress wages, extract increasing labor, and undermine efforts to organize. But Horkheimer's emphasis is less on Marx's interpretation of the necessary relation between the reserve army and the (barely) employed, and more on the changing nature of worker consciousness brought on by persistent unemployment. Capitalism has always generated a lower stratum of workers, the unorganized and unpolitical lumpenproletariat, which Horkheimer describes as a "relatively insignificant segment from which the criminal element is recruited" whose character was defined by "obvious qualitative contrast" with the organized proletariat.[4] But this distinction among the exploited begins to dissolve with extreme levels of unemployment. In the past, class division was characterized by a "steady transition between those who worked and those who didn't," and if someone was out of work, they "might be hired the next day, and the man who had work was much like his unemployed colleague when he lost it."[5] By the late 1920s, the period of rapid, if relatively dependable turnover was over, and with it the solidarity of the proletariat begins to erode. It is no longer a matter of high turnover, but something far more ominous, a "hopeless existence" of unemployment "from birth on."[6] The line between lumpenproletariat and proletariat dissolves and in its place is a condition of existential unemployment.

In this new situation defined by the sheer "wretchedness" and "utter hopelessness" of proletarian existence, revolution becomes a matter of "individual" rather than collective concern.[7] Workers do not want to risk even the barest forms of political organization as it might threaten their already precarious situation. It is under these conditions that unions become an increasingly conservative force, to a degree seemingly unimagined under the terms of Kautsky and Lenin's cautions about the "labor aristocracy."[8] "For the employed workers whose wages and long-term membership in unions . . . assure a certain, albeit small, security for the future, all political acts involve the danger of a tremendous loss," Horkheimer writes.[9] Unions close ranks as workers clutch the tenuous security they offer. Under these changing terms, the proletariat defined by "security," the unemployed by "hopelessness," Horkheimer inaugurates a large-scale reversal of the traditional Marxist order: it is the unorganized and unpolitical lumpenproletariat, the terminally unemployed who become the agents of revolution. The unemployed, unlike unionized workers, have nothing to lose "but their chains."[10] The unified proletariat are divided against one another as the unemployed are redescribed as the revolutionary force, while the employed (both poor and well-off) emerge as latent capitalists. For Horkheimer, what is alarming is the fact that the new marginalized element has "no understanding of theory."¹¹ They are disorganized, unpolitical, young, often violent, and uneducated. They lack the "human qualities" necessary to implement socialism. Here is the basic dilemma: the lumpenproletariat has a "direct interest" in socialism but lacks "clear theoretical consciousness," while the (barely) unionized worker has (apparently) a less immediate need for socialism but deeper theoretical consciousness. At the center of Horkheimer's analysis is the remarkable and fateful assertion that "work and misery no longer come together, people no longer experience both."¹² Those who work enjoy a degree of security; those who do not live a life of sheer suffering, a suffering that emerges as an untapped revolutionary potential. These are the revised terms of analysis that authorize the now canonized claims, which emerge forty years later in essays like Herbert Marcuse's "Liberation from the Affluent Society" (1967). According to Marcuse, "The insanity of the society . . . is the degree to which it is capable of conquering poverty and reducing the toil of labor and the time of labor and of raising the standard of living."¹³ On this account, it is insane to ease the lives of workers; it is insane to rid society of poor people (by giving them jobs) because those formerly revolutionary subjects find themselves fully "integrated" (a word in obsessive circulation in Frankfurt School writings) into capitalist society.¹⁴ Not only do the employed avoid revolution, they are reactionary because their lives are "comfortable."¹⁵ Marcuse relentlessly denigrates the revolutionary potential of the proletariat. According to Marcuse, "the most important single item" to understand is the "changing composition of the working class in the United States."¹⁶ The new threat is not "impoverishment" but rather the "high standard of living on an enlarged scale, which ushers in the end of capitalism."¹⁷ By the end of his life, Marcuse concludes that notions of capitalist integration do not go far enough to explain the situation of the worker:

> To say that the proletariat is integrated no longer does justice to the existing state of affairs. Instead, one must go further in one's formulations. In present day late capitalism, the Marxist proletariat, in so far as it still exists at all, only represents a minority within the working class. The working class, in terms of its consciousness and praxis, has been embourgeoisified to a great extent.¹⁸

If Marcuse rejects the proletariat, he then shifts his attention to the potential of *minority groups* to comprise a new revolutionary force. Marcuse describes the shift as emergent *within* the working class, as there has "always been an antagonism between white labor and black labor."¹⁹ The former side with capital, the latter with liberation. "The radical opposition [today] is very much limited to minority groups. The liberation struggle of the Blacks, as *one of* the minority groups, understands itself as being in the same anti-capitalist front with student movement, the younger workers, the women."[20] Notably, Marcuse warns these putatively "anti-capitalist" groups lack "unity in action" and have no "comprehensive organization" to create even a minimally "unified strategy." Kellner and Pierce sum up the two sides of Marcuse's attack on the "fetishized concept of class":

> Marcuse insists that today the industrial working class is no longer the radical negation of capitalist society and is therefore no longer the revolutionary class. It has no monopoly today . . . on oppression and immiseration, and is in fact better organized, better paid and better off than many members of racial minorities, women, and service, clerical and agricultural workers, as well as the unemployed and unemployable.[21]

It is my contention that whatever disagreements roiled the ranks of the Frankfurt School—no doubt the differences among Horkheimer and Adorno and Marcuse were substantial—there was deep assent among them when it came to an understanding of the compromised nature of the proletariat and the revolutionary potential of minority groups.

Virtually everything that emerges from the Frankfurt School from 1940 on takes up both sides of the new account: exhibiting the fully "integrated" character of the proletariat and outlining the revolutionary potential of the minority. On the question of capitalist integration, it is anything but a coincidence that it is in 1940—the moment Adorno turns his attention to the plight of the Jews—that Horkheimer begins to develop his broad-ranging and influential "theory of rackets." Under late capitalism, "all have become employees, and in the civilization of employees" everyone loses their "dignity."[22] In this new order "rackets control everything . . . according to plan, the capitalists through conflicts among each other and with the unions."[23] In "The Authoritarian State," also of 1940, Horkheimer pens a slogan for the new political program: "The revolutionary vision of emancipation continued to live on only in the slanders of the counter-revolutionaries."[24] On this account, it is the counterrevolutionary who creates the space for revolution, and the traditional revolutionary—the proletariat—is an agent of conservatism. The dispossessed—for Horkheimer and Adorno it is the plight of the Jews, for Marcuse and others it is an array of minority groups, even or especially if they have little "clear theoretical consciousness", replace the proletariat as the new revolutionary stratum. The marginalized are defined by their oppression, not by their class position, and while the marginalized largely overlap with a class position—Blacks and Latinos are significantly overrepresented in the bottom quintiles (so redistributive policies would have a disproportionately positive effect on their class situation)—it bears no necessary connection with class.

PROLETARIAT TO JEW: FRANKFURT SCHOOL TO SARTRE

At the same moment that Horkheimer and Adorno were developing their account of anti-Semitism—an account solidified with their cowritten analysis of the "Elements of Anti-Semitism" (written in 1944 in Los Angeles) for the *Dialectic of Enlightenment*—Jean-Paul Sartre was writing his astonishingly influential *Reflections on the Jewish Question* in France (1946).[25] To this day, Sartre's book remains among the most influential accounts of racism and antiracism ever written. Sartre's book is divided into two long chapters and two short ones. Chapter three, the centerpiece of the book, considers the question "What is a Jew?" Sartre reviews at length the range of interpretations that putatively define the Jew, focused on the seemingly intertwined notions of heredity, race, ethnicity, culture, and religion. But Sartre rejects them all one by one. None of these elements define the Jew, it "is neither their past, their religion, nor their soil that unites the sons of Israel."[26] Here he announces his basic thesis: "If they have a common bond . . . it is because they have in common the situation of a Jew, that is, they live in a community which takes them for Jews."[27] In answer to the question "What is a Jew?," he answers, "The Jew is the one whom other men consider a Jew."[28] They are, in other words, *negatively* defined. There is no fact of the matter that makes one a Jew, one is Jewish insofar as others see them that way. As my grandfather used to say to this lapsed Jew, "Hitler thought you were a Jew," or as Sartre puts it, "The anti-Semite . . . *makes* the Jew"[29] (emphasis in original). "Jews," Sartre declares, "have neither community of interests nor community of beliefs. They do not have the same fatherland; they have no history. The sole tie that binds them is the hostility and disdain of the societies which surround them."[30] The significance of this visibility for others—Sartre's refashioning of the Hegelian "Master and Slave" dialectic—emerges with the class position of the Jew. French Jews, he writes, are "members of the lower or upper middle class" and they are largely employed in the service sector, what Sartre calls "vocations of opinion."[31] Their class position makes them highly visible; they are employed in vocations that require them to "seduce, to captivate, and to retain confidence"; there are a "thousand little dance steps" necessary to "attract a customer."[32] Because the Jew is so visibly "dependent on other men," he is never at any moment allowed to forget that he is different, that he is a Jew.

Sartre's text is saturated from beginning to end with a metaphysical degree of pessimism. The Jew "cannot free himself no matter what he may do";[33] once the word "Jew" "appears in his life" it will "never leave again";[34] "no matter what he does, he is and will remain a Jew";[35] the "Nazi ordinances only carried to its extreme a situation of which we had formerly accommodated ourselves very well";[36] no matter the "greatest success [it] will never gain him entrance" into society;[37] finally, he concludes, "Such, then, is this haunted man, condemned to make his choice of himself on the basis of false problems and in a false situation," "everything he does turns against him."[38]

Whatever barriers confront the worker, they pale in comparison to those of the Jew. The worker's "situation is different" because he can "disdainfully reject the values and the culture of the middle class; he can dream of substituting his own."[39] The Jew, by contrast, "belongs" to the class that rejects them. "He can . . . acquire all the goods he wants, lands and castles . . . but at the very moment when he becomes a legal proprietor, the property undergoes a subtle change in meaning and value"; it magically becomes "Jewish" property.[40] The Jew "possesses nothing," because everything he touches becomes tainted with otherness.[41] Like the Frankfurt School theorists, Sartre conceives the central social ills as affecting marginalized groups. Moreover, those groups are categorically separated from their class position. On this account, the poorest (non-Jewish) worker is in a better condition than the richest Jew.

For Sartre, there is no point in trying to persuade anti-Semites of the errors of their ways. It is of "no importance" that anti-Semites harbor "erroneous notion[s]," it is "vain" for the Jew to "argue about his culture, his accomplishments," as the anti-Semite is not susceptible to reason.[42] Given the depths of this impossible situation the Jew is forced to endure, what possible recourse do they have? In one of the most remarkable and influential theses ever penned in the anti-racist literature, Sartre insists that the victim must not only accept but *affirm* the terms forced upon them by the racist. If every form of counterargument fails, because it is not based in reasons to begin with, then the only option is to *double down on the terms provided by the racist*, what Sartre calls "anti-racist racism."[43] The Jews, on Sartre's account, are compelled to "exalt racial qualities" as the only cogent response to a racist culture.[44] Famously, Sartre describes this situation as an existential decision: "He must decide: does he or does he not consent to be the person whose role they make him play?"[45] The victim of racism must "make reply" to the culture "by choosing himself."[46] To be a Jew in an anti-Semitic society one can choose to live "authentically" or "inauthentically." "Authenticity" means "to live to the full his condition as Jew; inauthenticity is to deny it or to attempt to escape from it."[47] The authentic Jew is "the one who asserts his claim in the face of the disdain shown toward him."[48]

The remainder of Sartre's account is devoted to the efforts of the inauthentic Jew to escape his situation, to fail to recognize and own up to the reality that constrains him. In a remarkable and fateful turn, Sartre construes the deepest form of denial as the Jew's commitment to reason and the universal.[49] The "royal road of flight" from their situation is to "espouse a conception of the world that excludes the very idea of race."[50] The attempt to deny race is nothing but "an attempt to conceal from themselves their own situation."[51] For those that believe that reason is "the same to all," that "there is no French truth or German truth, there is no Negro truth or Jewish truth," Sartre sees psychological repression run amok.[52] Belief in reason is a form of denial, as the "best way to feel oneself no longer a Jew is to reason, for reasoning is valid for all."[53] It is hard not to see Sartre's argument here as an instance of race reductionism. He asserts that it is "not by chance" that a "Jewish philosopher" (Léon Brunschvicg) "brings together in his writings the progress of reason and the progress of *unification* (unification of ideas, unification of men)"[54] (emphasis in original). What is the difference between the anti-Semite and the anti-racist here? Is this "anti-racist racism" or just racism? If every thought of a "Jewish" philosopher—one that makes no philosophical claims along those lines—is reducible to their Jewish condition, the lines between anti-racism and racism begin to blur.

Sartre draws his account to a close with a detailed assessment of the Jew's relation to money, a classically anti-Semitic trope. According to Sartre, the Jew embraces contractual, abstract forms of capitalism as a "counterattack" to their denial of social standing by anti-Semites. If the "Jew loves money," Sartre writes, it is because "money often assumes the abstract form of shares of stock, checks, banks deposits."[55] "Appropriation by purchase," he continues, "does not depend on the race of the buyer; it does not vary with his idiosyncrasies."[56] Remarkable though it is, Sartre's less-than-critical rehearsal of Jewish stereotypes is meant to stand in direct contrast to his denigration of rational argument. In Sartre's race-saturated universe, stereotypes are liberatory, while rationally dismantling them is construed as ideological.

The final paragraphs of Sartre's analysis are a plea for the Jew to "abandon the myth of the universal man" and to understand his situation as a "damned creature."[57] He must learn to accept a world defined by "irrational divisions" and in accepting it make "some of these values and these divisions his."[58] The authentic Jew will take "pride from his humiliation," and in doing so "he takes away all power and all virulence from anti-Semitism."[59] A well-known instance of Sartre's position is Lenny Bruce's infamous comedic routine consisting of a stream of racist slurs. The idea being that through repetition a racist word "would lose its impact." "Saying nothing," by contrast, "gives it power."

Although it has been little remarked upon, Adorno immediately responded to Sartre's account in chapter one of *The Authoritarian Personality* of 1950. In his unpublished "Remarks on *The Authoritarian Personality*" of 1948 Adorno offers a detailed and flattering assessment of Sartre's position. It turns out there is little daylight between their accounts: "Of all the philosophical discussions of the problem known to us, this study comes closest to our own interpretation of the anti-Semite."[60] Adorno notes how "amazing" it is to see how deeply Sartre's claims "coincide with our own interpretation down to exceedingly concrete details."[61] Sartre's command of literary psychology—centered on the works of Stendhal, Flaubert, and Proust—nullifies the "ideological" errors in his philosophy.[62] So even if Adorno rejects the "main tenet" of Sartre's philosophy, his commitment to the existential "decision," an idea that leads Sartre to an overly individualistic interpretation of anti-Semitism, Adorno discovers the "element of truth" in Sartre's account of the "freely self-chosen" attitude of the anti-Semite. "Individual anti-Semitism," Adorno writes, "is switched on and off," the repressed and destructive libido is "free floating," and the weak ego (someone who recognizes the insecurity of his situation) needs shoring up, something that the "pseudo-rational ideology" of anti-Semitism provides.[63] Adorno, that is, renders the entirety of Sartre's position compatible with his own, even redeeming the seemingly ahistorical and asocial dimension of "free choice." On the question of anti-racism, Adorno and Sartre share a great deal in common. Above all, both are committed to the notion that anti-racism not only cannot be understood under traditional Marxist terms of class analysis, but, far more centrally, class analysis *obscures* the basic nature of racist discrimination. And racism, first as anti-Semitism, later as anti-Black racism, becomes the privileged form that violence takes in the postwar capitalist countries. It would hardly be an exaggeration to say that the twined anti-racist positions of the Frankfurt School and Sartre define the central outlook of the anti-racist humanities from this point forward.

AMERICAN SOCIOLOGY AND THE COLD WAR CONSENSUS

The extent to which sociology and anthropology in the 1950s defined itself against an analysis of class conflict has yet to be fully understood. No doubt the dominant voices in American sociology—C. Wright Mills, David Riesman, William Whyte, Vance Packard, John Kenneth Galbraith, Paul Goodman, Daniel Bell, John Keats, and Maurice Stein among others—and anthropology—Ruth Benedict, Geoffrey Gorer, Karen Horney, Abram Kardiner, Margaret Mead, Edward T. Hall, and Ashley Montagu, many of them identified with the anti-racist work of Franz Boas—played a central (if sometimes contentious) role in the elaboration of a Cold War liberal consensus. It is my contention that the most cogent explanation for the degree and depth of the consensus is to see it as emerging from an understanding of the claims made by the Frankfurt School and Sartre in Europe. Sartre's *Anti-Semite and Jew* appeared in English in 1948, and the Frankfurt School was already well-established in Los Angeles and New York City where they shaped the nature of sociological thought in the 1950s. Erich Fromm's *Escape from Freedom* of 1941 was one of the most influential sociological texts of mid-century, bringing the ideas of the Frankfurt School into popular consciousness. Not surprisingly, Fromm imported the conventional wisdom about unions and the "insignificance of the individual":

> Many unions . . . have grown into mammoth organizations in which there is little room for the initiative of the individual member. He pays his dues and votes from time to time but here again he is a small cog in a large machine.[64]

The main ideas imported from Europe—about the integrated nature of the proletariat and revolutionary potential of minorities—could not find more fertile soil than in the Cold War context of the United States. After 1948, the mainstream of "left" sociology, voluntarily and involuntarily, erased positive references to Marxism or communism.

Consider, for instance, the recently recanonized 1955 collection *The New American Right*, edited by Daniel Bell and expanded in 1962 as *The Radical Right* (the first use of the term). As Bell notes up front, there is a "thesis" that drives the authors of the study: "This is a turbulence born not of depression, but of prosperity."[65] Richard Hofstadter makes the point blunter still: we are "confronted from time to time with a wide range of behavior for which the economic interpretation of politics seems to be inadequate or misleading or altogether irrelevant."[66] Whatever contemporary value this collective study might have in diagnosing so-called right-wing populism, what it more directly suggests is the origins of a liberal anti-populist consensus. (One might be forgiven, for instance, for seeing the book as *The Radical Left*, so deeply is it devoted to a critique of the "extremist" left.[67]) A thesis runs throughout the book, that the new right is driven, as David Riesman puts it, not by class insecurity but by an "unsatisfying quality of life." This dissatisfaction is a *product of* the affluent society, a prosperous society which put them in "possession of many of the insignia they have been taught to associate with the good life."[68] Not despite, but by virtue of, their relative affluence, they are roiled by unease, restlessness, resentment, and anger. Or, as Hofstadter puts it in his "The Pseudo-Conservative Revolt"—a study that draws "heavily upon" Adorno's *The Authoritarian Personality*—the new right is a "product of the rootlessness" of American life, above all, it is an expression of the new "peculiar scramble for status," an "uncertainty" that is split off from "economic and political causes."[69] Seymour Martin Lipset, in his "The Sources of the 'Radical Right,'" writes of "prosperity-born bitterness" among "'Tory' Workers."[70] Lipset, following Hofstadter, makes a basic and fateful distinction between "status politics" and "class politics." Status politics, he writes, "becomes ascendent in periods of prosperity . . . and when many are able to improve their economic position." Summing up the situation, Lipset concludes that status politics belongs to those "already possessing status who feel that rapid social change threatens their own claims to high social position, or enables previously lower status groups to claim equal status with their own."[71] Lipset, like others in the volume, attacks in equal measure the "extreme left and right," observing how McCarthy's origins lie in the leftist movements of the 1930s.[72] Lipset sums up a consensus view of the volume as a whole, and one that was widely shared among sociologists at the time:

> so similar are the political approaches of the radical right and the communists that one may fittingly describe the radical right doctrine as embodying a theory of "Social Communism" in the same sense as the communists used the term "Social Fascism" in the early thirties.[73]

A more subtle effort to carve out an anti-Marxist mode of sociological analysis emerges with the highly influential work of Riesman. Writing in 1951 for *Phylon*, a magazine founded by W. E. B. DuBois and based at Atlanta University, Riesman offers a defense of "marginality," pushing against the "prevailing attitude" of social scientists who aim to "abolish" marginal social positions.[74] In "Some Observations Concerning Marginality"—an essay later published in his 1954 collection *Individualism Reconsidered*—Riesman defends what he calls "secret" or "undefined" marginality, the important social role played by those who "subjectively fail to feel the identities expected of them."[75] These new identities are construed as a subset of a broader cultural shift, "new hierarchies [are] springing into existence, under which the older, relatively clear hierarchies of class and caste become amorphous and diffuse."[76] Increasing "economic abundance," which takes pressure off the need to survive, gives rise to heightening levels of interpersonal awareness, new modes of understanding how "one is different, in secret and subtle ways."[77] He charts the rise of "brown and mulatto societies" all with "various shadings of slight difference from each other," describing a social order that is increasingly attuned to "more subtle differentiation than the older ones of sheer economic and social class."[78] On this account, Riesman offers an unexpected, but also largely authorized, gloss on Sartre's *Anti-Semite and Jew*. Riesman understands Sartre's crucial claim that the Jew is someone "created by the expectations of the anti-Semite" as signaling the opportunity for individual self-creation. Given that Riesman is invested in *expanding* racial categories, Sartre's pessimistic sense of the inescapable condition of Jewishness for the Jew is refashioned as a heroic form of self-production, a version of what is now simply called identity politics. Sartrean pessimism gets repackaged as liberal self-discovery. Riesman observes how "Jews . . . have enjoyed the very risks of their marginality," lamenting how social scientists "look only at the punishing aspects" of marginality.[79] Not unlike Sartre, Riesman goes on the offensive against those who wish to "erase Jewish marginality," those who aim to "'normalize' the Jewish situation."[80] By normalizing Jewishness, Riesman is referring to pressure groups on "both sides of the ethnic line" that attempt to iron out differences among the Jews. Religious conversion, Zionist nationalism, "artificially sustained Jewish and Yiddish usages," and the embrace of "Jewish folksiness" are ways of erasing the marginal status of the Jew by giving them yet another fixed identity.[81]

Riesman's critique of racial unity, and racial leaders, extends only as far as culture. He observes how the "middle- and upper-class Negro, Italian, Jew, or Slav" is often "forced . . . from outside, to confine his sociability 'voluntarily' to his 'own' group, and to obey the leisure styles of that group."[82] The problem, as Riesman sees it, is with "cultural dictators," those who enforce constraints on the various lifestyles within an ethnic group. If cultural leaders are suspect, Riesman has nothing but praise for race leaders. Riesman observes how Booker T. Washington's "whole career could be described as an effort to turn the Negro away from dependence on tradition-direction toward dependence on inner-direction." His "strong emphasis on thrift, diligence, and manners" stands as a "remnant" of a vast literature devoted to "improving 'character.'"[83] Suffice to say, Riesman offers nothing in the way of a class analysis, finding it sufficient to point to inner-directed "character" as the path to success or failure. Riesman, in other words, offers his own contribution to the rising tide of underclass ideology, an ideology that purposefully misconstrues the class situation of minorities as the product of "character" or values, rather than political economy.

And what about lower-class ethnic groups, the ones not susceptible to cultural control? These ethnic groups "are the ones who liberate the majority." America's "play patterns may suffer," Riesman writes, "from the lack of . . . stimulus and élan when there are no more immigrants."[84] "Ethnics," he continues, "are invited to add to the variety of the nation by retaining the colorful flavors of their 'racial heritages.'"[85] Riesman's rather pathetic commitment to culinary diversity suggests the flimsiness of his substitute for class analysis. As Riesman sees it, an abundance economy signals the end of the class system, the moment that provides the opportunity for the full flourishing of diversity. As class differences cease to exist, class is transformed into an ethnic category, one that is subject to the same demand for tolerance as racial diversity.

At the center of Riesman's analysis is an effort to eliminate class as an economic category and to replace it with a vision of pluralistic difference. To make his point he draws on a recent experience at the University of Chicago. He observes how middle-class students—he describes them as "rapidly self-emancipating people"—feel increasingly compelled to "erase any feelings of prejudice." The prejudice he is referring to is "against those of different class and ethnic background"; the elision of the two terms is crucial. In the pressure to erase prejudice,

> students sometimes fail to realize that they are being asked to cross both class and ethnic lines at the same time—the situation appears to them to involve only the ethnic line. A middle-class boy from a small Midwestern town may be confronted with a Jewish boy from Brooklyn who is of working-class parentage, but the former may define the encounter as a test of his ability to shed any latent anti-Semitism; he fails to see that class and rural-urban differences may be much more important. Or again, an upper-class white girl may meet a lower-middle-class Negro boy and be horrified at what she thinks is her own race prejudice, since all the marginalities in the meeting have been packaged under the single ethnic label. People may even break down—I have seen such cases—out of a feeling of inadequacy to rise to such demands put on their tolerance of differences, because they do not realize how great and many-sided those demands are.[86]

At first glance it appears Riesman is asking his audience to distinguish between class and race and to see how the former has been effaced by the latter. Class disappears as marginality has been "packaged under the single ethnic label." Riesman seems to be asking his audience to consider the ways in which ethnic identity has subsumed every other form of marginalization. But this is not at all Riesman's point. His aim is not to show how ethnicity has become the privileged form of marginalization but to illustrate how class itself—for Riesman there are only varieties of middle class—is a lifestyle category that needs to be recognized alongside ethnicity. The prejudice that concerns Riesman is the lack of tolerance toward the "many-sided" nature of a minority's "class and ethnic background."[87] What does it even mean to "cross" the class line, assuming we know what it means to cross an ethnic line (tolerating different appearances, beliefs, and practices)? It certainly does not mean that the richer student hands the poorer student their money. The struggle Riesman describes, the one that leads some to "break down," stems from a "feeling of inadequacy" toward the lower class, an inadequacy to rise to "demands put on their tolerance of differences." But the difference between the well-off student and lower-middle-class student is neither a product of, nor can be fixed through, feelings of tolerance or intolerance. Whatever difficulties confront the intolerant student in their meeting with a lower-class kid (we are only given the richer kid's perspective), they are surely of a different nature from the economic difficulties that face the lower-middle-class kid. Because Riesman imagines that the class system has been more or less fixed—that "we in America now live in what in many ways is a great age" defined by the "relative affluence of millions of people"[88]—he cannot conceive of class struggle as anything but the lingering groupthink of elite intellectuals.

HOLLYWOOD AS COLD WAR SOCIOLOGY: THE CASE OF ELIA KAZAN

A full-scale analysis of the vast sociological literature of the 1950s is well beyond the confines of this chapter. At this point I will turn my attention to one of the most popular forms of dissemination of the liberal Cold War sociological consensus as it appears in the films of Elia Kazan, one of the most critically acclaimed filmmakers of postwar Hollywood. Kazan's work loosely, but conspicuously, draws on the current anthropological and sociological literature. His *A Face in the Crowd* is named after Riesman's 1952 work *Faces in the Crowd: Individual Studies in Character and Politics*. And if that's not on the nose enough, consider how the only redeemable character in *A Face in the Crowd*, Mel Miller (Walter Matthau), a liberal staff writer at a radio station and the only character skeptical of "Lonesome" Rhodes's populist schtick, flaunts his devotion to the latest expressions of liberal sociology. We are shown Mel on the phone with the woman who discovered Lonesome, Marcia Jeffries, as she is beginning to have doubts about Lonesome's character. We see the writers' room and on the wall is a large blow up of Lonesome's head as the writers throw darts at it. Directly below his face is another large poster that says "Escape from Freedom," announcing the title of Fromm's 1941 book. Never mind the absurdity of anyone having a poster with the title of Fromm's book; this is an graphic form of virtue signaling, advertising Kazan's up-to-the-minute liberal credentials to a bourgeois audience.

Kazan's earlier film *Gentleman's Agreement* of 1947 sets the standard for his career as a whole and it was undoubtedly among the most popular anti-racist films of the postwar era. The story follows Philip Green (Gregory Peck), a writer who is recruited by a magazine to write a series of articles on anti-Semitism in America. Finding it difficult to get information on anti-Semitism he pretends to be a Jew, so he can experience racism at first hand. As he quickly discovers, anti-Semitism, of a genteel, liberal variety, pervades every aspect of bourgeois life in New England (the film is set in New Canaan, Connecticut). Among the various revelations Green (and the viewer) has about the depths of anti-Semitism is a conversation Green has with the Jewish professor Fred Lieberman (Sam Jaffe). For Kazan, the fact that professors at Yale go to elite parties in New Canaan suggests the kind of order he aims to defend; this society is under indictment for its *racism*, not its class character. Lieberman is a scientist, and he is on a "crusade" to change the world's attitude toward Jews.

> *Lieberman:* I'm starting on a new crusade of my own. I have no religion, so I'm not Jewish by religion. Further, I'm a scientist, so I must rely on science . . . which shows me I'm not Jewish by race . . . since there's no such thing as a distinct Jewish race. There's not even a Jewish type. Well, my crusade will have a certain charm. I will simply go forth and state I'm not a Jew. With my face, that becomes not an evasion . . . but a new principle—a scientific principle.
> *Green:* For a scientific age.
> *Lieberman:* Precisely.

Here, Lieberman is singing the gospel of contemporary liberal anthropology, an attitude most famously described by Ashley Montagu in his best-selling 1942 book *Man's Most Dangerous Myth: The Fallacy of Race*. Montagu's position was canonized beginning in 1948, when, as a member of UNESCO, he was charged with defining "race" as an unscientific category.

The results emerge with the 1950 UNESCO statement on "The Race Question." The statement opens as follows:

> Racism is a particularly vicious and mean expression of the caste spirit. It involves belief in the innate and absolute superiority of an arbitrarily defined human group over other equally arbitrarily defined groups. Instead of being based on scientific facts, it is generally maintained in defiance of the scientific method. As an ideology and feeling, racism is by its nature aggressive. It threatens the essential moral values by satisfying the taste for domination and by exalting the contempt for man.[89]

To describe racism as an expression of the "caste spirit" is at once to broaden its reach and empty it of specific purpose, a point made at length by Black Marxist sociologist Oliver Cromwell Cox in his seminal work *Caste, Class, and Race* of 1948. For Cox, writing at the farthest extreme from the liberal consensus, the "most insidious" analogy between race and caste "rests in the idea of life membership in each group."[90] Such a view made it seem like Whites and Blacks were "equally interested" in protecting their color and, therefore, in segregation. The whole point of caste theory, as Cox saw it, was to "lump all white people and all Negroes into two antagonistic groups," a situation "very much to the liking of the exploiters of labor."[91]

Most readers construe the efforts of UNESCO and related anti-racist measures at mid-century as producing a crucial new distinction between the old, scientifically debunked, biological view of race and a purely social notion of ethnicity. Point 6 of the UNESCO statement, perhaps for the first time, makes this distinction clear. Because "cultural traits" have "no demonstrated genetic connection with racial traits" it would be better when "speaking of human races to drop the term 'race' altogether and speak of *ethnic groups*"[92] (emphases in original). These newly described ethnic groups "do not necessarily coincide with racial groups." To say these groups do not "necessarily coincide" with racial groups has a strange way of reinforcing the very point they putatively want to critique: that race is a "dangerous myth." At no point do they make the claim that race is plainly false, nor that ethnicity is strictly a social construct, and therefore identical with changing beliefs and practices. The distinction between race and ethnicity is not clarified, because it cannot be clarified. (Consider, for instance, a notion like "black culture," a term that freely, but also incoherently, conjoins biology and culture.)

What purposes, then, does ethnicity serve? Here again, Kazan's Professor Lieberman helps clarify the point. Lieberman has just outlined Montagu's point that race is a scientific myth. On this account, if a Jew is not religious, he is not a Jew at all. That is the nature of Lieberman's crusade. But the crusade will have to wait because the world is not ready for the truth. If racism persists, no amount of science will free mankind from the myth. Here, Lieberman turns from Montagu's anthropology to a pure expression of Sartre's Jew as the true antidote to a racist society.

Lieberman: There must be millions of people nowadays who are religious only in the vaguest sense. I've often wondered why the Jewish ones among them still go on calling themselves Jews. Can you guess why, Mr. Green?
Green: No, but I'd like to know.
Lieberman: Because the world still makes it an advantage not to be one. Thus, for many of us, it becomes a matter of pride to go on calling ourselves Jews. So, you see, I will have to abandon my crusade before it begins. Only if there were no anti-Semites could I go on with it.

The "no such thing" account of race will have to wait and in its place is a politics of "pride"—affirming one's solidarity with others who suffer under the same myth. Kazan is following here Sartre's declaration at the end of *Anti-Semite and Jew*, that the contemporary Jew "derives his pride from his humiliation."[93] Montagu's ethnic group joins hands with Sartre's authentic Jew.

If Kazan is preaching the new anthropological gospel, he is also affirming the position of Sartre's *Anti-Semite and Jew*. For Lieberman, it is a matter of pride to be a (nonpracticing) Jew, even or especially if the science tells him there is no such thing. Because the world "still makes it an advantage not to be" a Jew, the only authentic response, the only responsible thing to do, is to deny the advantage and take one's place among the hated, to become a Jew especially if there is no such thing.

FROM "CONTENDER" TO INFORMANT

The setting and scene for Kazan's 1954 *On the Waterfront* is starkly different from the world of genteel elites. But the superficial distinctions between New Canaan and Hoboken, bourgeois elites and longshoremen, fall away with Kazan's liberal account of postwar America. The casual and genteel racists of New England are replaced by the violent and corrupt Jersey union. But as the worldly Professor Lieberman makes clear, for Kazan, the elite are not the problem, it's their *racism* that's a problem. Kazan wants to make the world safe for elites like Lieberman. Nothing of the sort can be said for Kazan's view of union workers in Jersey. Rife with corruption and extortion, not only does Kazan refuse to offer a nuanced picture of union life, but as Orson Welles rightly put it, he ultimately "celebrates the informer."[94]

The film follows the struggles of Terry Malloy (Marlon Brando), a dockworker, and follows his path away from crime, renouncing the corrupt union run by Johnny Friendly (Lee J. Cobb). Terry's brother Charley (Rod Steiger) is Friendly's right-hand man, and it is Charley's murder by Friendly that convinces Terry to testify against Friendly thereby bringing down the union. The theme of the film is corruption among the working class, who are depicted as mob-soldiers or mob bosses. Although commentators have failed to notice, it is also a film about race and continues the anti-racist themes of *Gentleman's Agreement*. Terry falls in love with Edie Doyle, an Irish-Catholic teacher-in-training (her brother was killed by Friendly, after Terry set him up). Terry goes on a date with Edie at an Irish bar, a scene that presents an alternative vision of sociality to the mob mentality on the dock. When they walk in, the radio is playing a baseball game, the bartender informing them, "Well, what do you know—Jackie just stole home." Terry says, in a wry act of solidarity, "I wouldn't mind doing that myself." Here at the bar, among the Irish, a Black baseball player, drunks, and outcasts, Terry finds *his* home. It is an alternative America, one comprised of radical individuality, and it is meant to stand in the sharpest contrast to the empty sociality of the dockworkers, who identify in terms of a paycheck.

Kazan's next major film *A Face in the Crowd* (1957) exemplifies the basic tendencies of race and class thinking at mid-century. Like *On the Waterfront* it would be wrong to think of the film as "about race," which it manifestly is not. And yet the film is curiously and unmistakably bookended by a vision of race that is not only compatible with the claims of the earlier films but shows how race, and the elision of class, continues to structure Kazan's basic outlook.

The story focuses on Larry "Lonesome" Rhodes, a drifter who we first meet passed out on the floor of an Arkansas jail. Radio journalist Marcia Jeffries (Patricia Neal) is visiting the jail, looking for undiscovered talent. Marcia is clearly slumming it; she is a privileged student looking for "authenticity" among the dispossessed:

> I went to Sarah Lawrence College, I majored in music. I learned that real American music comes from the bottom up. When Gershwin played at the New York it was black tie music . . . but the real beginning of it was in folks that never owned a tie.

Marcia has a facile understanding of class, although it is unclear whether Kazan has anything more sophisticated to offer. Unlike the New Canaan elites in *Gentleman's Agreement*, Marcia is at once risible in her naivete but also, as the film progresses, heroic. If we are tempted to judge the rich girl for slumming it among the drunks and drifters, by the end of the film all of our scorn is reserved for Lonesome.

Marcia discovers her singer-entertainer diamond in the rough with "Lonesome" Rhodes (a name she gives him). Marica offers him a radio contract and the sheriff offers to set him free. The sheriff pokes around, investigating his options.

Sheriff: Hey, you, you can do something [pointing to a Black man in a jail cell].
Prisoner: I got black skin, but I ain't no minstrel.

The Black man is the only one behind bars; the White prisoners are free to roam about. Lonesome accepts Marcia's offer and waltzes out of the jail, poking fun at the inmates left behind, stopping to take a subtle dig at the Black man in the cell.

Lonesome: Bring on old Big Jeff, the sheriff of Pickett, Arkansas . . . with his big old fat key. To open up this nasty, filthy jailhouse . . . and make a free man of me. You got any objections to being a free man in the morning?
Prisoner: No, sir, I ain't.

Lonesome is free, the Black prisoner is not. But the prisoner, unlike Lonesome, retains his inner freedom, his refusal to play the minstrel, a theme that returns at the very end of the film. Lonesome, as the story unfolds, sells himself to the highest bidders and comes to inevitable ruin. A crucial aspect of the story—at least for Kazan—is that Lonesome has nothing but contempt for his audience, an idea that is given pride of place in the trailer for the film. When Lonesome begins to find fame, we watch him leave the town that made him famous, waving to his rapturous fans. When he turns away from the crowd, he tells Marcia under his breath how glad he is to "shake that dump." Marcia is mortified (although not mortified enough to drop Lonesome). By the end of the film Marcia has had enough of his contempt and keeps his mic open during a commercial break so the audience can hear him spew his disdain on air. In a fantastical image of the "truth shall set you free," Kazan shows audiences across the country shunning Lonesome in disgust, direct confrontation with the truth rights all wrongs. By the end, Lonesome is a drunken outcast once again, just as at the beginning.

It is at this point, in the final moments of the film, when Lonesome is shunned by society, that Kazan reintroduces race. When he hears that his audience is turning on him, we watch Lonesome break down in his mansion, grabbing the lapel of one of his (numerous) Black servants, shouting, "Say you're gonna love me, you're gonna love me. . . . What's your name?" The servant offers nothing but a blank stare, which enrages Lonesome as he yells, "Get out! Get out! Get out, you black monkeys! You turn my stomach. Get out!" Lonesome's racism is meant to take the audience by surprise. Up to this point, Kazan has made no effort to depict Lonesome as a racist, more like the opposite. Early on in the film Lonesome seemingly embraces a fantasy of racial leveling. During his radio program Lonesome tells listeners that his boss's pool is open to the public. What follows is a comic scene where all the kids in the neighborhood, conspicuously including all races, jump and splash in the boss's pool. But as the finale makes clear, Lonesome only pursues equality when it suits his purposes, when he has something to gain from it. It is crucial for Kazan that Lonesome is revealed as a racist, someone who is full of contempt even or especially for those who adore him. He is beyond saving, and he is not saved. For Kazan, Lonesome epitomizes the dangers of populism. And for innumerable recent commentators—see, for instance, Jake Tapper's "Why Americans Fall for Grifters: A Warning from a 1957 Film" in *The Atlantic* (2020)—*A Face in the Crowd* is lauded for its prescient understanding of Trump-style populism. Kazan is careful to indicate that Lonesome is an opportunist; without the slightest hint of political commitments, he sells himself to the left and the right. And for those that imagine the problem in the 1950s, or today, is so-called populism, and not liberal policy, Kazan offers a prophetic vision of the future. But what Kazan actually foretells is a world where class is erased and meaningful distinctions are matters of personal identity. The heroes of Kazan films, as they are in Cold War sociology—German, French, and American—are *individuals*, those who resist "the crowd."

What kind of politics emerges from this fictional paradigm? Consider Kazan himself. In 1952 he famously testified before the House Committee on Un-American Activities, identifying eight (former) communists in the film industry. It was this testimony that inspired Orson Welles to publicly denounce him as a "traitor." "He is a man who sold to McCarthy all his companions at a time when he could continue to work in New York at high salary," Welles says, careful to note Kazan's own class position. Welles draws the crucial connection between Kazan's art and his politics: "And having sold all of his people to McCarthy he then made a film called *On the Waterfront* which was a celebration of the informer." If *On the Waterfront*, as many believe, is a response to the criticism he received for testifying for McCarthy, then it is more like doubling down than a change of heart. Kazan's hero is Welles's scab informant. Terry—it's one of the most famous lines in film history—wanted to have "class," wanted to be a "contender" (in boxing, the individualism of the sport is to the point). Instead of being a contender, he was an informer, and having "class" meant selling out his class. Kazan, and the affluent society of sociologists of the 1950s and 1960s, defended the rights of the contenders, the individualists against the populist crowd. But instead of freeing the individual, they authorized a world of diverse, individuated agents perfectly suited for mass exploitation.

NOTES

1. I take up a similar set of questions concerning this quote in "Class into Race: Brecht and the Problem of State Capitalism," *Critical Inquiry* 44, No. 1 (Fall 2017): 54–79. My discussion here continues the line of argument there.
2. Adorno, quoted in Collomp, 2011, 422.
3. Tiedemann, quoted in Jacobs, 2015, 60.
4. Horkheimer 1978, 61.
5. Horkheimer 1978, 61.
6. Horkheimer 1978, 65.
7. Horkheimer 1978, 62.
8. Lenin quotes from an 1858 letter from Engels to Marx about the English situation: "The English proletariat is becoming more and more bourgeois, so that this most bourgeois of all nations is apparently aiming ultimately at the possession of a bourgeois aristocracy, and a bourgeois proletariat as well as a bourgeoisie" (Lenin 1939, 107).
9. Horkheimer 1978, 61.
10. Horkheimer 1978, 61.
11. Horkheimer 1978, 62.
12. Horkheimer 1978, 62.
13. Marcuse 1969, 181.

14. Lucien Goldmann sums up the point about "integration," a point made *ad nauseam* by the Frankfurt School, in his contribution to *To Free a Generation*: "The dominant strata succeed in deflecting the discontents of the workers and even of cadres—and I refer here to the analyses of Marcuse, [Serge] Mallet and [André] Gorz—preventing people from becoming conscious of the fact that their discontent is not only situated at the level of consumption and income, but that behind this lies another malaise, more vague, perhaps, but more general; a maladjustment of the human structure to a social reality which does not allow it to express itself and to develop. So ultimately the conflict can be resolved and the individuals integrated by conceding them a slightly higher income and an improvement of their material situation" (Goldmann 1969, 133).

15. Marcuse 1969, 181. Along these lines, Horkheimer decries Marx and Engels for their "teaching that the struggle for higher wages and shorter hours of work would finally put an end to the prehistory of mankind." Horkheimer describes the pursuit of wages and leisure time as a "pathetically secularized Messianism, infinitely inferior to the authentic one" (Horkheimer 1978, 231).

16. Marcuse 2015, 40.

17. Marcuse 2015, 48. Marcuse's misguided theoretical analysis is tied to an equally mistaken material analysis, as when he insists that there has been a "tremendous decline in self-employment in American society" (Marcuse 2015, 46).

18. Marcuse 1978, 150. As Douglas Kellner and Clayton Pierce note, "Marcuse was probably the most tenacious and unyielding critic of the Marxian concept of the 'proletariat' as the privileged revolutionary subject" (Marcuse 2014, 63).

19. Marcuse 2015, 67.

20. Marcuse 2015, 214 (emphasis in original).

21. Marcuse 2014, 62.

22. Horkheimer and Adorno 2007, 123.

23. Horkheimer 1978, 231.

24. Horkheimer 1982, 96.

25. The book famously emerges from and elaborates on his "Portrait of an Anti-Semite," which appeared in *Les Temps modernes* in November 1945.

26. Sartre 1948, 67.

27. Sartre 1948, 67.

28. Sartre 1948, 69.

29. Sartre 1948, 69 (emphasis in original).

30. Sartre 1948, 91.

31. Sartre 1948, 73.

32. Sartre 1948, 73–74.

33. Sartre 1948, 74.

34. Sartre 1948, 75.

35. Sartre 1948, 76.

36. Sartre 1948, 77.

37. Sartre 1948, 80.

38. Sartre 1948, 135, 141.

39. Sartre 1948, 81.

40. Sartre 1948, 82–83.
41. Sartre 1948, 83.
42. Sartre 1948, 82
43. Sartre 1988, 296.
44. Sartre 1948, 85.
45. Sartre 1948, 89.
46. Sartre 1948, 90.
47. Sartre 1948, 91.
48. Sartre 1948, 91.
49. Sartre 1948, 109, 111.
50. Sartre 1948, 110.
51. Sartre 1948, 110.
52. Sartre 1948, 111.
53. Sartre 1948, 111.
54. Sartre 1948, 113 (emphasis in original). Sartre goes on to make similar claims about the work of Henri Bergson, although this time it is a more tortured argument. Sartre must make Bergson into a rationalist philosopher in order to show how he too flees his authentic condition as a Jew (Sartre 1948, 115–16).
55. Sartre 1948, 126.
56. Sartre 1948, 126.
57. Sartre 1948, 136.
58. Sartre 1948, 137.
59. Sartre 1948, 137.
60. Adorno 2019, lviii.
61. Adorno 2019, lviii.
62. Adorno 2019, lix.
63. Adorno 2019, lx.
64. Fromm 1941, 126.
65. Bell 1964, 47.
66. Hofstadter 1964, 98.
67. In his contribution to *The New American Right*, Peter Viereck offers a banalized version of Frankfurt School cultural criticism, lamenting how "paeans of economic prosperity ignore the psychological starvation, the cultural starvation, the mechanical mediocrity of too-efficient bigness" (Viereck 1964, 182). Whatever gains are achieved through "relative political freedom" end in losses as "Big Business" "robotizes [the masses] into a tractable, pap-fed, Reader's-Digested and manipulated mass-culture" (Viereck 1964, 182–83).
68. Riesman 1964, 134–35.
69. Hofstadter 1964, 77, 83, 81.
70. Lipset 1964, 347. Lipset took his critique of economic analysis further in his reactionary assessment of what he calls "Working-Class Authoritarianism" (Lipset, "Democracy and Working-Class Authoritarianism," *American Sociological Review* 24, no. 4 [August 1959]: 482–501).
71. Lipset 1964, 308–309. Lipset takes up Hofstadter's basic distinction between "interest politics" and "status politics" (Hofstadter 1964, 84).

72. Lipset 1964, 332.
73. Lipset 1964, 330.
74. Riesman 1954, 153.
75. Riesman 1954, 154.
76. Riesman 1954, 156.
77. Riesman 1954, 156.
78. Riesman 1954, 157.
79. Riesman 1954, 159.
80. Riesman 1954, 159.
81. Riesman 1954, 159, 160.
82. Riesman et al. 1953, 323–24.
83. Riesman et al. 1953, 117. The crucial point of reference here is Judith Stein's critique of Washington and related figures, "'Of Mr. Booker T. Washington and Others': The Political Economy of Racism in the United States," *Science and Society* 38, No. 4 (Winter 1974/75): 422–63. One of Riesman's coauthors, Nathan Glazer, was one of the principal architects of the central document of underclass ideology, *The Negro Family: The Case for National Action*, otherwise known as the Moynihan Report of 1965. Glazer and Daniel Patrick Moynihan cowrote *Beyond the Melting Pot: The Negroes, Puerto Ricans, Jews, Italians, and Irish of New York City* (Cambridge, MA: MIT Press, 1963), which formed the crucial basis for *The Negro Family* of two years later. See Touré Reed, "Why Moynihan Was Not So Misunderstood at the Time: The Mythological Prescience of the Moynihan Report and the Problem of Institutional Structuralism," *nonsite.org* 17 (2015).
84. Riesman et al. 1953, 324.
85. Riesman et al. 1953, 323.
86. Riesman 1954, 160.
87. Riesman 1954, 160.
88. Riesman 1954, 135.
89. UNESCO 1950, 3.
90. Cox 1987, 8.
91. Cox 1987, 22.
92. UNESCO 1950, 6 (emphasis in original).
93. Sartre 1948, 137, see also 90.
94. See Orson Welles's interview with Henri Behar, Paris, February 24, 1982, https://www.youtube.com/watch?v=Z6DC4AjTG2M.

Chapter 2

The Dubious Wonder of Identity
Robert Pfaller

A substantial proportion of neoliberal pseudo-policies and the sensitivities they fuel are based heavily on questions of (cultural, ethnic, religious, sexual, etc.) identity. If you cannot offer people decent prospects for the future, just deflect their attention to their past, their origins, or the point at which they currently are. The following chapter addresses some of the contradictions and paradoxes inherent in questions of identity in order to pursue the follow-up question of what kind of organization of social illusions has led to the currently widespread preference for transience and the indefinite.

"I'M NOT ABOVE ANYTHING. IT WOULD REALLY HAVE TO BE SOMETHING!" SOME VARIATIONS, DIGRESSIONS, AND DIVERTISSEMENTS ON IDENTITY

It was at the height of postmodernity, during the late 1990s—when universities, above all in the United States and the United Kingdom, outdid one another with increasingly new measures to ensure the identities of all those involved in their educational programs would be treated respectfully and considerately—that the economization of universities was in full swing[1]. The outcome was that everyone involved with higher education would, from now on, be permanently monitored and checked and would constantly have to report on their activities. (Perhaps the two developments were even connected, for it was more or less the same kind of people who benefited the most from both and who now established themselves within the new score-counting apparatuses of control, and the mostly box-ticking and tally-counting apparatuses guaranteeing equal gender-based, etc., treatment.)

A colleague from Austria who worked as a lecturer at a British university and who came under pressure to report on her teaching activities came up with a fabulous response at the time. She simply said, "This is against my culture." Even more fabulous was the fact that her university board actually accepted this argument and immediately exempted her from any accountability and evaluation procedures. So, at the height of postmodernity, the reference to her identity was enough to even dodge the postmodern evaluation squadrons.

This example aside, I never quite understood why identity became so important to people who have learned to think in political categories. I realized more and more that struggles for the adequate recognition of an identity never benefited the entire identity group but only those who spoke on its behalf (often without actually being part of that group).[2] Yet even if an entire group were to have subsequently achieved comprehensive social recognition of their identity, I would have still asked myself whether this really was such a great achievement.

Why were people just fighting for recognition all of a sudden? And not for equality?[3] Is recognition not, as Nietzsche replied to Hegel, a demand of slaves?[4] And why were they fighting for the right to be as they were presumed to be? Why not at least also for the right to be different, too? Or, say, why not for the right to be addressed and treated without *any* reference to one's suchness or some assumed identity? And why does their *being* matter to these people so much suddenly? Might it be possible that this question was only invented as a distraction from the question of *having*, or, rather, *not having*?

During the late 1990s, I was working at a public US college. A few days into the job, I was sent to one of the university's admin departments, initially unaware of the purpose of my visit. An official asked me what my "race" was. I was slightly dumbfounded for a second. Up until then, I had thought only the Gestapo would ask me such a question.

I politely replied that, to my knowledge, my "race" had never been ascertained. And I inquired as to whom I would have to ask to find out. My GP? The official slid the form across the table and told me to just mark the right one. Besides the terms "African" and "Hispanic," which I had heard before, there were others, too, which I had never come across, like "Caucasian."

I thought very hard about how to answer. Austria and Spain had at one point in the past been one and the same country. And, owing to my dark hair and complexion, some friends in the Mexican neighborhood in Chicago where I lived had already jokingly asked whether I might perhaps be a "greasy spoon" (a gringo term for Mexicans) myself. So, was I in fact "Hispanic"? I hesitated, unsure what to do. The official began to lose patience with me. She took the form and marked "Caucasian." I asked her what that even meant. She explained that "Caucasian" simply meant "white," and by hesitating, I had clearly proven that I was White, because Whites, she said (her skin tone was in fact far lighter than my own), always messed about when it came to this topic.

Eventually, I asked what this whole process was good for in the first place. To protect me from discrimination, the official replied politely. So, in order to be protected from discrimination, I was discriminated against, that is, my identity was singled out from among other identities (and, incidentally, bad-mouthed without hesitation).

Workers whose native language is Turkish have been perceived as Muslims in Austria since about the mid-1990s. And all the problems these workers may have with others, or that others may have with them, are declared problems of religion or culture. This is a fairly recent development. Up until the mid-1990s, these workers had been perceived mainly as communists. At the time, they often formed the largest and most entertaining contingents at the demonstrations marking May Day, alongside the similarly large and entertaining Kurdish groups (which, however, all international solidarity aside, marched neatly separated from one another).

So, the fact that the problems that had also existed in the past started, from about 1995, to be reframed as problems of cultural or religious identity was a new phenomenon. I, for my part, could remember that the same or similar conflicts had already been around at a time when there had not even been any, or only very few, native Turks in Austria. Even back when everybody was a native German speaker in Austria, you were not allowed to play with certain other children and the respective parents would not speak to each other either.

When sculptor Alfred Hrdlicka's Memorial against War and Fascism was installed in Vienna in 1988, two rather distinct groups were outraged at his bronze sculpture of the "kneeling, street-washing Jew": on one side was the Jewish Community, on the other were those Austrians whose worldviews most strongly echoed those of the erstwhile Nazi perpetrators. This situation made it plain to me for the first time that two opposing groups, no matter how hostile they may be toward one another, can still have something in common despite their conflict—for example, that they do not wish to be reminded of a particular fact.

Such a scenario is reminiscent of a scene in Sergio Leone's Western movie *The Good, the Bad and the Ugly*, when the protagonists witness a battle of the US Civil War. In the scene, both Union soldiers and Confederates are dug in along both banks of a river and engaged in the most murderous firefight. Yet both armies take great caution to spare the wooden bridge that spans the river and which they rely on to launch their mutual attacks. But then our two protagonists put an end to this eerie alliance with the use of dynamite. The warring parties themselves, however, would never have violated this aspect of their tacit agreement.

In my view, the same seems to apply to certain conflicts in the suburbs, where a migrant "underclass" lives side by side with a nonmigrant "underclass." It appears as if there is a strong interest shared by all conflicting parties involved in framing their conflict as cultural or related to identity. Both sides, migrants as much as the politically right-leaning nonmigrants, seem to find this more flattering than, say, comparing their conflict to those which also took place between two culturally homogeneous groups just a few decades ago. It would entail describing this conflict as one between low-wage groups that are *more* versus *less* willing to advance socially or between those groups who have advanced upward to some extent and those who have not. Needless to say, such a conflict may well be more difficult to solve than one that is carried out in forthright terms, for it would imply persuading the involved parties and actors to first abandon their tenderly maintained, misleading narrative of the conflict—e.g. as a cultural, religious, ethnic, etc.[5]

In Austria, which used to be a traditional bureaucratic state run by an apparatus of civil servants, a new practice was introduced around that time, which may well have served as a blueprint for postmodern identity politics. All civil servants—but also all other people whom the state wanted to motivate to remain loyal to it, or rather, its political representatives, for a meager income— were given cost-effective but fancy-sounding titles instead of money. The long-standing administrative officer or civil servant became a "councillor of the Chancellery" (*Kanzleirätin*), the senior grammar school teacher became the "senior councillor of Studies" (*Oberstudienrat*), the accomplished entrepreneur willing to donate to the respective party received the honorary title of "councillor of Commerce" (*Kommerzialrat*), the long-serving school superintendent became a "councillor of the Government" (*Regierungsrat*), the unsuccessful older artist was made "professor." And even in the broader social context of postmodernity, eroded by neoliberalism as it is, it is common to give pleasant-sounding names to rather unpleasant matters, things, or tasks. The cleaner was elevated to the "room carer" (*Raumpflegerin*), the waiter was made "catering specialist" (*Gastronomiefachkraft*), the garbage incinerator became the "waste disposal facility," the expulsion of students from university at the end of a new, shorter study program was termed "lifelong learning," and people who were regarded as disabled in the past became people with "special needs," and so on.

Instead of ensuring that women are paid the same wage for the same labor, great efforts are made for them to look increasingly similar to men and be treated as rudely as men in cultural interactions; beyond that, they are supposed to be appeased by receiving gender-specific titles—which, incidentally, means that precisely in those instances where there was no differentiation previously, as in the academic titles like "MA," "Dr.," or "Prof.," the classic gender discrimination has now been made complete, with women being depicted as different, special, and requiring particular mention.[6]

Those disadvantaged by social injustices are treated as if they had no problems other than being referred to by a special, in most cases highly sensitive, name. And what is more, the bureaucracy tasked with implementing such (linguistic) measures then claims, with a kind of "magic worldview," that these better names can also lead to better conditions in life. Upon a more sober inspection, however, we must acknowledge that the better conditions have not only failed to materialize in most cases: the more appealing verbal label has rather—and this can be easily explained from the perspective of a theory of "two worlds"[7]—replaced any kind of real improvement. In fact, the conditions have remained as bad as before precisely *because* there are better names these days.

What we are being spared are designations that accurately depict the conditions. As if we were too sensitive to stand the truth. One thing seems rather conspicuous: the harder the conditions get, the more we are treated as wimps. Perhaps it is an attempt to prevent us from coming up with the idea of standing up against the hardening of conditions.

Is it really the pinnacle of happiness, the maximum of socially redeemable entitlement, to always be designated and treated as what one is—and as nothing else? A French joke may illustrate this matter: What is the difference between politeness and tactfulness? The answer: Politeness is when you encounter a naked woman behind a door in someone else's apartment and say, "Pardon, Madame." Tactfulness, by contrast, is to say, "Pardon, Monsieur."

When, for example, some gender or queer movements today, in their struggle against alleged "heteronormativity," fight to no longer define gender as a binary, charged difference, but instead as a calm continuum, the question remains as to what would constitute respectful treatment of those who situate themselves somewhere in the undefined middle of the continuum. Should they be addressed as such (and, if so, using what term)? Or would it not be far more tactful to grant them a masquerade and allow them to claim an existing gender role, even though they may not exactly fit this role for biological reasons or because they do not identify with it? There seems to be a tendency among Protestant cultures to privilege the genderless, or the undefined, which would correspond to both the fundamentalist Christian hostility toward any sexuality and the truth-mongering distrust against social pretenses and playful, polite forms of interaction. Correspondingly, activists whose habitus somewhat resembles that of a pastor's children demand the universal right to genderless designations. In Catholic cultures of pagan origin, by contrast, this is viewed quite differently. The so-called she-males in Barcelona, for example, who feature as main characters in the films of Pedro Almodóvar and Nazario's cartoons, attach great importance to being treated as ladies. After all, a gender role entails not only "normalization" or duties and responsibilities but also certain privileges that may be quite pleasant, such as being greeted with a kiss on the hand or for others to hold open the door.

In this sense, the so-called struggle for identity in postmodernity must be understood as a typical neoliberal political strategy. It encourages individuals to select an identity and then limit themselves to it.

They are not even to imagine or claim anything that goes beyond this ascription; nothing that would make them not only people with private interests and family or ethnic ties, or sexual limitations, but rather also cosmopolitan, global citizens, *Citoyens* or *Grandes Dames*. Any universalism is to be alien to them. And any critical rupture with one's own roots or cultural backgrounds as well. Slavoj Žižek, by contrast, has noted quite succinctly that the slogan of revolutionary solidarity today is not: "Let us tolerate our differences." According to Žižek, the issue is "not a pact of civilisations, but a pact of struggles which cut across civilisations, a pact between what, in each civilisation, undermines its identity from within, fights against its oppressive kernel."[8] If there is something about us that we need to fight for, it is not our mundane identity, but that which is universal about us, that allows us to critically reflect on this identity and potentially even break with it.[9] And to show solidarity with others who do the same.

As Richard Sennett once wrote, "Civility exists when a person does not make himself a burden to others."[10] We ought to complement this principle with its counterpart: it is just as uncivilized to define somebody by their alleged self and to burden them with it.

THE THRILL OF INDETERMINACY: VAGUE IDENTITIES, DECEPTIVE FREEDOMS, PERSISTENT CONSTRUCTIONS

From superstition to the confession of faith: the more you believe in something, the more this something turns to nothing.

One of the stories that postmodern ideology likes to tell about itself is that it is the epoch in which no one believes in "grand narratives" anymore. We must treat this story with the utmost caution; although it may seem that humanity is becoming more intelligent, this is certainly not always true when humanity believes it to be the case.

Psychoanalyst Octave Mannoni has presented a remarkably elucidating theory in this regard. In his essay "I Know Quite Well, but Still . . ." he discusses the example of an African mask cult whose observant followers report to the ethnologist that they themselves have no idea what the cult actually means, as the concomitant faith has disappeared.[11] The informants say that people *once* believed in the masks.

Instead of pursuing the hypothesis of a destroyed culture, Mannoni proposes considering this situation, this bizarre discrepancy between the nonexistence of the actual faith and the continuation of the mask ritual, as the normal state of the mask cult: the cult had always been practiced in the knowledge that the original faith was attributed to an earlier epoch. As Mannoni rightly notes, there are many situations in our culture, too, in which an illusion is maintained without anyone being able to say who actually believes in it: when we see a magic trick performed on stage, for example, we are quite aware that there is nothing supernatural about what is happening, and yet we are delighted by the "perfect illusion" of the trick. Mannoni refers to this type of illusion, of which there are no actual bearers, as *croyance* (a term that may best be translated as "belief" in the sense of "superstition"), and he distinguishes between the *croyance* and the *foi* ("faith"), the confession of faith, for which we shall always find proud bearers who will declare that they believe in something greater, or, rather, something that they consider to be just that—God, or human progress, or the self-regulation of financial markets.

That is to say, the confession of faith (*foi*) always rests on the principle of identifying with the illusion. The forms of superstition/belief, the *croyances*, might be quite enjoyable, but they do not allow for identification. Faith produces self-esteem; superstition arouses lust. Or, to put it in psychoanalytical terms, faith operates at the level of the ego-libido, superstition/belief at the level of the object-libido.[12]

Mannoni's deliberations allow for some far-reaching conclusions. The first insight is that the more illusions exist in colorful and material forms—such as an elaborate mask cult—the more they manifest in the form of *croyances* and are, moreover, addressed to an undefined bearer.

However, as soon as one starts believing in the illusions, they fade, become abstract, and lose their materiality. The history of religions illustrates this: In ancient polytheism, the gods and goddesses are specific. They display difference, they are visible (at times), and have a gender, needs, follies, an inclination to drunkenness, and so on. But people do not really believe in them; rather, they tell each other amusing stories about them. Only when people start believing do the gods lose their difference, their concreteness and visibility. In the later, so-called secondary religions, there is only one, invisible, asexual, omniscient, and apparently always sober God.[13]

This aspect contains the second major consequence of Mannoni's theory: superstition/belief can be found in all cultures. Faith, however, is a later achievement, which can be found only in some cultures. Not all cultures develop the ambition to believe in the illusions they create.

And this means, *third*, that faith in earlier epochs was not stronger, but weaker, more casual. Mannoni thus contradicts the widespread myth of the "enlightenment process," according to which people in medieval times lived safely in their content, naive faith in God above, whereas we, in our modern times, roam the world in a kind of "transcendental homelessness." The reality seems to have been quite contrary: in the past, people merely had ways of representing the illusion (and they may have referred to this illusion with the amusing awareness that people in the past actually believed in it); only later did they begin to abandon the representation, as they increasingly wanted to believe in these illusions.[14]

Here, Mannoni's insights concur with Max Weber's findings concerning the "disenchantment of the world."[15] Weber also sees the cause of this process, which robs the world of all the charming glamour of materialized illusions, not in science or materialist philosophy, but rather in a religion that is based on a greater sense of identification: Protestant Christianity.

That which likes to conceive of itself as an enlightenment process is thus anything but an increase in rationality or the shedding of faith-based identifications; it is rather a process of more intense identification—a process of internalization that no longer tolerates pleasure because of the desire to solemnly believe, and which is therefore hardly able to believe in anything any longer, precisely because it is so keen to believe. The stronger the identification with the illusion, the less imagery is attached to the illusion.

And that is precisely the context in which we must understand postmodernity's proclamation of the end of grand narratives. The feeling is real, and yet it is deceptive, as it does not imply the end of all illusion but rather a new stage of this heightened sense of identification. We are witnessing a process in which individuals are increasingly encouraged to identify with their illusions. However, because of a more intense identification, the object of illusion itself is lost. The satisfaction of the ego-libido comes at the price of the object.

That is why those with a strong sense of identity, the "highly identified," persuade themselves that they do not believe in anything or that they doubt everything. Yet as we know from Descartes, a general doubt about everything always entails the self-assurance of a skeptical self. And this self-(re)assurance is not simply a cognitive quality; it is, above all, also a libidinous cathexis. It corresponds to strong emotions: We are—UNFORTUNATELY—unable to believe in anything because we—HURRAY!—believe so strongly in ourselves and have to reassure ourselves of this constantly through our skepticism.

Of course, this forced ego-libidinous lust is not as exciting as the object-libidinous exhilaration offered by masks, magic tricks, or silly stories about gods. Rather, as Freud already pointed out, what is dominant here is the manifest "pain" (*Unlust*) that cannot be abandoned—that "neurotic 'pain'" which Jacques Lacan ambiguously termed "jouissance" (enjoyment).[16] The skeptic who cannot believe in anything and will not participate in any kind of playful foolishness, because they always have to be so sensible, lives under the diktat of a tyrannical superego that torments them with the merciless order to "enjoy!"

The Subjection Effect:
The more one wants to believe in oneself,
the less one can bear being something specific

The typical postmodern preferences for floating subjects, for broken, queer, crossed, evolving, and other indefinite identities, must be seen in this light:[17] to use Althusser's theory of ideology, they are forms of intensified subjectivization, that is, the intensified ideological recruitment and subordination of individuals. These indeterminacies represent intensified "subjection effects" (*effets d'assujettissement*).[18]

According to Althusser, the subjection effect does not simply come into play when an individual assumes a symbolic mandate along the lines of "Yes, it really is me! Here I am: a worker, entrepreneur, soldier!"[19] (and we could continue this list with, say, professor, artist, transsexual being, etc.). It appears only when an imaginary reversal takes place: that is to say, when individuals think that "they have always been subjects"; when they think that they have freely chosen their position and have assumed the mandate as already existing subjects.

That is why the possibility of a "performative restructuring" of a symbolic role in particular, conceived by Judith Butler as a liberating perspective, does not lead us out of the subjection effect, that is, the ideological subordination of individuals, but rather straight into it. Individuals become "subjected subjects" precisely at the point at which they sense that they can independently determine their role.[20] In this aspect, Althusser's theory of ideology strictly follows the doctrine of Spinoza on the deceptive, imaginary sense of free choice. Spinoza wrote,

> But if, however, we had not found out that we do many things which we afterwards repent, and that when agitated by conflicting emotions we see that which is better and follow that which is worse, nothing would hinder us from believing that we do everything with freedom. Thus, the infant believes that it is by free will that it seeks the breast; the angry boy believes that by free will he wishes vengeance; the timid man thinks it is with free will he seeks flight; the drunkard believes that by a free command of his mind he speaks the things which when sober he wishes he had left unsaid.[21]

The same applies under postmodern conditions: the broken identity believes it is broken as the result of a conscious choice, and the indefinite gender believes that it is so by choice. This sense of free choice increases in relation to the vagueness and indeterminacy of its object. A greater sense of free choice makes it far easier to be something vaguely defined or indefinite than something definite. Here, again, the coerced ego-libido effectively cancels out the materiality of its object.

This is what sociologist Richard Sennett has referred to as the "tyrannies of intimacy" in his book *The Fall of Public Man*,[22] and that makes his theory all the more topical, especially given the scenario of a neoliberal economy and a corresponding postmodern ideology.

The Tyrannies of Intimacy—and the Triumph of Idiocy

The fact that large parts of the population in Western societies have been preoccupied with questions concerning their identity since the early 1990s must be regarded as one of the central achievements of neoliberal ideology. As long as everybody is contemplating what they want to be, they no longer have the capacity to think about what they may wish to have. And this is indeed useful when people are simultaneously being stripped of things that will no longer be available to them in the future, such as democratic participation, work and income, education, infrastructure, social security, pensions, or even dignity and elegance.

This neoliberal ideology of obsession with one's identity, however, not only serves to distract from other crucial questions. It is itself part of the destruction and privatization of public space that is so characteristic of neoliberalism. *The question of identity arises in all those contexts where the previous distinction between public role and private person, between public and private space, has been liquidated* (as well as in all those contexts where the last residue of this distinction can be proactively, "performatively" liquidated simply by raising the question of identity).

Richard Sennett has shown that the public space that existed in Western societies ever since the time of the Renaissance was a theatrical space: everybody had a role to play in this space, and this playacting served the function of sparing others an encounter with the actual private person. According to Sennett, that is what the virtue of civilized behavior that characterized public space was all about: "Civility is treating others as though they were strangers and forging a social bond upon that social distance."[23]

In contrast, the so-called performative turn, so characteristic of postmodern ideology, consists of the suspension—as is common in the genre of performance more generally—of the theatrical separation between person and role. Now everybody wants to play themselves. And everybody feels fully liberated when they can act as themselves. Or, to put it in terms of ideology theory, everybody is encouraged to play nothing but themselves and to feel liberated when they need to be nothing but themselves. Sennett refers to this ego-libidinous preference by the psychoanalytically correct term of "narcissism."

Considering the example of private TV channels, we can easily see what this means: unlike in the past, everyone can now actually make it on screen—even the nude, the incompetent, the insignificant, the drunk, and so on. Yet, at the same time, this is only possible if they reveal nothing but their private quirks and refrain from seizing the opportunity to speak about something that is of general relevance. Here, we can see that Sennett's distinction between private person and public role coincides with the distinction between *bourgeois* and *citoyen* that emerged from the French Revolution. With regard to the TV example, this shows what is lost when television broadcasting no longer entails any public dimension and people are no longer to appear on TV in public roles. They are then treated exclusively as bourgeois—or, as it was put in ancient Greece, as idiots, that is, as those who are concerned with nothing but their private matters. (Given the existence of so-called reality TV, Michel Foucault's theory of sexuality must be considered in a new light: it is not simply the theory of a [governing] power that encourages speaking about and confessing to an identity instead of simply using repressive force; it is rather, above all, also a theory of an increasing subjectivization of individuals that makes it easier to deny them a public role.)

This limitation and *homogenization*[24] of the "other" as a mere idiot is what postmodern ideology mistakes for "tolerance." The characters of Ali G and Borat performed by comedian Sacha Baron Cohen clearly illustrate the effects of this so-called tolerance: if you treat someone as if they were nothing but their idiotic identity, if you deny them the ability to transcend this identity in favor of a role and to adopt civilized behavior in public, then you are literally racist. Postmodern racism consists of reducing the other person to their mere identity, hence not expecting the least of them and homogenizing them as idiots—for instance, the uncultured Kazakh; the monumentally moronic rapper; the pornography-consuming member of the underclass; the student from an uneducated background; the religiously, ethnically, sexually, and so on, sensitive; or those vulnerable to "micro aggressions."[25]

Postmodern "tolerance" grants every individual the unlimited right to be an utter idiot. (Hence the boom in self-help literature, albeit not without irony: *The Complete Idiot's Guide to Understanding Ethics* or *Derrida for Dummies*, etc.) Today, we ought to counter this with a phrase taken from Hannah Arendt, modified to offer a counter-principle: nobody has the right to be a complete idiot. And no one has the right to treat anyone else as such and to expect nothing of them.

"PLAY YOUR ROLE WELL"

Remember that you are an actor in a play,
The character of which is determined by the Playwright [. . .]
For this is your business, to play admirably the role assigned to you;
But the selection of that role is Another's.[26]

Being something else besides oneself means playing a role. As in any play, this theatrical performance of the public role entails at least two dimensions that may seem problematic under the narcissistic conditions of postmodern ideology, so precisely identified and analyzed by Sennett.

First, play always implies that you have to try to *play well*. Whoever fails to help maintain the fiction of the play—and the belief that a successful play is somehow of crucial importance—is a spoilsport. This means that any play entails an ideal and may even demand compliance with such an ideal from the playactors. What this also means, then, is that one can be more or less successful at the activity. A gender role, for example, is by no means adequately played through favorable biological premises or a careful (identity) construction alone. One must also artfully master the role, and this takes practice.

Under narcissistic conditions, this demand for the ideal performance of a role is experienced as offensive. The fact that one is expected to feel satisfaction and happiness not only for what one is but for what one can do is perceived as an unnecessary, cumbersome theatrical detour, if not as downright heteronomy.[27] It is far easier to create a new role than to practice a difficult one. Narcissists always wish for a good role instead of following the Stoic Epictetus, to whom it is far more important how that role is played. That is the reason why many postmodern narcissists—acquiescing to the interminable and merciless tyranny of their superego—are currently permanently and compulsorily preoccupied with the reconstruction of their role and thus never achieve the object-libidinous pleasure of at least approximating their ideal in isolated instances as a result of skillful play. After all, the latter is precisely the pleasure one can hope for in this context. As Sigmund Freud notes, "There is always a feeling of triumph when something in the ego coincides with the ego ideal."[28]

Yet if the ideal must be disparaged because of its discrepancy with the ego which is perceived as offensive, then the individual prevents themselves from attaining the potential pleasure—and only hands the tyrannical superego an evil triumph. If there are no gender roles that could be played well or poorly and everybody is nothing but their own little unique snowflake, then no one is ever able to play any role well; nobody is ultimately happy and satisfied, but instead unhappy beyond relief. Sennett's insight underscores this aspect, as he notes that narcissism possesses "the double quality of being a voracious absorption in self needs and the block to their fulfilment."[29]

This is the reason why no identity is ever fully owned by anyone. Such an idyllic, fully owned identity exists only as a fantasy if it is prevented from manifesting itself in reality, for example, through oppression or marginalization. By contrast, as soon as it can be realized, that is to say, publicly displayed, it is already at the point where it possesses its own rules and regularities that no longer correspond to the wishes of the ego, which is why its masterful performance is so crucial. Only if one's own identity is oppressed or marginalized can this fact be dismissed. At that point, the "other" becomes a "thief of enjoyment";[30] he or she helps us maintain the idyllic image of our oppressed identity. The "other" is also the only reason why we can imagine the satisfaction with our identity that we could enjoy in the absence of that "other"—spared from any demand for ability as we would be.

Furthermore, this is the reason why negative identities in particular become so popular under narcissistic conditions, as psychoanalysts Béla Grunberger and Pierre Dessuant established in their comprehensive study on narcissism, Christianity, and anti-Semitism: everything that is material and may imply certain rules and laws is unbearable for narcissism.[31] As a result, only substance and content that do not impose any kind of positive rules or requirements concerning abilities are adequate for a total, narcissistic identification: this is why the current heroes and heroines of talk show TV and popular culture consider the most intimate thing they can confess to be related to their indefinite sexual identity, their metrosexuality, their "Low Desire Syndrome," or their post-sexuality.

"GO BEYOND YOUR PRINCIPLES!"

The second dimension of the play that may seem problematic, or indeed unbearable, under the narcissistic conditions of postmodern ideology lies in the fact that the performance of the public role always entails a certain imperative. It orders an individual to overcome their personal boundaries concerning shame and morals; as Freud once clairvoyantly remarked, plays are "excesses provided by law."[32] In the absence of such an imperative of excess, the sexually liberated, informal post-1968 generation, for example, who were raised in antiauthoritarian ways, use (at least in German) the casual and somewhat obtrusive, informal "you" (*Du*) to address each other, but nevertheless tend to always dance by themselves in the club, while, on the other hand, more conservative-socialized people, who are subordinated to very strict rules of politeness, are able, thanks to these very rules, to dance across the ballroom cheek to cheek with a complete stranger at the Vienna Opera Ball.

The rules of culture are not interdictions; they do not prohibit individuals from doing anything, they rather demand something from them, which the latter would never do by choice. That is precisely why we need the rules and imperatives of culture—as enabling conditions of lust, a resource of lust; because—as Freud acknowledged in his *Essays on the Theory of Sexuality*—we ourselves are inhibited.[33]

CONCLUSION

This is the backdrop against which we must assess the current fascination with alleged indeterminacy and those fashionable themes that have haunted the diverse areas of cultural studies and led to the formation of increasingly diversified subdisciplines. To conclude, I would like to briefly make two dangers of misjudgment explicit that appear particularly contingent.

(1) "Oh, Poor Me!"

First, the proclivity for indefinite identities is a typical phenomenon among privileged groups. Fully in line with the fundamental narcissistic principle identified by Grunberger/Dessuant, the weak always appear as the righteous. That is why the privileged make an effort to point out their own *un*privileged features and elevate them above all those many other aspects on the basis of which they would have to consider themselves privileged. Here, a potential truth becomes ideological as a result of being used to conceal many other truths that are perceived as being embarrassing. One seeks to realign one's own alleged moral misalignment as a privileged individual in a narcissistic way through self-imagination as a victim.

(2) "Reinvent Yourselves in New Ways!"

Second, narcissism, in theory, seeks not to solve problems, but to avoid them. This leads to the seemingly benevolent, yet really always, abusive and selfish interest in minoritarian or marginalized groups: those who do not suffer from a given problem become the model of salvation for those who do—for example, homosexuals for heterosexuals; lesbians for "breeders"; post-sexuals for sexuals; the indefinite for the definite; and so on. So, instead of devising rules under which heterosexuals could, under more liberal conditions, freely display pleasure among one another, much is enthusiastically discussed about the constructedness of gender identity or sexual orientation, which tacitly signals to those suffering from illiberal conditions: "It is people's own fault if they are unable to reconstruct themselves in a different way these days—as lesbian, gay, trans, inter- or asexual."

In contrast to this, we may recall that constructions are by no means easily modifiable just because they are constructed. The changeability of things and relations depends not on whether they were historically produced or simply encountered in their pristine form. It depends on their own persistence. Gender theory in fact consistently fails to recognize one type of particularly persistent construction, thereby repeating a mistake attributed, perhaps with a certain justification, to a psychoanalysis focused above all on the petty bourgeois family.[34] It ignores the manifold social, including intergenerational, institutions of sexuality, which are so closely interwoven with the relations of ownership.

Through its focus on sexual identities and orientations, gender theory overlooks—as you would expect from a neoliberal perspective—the fact that gender relations take effect not only between individuals. Rather, sexuality inevitably comprises intersecting economic and legal parameters which extend into the most comprehensive organizational forms—as Friedrich Engels masterfully summed up in the title of his work *The Origin of the Family, Private Property and the State*.[35]

And this is also true, as Deleuze and Guattari have correctly noted,[36] even for the seemingly most intimate desires. Even they are pervaded by these structures. One crucial determinant of sexual desire is therefore the choice of institution—that is to say, the question of whether one wants to live in a monogamous or a polygamous relationship; whether a relationship should be one of long-term or serial monogamy; whether partners wish to have children together or not; whether or not one wishes to meet a partner's parents and siblings, and so on.[37] As a result of the misleading focus on questions of identity and orientation, the political problem of the formation of sexual institutions has been largely neglected and left entirely to the political opponent. While polemicizing against an alleged "heterosexual matrix," it was overlooked not only that the tolerance of homosexual relationships is quite common even among more isolated social environments but also, and most importantly, that the ground gained in the wake of 1968 for free(er) love and the corresponding social form of partnership has, for the most part, been lost. Today, the monogamous couple, ideally involving procreation, has become as dominant as rarely before—it has become "the only game in town," even for many homosexuals—and, as the tyrannical "monogamous matrix" that it is, dismisses all other forms of romantic relationship as unthinkable and unspeakable, and it does so to an extent that women without children must today once again put up with raised eyebrows and perplexed questions.[38] Instead of indulging in the possibilities of one's own indeterminacy, we should all focus our attention on the hard, utterly definite, albeit not unchangeable, social relations that have imposed their schema on love in the twenty-first century.

Translated by Jan-Peter Herrmann

NOTES

1. This title comes from an—as far as I am aware—unpublished poem by my friend Carl Hegemann, who once read it to me.
2. On this, see the insight by Cora Stephan, who soberly notes, "The women's movement benefited only its leaders and officials" (Stephan 1993, 26).
3. The most lucid remarks on this matter once again come from Slavoj Žižek, see Žižek 2008, 140; see also Fraser and Honneth 2004.
4. On this, see Nietzsche: "We can see it as the result of a tremendous atavism that, to this day, ordinary people still wait for an opinion to be pronounced about themselves" (Nietzsche 2002 [1886]: 157 [261]); "The slave only conceives of power as the object of a recognition, the content of a representation, the stake in a competition, and therefore makes it depend, at the end of a fight, on a simple attribution of established values" (Deleuze 1983, 10).
5. On the deceptive labeling of conflicts as "cultural" or "religious" see also Meyer 2001; Balibar 2012.
6. Karin Fleischanderl criticized this quite shrewdly in an op-ed article (https://www.derstandard.at/story/1350261586642/wozu-ist-das-binnen-i-gut, accessed July 13, 2021). She writes, "For all those reasons (listed), I can only perceive the 'internal I,' the -a in *Magistra* and the -in in *Doktorin* [the female form of 'Doctor' in German] as mockery. Why do I constantly have to let myself be marked, why do I constantly have to be told that I'm a woman, a woman, a woman, a woman, as there is no-one (neither me nor anyone else)—let alone the internal I, the -a in *Magistra* or the -in in *Doktorin*—who could liberate me from the more obvious disadvantages of being a woman? I would have to cease being a woman if I wanted all that money, power and prestige. Is someone trying to spite me by really rubbing it in with each letter addressed to 'Frau Doktorin'? This doubling of the female markers alone already sounds like someone is trying to mock my titles through ironic exaggeration. The internal I, for its part, sounds as if we had finally overcome the drudgery of gender difference and all become sisters: *HerausgeberInnen*, *LehrerInnen*, *BundesministerInnen* [inclusive German plural forms of 'editor,' 'teacher,' 'federal minister']. And why is it that in the very environment where I have managed to escape my gender identity as far as possible, namely in the academic context, I am reminded most strongly of the fact that I am a woman?"
7. See Pfaller 2012.
8. Žižek 2008, 157.
9. On this, see also Meyer 2001, who emphasizes that modernity is not identical with Western culture, but in fact only emerged as a result of a break with this culture during the seventeenth and eighteenth centuries.

10. Sennett 1977, 269.
11. Mannoni 1985, 9 ff.
12. See Pfaller 2014, 167.
13. On the distinction between "primary" and "secondary religions," see Sundermeier 1999; see also Assmann 2003, 11.
14. See Pfaller 2014, 61 ff.
15. See Weber 2004, 30.
16. See Freud 1961 [1920], 22; Lacan 1999 [1959–60], 165 ff.
17. See, for example, the well-written volume by Andreas and Frankenberg (eds.) 2013.
18. See Althusser 2014, 199.
19. See Althusser 2014, 195.
20. See Butler 1990, 128 ff.; see also Fischer-Lichte 2008, 30 ff.
21. Spinoza 1954 (1677), 132.
22. See Sennett 1977.
23. Sennett 1977, 264.
24. On the concept of the homogenization of the other, see Pfaller 2012, 8 and 88.
25. On the "multicultural" version of racism in postmodernity, see Balibar 2011, 17–28.
26. Epictetus 2018, Chapter 17.
27. Just to give an example: a review of the book *Boys Don't Cry* by Jack Urwin reads, "Jack Urwin has had enough. Not only should the strong man be allowed to cry or take parental leave, Urwin asks why men even have to be strong at all. Why are we still guided by stereotypes, even though we would be so much better off without them?" See https://www.perlentaucher.de/buch/jack-urwin/boys-don-t-cry.html. Accessed July 13, 2021. And that is precisely the question: Would we really be better off without stereotypes? Are we not witnessing the very opposite in postmodernity? There are countless desperate people who have lost any kind of stereotype, and, on the other hand, masses of fanatics who would prefer to cling to an idiotic stereotype instead of not having one at all.
28. Freud 2012 (1921), 54.
29. Sennett 1977, 8.
30. Žižek 1993, 203–204.
31. See Grunberger and Dessuant 2000, 107; 120 f.; 203.
32. Freud 2012 (1921), 53.
33. See Freud 1953 (1905), 231.
34. See Deleuze and Guattari 1983, 51 ff.
35. Engels 2010 (1884).
36. See Deleuze and Guattari 1983: 30 ff.; 74; 377.
37. See *Madam, I'm Adam. The Organization of Private Life*, ed. Piet Zwart Institute and University of Art and Design Linz, Department of Experimental Design, Rotterdam, Linz, 2003.
38. See Pfaller 2012.

Chapter 3

The Meaning of "Gender" in Current Debates of the Left

A Discussion between Elena Louisa Lange, Joshua Pickett-Depaolis, and Jane Clare Jones

Elena Louisa Lange, Joshua Pickett-Depaolis, and Jane Clare Jones

1. In recent years, the view that gender is a "social construct" has no longer been confined to Gender Studies as an academic discipline but become a widespread view within the academic left. At the same time, however, the concept of "gender," especially in Marxism-feminism, has become something we dare not to question, a concept that would belong to Plato's realm of ideas: the idealist idea of gender as authentic and original, according to which both the world of work and private life are organized. Often, in this sense, the argument that "work is organized by gender" (Kathi Weeks) is tautologically explained with "gendered work." The "gendering of work" then seems like something from which no human, male or female, can escape. How do we square the circle of understanding "gender" as a "social construct"—as something that is contingent and object to historical change—with viewing gender as a rigid conditio sine qua non to human life in general?

Jane Clare Jones: I think the short answer is that we don't square the circle—the view that gender is an inner authentic essence that must not be interrogated is incompatible with the traditional feminist view that it is a social construct. This conceptual incongruity seems not to be noted by many advocates of what I would call transgender ideology, who seem to simultaneously maintain that gender is both constructed and an innate essence, and from our perspective, this only makes sense if what they are referring to "gender" or "gender identity" is just human personality in its identification with the social norms of gender. Given that gender-critical feminism considers the social norms of gender to be an oppressive structure, and one that functions to socialize women into fulfilling the role of a service class to male needs, we evidently don't think that encouraging people to essentialize or reify their identification with gender is a progressive move. Rather, we would advocate for all people to be free to express their individual personalities in defiance of, or through a process of disidentification with, gendered normativity. One of the fundamental problems with the transactivist reification of gender is that it ceases to have, and in fact, makes impossible, a structural and material analysis of why gender exists and whose interests it serves. And although she originally advocated a performative, nonessentialist notion of gender, this is also what is effectively achieved by Butler's intervention—gender is no longer a system which serves the interests of a sex-based class system which extracts resources from females, and becomes a purely discursive structure which exists for no particular reason, and which is unjust only insofar as it differentially distributes intelligibility between gender-conforming and nonconforming people. Notably, women are not thought to be more disadvantaged by this system than men, and insofar as both are thought to be "intelligible" within the "gender binary" they are both equally "privileged." The oppression of women in general, and the issue of the sexual division of labor in particular completely drops out of the picture here, along with any account of how women are socialized to engage in a self-abnegating prioritization of the needs of others, and how this results in women doing a massively disproportionate share of the labor of social reproduction. I think Nancy Fraser's distinction between the politics of recognition and the politics of redistribution is a useful way to think about this. Effectively the contemporary discourse has replaced an analysis of material oppression with one of representational marginalization (which it has falsely conflated with oppression) and reduced the mechanics of this to "exclusion" and individual "bigotry" rather than class-based exploitation (obviously I am understanding "sex" here as an axis of class relations). Then, rather than directing its demands at changing exploitative structures, it becomes obsessed with representational justice and engages in extreme puritan witch hunts in effort to hunt down and cleanse the souls of those whose "privilege" and "bigotry" is, it thinks, the origin of all the worlds' injustice. This is rank idealism. And it is little wonder why the institutions of capital are so eager to encourage it. It costs them nothing to add a little social justice window dressing and deflects attention away from the inveterate exploitation of both the planet and labor, which continues apace.

Joshua Pickett-Depaolis: Conservative essentialist naturalization and postmodern social constructivism converge in a reactionary valorization of "difference." The ideological structure of gender which finds its basis in a sexual division of labor that capitalism tends to erode is continually rearticulated. Whether gender is correctly understood as performative or mystified as indissoluble from biology or "divine will," all sides agree the show must go on. Sexual preference whether that be in choice of partner or of self-identification and modification become a "political" battlefield par excellence for a society in which the only substantively political question—which class will hold state power—has been resolved decisively in favor of the bourgeoisie. Feminist critique of "toxic masculinity" and heated debates over "preferred pronouns" and the sex industry compensate for the passive acceptance of the "universal prostitution" which is the common "lived experience" of most men and women today. Most of us must sell our labor power, and the naturalization of this relation and its increasingly onerous terms is precisely what the morbid gender and sex fixation of the culture warriors serves to obscure. The gendered disparities which persist within that relation can only be resolved by working-class unity. Positing an illusory community of interest between women can no more resolve them than national liberation movements can resolve uneven development on a global scale. The Marxist capitulation to feminism's idealist conception of gender is part of a general capitulation to bourgeois politics which also has its effect on the philosophical front.

Elena Louisa Lange: I agree with Jane that the logical and factual contradiction between gender as "socially constructed" and gender as a primary determination of individuals cannot be solved. There is a profound contradiction in claiming, on the one hand, that the concept of gender was "fluid," and then propagating the necessity for the "transitioning" of "gender-nonconforming" young people, even children. Either it is "fluid" or it is determination "wrongly ascribed," but it cannot be both. Marxism-feminism, however, collapses sex and gender on a regular basis. Because it often reproduces gender stereotypes, where it should question them, and because, in this very process, it loses its Marxist or historically materialist angle, I would even go a step further and argue that Marxism-feminism today, in proponents such as Nancy Fraser, Cinzia Arruzza, and Tithi Bhattacharya, but also many "original" or older representatives like Silvia Federici, Selma James, or Joanna Brenner, is neither Marxist nor particularly feminist. Let me explain.

"Family" is a precarious concept. Under neoliberal rule, we have for a long time seen the erosion of the family, particularly in the working class. In Asian mega factories, for example, the reproduction of labor power does not take place within family structures at all: workers' barracks and "employee housing" for, for example, Foxconn and Toyota workers are the rule, with men and women living in separate dorms. The production of relative surplus value has lowered the value of labor power and made it impossible for workers worldwide to live off one wage alone. Gone is the idyllic family structure of Fordism and even post-Fordism. At the same time, the outsourcing of household tasks has taken a more global character, because relative surplus value production does not only lower the value of labor power but also of means for childcare, and so on. This is the logic of real subsumption. Everyone is at the mercy of increasing commodification, even of the most "private" tasks. Yet, in the strange world of the 1950s that many Marxist-feminists inhabit today, where all men have wage-jobs and all women are stay-at-home mums—a distorted reality, which may be true for segments of the middle class but is hopelessly distorted for workers—women have the complete burden of reproduction. The problem, however, goes further. Authors like Federici and Brenner do not only *describe* a reality, but they also cling to this antiquated separation as a fact, as something that *structures* social reality. The strange concession they make to a rigid concept of gender—the woman's place is to "follow timidly behind the man, carrying groceries, babies, and diapers" (Nancy Hartsock)—is quite astonishing. But it is never questioned—otherwise, the argument of "gendered exploitation" would be difficult to defend. Joanna Brenner even argues that "biological differences condition women's participation in economic/political life"—a clearly conservative, anti-feminist talking point that justifies the lowering of wages for women. Furthermore, this kind of argumentation takes place against the background of completely ignoring the impact of real subsumption that Joshua pointed to, but also of an *emancipatory perspective*. I would therefore say that Marxism-feminism, despite its own claims, is neither feminist in the sense of seeking emancipation from rigid gender norms nor Marxist. The latter point, I think, is worth returning to.

2. Both historically and theoretically, the relationship between Marxism and feminism has always been strained. Rosa Luxemburg was notoriously critical of feminism, Marxist historian Ellen Meiksins Wood said that "capitalism is uniquely indifferent to the social identities of the people it exploits," while the Combahee River Collective subordinated class within the trinity of "race, class, and gender" now known as "intersectionality theory." And today, many anti-bourgeois feminists, such as Jessa Crispin, identify capital with the patriarchy. Where does class politics end and identity politics begin?

Joshua Pickett-Depaolis: I think we must be clear that the gender relation is not a class relation. Most traditional societies were undergirded by a systematically formalized subordination of women to men: a subordination which bore much in common with the fixed relations of personal domination which also characterized the defining *class relation* of these societies. With the rise of capitalism these fixed estate statuses are displaced by the abstract equality of commodity owners as the mode of appearance of the class relation. There follows a tendential actualization of equality between men and women on the ground of emancipation within civil society. Far from men exploiting women as a class, the inherent trajectory of capital is the reduction of men and women to a common waged position. Communists, like bourgeois democrats, support the furthest extension of this process and the elimination of all obstacles to its realization (free access to divorce and to abortion, substantive criminalization of domestic violence and marital rape, etc.). However, unlike bourgeois democrats we understand that, taken *by itself*, the fullest actualization of abstract equality is at the same time concrete inequality. This concrete inequality between buyers and sellers of labor power can only be eliminated by the *class struggle* of male and female workers together—not for emancipation *within* bourgeois civil society but for the *abolition* of this society. In this context, the feminist identification of gender with class confuses the struggle for democratic rights with the struggle to abolish democracy. By the same token transactivists are not wrong to see gender as an incidental performative activity and to demand that individuals have the right to modify themselves in conformity with the type of performance they prefer. Yet, they are wrong when they assign a "subversive" significance to such modification. Like feminists, their vision of freedom stops with the actualization of bourgeois civic emancipation. The shared ground of feminism and queer theory is the mystification of the class contradiction which defines capitalist society in favor of the valorization of a struggle against oppression which is completely compatible with the human rights ideology of the neoliberal counterrevolution. As Alexandra Kollontai (often perversely depicted as a "feminist" in postmodern "left" circles) observed concerning the former movement,

"What is the aim of the feminists? Their aim is to achieve the same advantages, the same power, the same rights within capitalist society as those possessed now by their husbands, fathers and brothers. What is the aim of the women workers? Their aim is to abolish all privileges deriving from birth or wealth. For the woman worker it is a matter of indifference who is the "master," a man or a woman."

Jane Clare Jones: So of course, what I am going to argue is that the difference between class and "identity politics" is to be found in whether you are organizing around an axis of material structural oppression which functions through exploitative class relations, or whether your object of concern is "marginalization" rather than oppression, with a particular focus on representational marginalization. I've recently returned to working with the debates between socialist and radical feminists in the 1980s, which I confess have always somewhat baffled me, given that it makes little sense, other than as a point of theoretical prejudice, to deny the homology, and intertwining, of exploitative relations in the sphere of production *and* reproduction, and how the patterns of extractive dominance reproduce and reinforce each other in both spheres. From my perspective, the fundamental thought of materialist analysis is that social relations arise through the historical development of various modes through which humans meet their needs. These needs are obviously in the first instance material, and as Engels recognizes in the *Origins of the Family* include the immediate reproduction of life, but are also, as is evident in the articulation of the ethical critique of estranged labor, "spiritual," insofar as human species being needs to see itself externalized through its sensuous and material work with the world, and this is true of work done both under the conditions of wage slavery and work which is unpaid. Evidently then, I am going to reject the assertion that social relations organized along the axis of sex (not gender) are not a class relation. And indeed, the way Joshua frames this claim—namely, "I think we must be clear that the gender relation is not a class relation"—confronts us with a useful example of a place where discursive appropriation stands in direct relation to material appropriation. If we want to elaborate a critique of "idealist" politics, we need to do something far more complex than merely thinking that claims about discourse have a priori nothing to do with material relations (for instance, "pronoun protocols" are manifestly idealist, analysis of how "toxic [I would say patriarchal] masculinity" is implicated in violent sexual appropriation is not). Indeed, what I draw from Marx's ethical critique is the thought of human species being as shaped through the dialectical working of ourselves on the world and the world on us. Indeed, I take this thought of the constant interactivity of human and world, or matter and idea, as fundamental to all social analysis. While, therefore, ideology arises from material relations, it also transparently functions to disseminate, perpetuate, and exculpate those relations. That is, the interaction between matter and idea is a two-way street. The question is, does this discursive gesture map a material and structural one, or is it simply a claim about recognition which is confined only to the ideal, and is principally concerned with representation-qua-expression of "who-you-really-are," that is, the assertion and demand for recognition of an ideal, individualist identity?

In this case, what resides in the "we" of this assertion is the assimilation of the interests of female people as a class to the interests of the dominant class, and furthermore, we might argue, an expression of the interests of that class in denying their interests in the material exploitation of female people's bodies and labor. Indeed, this is made explicit when it's asserted that the interests of female people as a class are "illusory." This "we" here then is not "just discourse," and refusing it is not "just idealism." It is a mark of linguistic assimilation which stands in indexical relation to the material assimilation of female people's subjectivity, needs, desires, labor, and bodies, to those whose class position resides in reducing women to resource. Here also we see that the invocation of "difference" is not merely a "reactionary valorization," but can be, rather, a refusal by a subordinate class to have their interests assimilated to the dominant class. A rhetorical invocation of "difference" may, for example, in concrete terms, mark the place where a woman says "no" to a male person's expectation of domestic or sexual service. The place where she asserts, "I am a human being with my own material and spiritual needs, my interests are not yours and will not be subordinated to yours."

I must confess then that I find nothing here to evidence the suggestion that the assertion of a sex-class relation is idealism, or indeed, a "capitulation to bourgeois politics," beyond assertion. Evidently if you define material relations as pertaining only to production one will reach that conclusion, but this is circular, unless a compelling argument is given as to why the material appropriation of women's bodies and labor (both by men and by capital-mediated-by-men) should not count as a relation of material exploitation, or why only relations of material exploitation which function through the site of production should be centered in any analysis concerned with more just social relations. It's illustrative here that Joshua's critique of feminism seems to take as its object only liberal feminism, whose "vision of freedom," as he rightly says, "stops with the actualisation of bourgeois civic emancipation." This is precisely the reason for the rejection of liberal feminism by those working in both the radical and socialist feminist traditions, or those, like me, who consider themselves to be thinking at the intersection of those two branches and working to develop a synthesis we might like to call "radical materialist feminism." Indeed, we take as axiomatic the need to destroy all three axes of extractive relation—class, sex, race, and so on, and note, we consider this to be "intersectionality proper" rather than the corrupted "woke" kind which has, of course, confused relations of material exploitation with a range of marginalizations that do not index sites of material class-based extraction (and as I suggested in my earlier response, this confusion does play directly into the hands of those with interests in maintaining all three kinds of extraction in their interrelation). The "vision of freedom" of a radical materialist feminism would then incorporate the overthrow of class relations mediated through the site of production. However, our conviction that this historical iteration of extractive relation rests on an older historical form which developed during the agricultural revolution through the intertwined appropriation of women's bodies and the land—the conditions of accumulation which first produced class society in the pure Marxist sense—suggests to us a singular focus on "class-qua-production" is entirely inadequate to undermining male people's exploitation of women's bodies and labor, and indeed, is also inadequate to transforming the extractive class relation mediated by production itself. If we are serious about social transformation, we must address ourselves to the fact that social relations arise through the interaction of human need and particular modes of meeting those needs and interrogate why certain modes have developed and been perpetuated. This calls us to think through human need as a complex material/spiritual composite—for instance, the historical fact of accumulation beyond all material need cannot be itself explained only as "material," and accumulation is clearly meeting needs for esteem, status, and social and political power. Indeed, this is one factor in the persistence of accumulation even while it threatens to destroy the material conditions of its own existence, and why, even when as predicted, it reaches its material limits, it will respond with—ultimately untenable—virtualization. The fundamental question must be, "Why do our social relations take the form of extraction/exploitation/dominance in its various historical iterations?" I do not think that a "class reductionist" form of materialist thinking has an answer to that question.

Joshua Pickett-Depaolis: What differentiates the working class as a social grouping within capitalist society? It is a grouping which is compelled by its separation from the means of production and its lack of reserves to sell its labor power to the representatives of capital. The working class as a group is defined by an objective, structurally determined obligation to perform surplus labor for the benefit of capital. Someone who does not face such an obligation is by definition not a part of the working class. Speaking scientifically without cultural or moral colloquialisms the term has no other content. Moreover, this structurally determined obligation forms the entire substance of capitalist society. Now let us ask what differentiates women as a social grouping within capitalist society? Nothing. Many (but certainly not all) women perform a disproportionate share of domestic labor within families and often face interpersonal violence intended to enforce their subordinate role in such circumstances. However, this is not a situation which *necessarily defines* all women as a grouping within capitalist society and this situation could be abolished without eliminating any of the structural characteristics of that society. We would certainly be on shaky ground in arguing that a single professional or a woman married to a man who does her housework is no longer a woman though such an argument would hardly be more far-fetched than the assertion that personal equality between men and women would spell the end of capital. On the contrary a worker no longer compelled to sell their labor power is self-evidently no longer a worker and concrete equality between workers and capitalists means the elimination of both categories. It is for these reasons that women do not constitute a social class within capitalist society. Women as *a group* share no common position in either the production of surplus value or family life. In fact, today to be a woman (or a man) means very little. That is precisely the emancipation which capital has brought, and which should be defended and extended against regressive currents. However, as I noted, the defense of bourgeois emancipation does not separate communists and liberals. Rather, it unites them. The critique of the oppression of women which underpinned prior class societies, like the critique of religion or aristocratic privilege, is the critique which the democratic bourgeois launches against its predecessors. It can well afford to make such critique because its existence depends upon none of these outmoded social forms. There are good reasons why the WEF or the UN condemn the unequal treatment of women seven days a week but are hardly likely to denounce the existence of a market in labor power. The reason why, as Jane notes, I direct my critique against liberal feminism is because I consider liberal feminism as the only substantive form of feminism. Precisely because women do not share a common position within capitalist society any defense of the interests of women per se can only be a defense of the democratic rights which apply to women in general. It cannot be a demand to transform the existing production relations which many women have objectively grounded reasons to defend. Moreover, Marxism as the ideology of universal emancipation based on the class position of the proletariat requires no feminist "amendment" to struggle against the oppression of women.

Elena Louisa Lange: I think the question is best answered when you consult the historical and theoretical works by socialists like Clara Zetkin and Rosa Luxemburg on the "woman question" and you compare it to the works by so-called Marxism-feminism today. For Zetkin, as for Luxemburg, the issue was the abolition of capitalist relations of production, not "women's rights advocation." But Zetkin did not see enough consciousness of that difference—that is, class consciousness—among women of the working class. Therefore, she organized socialist women groups, always making it clear that "the ends of communist men are our ends, our tasks." The ends, for Zetkin's program, were to reach out to the working class as a whole. You don't find these appeals to unity in current Marxism-feminism, which holds an identitarian, and therefore sectarian, approach to society. It only makes cosmetic demands for a better material base to satisfy a moral program: women should be equal to men. In essence, prominent Marxist-feminists today promote a *politics of resentment*, not a politics of emancipation. I think it fundamentally rests on the false assumption that men "have it better." But as Marx said, "To be a worker is not a piece of luck, but a misfortune." Trying to erase differences *within* the exploited class, but leaving *exploitation itself* unscathed, is the political project of most Marxism-feminism today. But then of course the question pops up *why* women lack a certain level of class consciousness, as Zetkin believed. And here, I see Jane's point that the "material appropriation of women's bodies and labour" in a specifically capitalist way may have put women in an inferior position to gain an understanding of their own social position. In industrialized Europe, there were many women in factories at the time—and there are even more so today, globally. But most women workers were and still are engaged in nonindustrial jobs or in industries based on domestic or care work. The character of this work, in schools, childcare facilities, or nursing homes, and its spatial separation from the larger proletarian workforce may not be conducive to unitary organization in large numbers. In addition, the fact that women give birth has proven to be a direct impediment to struggle for higher wages. Capitalists argue it is not their burden to compensate for the risks of a loss in profits when women miss out on labor time. Women's bargaining power in wage struggles is often compromised by this natural impediment. Of course, this argument is deeply cynical, as it subsumes the conditions of a normal personal, as well as social development, namely having children, to the profit interests of capital—an interest that cannot be disentangled from its interest in having a supply in labor power. But capitalism, in that sense, is cynical—and not only in Zetkin's time. So, while I agree with Joshua that women are not a separate social class—in fact, this would put women like Ursula von der Leyen in the same category as the Bangladeshi textile worker—I also agree with Jane that the class consciousness of women may under certain conditions rest on different terms than that of men. The bottom line is that capitalism is harmful—for both men and women. To advocate for separate politics regarding the abolition of capitalist relations of production is counterproductive, I think.

3. One of the most controversial things you can say in public today apparently is that "men are not women." Saying that there are two sexes, that only women can give birth, or even just using the term "woman"/"women" will quickly put anyone on the blacklist. The socially preferred terms "individuals who menstruate," "uterus/cervix havers," "chest-feeders," "bleeders," or "womxn," all aimed at "gender-inclusive" language, have become advised terms in social management and technocratically oriented institutions like the UN. People who defend the definition of "woman" as adult human female are publicly excommunicated. We would be interested in hearing why you think this happens. Not so much whether powerful institutions are right or wrong in purging language that is allegedly "insensitive" to gender-inclusivity—but why late capitalist society is so obsessed with "gender," and even more so, it seems, than with "race." This goes so far that the perhaps rightful concern for the actual day-to-day discrimination of "gender-nonconforming" people is completely subordinated to using "correct pronouns" and "gender-inclusive language" in daily debates. What are the power structures behind this extreme focus on gender? Have the contradictions of capital become so apparent that it needed a false mirroring in genderism to overcome its own crises?

Jane Clare Jones: I think this happens because male people want something, they want something that women have, and we live inside a power system which prioritizes male people's needs over female people's needs and assumes that female people's role is to accommodate the needs and desires of men. The name of this system is patriarchy. It is a system of sex-based oppression that functions through a hierarchical structure of roles, status, and values known as gender. Unlike the superficial idea of gender used by radical queer theorists and transactivists, the deep structure of patriarchal gender hinges on the inculcation of male entitlement and female service, which, as I suggested in my previous answer, produces a system in which male people exploit the bodies and labor of women. In this specific case what male people want is the fulfillment of their desire to be a "woman"—and it must be understood here that this is entirely about patriarchal projections of "woman," and nothing whatsoever to do with existing female people. As Luce Irigaray, following de Beauvoir, so keenly perceived, within the symbolic system of male power, actually embodied female subjects do not exist. What exists is "woman," an image produced by weaving together both the fantasies and the disavowals of the patriarchal male subject. The aim of transgender ideology is to redefine women in law and public policy based on "gender identity," that is, based on patriarchal projection. This entails the political erasure of woman as a sex-class, and hence, as you indicated in your question, the disassembly of women into organs and functions in those instances in which female people need to be referred to as a group. As this dehumanizing language suggests, this conversion of women from a sex-based to a gender identity–based class is a harm to existing female people. First, because it occludes sex and sex-based exploitation, and, second, because patriarchal projection undermines the humanity of female people and positions us an exploitable resource. As gender-critical feminists have made evident during this conflict, we will not consent to being redefined by the mechanism of our own oppression. It turns out, however, that the patriarchal contempt for the subjectivity of actual women is so deep and entrenched that our institutions did not even stop to consider whether female people needed to be consulted about their own definition in law, and large numbers of people are still apparently incapable of countenancing that women have a legitimate political interest in their own political existence. At its heart, the "gender war" is a straight up down conflict between male desire (centered on "woman" as a male projection) and the actual existence of female people. And what has been revealed is that many people reflexively assume that male desire, and male projection, should be prioritized over women's existence, and moreover, that women who refuse to comply with this self-abnegation are "evil bigot witches" who should be righteously sanctioned. This is the purest unconcealment of the core mechanism of patriarchal dominance many of us have seen in our lifetimes.

There are also capitalist interests in disseminating and amplifying the trans ideological project, because contra Joshua's analysis, feminism cannot be reduced to liberal feminism, and a radical materialist feminism which understands sex as an axis—indeed as the patterning structure—of material extraction, is a threat to the generalized system of exploitation. It is a central tenet of our analysis that males who think themselves concerned with justice but refuse to grasp the centrality of the male appropriation of women to the structure of extractive dominance are motivated by maintaining their interests in that appropriation. This, in fact, was the fissure that led to the development of radical feminism out of more traditional forms of leftism, and it is also the axis of tension between gender-critical women and the "progressive" male trans allies we often refer to as "woke-bros." In both cases, feminist women are confronted with men's refusal to acknowledge their interests in, and complicity with, the sex-based appropriation of women, which both serves their individual needs and underpins all economy. Women's reproductive labor is the ground of the entire system of extractive economy, and capitalism is only one historical variant of that system of extraction. It is women who make the labor force, women who maintain the labor force, and without women's reproductive and socially reproductive labor, *there is no labor power, no surplus value, no economy at all*. Capitalism has always been hospitable to forms of liberal feminism which largely focused on the representation of women in the workforce and legal equality within the existent system (and indeed, if you define that as the only substantive form of feminism then you can claim feminism is bourgeois). It has, however, never been able to accommodate radical and materialist feminist demands for the recognition and equitable valuation of women's reproductive labor. It is therefore entirely in the interests of capital to collude with an ideology which would make the analysis of sex-class exploitation *verboten*, and which appears to address issues of "social justice" through purely idealist and representational gestures which present no challenge to material exploitation.

Elena Louisa Lange: Unlike perhaps some of my peers, I think the question of the asymmetric public discourse over the foremost identitarian markers "race" and "gender" poses a challenge to a Marxist historical-materialist class analysis. What does this infatuation with "gender" and transgenderism signify today? Cui bono? It is not as simple as it looks, in my view. One thing that is sure, however, is that current politics—and policies, like the Gender Recognition Act—hurt women as a group. This is obvious from how free speech is curbed mostly in relation to expressing women's interests, like fairness in sports competitions, or the right to certain safe spaces like rape shelters. I agree with Jane on this point. On the other hand, however, I must admit I find Jane's *explanation*—that the patriarchy has a specific interest in sex-based oppression for the reproduction of capitalist productive relations—not very persuasive. Again, women are not a class. *Working class women* are—as well as *working-class men*. Overthrowing capitalist relations of production is not in the interest of someone like Christine Lagarde or Angela Merkel. Saying that these women belong to the "patriarchy," too, is to conflate sex and class, the latter defined as the position one assumes in the process of production, either as the owner of labor power or as the owner of means of production. These positions in the production process define one's class position, which is independent of one's sex or gender. So, while I agree with Jane's diagnosis, I would offer a different explanation.

But as I said, it is not so simple as it looks. This becomes clear when we recall the asymmetry of how "race" and "gender" are treated in the consciousness of the neoliberal subjects and the "leftist" discourse they propagate. The public outcry about Rachel Dolezal's "exposé" in 2015 signifies something quite elementarily self-contradictory in the way "identities" are perceived here. Dolezal was publicly ostracized for "falsely" "passing as black," while approximately during the same time, Caitlyn Jenner became a celebrated "transgender" personality, designated as "bold" for posing in Vanity Fair and receiving the stately praise of someone like then president Obama. As Adolph Reed Jr. noted in his brilliant "From Jenner to Dolezal: One Trans Good, the Other Not So Much" (2015), it is obviously "OK to feel like a woman when you don't have the body of a woman and to act like . . . a woman, but it's wrong to feel like a black person when you're actually white and that acting like you're black and doing your best to get yourself the body of a black person is just lying." The "mind-bogglingly wrongheaded" assessment of this asymmetry as one being "voluntary" (racial identification) and the other being "involuntary" ("gender self-ID") —"people's decision to transition is almost always involuntary," as Meredith Talusan noted (quoted in Reed Jr.)—not mentioning the presupposed paternalism of this view, has been pointed out by Reed, for it ultimately implies that gender and sex would need to be confounded, making sex disappear, so that gender could emerge as an *essential trait* of human biology. Only on this basis of a *naturalization of gender*—not sex!—could someone obviously "involuntarily" make a decision based on feelings of being trapped in the wrong body. We are ultimately confronted not only with a simple but a *double topsy-turvy view* of the truth: first, instead of stating the obvious, namely that "race" *does not exist*, it is very much essentialized and declared an immutable trait of humans, while biological sex, which *does exist*, is treated as *nonexistent*. Second, gender receives the status of something innate and immutable, while it is also *completely arbitrary*. The insanity of one of these views alone would be something to behold, but in the mainstream leftist discourse on transgenderism, both are supposed to apply. What is happening here? Obviously, as Reed noted, "naturalized categories of ascriptive identity that sort us into groups supposedly defined what we essentially are rather than what we do" is key to understanding how identitarianism works to not only *obscure* but *replace* class politics. In this neoliberal-managerial ideal vision, we are nothing but atomized individuals whose "very own" identity not only makes broader coalitions based on solidarity against the powers of the state and capital impossible—it makes an *understanding of capitalist society* impossible. And that is its foremost goal. The replacement of working-class politics by identity politics is a formidable example of class war against the workers who are left with nothing but the self-perception of individual consumers and choice-makers on the ever-growing market of particular identities, which, to perfect the circle, contribute to an expanding supply and demand of commodification. The bad news for women is this: in a world where imagined identities replace class, and which forms a market on its own, a market that must grow and yield surplus value, "something's gotta give." And women are, in an ironic, but very precise, sense, the victims of this market expansion of ever-newly fabricated identities. They are *collateral damage*. Let us just recall how, initially, trans rights and women's rights were both simultaneously on offer on the smorgasbord of urgent social justice issues a few years ago. But not anymore. The incompatibility of the two, despite the incompatibility of its own theoretical assumptions, has been acknowledged by the trans community. Women's rights have been pushed out of the market, mediated by internet platforms and the usual corporate media culture war alarmism. In other words, the obsession with "gender" as a terrain, in which late neoliberalism's insatiable drive to marketization of even the most intimate personal phenomena can be freely exercised—the commodification of "feelings" in the strictest and most intimate sense—is a *class project*, whose collateral damage happen to be women who insist on the reality of biological sex, a project no longer deemed up-to-date with the latest valorization interests of capital. The upshot of this analysis—which I hope to expand on in more detail, but for which the space here is limited—is that identity politics hurts everyone: in varying degrees, yes, for women insisting on "old-fashioned" biological truths happen to present a particular obstacle to fostering new marketization campaigns. But at the end of the day, the autonomization of the law of value, which requires submission to the logic of market expansion, hurts all—also the "trans community" who have been psychologically blackmailed (or "gaslit," to use the fashionable term) into accepting this regressive vision of society as a form of "liberation." For it is not liberating. It is much rather a perfection of servility in the shell of "emancipation" and the disguise of progressivism.

Joshua Pickett-Depaolis: An essential aspect of the development of the capital relation is the tendency toward the increasing universality and fluidity of the individual. As I noted earlier, precapitalist class societies were characterized by a rigid division of estates that assigned individuals to fixed positions within personal relations of domination and subordination. In correspondence with this articulation of the relations of class exploitation, women and men were strictly divided into "complementary" social roles and the submission of the individual to these roles was ensured through the sanctification of these positions as "eternal" metaphysical categories.

From the above standpoint Jane's positions errs through a failure to recognize that the premise and result of capitalist production itself is a tendential decomposition of these categories. The increasing fluidity of gender identity far from being an attack on women by men expresses a movement toward the overcoming of both by a free individuality in which biological sex is increasingly denuded of social significance at the same time as it becomes increasingly susceptible to technical modification. This is the exit from the horror of the "state of nature" which capitalist development makes possible. As can be seen from polling data in perhaps the paradigmatic advanced bourgeois society, the United States, with each generation an ever greater minority identifies as LGBT. This trend reflects the qualitative advance in personal freedom produced by the social movements of the 1960s. It is within this context that the increasing trend of gender self-identification and the codification of access to sex reassignment as a right is to be understood. It is neither "male exploitation" (an especially strange formulation considering the existence of transmen) nor "damage," collateral or otherwise. It is, on the contrary, a great democratic victory. And one which reflects the contribution made by feminism to the actualization of freedom within the limits of bourgeois emancipation. It is perhaps ironic considering current alignments on the "left" that contempt for free speech and mockery of "preferred pronouns" share a common conceptual origin—a one-sided and distinctly un-Marxist hostility to the freedom of the universal individual within capital. Elena's condemnation of the spread of commodification to the realm of sexuality fails to recognize the progressive aspect of decomposition it embodies. It is the fixed distinction between men and women historically inextricable from the restriction of individual freedom by relations of personal domination which obstructs the unification of the working class. The reduction of biological sex to a matter of indifference and gender to a question of personal choice is on the contrary a necessary basis for the undifferentiated unity of free individuals.

My case for the overcoming of capital is not made on behalf of the fixed metaphysical categories, which once subsumed the individual and which commerce thankfully corrodes. Rather, this is the concern of reactionaries who seek to further mystify the governing contradiction of modern society by shoring up outmoded ideological forms. It is worth noting here that perhaps the most prominent strain of the critique of "gender ideology" in the West is that expressed by the Catholic Church. In this sense one could fairly argue that those who insist on the right to sculpt their identities and their bodies as they see fit are continuing the struggle for bourgeois self-ownership which began with the Reformation.

I defend the democratic rights of sexual minorities for the same reason I demand equality between men and women: because the actualization of these demands represents the greatest possible extension of freedom within capital and the completion of the bourgeois revolution's sacred task of destruction. The attack on "gender ideology" implemented by a "holy alliance" stretching from the most reactionary religious denominations to national-populist parties and governments should be understood for what it is—a new *vendeé* against emancipation.

The fact that, like the Jacobins, today's liberals are irreconcilable enemies of the workers and that their defense of democratic right is couched in a metaphysics just as mystifying as the natural law critique of feudalism should not make us lose our bearings. Just as I don't hesitate for a moment in supporting conservatives when they defend the right to bear arms and attack social media censorship, I am equally shameless in backing the neoliberal center left when it defends sexual freedom against medieval barbarism.

Chapter 4

Mourning and Melancholia

The Millennial Left between New Left and Old Left

Anton Jäger

The covers came in a fierce, fluorescent hue—orange, yellow, red, blue, turquoise, pitch black. Their titles were usually short, jotted at the top, with authors' names at the bottom. They usually came without illustrative accompaniment. Bobbing across central London, a group of protesters clad in black carrying anarchist flags had come equipped with a specific item—*books*—to fend off the steady police presence in the city center. They carried colored cardboard shield, emblazoned with the titles of monographs from the critical theory canon. The concept of the "book bloc" had been introduced a month earlier in 2010, by students demonstrating against Berlusconi's education reforms in Italy, when the streets of Rome filled with works such as Plato's *Republic* and Deleuze and Guattari's *A Thousand Plateaus*, but also *Moby Dick*, *Don Quixote*, Petronius's *The Satyricon*, or Luther Blissett's *Q*. A month later a so-called Book Bloc descended on London, sometime after the Conservative-Liberal Democrat government announced its fierce spending cuts for the country's education sector and an increased cap on tuition fees. Its range of authors was wide, including the papier-mâché shields of Rachel Carson's *Silent Spring*, Marcuse's *One-Dimensional Man*, Adorno's *Negative Dialectics*, and Ivan Illich's *Deschooling Society*: all countercultural classics.

Next to this New Left canon, the shields also included some more recent acquisitions, one of the more conspicuous being Mark Fisher's *Capitalist Realism*. Published a year before in 2009, Fisher's book received great critical and commercial acclaim, already an established classic in the student movement of 2010. Somewhere between a Dadaist performance and a guerrilla offensive, the book bloc protest at which Fisher's essay figured also offered a representative snapshot of a specifically new, millennial left:

academic, intellectualist, interested in theory, but still openly militant, with a belief in transformative change and institution-building, which went far beyond the sub-ironic sensibility that ailed the earlier, Gen-Z cohort—or the aggressive, ostentatious conformism of baby boomers.

Few writers offered more durable inspiration to this new "millennial" left than Fisher himself. In the 2000s, his blog[1] was a holdout of critical thought in a miasma of neoliberal and academic groupthink, an outpost of a mature, digital counterculture. His *Capitalist Realism* (2009) offered a snapshot of the political and social landscape left behind by the Great Depression, just after Cameron's Conservative government inaugurated its decade-long drive for austerity. Later books—*Ghosts of My Life* (2012) and *The Weird and the Eerie* (2017)—proved belated classics. His writings inspired the British student movement in 2010 and 2011 which went on to storm the Tory headquarters in central London. Fisher's influence was never exclusively British, however, and steadily fed into the deeper dynamic of protest swarming across the globe in the long 2010s. In 2011, the so-called populist explosion of the 2010s still appeared as a predominantly right-wing affair. Tirelessly applied to right-wing politicians in Europe and North America, the last ten years have also seen the word "populism" move to a new set of characters however: the left. From Greece's Syriza to Spain's Podemos, to the Labour Party under Corbyn in the United Kingdom, to Bernie Sanders in the United States, a left populist hype took off on both sides of the Atlantic after 2008. All broke with the conservatism of the Third Way or the sectarianism of smaller left parties. As with so many contemporary phenomena, its roots could be traced to the big bang of 2008, whose fallout was diagnosed in *Capitalist Realism*. Long predating the 2008 financial crisis, however, there lurked a deep political and psychic transformation: the secular decline of collectivity, flagged by the slow fall of mass parties in all developed democracies. Left populism stood out as the short-term product of the crash and the long-term child of the long disorganization. More than a decade ago, the bottom dropped out of the global financial system. Its epicenter was American, but the aftershocks quickly reached Europe and shook the core architecture of the Eurozone. As European elites began implementing harsh austerity programs to reckon with their rising public debt, a new generation of activists took to streets and squares demanding a better life. Mainstream parties had lost their members and hemorrhaged support. From Occupy to the Indignados to the British anti-fee movement to the Greek Squares, these protests thrived *next* to the social democratic parties which had dried out and sold out or tried to retake the parties in question. Their mode of engagement was presaged by the "non-movements" that arose out of the early labor militancy of the Arab Spring. By 2012, however, most of these movements realized their demands were not being met; activist energies on the squares were going to dissipate. Austerity was to continue unabated.

Left activists from Pablo Iglesias to Jean-Luc Mélenchon decided to reach for a new toolbox: inspired by Latin American precedents and the writings of Ernesto Laclau and Chantal Mouffe, the Atlantic left decided to go populist, beyond the paeans to horizontal organizing found in Toni Negri and Michael Hardt. Yet Fisher also steadily became a natural point of inspiration for a new generation of radicals—the millennial left. But like this millennial left, to which he provided inspiration, Fisher's own oeuvre and the left populist politics it spawned was also characterized by a chronic, internal instability. On the one hand, his thought harked back to the epigones of what Alberto Toscano called '73 thought,' the (chiefly Francophone) contingent of writers who saw the slowdown of capital accumulation after the oil crisis as the cue for the fact that capital was returning to a conservative mode. Growth rates were plummeting, consumerism was out of fashion. Instead of clinging to an outdated model of state-tended capitalism, workers had to go on the offensive and take capitalist dynamism at its word. They had to push capital to be more progressive than it could be. Fisher also had little time for the romantic anti-capitalism that eulogized an Adamite world of feudal innocence before the market revolution—a tendency within a sector of the New Left he always remained wary of, exemplified by sections of the ecological movement. Fisher was conditionally critical of this New Left, yet his own oeuvre acknowledged deep debts to their theoretical achievements and concerns, from Marcuse to Lyotard, Félix Guattari to Angela Davis.

"We don't have to choose between class politics and anti-authoritarianism any more than we need to choose between Gramsci, Deleuze, and Guattari," Fisher noted in 2014. "Class politics must be renewed and resumed," in his view,

> not simply revived as if nothing has happened. In a Gramscian mode, we need to take institutions seriously again. Mainstream media are still where our sense of reality is produced; and despite all the claims about the waning of the state, parliament still has power over life and death via its control of the military, health services and social security. Yet these institutions cannot be renewed from within—it is necessary to articulate the institution and the forces outside them.[2]

Here was a delicate attempt to combine the best of the New and Old Left and to drag the millennial left out of the morass of "capitalist realism" along the way.

At the same time, Fisher's writing presented a constant, careful balancing act between two left-wing legacies. Not a millennial himself, his generational distance to the Corbynites gave him to a political panorama between two organizational moments whose transition he had experienced in full. He was equally critical of both. For instance, Fisher remained acutely aware of the tacit and even open convergence that this mode of neo-leftism had engaged with the new neoliberal order. Much of the New Left had prefigured the anti-institutional energies of the later neoliberal moment, seeking to tear down the confines of race, nation, gender, and class, which had locked the working class into its Fordist cage. The New Left might have been no direct factor in *causing* the neoliberal turn, as Fisher warned (the case for complicity can only be made for a handful of opportunists, he noted, whose dalliance with the left was always more oedipally targeted against their bourgeois forefathers). But the case for an essential *compatibility*—or rather, uncomfortable comfort—was undeniable: while the New Left opposed the neoliberal counterrevolution, it also contributed to the weakening of oppositional energies that could have halted the marketization of the social set in by the neoliberal era.

More than that, the anti-organizational enthusiasm of the New Left seemed to silently *sanction* the neoliberal rollback of the state, hoping that Thatcherite "de-stratification" would open breathing space for left militancy. The final product was tragically different, of course: rather than opening new spaces for left militantism, neoliberalism neutralized mass politics itself and radically constricted the space for radical action. Culturally the setback was equally dramatic. Unable to kick-start growth or stimulate real innovation, and no longer disciplined by a disorganized opposition, neoliberalism increasingly turned to the state to enforce its hope for freedom through marketization. Economically, this meant a zero-sum expansion of rentiership, in which former council housing owners bought houses and could offset wage stagnation by relying on rental incomes. On the level of popular culture, it meant an even deeper collapsing of a postwar working-class hegemony into a nebulous "mass culture," in which television, music, and the arts were overtaken by a deep and abiding retromania, a passion for the old masquerading as an addiction to the new. Since the gutting of welfare provisions that made working-class involvement in the arts a viable option, the worlds of *Kultur* had been radically recolonized by the British professional classes. Their own capacity for cultural self-invention and fashioning, however, were radically curtailed by the absence of a working-class threat in society, which had forced the cultural responsibilities of cultural leadership on them. Instead, they took to parasitically aping the styles and mores of a previous phase of popular modernism. In the music of the Arctic Monkeys, Kaiser Chiefs, and even the earlier Britpop sensations of Oasis, Fisher found a bland recycling of a moribund mass culture was now the rule.

Fisher never took to blaming or dismissing the New Left for this world-historic stagnation, however. Instead, he recognized the New Left as a rational response to the petrification and "over-statification" (*étatisation*) of an Old Left. This held as much for economic as political matters. Economically, the emphasis on a breadwinner model of industrial development marginalized and cornered imperial and gendered subjects left out of the Fordist regime. Culturally, it relied on a rigid model of humanism and cultural advancement, which saw the West's bourgeois patrimony as the primary proletarian heritage, to be tended and even reinvented by an ascetic proletarian culture. The original Fordist compromise which this Old Left had constructed could not contain the libidinal energies it was spawning. In the aftermath of the failed world revolution from 1917 to 1923, the global working classes (or, to be clear, their representatives) struck a deal with their respective national bourgeoisies. Instead of transcending capitalism, they sought to construct a model of social citizenship within the confines of a capitalist order.

Rather than socialist revolutionaries, national labor movements turned out to be the delayed executioners of stubborn ancient regimes. Stalin's repartition of the Junker lands, the Austrian social democrats' breaking up of the old Habsburg estates, and the further liquidation of the peasantry in France effectively brought the old order to an end—a task which an older liberal bourgeoisie had never proven capable of. The size of the achievement should not be underestimated, as Fisher always clarified. The granting of general suffrage, the construction of a rudimentary welfare state, and the recognition of syndical freedoms all spoke to a deep victory in defeat for the twentieth-century working class: while the constrictive horizon of capitalism could not be transcended, the proletariat could achieve a degree of humanity under its aegis. "Man" as a worker could be humanized, even within an inhuman system. By the late 1950s, however—when the percentage of industrial workers hit its peak—the cracks in this consensus were already becoming plain to see. The consumerist rights gained by national labor movements spawned a new youth culture unwilling and unable to achieve integration in Fordism. The "integration" their forefathers had indirectly fought for, a grandiose index of defeat, was beyond their reach.

Fisher's own oeuvre can be seen as a delicate therapeutic attempt to work through this tension. Neoliberalism had recuperated the antinomian energies of the New Left, channeling their anti-institutionalism into a neutralization of politics as such. The individualization of politics, the pulverization of old collectivities, and the shattering of social citizenship led to an overall demobilization. At the same time, a return to the rigid economism of the Old Left was not viable. The usual response to this shock was a form of "depressive hedonism" only partially broken by the 2008 shock, when left populism sought to reclaim the questions of both New and Old Left. What remained was the mere pressure of negativity: "this" cannot continue, "this" I will not endure. Fisher's support for the Labour Party, his cautious optimism about the Brexit revolt, and his enthusiasm for left populism saw a left which finally returned to the question of power.

In a 2020 piece for The Platypus Review, Ephraim Carlebach has sought to further tease out these distinctions in Fisher's thought. To Carlebach, part of the millennial left has willfully "forgotten" Fisher's insights, opting for one side of the dialectical binary without ever working through the tension. Fisher's attempt to "put the Old and the New Left back together again" in his view was "not an act of remembering but an act of forgetting: forgetting that the old Labour Left, which the Stalinist Communist Party supported, was never about overcoming capitalism, but as Fisher puts it, 'mitigat[ing] its worst excesses.'"[3] As Carlebach notes, "Fisher . . . was susceptible to the shockwaves of 2016," since it was "premised on (anti-)neoliberalism to such an extent that the crisis of neoliberalism melted away his earlier circumspection. He therefore sought "alternatives for post-neoliberalism" in a "soft-left social democracy" fused with a New Left sensibility.[4] To combat a form of "'deflationary consciousness,' Fisher then sought to "turn to forms of 'consciousness raising' salvaged from the 60s-70s New Left under the rubric of 'acid communism,' the title of the book he was planning at the time of his suicide"—"a remarkable reversal of (an) earlier position," which saw a dialectic of defeat leading the counterculture to culminate in neoliberalism.

Carlebach rightly points at the intrinsically *political* nature of Fisher's conundrum. Rather than present these tendencies as intellectual deviations, however, both can be understood as expressions of two political moments, two different expressions of a different capitalism. The millennial left stood out as the legatee of two consanguineous but still oedipally entwined bloodlines: an Old Left dedicated to institution-building, the dignity of labor, and the labor movement, and a New Left opposed to institutionalization, skeptical of labor, and seeking to represent the "movement of movements" rather than a monolithic labor movement. Teetotalism and psychotropic drugs, spontaneity and discipline, basic income and Stalinist planning, and deterritorialization and reterritorialization here vie for predominance within the same ideological brain. Aaron Bastani's dreams of full automation, Peter Frase's plea for a "weird" socialism, Jodi Dean's defense of comradeship against networking, a neo-Foucauldian critique of the prison coupled with welfare state nostalgia, Asad Haider's attempt to square "class" and "identity," and Jeremy Gilbert's acid communism here combine with a plea for a return to the party and an emphasis on electoral work.

Left populism—the project of the millennial left—was the largest attempt to break this Gordian knot. On the one hand, the left populism put forward by the millennial left arose precisely as a *rejection* of these "anti-political," movementist impulses that funneled the Occupy movement. The idea that one could "change the world without taking power" now appeared dangerous and ludicrous even, punctured by the dissipating energy of the *Indignados* marches. One day the protests would fizzle out: the mere "carnivalesque background noise" that could only function as a sort of shrill basso continuo in the background of neoliberal globalization.[5] If the left was serious about power, it had to think about politics as beyond the street: in the town hall, the parliament, the party, the central bank, and the trade offices. This also implied a much stronger return to Old Left themes, however, and question of discipline and verticality which had been banished for long. This effect did not take long to take off. At the same time, the combination of discipline, a paean to older forms of comradeship, twined badly with the long years of marginality which the left had sheltered in during the end of history.

Fisher's consciousness of this tension came out most strongly in his writings on the phenomenon of "cancel culture," exemplified by his 2014 piece for *The Northern Star* on "Exiting the Vampire Castle." On the one hand, the dynamics of online engagement on Facebook and Twitter appeared positively totalitarian in their strict policing of language codes and registering of minor transgressions. Fisher recognized them as a form of rigid party discipline without an actual party. Or they were an attempt to generate a culture of internal discipline without stipulating a worldview to which that culture had to function. On the other hand, their erasure and uneasiness about class stood out as an unfortunate product of the New Left's embrace of pluralism against a monistic workerism. Unlike the deadening television culture of the 1990s, the internet was *dialogical* and not monological, opening spaces of discourse closed and unavailable before. Fisher's own nostalgia for an earlier, frontier-phase of the internet, in which academic writing could be undone of its jargonesque confines on the "blog," testified to this. Yet the new, post-2008 internet also seemed to undo this original emancipatory promise, reducing the space of experiment and instead seeking panoptical control without a center. The result was what Fisher termed "Stalinism without utopia": an ascetic ethic, with highly judgmental norms for interpersonal engagement, rigid enforcement of sexual mores and libertine abstentionism—now mediated through new digital platforms—but without the utopian calculus which could justify the cruelty of the commissar and the party official. Aggressive vulnerability, as Pavlos Roufos calls it, stood out as an expression of a highly individualized political culture in which collective solidarity and control can only be reached through moralist hectoring.[6] Fisher himself pleaded for a fusion between the Old and New Left, hoping that the millennial left could occupy both the square and the parliament, the blog and the worker's journal, Twitter and the newspaper and support basic income and universal health care and acid communism and teetotal workerism. There was always a perverse and a positive version of this fusion: the anti-utopian Stalinism of the extremely online and the Corbynism which came close to winning a majority in the Commons in 2017.

This left populist attempt to synthesize the Old and New Left also operated in parameters which were not of its own making—a relation of essential heteronomy. We could typify the neoliberal state produced in the wake of the defeat of the Old and New Left, and also the state confronting the millennial left, as "hard and hollow." The era of post-history and "capitalist realism" witnessed a fargoing weakening of the state's "internal sovereignty"—the ties that link states to institutions such as unions, churches, and parties and allow the latter to exercise power over the former. States appeared powerful and capacious, mainly in their executive branch, but insulated from any of the substantive pressure from below exemplified by the older, organizational Left (the COVID-19 crisis has even exposed the ails of this subcontractor state, the "Thousands on thousands of sharks, swarming round the dead leviathan, smackingly feasted on its fatness"). As Fisher and other critics always noted, the aim of contemporary left populism was to rethink mobilization for an age of demobilization. In this sense populism was the product of a "hard but hollow" environment, an attempt to break the iron grip of the neoliberal state with little to no resources at our disposal to do so. The neoliberal state started as an interventionist experiment to shield the market from mass democracy; this was its avowedly "hard" side. But it could not do so while remaining beholden to a variety of popular interest groups, which were clamoring for checks on that very market. Therefore, it also had to be "hollow," undone of its ties to social actors below. Mass party democracy was hampering a renewed drive to capital accumulation; the only solution was to neutralize the state and turn it from an active player into an impartial arbiter. This cutting operation was as drastic on the right as it was on the left. As James Heartfield describes it,

> To defeat the working-class challenge of the seventies, the elite tore up the old institutions that bound the masses to the state. Class conflict was institutionalized under the old system, which not only contained working class opposition but also helped the ruling class to formulate a common outlook. What started as an offensive against working class solidarity in the eighties undermined the institutions that bound society together. Not just trade unions and socialist parties were undermined, but so too were right-wing political parties and their traditional support bases amongst church and farmers' groups. Middle class professional groups lost their privileged position.[7]

The result was the infamous "void" described by Irish political scientist Peter Mair—a "demobilized" citizenry forced to rely on the market for meaning and survival, only taking cues from the state as to how to maximize its competitive positioning. Collective agency was abdicated to globalization, and institutions were passé. In the 1990s, most of the left willfully participated in this shift, trading working classes for "multitudes" and the market for "the network."

Populism tried to take stock of this new situation by building on this void. As Fisher noted, this is again unsurprising: men make their own history, but not in circumstances of their own choosing, as Marx already knew. Any critique of left populism which does not account for this fact will be of little help to us today. The scholarly term for this "hard but hollow" environment is "disintermediation"—the cutting of the intermediate ties which tie individuals to each other on a horizontal level but also tie individuals to larger institutions higher up, on a vertical level. Parties had atrophied, unions lost members, and churches ran empty. After 2008, the process was hardly reversed. The left first hoped that mass misery would breed mass militancy, but this response failed to materialize. When no class came into being, a collective collage of identities seemed to offer succor, as Fife and Hines note. But such a collage always had a strong anti-materialist bent and therefore missed the very crux of the austerity moment. "Because left populists (did) not locate oppression as the result of non-subjective structural dynamics," they note, and "see class as just another identity category, the left populist project becomes not a confrontation between classes" but instead "a sort of amorphous yelling for recognition that, if we believe in it, will magically change culture."[8] From *Occupy* to the clown posse, the affirmative festival was the primary figure of our age.

The left populist's response to the neoliberal situation appears, in this framing, as a compulsively optimistic defense which tacitly accepts the neoliberal order by inviting everyone to a flattened bacchanal with the hopes that the unity of various oppressed groups regardless of class will result in a capable change-agent. Even though members of such a coalition might have conflicting economic incentives, if we can all just "recognize" one another in contingency—think acid communism—and legitimate one another's identity, then, in our collective ecstasy, a positive new reality will emerge. Quintessential for this left populist response to depressive hedonism into compulsive bliss is an attitude such as this: "Everyone is so excited, so happy to be together, and so swept up in their shared emotional experience that there simply isn't space for strategic quibbles." As Fife and Hines note,

> The excited bacchanalia of the hyped left populist party often ends in predictable tears—with accusations of misrecognition, and active exclusion of those who can't or won't keep up with whatever floating signifier signifies knowledge of the latest link to be added to (Laclau's) "chain of equivalencies."[9]

By the end of his life, Fisher himself was moving away from one side of the dialectical tension, from old Labor discipline to acid communism. This tendency relived a natural upsurge after the defeat of the Corbyn insurgency in December 2019. Its focus on libidinal release as the aim of politics and its distaste for mediating structures also seemed to twine with the anti-racist protest wave of 2020. Fisher would probably have greeted this wave as salutary and necessary but also recognized its limits vis-à-vis the previous left populist episode: its lack of organizational duress, its institutional agnosticism, the residual presence of a militant liberalism in its ranks, and its incapacity to build broad majoritarian support for its program. In early 2021, the fusing of this anti-racist sensibility with an earlier wave of support for Palestinian liberation seemed to send the left back into the future. The protest harked back to the alter-globalization protests of the 2000s, but not in a new sheen, and without consciousness of the populist intermission.

The COVID crisis also appeared vastly different from the 2008 crash, however. If 2008 consisted of dimming the lights after an electric fault, this is more like pulling the plug. The festivals of the 2000s might have resembled labor camps, but they could not do with any social distancing—the point was to generate the illusion of "massness" in an age after mass politics. The COVID crisis, however, is the final solvent of the "masses." Finally, the left's real trauma might be that neoliberalism died without them killing it, delaying Fisher's exit from capitalist realism into a deepening of a previous capitalist unrealism. "Agency" now seems to reside with an inhuman agent, reminiscent of Heidegger's claim that "only a God could save us now." The left waited for ten years for someone to finally bury the neoliberal settlement; no one of adequate power arose, and now an extra-human agent will take care of it.

Capitalism has always had "private" and "public" moments. As the intellectual historian Howard Brick noted in his *Transcending Capitalism*, "There is a two-sidedness to capitalist social development that socializes and privatizes simultaneously."[10] The ambiguity of capitalist "social development," therefore, is that it

> may spawn an illusory faith in the progressive promise of the status quo, but it also fosters the confidence, at the heart of Marx's historical vision, that a break toward a new, genuinely "associated" mode of production can follow based on institutional resources provided by capitalism itself.[11]

In 2021, states indeed seem to be moving from a private into a public capitalism. It is tempting to view the moment like Karl Polanyi, who saw a twisted hope in the fascist "countermovements" which arose in the 1930s. The very tension between property relations and productive relations is what drives the system forward; contractions and expansions are a part of its very nature. Fisher's attempt was to extract a modicum of agency from this tension, combining the Old and New Left.

Undoubtedly capitalism's public moments remain objectively more interesting to the left than the private ones, as Fisher himself recognized about the original emancipatory avenues opened by the postwar moment. But they will always be an insufficient, though necessary, condition of positive change. Also needed, of course, are left strategy and organizing. Left populists didn't think the politics of class were enough, so they sought to craft a cross-class coalition against austerity. This strategy underestimated both the desire for normality in part of the population and the desire for agency in another (think Biden, Trump). In the time of COVID-19, the politics of survival will create a new universal, precarious subject. This subject can hardly claim more independence and now just wants bare survival. The tragedy is that any form of political independence will be forfeited for that survival itself.

What with the millennial left that sought to square the Old and New Left? With lockdowns active across the world, the long-awaited mass mobilization will have to be postponed. States demobilized their citizens for about thirty years. Now they will ask them to demobilize just a little bit more. Politicians, in turn, advised voters to realize their dreams of self-determination in the marketplace, through consumer sovereignty or the sugar highs of a credit boom. In the 2010s this model became infrastructurally untenable; citizens realized that there were other models of sovereignty out there, some of them majoritarian, others digital and affective. Those will have to be postponed as well. The market can no longer provide or protect, and the state will have to cushion the blow. The "hard" will become the "soft"—a move from states as the "armed wings of Amazon" to the "armed wings of Oxfam," as Richard Tuck has put it.

This shift also represents a sensitive blow to the "hardness-hollowness" paradigm set up by Fife and Hines. What we're seeing is the "softening" of the "hard but hollow" state built by neoliberalism, but without "filling" up the void. We will see increased administration and a return of planning, a more competent bureaucracy. States are unlearning thirty years of nudge theory and finessing their means of coercion. Production for use value appeared like a necessity again. The GOP moved leftward before the Democrats on cash transfers and credit provision, the latter addled by a typically neurotic liberal legalism. Once these interventions end, it will be hard to put the genies back in the bottle. There might even be some war socialism and transfers of labor; UBI is already on the horizon. After catastrophe capitalism, quarantine corporatism will become a lived reality for most of humanity.

But we will see little to no mobilization, and probably no "counter-hegemonic" subject. Instead, the West will witness the completion of the capsular civilization constructed by neoliberalism in the last thirty years. We can confidently expect the Houllebecqian nightmare we've been warned of. Without a massive stimulus package, the Corona crash will wipe out most of the small-scale service sector, from barbers to nail salons to internet cafés to specialty coffee bars. The only companies left standing will be Amazon and the large chains, now lording over a recalibrated subeconomy designed to deliver "essential" goods. This situation might just realize the dream of 1990s sociology and its "network society" described by Manuel Castells. Interpersonal contact will be replaced by mediations through machines. Experience will be increasingly restricted to emojis. Sexual pleasure will be outsourced, with porn addicts turning into ideal consumers of themselves.

Parts of the left will no doubt find some solace in this new world. As Philip Cunliffe notes, the future lies with an "avowedly passive, consumerist vision of socialism," in which citizens "get paid by the state to live under martial law as we supposedly work from home while living on the backs of an underclass that are compelled to work for Deliveroo and Amazon."[12] After some time, perhaps during the second or third wave, new ideological cleavages will reemerge: COVID-19 relativists will face COVID-19 absolutists against COVID-19 denialists. The first will want to see a quick return to normalcy triaged by age, suboptimizing the death rate and freeing up boomer assets. The second will want continued lockdown and enforced labor, a statist settlement that can keep the economy afloat while the middle class survives on its reserves and serenades on balconies (we could style it "lockdown liberalism"). The latter will build a religious attachment to the idea that COVID-19 was still a flu, that all of this was a state-induced collective panic, that someone will, in the end, cancel the hallucination.

Peter Sloterdijk once controversially typified the disabled "future subjects of humanity."[13] His prediction is *outré* but contains a kernel of truth. Our growing daily dependence on the "technological prostheses" dreamt up by the global market—sporadically celebrated as the advent of a new "cyborg" subject by the likes of Donna Haraway—is now completing the infantile revolution ushered in by a post-paternal capitalism. Clubs, cafés, and other sites of sociability would have to be redesigned to accommodate the new humans, and the anthropological type suitable to the new Corona capitalism will not be the "lonely crowd" but the cellular pod, the monadic embryo vegetating in a womb. The embryo's state will be "soft" but still hollow, drifting through its fresh, new, maternal void.

Any move toward a more "public" capitalism could obviously be welcomed from the left, and Fisher would have recognized the potential of an early pandemic statism. But "socialization" can happen both "from above" and "from below," much like Polanyi's "countermovements" could flow both from socialist and fascist impulses. Fisher's left needed more than the right kind of administration or a mitigation of capitalist excesses, much like it needed more than an assemblage of identities in the 2010s. Left populism was an attempt to do politics in a time after history, when the clash of classes and the bargaining of interests seemed both institutionally and intellectually impossible. The death of face-to-face sociability is unlikely to give a fresh impetus to new organizations (those hoping to kick-start a "Corona revolution" with an emergency ban on gatherings over five are in for a rough ride). The "hard" part of the "hard but hollow" neoliberal state might have ended. But the hollowness will probably persist; the void is widening rather than closing, gobbling up ever more space. It might take a while before history starts again. In his own, original essay on "Mourning and Melancholia," Freud diagnosed the same instability. "The most remarkable characteristic of melancholia," he noted, "is its tendency to change round into mania—a state which is the opposite of it in its symptoms." In its resulting "circular insanity," a "regular alternation of melancholic and manic phases" now afflicts the patient, both "wrestling with the same complex"—the traumatic loss of its "libidinal object." After the defeat of the Old and New Left, a new millennial left underwent an internal oscillation between mania and melancholia, swerving between compulsive optimism and a conscience of doom. No one provided a better analysis of this circularity, of optimism circling back into fatalism, of melancholia switching into mania and back, than Mark Fisher. The fate of left-wing politics in the twenty-first century still depends on a resolution of this tension.

Parts of this essay first appeared as an essay in Damage Magazine, see *"It Might Take a While Before History Starts Again," Damage Magazine (March 25, 2020), https://damagemag .com /2020 /03 /25 /it -might -take -a -while -before -history -starts -again/. Accessed June 30, 2021.*

NOTES

1. Now archived at http://k-punk.abstractdynamics.org/. Accessed July 1, 2021.
2. Fisher 2014.
3. Carlebach 2019.
4. Ibid.
5. Cited in Hammond 2019, 50.
6. Roufos 2018.
7. Heartfield 2014.
8. Fife and Hines 2020.
9. Fife and Hines 2020.
10. Brick 2006, 269.
11. Ibid.
12. Cunliffe 2020.
13. Sloterdijk 2014, 90–92.

Chapter 5

The Poverty of Immediacy
A Critique of the Communization Current
Joshua Pickett-Depaolis

In spite of Proudhon, the proletariat continues to see in the political revolution the most powerful means of achieving an economic revolution.

—G. V. Plekhanov[1]

Classes can be abolished only by the dictatorship of that oppressed class which has been schooled, united, trained, and steeled by decades of the strike and political struggle against capital—of that class alone which has assimilated all the urban, industrial, big-capitalist culture and has the determination and ability to protect it and to preserve and further develop all its achievements, and make them available to all the people, to all the working people.

—V. I. Lenin[2]

Communization theory first takes shape in France following the uprising of 1968.[3] Its various tendencies have raised important questions on the transformation of class composition within contemporary capitalism. However, the present chapter does not center its engagement with communization theory on its analysis of the current stage of capitalism. On the contrary, it interrogates the standpoint from which this analysis is produced. Specifically, it questions whether the standpoint of communization theory can be seen as in continuity with the Marxist tradition or whether it constitutes a permutation of reactionary anti-capitalism. My thesis is that the positions characteristic of the reactionary critique of capital are not only hegemonic within an explicitly non-Marxist "romantic left" (the spectrum of anarchist, ecological, feminist, and Indigenous critiques which flatly reject capitalist modernity) but also take on nominally Marxist forms. One of these forms noteworthy for its articulation of a non-Marxist conception of communism, in Marxist terms, is communization theory.

In the following I will show that, in fact, the anti-dialectical hostility of the communization trend toward the social totality constituted by exchange value, and its demand for an "authentic" class, which refuses articulation into any system of organizational mediations, situates communization theory firmly in the camp of reactionary anti-capitalism. This chapter will carry out an investigation of the hostility to bourgeois modernity, which defines the communization current. It is a trend of thought which in its effort to reconcile Marxist analysis with a passive adaption to the end result of class decomposition can be seen as the *ne plus ultra* of the "conformist rebellion." Taking negative critique to the horizon line where it unites with its opposite—the affirmation of the existent—it reassures rebellious intellectuals that the present order is not the work of man, but of fate.

It is indisputable that communization theory is a part of the communist tradition. The work of this current is clearly oriented toward the abolition of commodity production. However, communism and Marxism are not equivalent terms, and a specifically Marxist approach to the realization of communism is defined by two integrally linked theses. First, the realization of communism is dependent upon the development of capitalist production relations as a precondition.[4] Second, this realization is not simply a rupture with the reproduction of these relations but the actualization of their own emancipatory potential through an overcoming *from within*.[5] For Marx and for the Marxists of the Second and Third Internationals, these two points were foundational and unquestioned. They formed the basis of Marx's support for national liberation,[6] colonialism,[7] and warfare against feudal powers,[8] just as they were the premise for the polemic of the Russian Social Democrats against populism.[9] To be a Marxist in the nineteenth and early twentieth centuries was to be a partisan of capital as a precondition of communism. From its origins, Marxism confronted other currents of anti-capitalist critique which, rather than seeing capitalist production as the necessary basis of human emancipation, identified it as a corrosive force to be limited or destroyed. These currents ranged from the patriarchal small producer ideology of Proudhon to the agrarian communalism of the populists and the "feudal socialism" of Carlyle and Linguet.

What differentiates Marxism from other anti-capitalist currents is not a critique of wage labor but the insistence upon capitalism as not only the necessary *premise* of any emancipatory movement but containing within itself the possibility of a fully emancipated world. From the Marxist perspective, the generalization of the wage relation through its dissolution of prior limited communities, the production of a universal individual and an unprecedented development of productive forces form the premise of communism. This viewpoint is the systematization of a radical optimism which sees in the expanded reproduction of capital not mere horror but the growing possibility of a better future.

However, Marxism, like the dream of a better future it embodies, has been in decline for a long time. First, the failure of world revolution following the First World War narrowed the immediate perspective of the revolutionary movement from the transcendence of capital toward a defensive preservation of the balance of forces *within capital*, produced by the institutional crystallizations of the workers movement following the October Revolution.

Second, the integration of the organized workers movement within the global and national frameworks of capital reproduction obstructed the reconstitution of class subjectivity necessary to advance these gains toward rupture.[10] Finally, this integrated worker's movement was left defenseless in the face of the offensive of capitalist restructuring against its accumulated gains leading to the current period of class decomposition. This setback opened further space for the proliferation of communitarian movements, which systematically mystified the class contradiction. In this context, Marxism finds itself severed from a connection to worker struggle and in a permanent crisis of confidence. This has resulted not only in the increasing popularity of efforts to detach the project of universal emancipation from the mediation of class, party, and state, but in a retreat by much of the radical left from this project itself.[11] Here, the post-capitalist future is not understood as the actualization of universal freedom whose premises bourgeois civilization creates for the first time in history. On the contrary, this freedom is denounced as a mere ruse of domination, and liberation is identified with a return of the archaic community.

Despite its relative obscurity, we will take the work of the French collective *Théorie Communiste* as a case study, both because of its conceptual sophistication and its decisive influence on the work of other, more well-known exponents of communization, such as the academically influential UK-based writing group *Endnotes*.

THÉORIE COMMUNISTE'S REVOLT AGAINST MEDIATION

Communization theory, in the form articulated by *Théorie Communiste*, grounds itself in a critique of the theory and practice of the classical worker's movement. It is viewed as the product of a historically closed period of class struggle, allegedly superseded by the linear development of capital. *Théorie Communiste* terms this theory and practice "programmatism."

My engagement with *Théorie Communiste* will take the form of a commentary on selected lines of the text *Much Ado about Nothing*,[12] written as part of a polemic with fellow left-communist theorist Gilles Dauvé (1947–) who rejected their attempt to historicize communization as the product of the new stage in the class relation produced by the decomposition of the classical worker's movement.[13] I will focus on five aspects of the discourse of *Théorie Communiste*: (1) the conceptualization and critique of *programmatism*, (2) the conceptualization of the Marxist concept of *subsumption*, (3) the critique of *self-organization*, (4) the critique of *quantification*, and (5) the *activist quietism* implied by the above. It will become apparent over the course of my examination that the radical posture of *Théorie Communiste* (and by extension of the current it represents) conceals a passive adaption to the comprehensive defeat of the workers movement, which rather than being challenged is taken as permanent.

THE REJECTION OF PROGRAMMATISM

In *Much Ado about Nothing*, *Théorie Communiste* defines programmatism as follows:

> The theory and practice of class struggle in which the proletariat finds, in its drive toward liberation, the fundamental elements of a future social organisation which become the *programme to be realised*.[14]

The sweeping generality of this opening definition demands interrogation. Much as communization theorists condemn planning and accounting, here the articulation of any project for a future social reorganization, based on an anticipation from the dynamics of the present, is framed not as a general precondition of political action but as a historically determined and now superseded phase of the class struggle. The implication is the dissolution of rational synthesis within a pure immediacy. For *Théorie Communiste*, the development of capital has overcome the possibility of the articulation of a proletarian political trajectory. It has therefore overcome any possibility of constructing a subject internal to the social totality, which consciously masters this totality. The production of communism is not premised in a protracted synthesis of the general with the particular within the worker's movement. Indeed, this synthesis was a historically given limit. Now that it is has been overcome by the defeat of the workers' movement, communism appears "exposed" as a *directly emergent potentiality*.

This revolution is thus the *affirmation* of the proletariat, whether as a dictatorship of the proletariat, workers' councils, the liberation of work, a period of transition, the withering of the state, generalized self-management, or a "society of associated producers."[15]

For *Théorie Communiste*, the affirmation of the proletariat equates the affirmation of the value relation which already constitutes the present society, as I will show. Thus, programmatism was simply the reproduction of this society. However, the affirmation of the *proletariat* is *not* the affirmation of the *working class* as members of bourgeois society engaged in the sale of the labor power-commodity. Nor is the affirmation of the proletariat simply the affirmation of the *workers' movement*—which is to say, the subjectivity engendered within the struggle over the terms of the sale of the labor power-commodity. The affirmation of the proletariat is the affirmation of a political program for the overcoming of the value relation, which becomes operational through its fusion with the workers' movement. There is neither equivalence nor linear continuity within the trinity of working class, workers' movement, and proletariat. It is possible for the working class to form the social majority and the organized defense of working-class interests to be an exception, just as it is possible for a superficially strong working-class movement to exist in the absence of proletarian politics. Only if the distinction between them is not understood, is it possible to assign to proletarian self-affirmation the meaning which *Théorie Communiste* asserts.

The affirmation of the proletariat is not reducible to the affirmation of the worker as a term of the capital relation and a sociological group within bourgeois society. The working class is an objective *position* within bourgeois society; the proletariat is a subjective *program* for the actualization of that society's imminent emancipatory tendency through its overcoming. The spurious reduction of the latter to the former is a necessary premise for the polemic against "programmatism." *Théorie Communiste* contends that

> programmatism is not simply a theory—it is above all the practice of the proletariat, in which the rising strength of the class (in unions and parliaments, organisationally, in terms of the relations of social forces or of a certain level of consciousness regarding "the lessons of history") is positively conceived of as a stepping-stone toward revolution and communism.[16]

That is to say, programmatism is the constitution of the proletariat as a subjective force within the movement of capital, as an aspect of this movement. We can say that to set yourself against programmatism is to oppose the Marxist understanding of the proletarian revolution as the conscious self-overcoming of capital in favor of an anti-dialectical "pure" negation.

THE COMMUNIZATION VIEW OF THE MARXIST CONCEPT OF SUBSUMPTION

> Programmatism is intrinsically linked to the contradiction between the proletariat and capital as it is constituted by the formal subsumption of labor under

capital. At this point, capital, in its relation to labor, poses itself as an external force.[17]

This linkage between formal subsumption and "programmatism" is audaciously erroneous. For Marx, formal subsumption is a term which characterizes the subsumption of a "given, existing labor process" under capital without the transformation of the technical basis of the process, which to the contrary characterizes *real* subsumption.[18] The examples of such preexisting labor processes characterized by *formal* subsumption include "handicraft labor" and "the mode of agriculture corresponding to small scale independent peasant farming."[19] The parties of the Second and Third Internationals (the most prominent examples of the "programmatism" which *Théorie Communiste* sets out to critique) neither found their main base of support within workers in such preexisting processes nor saw such workers as their primary constituency. Moreover, their programs were premised not upon small-scale craft production but upon large-scale modern industry: real subsumption. In fact, the classical workers' movement and its revolutionary program was "intrinsically linked" not to formal, but to *real* subsumption. Though formal subsumption remained a significant feature of the societies within which the classical Marxist parties operated, their program was not the liberation *of* labor based on *formal* but rather liberation *from* labor on the basis of *real* subsumption.[20] This is how Engels characterized the technical and social basis for the communist movement in 1847:

> It has come about that in all civilised countries almost all branches of labour are carried on under the factory system, that in *almost all these branches handicraft and manufacture have been ousted by large-scale industry.*[21]

The Erfurt Program of German Social Democracy characterized the level of development of productive forces, which formed the point of departure for its program in 1891, as follows:

> Along with this monopolizing of the means of production goes the crowding out and scattering of small production, *the development of the tool into the machine, and a marvelous increase in the productivity of labor.*[22]

And here is how the Communist Party of the Soviet Union (CPSU) described the technological basis of its own program in 1919:

> The sphere of dominion of capitalist production relations is extending wider and wider as the *constant improvement in technology*, by increasing the *economic importance* of *big enterprises*, leads to the squeezing out of the petty independent producers, to the conversion of some of them into proletarians, and to the

restriction of the part played by the remainder in the social and economic life and at times subjecting them to the more or less obvious, more or less burdensome dependence on capital.[23]

If any position within the classical workers' movement can be considered a form of consciousness produced by formal subsumption, it would be the apologia for small production expressed by Proudhon and the mutualists. However, classical Marxism (and syndicalism, for that matter) stand on completely different grounds—that of real subsumption. It is characterized by production processes within which

> [the] *social* productive powers of labour, or the productive powers of directly *social, socialised* (common) labour, are developed through cooperation, through the division of labour within the workshop, the employment of *machinery*, and in general through the transformation of the production process into a conscious *application* of the natural sciences, mechanics, chemistry, etc., for particular purposes, *technology*, etc., as well as by working on a large scale, which corresponds to all these advances, etc.[24]

The logic at work in this attempt to associate revolution as affirmation with formal subsumption is the valorization of a relative externality of labor to capital. For *Théorie Communiste*, the possibility of programmatism is found in this relative externality, because the "programmatic" revolution is not understood as capital's own self-overcoming. But in reality, the program of revolutionary transition finds its most favorable *objective* base in the maximum organic composition. However, the balance of forces between revolution and counterrevolution can no more be directly inferred from the objective stage in the development of the capital relation than the outcome of a wrestling match can be predicted by the physical statistics of the contestants. The assertion of an "intrinsic connection" between formal subsumption and "programmatism," when the opposite is the case, is the first mistaken premise of *Théorie Communiste*'s critique. I will now proceed to the second:

> For the proletariat, to liberate itself from capitalist domination is to turn labour into the basis of social relations between all individuals, to liberate productive labour, take up the means of production, and abolish the anarchy of capitalism and private property. The proletariat's liberation is to be founded in a mode of production based upon abstract labour, i.e., upon value.[25]

There is a continuity within classical Marxism of the self-overcoming of value as a programmatic position from the Second to the Third International.[26] However, the misunderstanding displayed here by *Théorie Communiste* is deeper than a failure to attentively read the texts of the tradition they critique. What they fail to understand is that the transformation of labor into the basis of social relations between individuals, the liberation of productive labor, and even the abolition of the "anarchy" of private property was not the final objective but the necessary precondition for the overcoming of value in the "programmatist" schema they criticize. Any conceptualization of emancipation which is not founded in full actualization and gradual transformation of a "mode of production based upon abstract labor" is, whatever its merits, not situated within the Marxist tradition. For *Théorie Communiste*, the liberation of the proletariat can only be its (false) liberation as value-producing labor— or its (real) liberation accomplished through the immediate destruction of value. The conscious mastery of the value relation as precondition of its qualitative transformation disappears. The overcoming of the value relation entails the fullest extension of this relation as a precondition. Communism is not a destructive rupture with the universalization of the value relation, but a *potential* actualization of the consciously willed freedom of the community of social labor this relation itself produces. *Théorie Communiste* and the communization current, more broadly, systematically confuse emancipatory self-overcoming and regressive destruction. A case in point is this passage:

> The revolutionary process of the affirmation of the class is two-fold. It is on the one hand conceived of as the rising strength of the proletariat in the capitalist mode of production and, on the other hand, its affirmation as a particular class and thus the preservation of its autonomy. In the necessity of its own mediations (parties, unions, cooperatives, societies, parliaments), the revolution as autonomous affirmation of the class (as a particular existence for itself in relation to capital) loses its way, not so much in relation to revolution per se, but in relation to this very affirmation. The proletariat's rising strength is confused with the development of capital and comes to contradict that which was nevertheless its own specific purpose: its autonomous affirmation.[27]

If the first term of this binary is the class in objective terms as the strata of the wage-dependent, then it cannot be "confused" with the development of capital, as it is an inextricable function of such development. The growth of the working class and the expansion of capitalist relations of production are not separable phenomena. And the expansion of capitalist relations is at the same time inextricable from the expansion of the *potential* for the development of a proletarian political subjectivity, characterized by the programmatic objective of transcending such relations. Moreover, the revolution is not simply the particularity of the working class "for itself" but the dynamic between itself and a general program for the transformation of the social totality. Here, the organized and conscious element of the working class transforms the constitutive substance of this totality by means of a qualitatively distinct structuration of state power—abolishing itself in the process. Proletarian politics has no unmediated identity with the interests of a given strata of wage workers. The general program of the proletariat and the interests of a given worker strata form two terms of a contradiction, which only annuls itself when the self-abolition of the class and hence of value is complete. As *Théorie Communiste* further contends,

> In the revolutionary period after World War I, of which the Communist Left in their practice and theory are the substantial expression, the proletariat finds itself ambushed by a novel situation: in its autonomous affirmation it confronts what it is in capital, what it has become, its own strength as a class *in so far as it is a class of the capitalist mode of production*.[28]

After the First World War, the organized working-class movement was split between the project of comanagement of the capitalist mode of production with the capitalist class (social democracy) and seizure of political power as the precondition for a transition to communist relations of production.

Two subjective class projects, that of the bourgeois workers' parties and that of the communist proletariat, confronted each other within the objective class terrain of the workers' movement.

However, *both* projects are manifestations of the working class as an element of the capitalist mode of production. The autonomous affirmation of the working class is not autonomy *from* the capitalist mode of production (an impossibility) but the merger of the scientific (proletarian) consciousness of the necessity of overcoming capital with working-class organization *within capital*. The struggle between revolution and counterrevolution is not and cannot be a struggle against capital, but a struggle *within* the capital relation over the political framework, within which the reproduction of this relation is to be stabilized or progressively abolished.

Counterrevolution stabilizes the political framework of reproduction of the capitalist relations of production. Revolution, to the contrary, affirms itself as a project for the imposition of the political framework required for the overcoming of these relations from *within themselves*, and on the foundation of their full actualization. The question of the abolition or reproduction of capitalist relations of production *never appears directly* in concrete actuality, but only through the mediation of the two political class projects. This is not a function of a given historical period in the development of capital, but a general function of the relation between the objective dynamic of the capital relation and the subjective articulation of the two political class projects within this dynamic.

The party is the organized anticipation of the potential transformation of capitalist relations of production into communist relations. This transition is distinguished historically from the development of commodity relations into capitalist production precisely by its conscious character. The possibility of actualizing the communist potentiality within socialized labor can be expressed only through the mediation of the programmatic aspiration of the revolutionary organization. This is because communism only has actuality at the level of the totality, at the level of the self-overcoming of the movement of capital as a *global whole*. This overcoming is not possible within the horizon of immediate struggles. It becomes real only in the articulation of a state project for its implementation. However, in *Much Ado about Nothing* we read,

> The rising strength of the class, in which labour presents itself as the essence of capital, is confused with the development of capital itself. All the organisations which formalise this rising strength, are able from the First World War onwards, to present themselves as the managers of capital—they become as such the most acute form of the counterrevolution.[29]

But the revolutionary program is the self-overcoming of the value relation *from within*. The distinction between the transition of capital beyond itself and the destruction of capital is that between the realization of Enlightenment and the romantic perspective of regression as liberation. The question at hand is the decision between the bourgeois management of capital, which seeks to stabilize the relation, and the proletarian management of capital which develops it beyond itself. For *Théorie Communiste*, the planned gradual abolition of capital is indistinguishable from "counterrevolution," because for them the "revolution" is a nihilistic destruction of the social totality constituted by exchange value. *Théorie Communiste* argues,

> In the years after 1917, revolution is still an affirmation of the class, and the proletariat seeks to liberate against capital its social strength, which exists in capital—a social strength on which it bases its organisation and founds its revolutionary practice.

But there is no "outside" to capital, and subsumption within capital means unprecedented freedom in comparison to traditional society. The question is whether this new freedom will be progressively liberated from the restrictions of exchange value through the political agency of the proletariat. The proletariat is not simply an entity in opposition to capital but a program for the fulfillment of capital's immanent tendency to overcome itself. *Théorie Communiste* further argues that

> the concept of programmatism historicises the terms of class struggle, revolution and communism. This enables us to understand class struggle and revolution in

their real historical characteristics, and not in relation to a norm; to overcome the opposition which is made between revolution, communism, and its conditions (those famous conditions which are never ripe); to abandon the dichotomy between a proletariat always revolutionary in its substance (revolutionary, in fact, as the subsequent period understands the term) and a revolution which it never produces; to construct the diverse elements of an epoch as a totality producing its own internal connections at the same time as its diversities and conflicts (between Marx and Bakunin, Luxembourg and Bernstein, etc.); and finally, to avoid ending up with a "revolutionary being" of the proletariat, whose every "manifestation" results in a restructuring of capital.[30]

The first problem in this analysis is that the October Revolution was in fact "produced" and formed the *basis* of the further development of the class contradiction, generating a proletarian state as its effect. *Théorie Communiste* cannot understand revolution as the progressive self-abolition of capital, implemented as policy by the proletariat, because *Théorie Communiste* cannot understand communism as *immanent* to the movement of capital. For *Théorie Communiste*, communism is a simple *moment* of automatic exit, or *separation* from capital, rather than a *conscious process* of appropriation and transformation. Communism is the transcendence realized through the actualization of the potential within the *dynamic of this relation itself*, not its immediate, and hence, unmediated destruction.

But *Théorie Communiste* assume that

> this workers' identity which constituted the *workers' movement* and structured class struggle, even integrating "really existing socialism" within the global division of accumulation, rested on *the contradiction between, on the one hand, the creation and development of labour power put to work by capital in an increasingly collective and social manner, and on the other, the (increasingly) limited forms of appropriation by capital of this labour power in the immediate process of production and reproduction.*[31]

The "cold war" period in the articulation of the class relation cannot be separated from the political rupture of the October Revolution and its effects. For the first time, the state project of the proletariat confronted the state project of the bourgeois on a global level. It is not that this configuration went so far as "even" to embrace the degenerated workers' states. On the contrary, it was a complex of the direct and indirect effects of the October Revolution, which created a balance of power within which a relative rigidity of labor markets with its furthest extreme in these states became a global norm.

This period was not the unmediated effect of a given organic composition but the product of the changed balance of political class forces produced by the workers' states. The features of this period, identified as characteristic by *Théorie Communiste*, are the product of the direct gains of the October Revolution in the form of the workers' states. They are also the indirect gains of the October Revolution in the form of class compromises developed in the context of the global imperialist containment strategy against the rupture that these states represented.

Capitalist development was constrained by the political limit of the workers movement whose most concentrated expression was the workers' states. That the workers' movement, articulated in unions, parties, and states, far from embodying a program for world revolution, functioned as the crucial component in the administration of a class compromise within the dynamic of capitalist development has no bearing on the fact that this compromise was the product of the pressure of workers against the valorization imperative and a *qualitative* advance in the proletarian struggle. *Théorie Communiste* however contends:

> There was a self-presupposition of capital, in accordance with the concept of capital, but the contradiction between the proletariat and capital couldn't situate itself at this level, in so far as within this self-presupposition there was a production and confirmation of a workers' identity, through which the class struggle structured itself as the workers' movement.[32]

For *Théorie Communiste*, the class struggle is no longer structured as the workers' movement, but in the period following neoliberal restructuring, assumes a form characterized by the predominance of diffuse struggles in circulation and reproduction. The premise of this argument is given by the defeat of the workers' movement characterized by the elimination of the previous concentrations of worker power in the production process. It is also given in the context of political defeat resulting from the elimination of the gains of the October Revolution, a capitalist class offensive facilitated by the development of the productive forces in terms of the new possibilities of restructuring of the process of production (automation, computerization) and circulation (logistics).

However, contra *Théorie Communiste*, we have not encountered a new subject or terrain of struggle. We have rather encountered a predominance of cross-class democratic movements and an absence of proletarian leadership in a relationship of mutual determination, with the weakness of the working class imposed by restructuring. In the postwar period of East-West confrontation and decolonization prior to neoliberal restructuring beginning in the 1970s, the bourgeoisie was on the defensive in the face of the balance of powers produced by the October Revolution. Following restructuring, the dynamic has shifted to the offensive of the bourgeoisie and the progressive elimination of both the workers' movement and proletarian politics.

The terrain has been set by the constraints of the given technical forces of production. But the balance of forces itself has been produced by the subjectivity of the two classes in relation to the systems of organization which represent them and mediate their interrelation within the movement of capital.

COMMUNIZATION THEORY'S CRITIQUE OF SELF-ORGANIZATION

> The decomposition of programmatism contains the increasingly obvious impossibility of conceiving the revolution as a "growing-over" of that which the proletariat is in capitalist society, of its rising power as a workers' movement. The process of revolution is practically and theoretically posed in terms of *class autonomy*, as so many ruptures with its integration, and of the defense of its reproduction. Self-organization and autonomy become the revolution, to such an extent that the form suffices for the content.[33]

From the Marxist standpoint not only is the possibility of revolution premised upon the growing strength of the proletariat (understood as the organized fusion of the workers' movement and scientific socialist consciousness) within capitalist society, but the transition to communism is the "going over" of capitalist society as a conscious process of self-transcendence. Revolution is not a radical destruction of the socialized production process of capital but its organized subordination to the dictates of the associated producers. This is both the precondition and the result of the qualitative transformation of its content.[34] It is a subordination which cannot be implemented directly but only through political mediations. In other words, the *political* autonomy of the proletariat is not the "self-organization" of workers in immediate struggles. It is the leadership of the party as the organized manifestation of the program of planned abolition of value over the immediate struggles of the working class, integrating them within the strategic perspective of the seizure of state power to implement the self-overcoming of value as *state policy*.

Théorie Communiste and the workerist positions it criticizes form two substantially identical articulations of economism. The first confuses proletarian politics with the wage struggle, and the second confuses proletarian politics with ruptures that produce self-reproduction outside the wage relation. In both cases, the mediation of scientific consciousness is rejected in favor of a fetishization of the immediacy of struggle.

There is no restructuring of the capitalist mode of production without a workers' defeat. This defeat was that of workers' identity, communist parties, and unionism: of self-management, self-organization, and autonomy. The restructuring is essentially counterrevolution. Through the defeat of a particular cycle of struggle—the one which opened in the aftermath of the First World War—it is the whole programmatic cycle which reached its conclusion.[35]

The crystallization of the proletarian state project into *degenerated workers' states*,[36] and the qualitative weakening of the labor movement internationally was a defeat for the working class and the proletariat whose effects we are still experiencing. However, the essential feature of the capitalist mode of production, the contradiction within the production of relative surplus value, remains determinate and can only lose this status as a result of its collapse or conscious elimination.

What *Théorie Communiste* characterizes as programmatism and erroneously identifies with the period in which formal subsumption predominated is the mode of manifestation of worker and proletarian subjectivity structurally given by capitalist production itself.[37] Its specific forms are modified both in relation to the level of organic composition within a given period of capitalist development and the historical particularities of national and regional social structures. But the essential schema of mediations remains. The relative absence or weakness of workers' organizations today is indeed a mark of a qualitatively new stage of the class struggle, characterized by neoliberal restructuring. Restructuring in conjunction with the secular increase in organic composition destroyed the concentrations of worker power in production and eliminated the wage guarantees which had been imposed by the impact of the October Revolution.

The fluidity of capital and flexibility of the wage relation which defines the current period is both cause for and effect of the atomization and disorganization of the working class. The weakness of the working class, in turn, stands in a bi-directional relationship to the absence of the proletariat as state project. This scenario *does* unfold within an objective situation characterized by the linear transformation of the organic composition of capital. The latter, in turn, transforms the class composition. *Théorie Communiste* and their co-thinkers are correct to note the impact of this aspect. Unfortunately, the real complexity of an exit from this unfavorable relation of forces is evaded by an appeal to the anticipation of a qualitatively new content embedded within contemporary struggles—a content which allegedly sidesteps the transhistorical necessity of organizational mediation, scientific consciousness, and strategic leadership by enabling an automatic rupture.

COMMUNIZATION THEORY'S REJECTION OF QUANTIFICATION

At this point in their exposition, *Théorie Communiste* proceeds to a direct response to certain points raised by the communizers who are opposed to their historicizing position. Some of *Théorie Communiste*'s clarifications are notable:

> The workers couldn't have had the liberation of labour as their perspective because they didn't want to work more for the boss. The argument is simply dumbfounding. Dauvé and Nesic don't understand the "affirmation of labour" as the "liberation of labour," that is to say the abolition of its situation of subordination. The "liberation of labour" is precisely the reverse of wanting to work more (for less money) for the boss. It is precisely not to consider wage labour as a positive reality, but as that which is to be abolished.[38]

Théorie Communiste understands that the revolutionary workers' movements of the past sought the abolition of wage labor and that this was the content of working-class self-affirmation. However, they clarify that it is this "liberation from labor" which they find inadequate. *Théorie Communiste* seeks not the liberation of social labor from capital but the elimination of the regulation and quantification inherent to socialized production in general. This regulation and quantification is the precondition for the maximization of free time without which the abolition of wage labor would be a step backward.[39]

They continue with a digression on Marx's interpretation of the Paris Commune:

> If Marx doesn't speak of the social significance of the transformation of the Commune's organs of management, and if he pretends that the Commune is exclusively a workers' government ("the finally achieved form of the dictatorship of the proletariat"), it is because, for him, the revolution is not where we, today, look for it—that is to say, in the independence of proletarian action and in its capacity to abolish itself in abolishing the capitalist mode of production—but in the capacity of the proletariat to represent the whole of society and its future.[40]

Today "we" look for revolution in the "independence of proletarian action and in its capacity to abolish itself in abolishing the capitalist mode of production"; yesterday Marx looked for the same in the "capacity of the proletariat to represent the whole of society and its future." For *Théorie Communiste*, the proletariat can no longer constitute itself within the social totality of capital as the organized embodiment of the political will to consciously overcome it from within but manifests itself in a merely negative exit from capital into self-subsistence.[41] They argue that

> the emancipation of labour is here conceived as the measurement of value by labour time, the preservation of the notion of the product, and the framework of the enterprise and exchange. At those rare moments when an autonomous

affirmation of the proletariat as liberation of labour arrives at its realisation (necessarily under the control of organisations of the workers' movement), as in Russia, Italy, and Spain, it immediately inverts itself into the only thing it can become: a new form of the mobilisation of labour under the constraint of value and thus of "maximum output."[42]

In the Soviet Union, the emancipation of labor was identified with the overcoming of value. This remained the case until the Stalinist reaction of the Thirties.[43] For *Théorie Communiste*, however, the quantification and maximization of efficiency, which forms the necessary foundation of communism as the potential of capital, is confused with the subordination of living labor. This is closer to Guénon than Marx.[44] The "control and management" of socialized production and circulation is conflated with its capitalist form and identified not as the terrain where the communist program is progressively implemented upon the basis of this form but as a limit to be overcome.

> It is true, there was never any "scope for a workers' capitalism," but that simply means that there was scope for a capitalist counterrevolution articulated within a workers' revolution based upon the seizing of factories, liberating labor, and erecting the proletariat as ruling class: a counterrevolution that was able to turn the latter's content back against it.[45]

Unlike emerging capitalist relations of production in feudal society, communist relations of production cannot emerge and proliferate within a social formation dominated by capitalist relations of production. Capitalist relations of production are defined by the subsumption of the production process under the movement of exchange value which previously circulated "in the pores" of traditional society. On the one hand, the development of capitalist relations of production is a precondition for the bourgeois revolution. On the other hand, communist relations of production are a potential contained within the development of capital itself. This potential is embodied in the party as the organization of the conscious will for its actualization. The seizure of state power by the party creates (assuming the objective base of sufficient development of productive forces) the foundation for a possible transition to communism, which has as its immediate premise the appropriation of the socialized process of production and circulation in its capitalist form by the proletarian state. In this sense not only is there "scope" for "worker's capitalism"—it is the only possible trajectory toward the realization of the self-transcendent potentiality inherent to capital itself.

The rupture with the capitalist social totality proposed by *Théorie Communiste* is a program for collapse of the productive forces, but from this, the subordination to the "conscious will of the producers" does not follow by necessity. Rather we are presented with a proposal for catastrophic regression into pre-bourgeois forms of life whose utopian pretensions communicate a proud indifference to vulgar matters of efficiency and comfort.

COMMUNIZATION THEORY'S QUIETISM

The limitation of the revolutions of the twentieth century was their containment within peripheral "weak links" of the imperialist chain, in which they were constrained to complete the socialization of production within the constraints of exchange value. Completing the transition to communism is no more possible within the borders of a single state (or bloc within the world state system) than within the confines of an individual economic struggle.

This containment produced by the *political* defeat of the revolution on a world scale in turn resulted in the *political* degeneration of the proletarian state project, which became both a cause for and an effect of the stagnation of the world revolutionary process. It is precisely this defeat and this degeneration which *Théorie Communiste* avoids subjecting to analysis, in favor of a schematic fatalism that is defined by predetermination between the binary poles of mere reproduction of capitalist production relations and their absolute, and immediate, negation.

For *Théorie Communiste*, the forms of political subjectivity of the working class are directly given by the corresponding stages in the linear development of capital. The contingency of the political within the constraints given by inscription within this trajectory disappears. From this standpoint, the question of "What is to be done?" is of no significance. The revolutionary minority is restricted to passive observation and contemplation of struggles whose essentially "theoreticist" content is not transformed by its incidental occurrence within the struggles themselves:

> In this sense, theoretical production, in all its diversities and divergences, is as much a part of the class struggle as any other activity which constitutes the class struggle. At that point, the question "What is to be Done?" is completely emptied of meaning; we no longer search to intervene in struggles as theoreticians or as militants with a constituted theory. That signifies that when we are personally implicated in a conflict, we operate at the same level as everyone else; and although we don't forget what we do elsewhere, the way in which we do not forget this is in recognising that the struggle in which we find ourselves is itself reworking, reformulating, and producing theory.[46]

That is say, even when the militants act within immediate struggles, they consciously dissociate theory and practice. They reduce their own practice to the preexisting level of the struggle and reject any function of synthesis between theory and practice. Here we see the unity between the rejection of political mediation and a crudely deterministic objectivism, which defines both *Théorie Communiste*'s project and that of the nominally Marxist branch of the communization tendency in general.

For *Théorie Communiste*, the classical workers movement and all the gains it won over a century of struggle were doomed to remain a mere affirmation of labor within capital. Now that this movement has come and gone, those of us cursed by the misfortune of critical consciousness should no longer ask themselves "What is to be Done?"—but instead "operate at the same level as everyone else."

If the classical workers' movement, whose death the communizer is so eager to pronounce, equated theory to dynamite for the communization militant, it is something akin to stamp collecting or bird watching. A private hobby only good for boring one's coworkers whose spontaneous adhesion to bourgeois ideology is best observed with a serene detachment. If the Last Man so feared by Nietzsche and Francis Fukuyama were compelled to try his hand at Marxist theory, he might have trouble matching such self-effacement. Exposed to the light of practice, the grand dream of a "total negation of capital" is revealed as the petty reality of an equally total negation of any substantive antagonism to the same. Though a firm rejection of this anti-political "passivity within activity" is no guarantee of success, tolerating it is a certain recipe for failure.

NOTES

1. Plekhanov 1977 [1883], 76.
2. Lenin 1974 (1919), 390. Emphasis mine.
3. For an early collection of texts which functions as a "bridge" toward the communization perspective see Camatte (1976) 1988.
4. Marx 1973 (1857–1858), 162. Marx 1965 (1874–1875), 633. Capitalism creates the possibility of communism as a universal association of free individuals for the first time in history. To deny this is schoolboy stupidity. Nothing is further from this perspective than hatred for capitalist modernity and nostalgia for communal stagnation.
5. Marx 1973 (1857–1858), 158–59.
6. Engels (1882) in Marx and Engels 1952, 117.
7. Marx 1979 (1853), 132.
8. Marx 1897 (1853–1856).
9. Individual citations could be multiplied but for our purposes it is sufficient to note that this polemic occupies a predominant place in the early work of both Lenin and Plekhanov.

10. In the following text the term "working class" will be used to characterize both the objective *position* of productive wage labor and its subjective *movement* to negotiate the terms of sale of labor power. The term "proletariat" will designate the contingent coalescence within the latter movement of a consciousness of the need to abolish the wage relation itself at the level of the social whole through the implementation of a revolutionary program. Regardless of the specific terminology employed to designate it a careful attention to this distinction is a necessary precondition for a literate reading of the classics of Marxist political thought.

11. This can be seen as the shared aspiration of a variety of approaches ranging from Lazerus's post-Maoist negation of the class line (Lazerus [1996] 2015) to the attack on "Marxism from the standpoint of labor" advocated by Postone and others (Postone 1993).

12. Endnotes 2008, 154.

13. A critique of Dauvé's more simplistic formulations is beyond the scope of this chapter.

14. Ibid., 155.

15. Endnotes 2008, 155. Emphasis added.

16. Ibid., 155.

17. Ibid., 156.

18. "Formal subsumption may be a prerequisite for capitalist relations of production to arise (and the fertile ground for the mystification of capital); however, it is *not* itself specifically capitalist. Something else aside the mere subjugation of the labour process under the directives of capital must happen in order for the *real*, for the *specifically* capitalist mode of production to develop" (Lange 2021, 509) (emphases in original).

19. Marx 1994 (1861–1864), 425–26.

20. For a classic examination of the concrete forms of formal subsumption in this context see Lenin 1967 (1899). For Kautsky's early articulation of "liberation from labour" as a programmatic objective see Waldenburg 1980, 77.

21. Engels (1847), 82 in Marx and Engels 1976. Emphasis ours.

22. Kautsky 1910 (1907) 8. Emphasis ours.

23. https://www.marxists.org/history/ussr/government/1919/03/22.htm. Emphasis ours.

24. Marx 1994 (1861–1864), 428–29 (emphases in original).

25. Ibid., 156.

26. See among countless examples Plekhanov 1977 (1884), 196, 327; Lenin 1977 (1894), 156; Bukharin and Preobrazhensky 1922 (1920), 72.

27. Endnotes 2008, 156.

28. Ibid., 156 (emphases in original).

29. Ibid., 157.

30. Ibid., 158.

31. Ibid., 159 (emphases in original).

32. Ibid., 160.

33. Ibid.

34. "To make things even clearer, let us first of all take the most concrete example of state capitalism. Everybody knows what this example is. It is Germany. Here

we have 'the last word' in modern large-scale capitalist engineering and planned organisation, *subordinated to Junker-bourgeois imperialism*. Cross out the words in italics, and in place of the militarist, Junker, bourgeois, imperialist state put also a state, but of a different social type, of a different class content—a Soviet state, that is, a proletarian state, and you will have the sum total of the conditions necessary for socialism.

Socialism is inconceivable without large-scale capitalist engineering based on the latest discoveries of modern science. It is inconceivable without planned state organisation which keeps tens of millions of people to the strictest observance of a unified standard in production and distribution. We Marxists have always spoken of this, and it is not worthwhile wasting two seconds talking to people who do not understand even this (anarchists and a good half of the Left Socialist-Revolutionaries)." (Lenin 1973 [1921], 334)

35. Endnotes 2008, 161.

36. By *proletarian state project* I refer to the workers' state as a dynamic process of self-dissolution tending toward the communist transformation of the production relations. By *degenerated workers' state* I refer to the state order resulting from the stagnation of this process and appearing as the characteristic political form of a high point of worker rigidity within the wage relation.

37. The development of capital is at the same time the development of the *working class* which, insofar as it becomes aware of itself as an interest group within bourgeois society, is defined by wage dependency and constitutes organizations in order to defend and improve its reproduction conditions ("trade unions"). The fusion of this movement with *proletarian ideology* produced in relative exteriority to it leads to the *party* as the organizational articulation between the immediate struggles over the reproduction conditions of labor power and the program of communist transition. The advance toward the implementation of this transition entails the construction of the dictatorship of the proletariat as the state form which organizes the self-overcoming of value. The validity of this strategic framework is unaffected by incidental transformations in class composition (like these discussed at length by communization theorists), however much tactical impact such transformations might have on the forms of the "trade union" struggle.

38. Endnotes 2008, 166.

39. "Even after the capitalist mode of production is abolished, though social production remains, the determination of value still prevails in the sense that the regulation of labour-time and the distribution of social labour among various production groups becomes more essential than ever, as well as the keeping of accounts on this" (Marx 1981 [1894], 991).

40. Endnotes 2008, 169.

41. In the schema of *Théorie Communiste*, labor, far from affirming itself in a worker's dictatorship over the social whole, simply exits society. The gain in conceptual simplicity is more than compensated for by the loss in practical applicability.

42. Ibid,. 172.

43. See Harrison Mark 1983, 8–12 for a brief discussion of Stalin's 1934 intervention on this question and its impact on Soviet economic doctrine. The premise that

the Bolshevik objective was state-managed commodity production is a myth of the ultraleft.

44. "According to the profane conception on the other hand, these qualities are no longer taken into account, and individuals are regarded as no more than interchangeable and purely numerical 'units.' The latter conception can only logically lead to the exercise of a wholly 'mechanical' activity, in which there remains nothing truly human, and that is exactly what we can see happening today" (Guénon [1945] 2001, 58).

45. Endnotes 2008, 172.

46. https://libcom.org/library/interview-roland-simon. Accessed July 1, 2021.

Part II

THE CULTURE OF THE CONFORMIST REBELLION— CULTURE WARS, IDENTITY POLITICS, AND ART

Chapter 6

Popular Sovereignty, Left Liberalism, and the Brexit Culture Wars[1]

George Hoare

In this chapter I contend that the Brexit process and its appearance as a prolonged culture war illustrates a number of important aspects of the British state and British politics, not least the political function of the Left in providing a "conformist rebellion" that appears to critique the status quo while in fact providing one of the most significant ideological defenses of it. First, I outline the context in which the Brexit vote and subsequent crisis occurred, specifically one of a political "void" of disconnected elites and voters. The emergence of this void is closely connected with the process of state transformation through which Britain moved from being a "nation-state" to a "member-state" of the European Union (EU). I then provide a brief account of the Brexit process, focusing on the ways in which appeals to popular sovereignty were criticized and delegitimated. Finally, I draw out some of the key legacies of Brexit in relation to popular sovereignty, the Left, and the possibilities for working-class power.

Throughout, I draw on the thought and political experience of the Full Brexit group of scholars and activists. Founded in 2018, the Full Brexit attempted to put forward a "political theory of Brexit" and an analysis of the Brexit process grounded in a defence of the 2016 referendum Leave result as a historic opportunity for democratic and economic renewal. It produced analyses of the current political moment, generated proposals for a post-Brexit Britain, and collected other Eurosceptic "Views from Europe" (including from Sweden, Germany, and France). The group also organized or co-hosted a number of public events, including the *Transforming Britain After Brexit* series of national events and a high-profile and well-attended launch event of Costas Lapavitsas's *The Left Case Against the EU* in December 2018.[2] For these activities, the group attracted considerable criticism, especially from the Left. At the London event of the *Transforming Britain After*

Brexit tour in March 2019, trade union activist Eddie Dempsey (one of the invited speakers) argued that

> whatever you think of people that turn up for those Tommy Robinson demos or any other march like that—the one thing that unites those people, whatever other bigotry is going on, is their hatred of the liberal left and they are right to hate them.

As a consequence, Eddie was subject to a range of attacks, including from Labour MP Clive Lewis, *Another Europe Is Possible* campaigner Michael Chessum, and journalist Paul Mason. The Full Brexit invited Lewis, Chessum, and Mason to debate the nature of the Left, the EU, and the Far Right but received no response.[3] Providing analysis throughout the Brexit process, the Full Brexit continued to produce analysis of the post-Brexit moment, with a particular focus on the COVID-19 pandemic.

CONTEXT: MEMBER-STATE THEORY

One of the starting points of the Full Brexit analysis was member-state theory. Developed by James Heartfield, Christopher Bickerton, and Philip Cunliffe, this theory explicated the ways in which European nation-states have transformed into EU member-states.[4] The nation-state, as one of the classic constructs of political modernity, represents a *vertically* integrated political unit in which the relationship between citizens and their representatives traditionally gives the state its political direction and legitimacy. Member-states, on the other hand, are *horizontally* integrated political units, in which legitimacy and policy direction are increasingly drawn from elites' relations with their European counterparts.[5] The movement from one to the other is often euphemistically called "European integration," which is in fact a political process that is intimately connected with domestic politics and polities.[6]

However, it is important to be clear that the transition from nation-statehood to member-statehood, and the accompanying democratic deficit of the latter, was not created by the EU. The EU is more accurately seen as an outgrowth of the withering of political representation within the nation-state, which preceded EU membership across the continent.[7] Falling voter turnout, party membership rates (with few exceptions), rates of party identification, and stability of partisan preferences in the (particularly Western) Europe of the later twentieth century led to a widespread distrust of politics and politicians pervading those nation-states.[8] Often, the blame for a lack of political engagement and trust was put on citizens themselves, attributed variously to increased consumerism, globalization, or the pernicious effects of media, with a general moral panic about apathy emerging as particularly marked in the mid-2000s.[9]

This period was marked not just by the disengagement of citizens but also by a dynamic that saw the simultaneous withdrawal of elites into an official and increasingly transnational world of public offices, with parties exhibiting a declining ability to play any mediating role between the people and their representatives. The political scientist Peter Mair's influential account captures this process as one in which parties became increasingly "catch-all" ones that appealed to the "center-ground" as elites increasingly abandoned their task of aggregating, organizing, and representing distinctive and opposed social forces. Voters, as this dynamic developed, increasingly withdrew into private life as parties were unable to offer distinctive alternatives or substantive policy differences. Consequently, elites came to search for legitimacy in sources other than popular sovereignty, understood as the mass participation of the citizenry in politics.[10] It is this need to adapt to declining popular sovereignty that explains the characteristic forms that neoliberal governance takes, from shifting the responsibility for decision-making to unelected bodies such as courts, regulators, or quangos to drawing policy inspiration from a range of transnational policy networks.[11] In the standard model of neoliberal governance, these transnational policy networks function through the creation of a set of overlapping transnational regulations (rather than supranational bodies), which member-states impose on domestic populations, transforming themselves in the process.[12] In this context, it is possible to see the unity of the European political class, and its shared modes of operation, as coming materially from their shared need to find legitimacy beyond domestic policies, and not just their ideological attachment to the European project.[13]

Although the disconnect between the citizenry and vehicles of political representation was not and is not a uniquely British phenomenon, the Full Brexit account of member-state theory had a number of important consequences specifically for interpreting the Brexit crisis that was to follow. It allowed the Full Brexit to develop a position that explained how almost all accounts of the UK's membership of the EU mistook the nature of that political institution.[14] In broad terms, the Right tended to portray the EU as a superstate that trampled on domestic freedoms, while the Left constructed an equally fantastical account of the EU as a "social Europe" that would act as a supranational protector of the working class against a domestic Conservative threat. As Hilary Benn, son of famous Eurosceptic Labour MP Tony Benn and himself also a Labour MP, put it in an article on the eve of the referendum itself, "If we leave, we would be handing control over to a Tory government beholden to its Eurosceptic. And who would pay the price? It would be workers, businesses, consumers, the vulnerable and, ultimately, the nation."[15] Others still, mainly on the Left, saw the EU as a historic peace project that looked to realize the hopes of postwar Europe for a lasting peace. In each case, the EU was fetishized, either by ignoring the small size of the EU administration and the role of national governments in EU politics, by overlooking the ways in which the EU constrains national governments' political programs, or by being blind to the real developments of the EU's relations with the rest of Europe and the world (from controversies over "Fortress Europe" and the EU's hard Mediterranean border to debates over an "EU army"). In particular, many on the Left were put in a position that involved considerable cognitive dissonance as the Brexit process developed: having previously criticized the Troika's handling of the Greek sovereign debt crisis or the refugee crisis, when the role of the EU in British politics was considered, there was almost unanimous support on the Left for remaining a member-state. The clearest illustration of this contradiction, which I explore below, came to be found in the logic of the "Lexit" position, which appeared to advocate for exiting the EU but in fact had the practical consequence of attempting to defend the status quo. In each case, the impact of "Europe" on British politics was seen as something "over there" in the workings and politics of the EU, rather than also, and perhaps more importantly, being "over here" in the sense of having an intimate relationship to domestic crisis.[16] In this sense, the Full Brexit account as grounded in member-state theory represented a considerable theoretical forward step compared with the standard (but completely correct) critiques of the EU as a neoliberal institution with a structural democratic deficit that functions to guarantee the interests of capital throughout the continent (and German industrial export capital in particular) while defending a brutally hard border regime in the name of (European) cosmopolitanism.[17] By emphasizing the process of state transformation involved in member-statehood, this analysis was able to develop a wider picture of the role of the EU in British politics that took into account the reciprocal relationship between elite and citizen withdrawal as mediated through EU membership. Nevertheless, it is still worth being clear that this account is not incompatible with one that starts from an honest empirical investigation of the practices of the EU, and, in particular, the rulings of the ECJ in favor of capital over labor that constitutionalize a neoliberal economic framework, which would be likely to reveal many reasons why those not utterly aligned with the interests of capital might want to leave its strictures.[18] In the British context, though, it is sufficient to say that a lack of understanding of the reality of processes of European integration would set the scene for a bitter and prolonged "culture war" over Brexit; the response of the liberal establishment in particular to the unexpected reemergence of political contestation would largely come to define British politics in the coming years.[19] The Full Brexit counter-position, developed through a range of analyses of the political situation that accompanied the

Brexit process, was not homogeneous. Nevertheless, there was in general an attempt to defend the democratic potential of the Brexit vote and the democratic capabilities of voters against a vast range of strategies (often from the Left) that looked to question the cognitive and moral worth of Leave voters, especially working-class ones, while at the same time providing a positive class-based analysis of British politics.

THE BREXIT CRISIS: A FULL BREXIT ACCOUNT

The Full Brexit account summarized above also gives an account of how the referendum itself is a response to the "void" of British politics. During the 2010s politicians came to be regarded as "out of touch" and unresponsive, with voters turning increasingly to populist parties, in particular the British Nationalist Party or the United Kingdom Independence Party (UKIP). The threat of UKIP to parts of the Conservative Party's electoral base prompted David Cameron in February 2016 to call a referendum on EU membership, aiming to extinguish UKIP's key appeal. Therefore, Brexit was never a "ruling class" or a "Tory project," but is instead better understood as a symptom of political decay and the Conservative Party's inability to respond to the threat of UKIP. In the referendum of June 23, 2016, a turnout of 72.2% saw 51.9% vote to Leave and 48.1% to Remain.

The immediate aftermath of the result, which was unimaginable for large parts of the political class,[20] saw an outpouring of bile against Leave voters, particularly from the Left. As journalist Laurie Penny saw it, it had been a "referendum on the modern world" in which those with a "frightened, parochial lizard-brain" had triumphed.[21] Academics saw the vote as one explained by cultural factors, specifically racism, imperial nostalgia, and "cultural backlash" against modern and progressive values.[22] In this context, Leave and Remain identities solidified, with only 6% of people not identifying with either Leave or Remain (compared to 21.5% with no party identity).[23] At the same time, a more or less coherent "Remainism" ideology emerged as an instantiation of the key patterns of Remain positions in the Brexit process.[24] First, the nation was distinguished from "Europe," with the latter equated with the EU and the former seen as a retreat to nationalism and xenophobia. There was a clear moral core to the argument, grounded in what Wolfgang Streeck calls the "sacralization" of Europe and the coding of Brexit as "anti-European."[25] Cosmopolitan supranationalism was counterposed to illiberal national sovereignty. Second, opposition to Brexit, and specifically a "damaging Tory Brexit," was legitimated as in the interests of the worst off in society. The working class (although class language was rarely used here) was seen as the *object* of politics, not the *subject* of politics. In other words, if the Left has always been an alliance of some sort between progressive liberals and socialists, then it has tended to see the working class as the object of politics (in terms of being the recipients of various welfare and redistributive projects) as well as the subject of politics (with the ultimate goal of working-class self-government). The latter view, to generalize, is held by the socialist wing of the coalition while the former view is associated with liberals and reformers of various sorts. Although these views have historically been combined in struggles for improved conditions of work and for democracy, by the beginning of the twenty-first century they had come apart entirely, with very few defenders of the idea of the working class as the history-making *subject* of politics on the Left in the course of the Brexit process. Instead, cultural ideas of community, belonging, and the nation (rather than a political definition of the working class as the collective subject of politics) came to fill that space as the ways in which the working class was understood by the British Left. These were largely the dominant terms of the Brexit "culture war" that developed after the 2016 referendum result.[26]

As the Brexit crisis dragged on, it was clear that the referendum result itself did nothing to alter the functioning of the British state as a member-state. Accordingly, some thinkers around the Full Brexit contended, it would always have lacked both the technical capacity and the political authority needed to implement and to take responsibility for the democratic vote of the Brexit referendum.[27] Decision-making had long been hived off to technocratic and depoliticized forms of national and transnational regulation whose only metric was promoting smooth and internationally competitive markets.[28] Consequently, Theresa May's weak Conservative governments, dominated by Remainers and having little enthusiasm for representing the popular will, were unable to make any progress.[29] As the Full Brexit pointed out, Brexit remained a *democratic moment* without a *democratic movement*: while the referendum expressed a moment of mass democratic participation, the crisis of representative democracy was so deep that there was no representative mechanism that could turn the crude political aggregate of 17.4 million Leave voters into a movement capable of subordinating political representatives to its will.

Eventually, The Brexit Party emerged as a populist challenger with no party democracy and only a thin program—a "creature of the void" that forced the Conservatives to replace Theresa May with a more pro-Brexit leadership.[30] In 2019, working-class voters finally broke the political deadlock by lending their support to Boris Johnson's Conservatives, on the promise to "Get Brexit Done"; however, this depoliticizing slogan revealed Johnson's desire to make Brexit go away and "get it done," and to attempt as far as possible to discharge any democratic energies stirred up by the

Brexit process.[31] Johnson's handling of Brexit displayed all the clear marks of member-statehood, with the nature of the UK's future relationship with the EU negotiated in secret and with parliament forced to ram through the Trade and Cooperation Agreement (TCA) without serious debate.[32] In other words, the Brexit vote as a democratic moment without a democratic movement did not entail democratic control of *how* Britain should leave the EU, and the process retained all the classic member-state governance traits of closed-door discussions (rather than public briefings or open discussions in parliament) and last-minute, unaccountable decision-making.

THE LEGACY AND MEANING OF BREXIT

Popular Sovereignty

The first legacy of Brexit was that it put the question of popular sovereignty as central to British politics. Brexit was a vote that encapsulated a felt loss of popular sovereignty, filtered through the discourse around immigration as a felt loss of control over the composition of the political community. The "Take Back Control" slogan was a masterpiece of political rhetoric, appealing directly to this sense of powerlessness while constructing an imagined previous period in which the people (presumably) had control. But the underlying radicalism of slogan is worth noting: control is something that needs to be taken (not given), and it does not set any limits to what control is held over. The injunction for ourselves to "take control" is at the center of any emancipatory politics, as it leads to collective mastery of the decisions that affect our lives, be they around our political institutions or our economic structures. This is why the Conservatives both struggled to master the Brexit process and then attempted to drain the political energies out of Brexit with the profoundly depoliticizing slogan of "Get Brexit Done." Faust-like, they had called up the dark powers of the feared British public and then fought mightily to banish them again when they threatened to drive things too far forward too quickly. Although the Eurosceptic wing of the Conservative Party was prepared to be a bit more radical (at least on the surface), the Remainer wing was not, and fought with the (dominant) Remainer sections of the Labour Party to depoliticize the process as much as possible.

On the theoretical level, the Brexit process had important implications for our understanding of "sovereignty." As Peter Mair notes in his *Ruling the Void* (2013), a familiar theme in the political science of the 1960s was that the people could end up being "semi-sovereign" to the extent that they could not exert control over political decision-making. In his empirical analysis of the actual levels of political engagement across Western Europe in the postwar period, Mair also explores the theoretical consequences of this material change by highlighting how the conception of democracy that emerged in this period tended to downplay the need for a popular component. In other words, a more limited and narrow understanding of democracy came to dominate, highlighting the importance of procedure and checks and balances on power (or of human rights) over any need for citizen engagement to generate democratic legitimacy. In the broadest terms, we can see here the replacement of an understanding of democracy linked with the socialist tradition with one linked with the liberal tradition, the latter of which has always sought to portray democracy as a system of protections for the individual against the concentration of (class) power or the "tyranny of the majority."

The account developed by the Full Brexit with respect to popular sovereignty can be distinguished from a more straightforward Tory Euroscepticism, as it sees the EU not as a foreign imposition on British democracy but instead as a domestic evasion of accountability, specifically through the ways in which it enabled members of parliament to acquiesce to their exclusion from the processes of lawmaking by the executive.[33] Accordingly, Brexit is a democratic step forward on this view to the extent that room to evade accountability for domestic representatives (by invoking the external constraints of the EU) is decreased. The issue of popular sovereignty was also present in the debate over a second referendum; as Richard Tuck argued, a second referendum would not just risk undermining the first result but also undermine parliament's political authority in a very fundamental way, since it would question the legitimacy of the electoral mandate that remains the ultimate source of power for parliament.[34]

The lens of popular sovereignty is also a useful one for interpreting the status of the relationship of the people to our representatives. Very few parliamentarians, or members of the political class more generally, were receptive to arguments grounded in popular sovereignty or democratic theory; legitimacy for decisions and political courses of action was not commonly felt by many to reside in any popular mandate. Instead, the 2016 referendum result (and those who voted for it) were the subject of constant attacks that attempted to delegitimize that vote. It is possible to move beyond the populist opposition of the people and parliament ("they don't represent us") to make the more fundamental point that this action by parliamentarians revealed a deep absence of political authority and stood as a defense of the trappings of member-statehood. Even before COVID-19 lockdowns, it was clear that Britain would continue to act as a member-state for a considerable time to come.[35] Although the 2019 election did see the defeat of certain anti-Brexit forces, the TCA maintained a core EU mechanism of unaccountable and secret intergovernmental rulemaking.[36]

Brexit and the Left: Culture Wars and Lexit logic

The second legacy of Brexit lies in the way it illuminated the positions and interests of the actors in British politics with extraordinary clarity. In particular, it showed the deep skepticism of the British Left toward any notions of democracy and popular sovereignty. Instead, the weight of the democratic vote for Brexit was undermined by a variety of strategies. One of these was straightforwardly to question the cognitive abilities of Leave voters, while another was to smear them with suggestions of racism, xenophobia, or even fascism. The most strident opposition to Brexit came from the Left, usually framed in internationalist terms or based on defending the material interests of the working class. At the same time, Brexit was constructed as project of the Conservatives or the ruling class more widely. In each case, the role of the Left around Brexit was to attempt to articulate a competing political logic to that of majoritarianism, whether framed in terms of defending minorities, enlightened reason, or a fundamentally conservative betting on the status quo against the possibility of change. In this sense, the British case is illustrative internationally, as in it the political role the Left plays in defending the status quo can be seen with exceptional clarity. The distinction between a "Left" position on Brexit and the Full Brexit one is succinctly illustrated by considering the term "Lexit." "Lexit" as a position was initially defended by the prominent Left-wing journalists Owen Jones and Paul Mason as the possibility of a Left-wing case for Brexit, but soon became the dominant term designating "Left" defenders of Brexit.[37] There are few more striking examples of the nature and ideological function of the "conformist rebellion" of the Left than Lexit. Lexit logic follows what we might suggest is the characteristic three-step ideological process of the contemporary Left: recognize flaws in the existing order, invoke a threat that renders change undesirable or impossible, and salve the consciences of those initially opposed while channeling them into support for the status quo.

First, a Lexit position started by detailing the widely accepted and deep flaws of the EU: its democratic deficit, its economic torture of Greece, the hard borders of "Fortress Europe," the tragic demise of numberless migrants in the Mediterranean, and so on. It was important that this was done with gravity and seriousness, and that the flaws were not skirted over, as this served to establish the defenders of Lexit as informed and serious critics of the EU. To quote an article from Paul Mason in the *The Guardian* written before the referendum,

> The EU is not—and cannot become—a democracy. Instead, it provides the most hospitable ecosystem in the developed world for rentier monopoly corporations, tax-dodging elites, and organised crime. It has an executive so powerful it could crush the left-wing government of Greece; a legislature so weak that it cannot

effectively determine laws or control its own civil service. A judiciary that, in the Laval and Viking judgements, subordinated workers' right to strike to an employer's right [to] do business freely.[38]

Continuing his critique, Mason writes,

> Its central bank is committed, by treaty, to favour deflation and stagnation over growth. State aid to stricken industries is prohibited. The austerity we deride in Britain as a political choice is, in fact, written into the EU treaty as a non-negotiable obligation. So are the economic principles of the Thatcher era.

The first step of the Lexit position, then, is a clear laying out of the problems with the EU and the corresponding strength of the Left case for exit.

Second, once the flaws of the EU have been established Lexit made support for Brexit *conditional* and specifically dependent on the Left leading the exit process. Brexit was, under Lexit logic, good *if and only if* it could be led by the Left; in this sense, Brexit could have been redeemed by the increased possibilities it could have given to a Corbyn government (in terms of the greater opportunity for state intervention in the economy outside of EU "state aid" rules). The Full Brexit position, however, was consistently that Brexit is inherently a progressive democratic development, since it is a necessary step away from member-statehood and toward popular sovereignty. The conditionality of the Lexit position depended on the politics of fear, and specifically on the threat of a "Tory Brexit," portrayed as an unregulated "Singapore-on-Thames" that would destroy workers' rights. As Mason writes in the article quoted above, having summarized the "principled" left-wing case for Brexit,

> Now here's the practical reason to ignore it. In two words: Boris Johnson. [. . .] If Britain votes Brexit, then Johnson and [prominent Leave campaigner and Conservative MP Michael] Gove stand ready to seize control of the Tory party and turn Britain into a neoliberal fantasy island.

In extremis, this threat is always what Elena Louisa Lange and Joshua Pickett-Depaolis have called the "fascism blackmail": those who are considering opposing the status quo need to be disciplined by the invocation of a threat of fascism.[39]

Third, Lexit logic led its proponents to advocate a political position of reluctant, heavyhearted, and slightly resentful defense of the EU. As Paul Mason concludes in the article quoted above,

> The EU, politically, begins to look more and more like a gerrymandered state, where the politically immature electorates of eastern Europe can be used—as

Louis Napoleon used the French peasantry—as a permanent obstacle to liberalism and social justice. If so—even though the political conditions for a left Brexit are absent today—I will want out soon.

Leaving aside any questions of Mason's reading of the role of Eastern Europe in the development of the EU, the conclusion here is clear: Brexit may be a good idea in principle, but the practical conditions to make a left-wing Brexit are not present. As the Brexit process developed, the Lexit defense of the EU became more explicit; EU came to be seen, quite incredibly, as an ardent defender of workers' rights rather than as a political-legal institution that systemically defends the interests of capital and undermines the rights that workers win for themselves in domestic struggle. Frances O'Grady, the general secretary of the Trades Union Congress or TUC, a federation of trade unions in England and Wales representing around 5.5 million members, argued after the Brexit vote that continued membership of the single market would be the best way to protect British workers after Brexit.[40] In Lexit logic, the lack of enthusiasm in defending the EU is important, as it allowed the People's Vote campaign (that advocated for a second referendum) initially to be dismissed as partisans before being embraced as comrades in the struggle for a "confirmatory referendum." Clearly, there is an operation of what Sloterdijk might call cynical reason here: since the flaws have already been pointed out, weighed up carefully, and then reluctantly accepted as the necessary "cost of doing business," any critique can be rejected as always-already having been understood, processed, and rejected as ultimately insufficient.[41] As the Left was never going to be in a leading position, it left activists free to oppose a "Tory Brexit," support a Labour Party openly advocating for a second referendum as the leading party of Remain, and disparage the Full Brexit as useful idiots for the Conservative Party for supporting a democratic vote.[42] At the same time, the logic of Lexit allowed those who understood the irreformable, structural flaws of the EU to acquiesce in support of it, salving their consciences or even presenting themselves as brave opponents of a damaging Tory Brexit.

Therefore, it is crucially important to distinguish a Lexit position that ultimately defended the status quo from a Full Brexit one that opposed it. While they might appear so close that any attempt to distinguish them would just be a case of "the narcissism of small differences," they in fact represent the dividing line between the Marxists (and their allies) on one side and the bourgeois socialists on the other. "Lexit" appears as a case in support of Brexit, but in reality it is a construct designed precisely to show its impossibility. "Lexit" is thus the conformist rebellion of the Left in a nutshell: its seeming criticisms of the existing order are one of the more effective ideological tools in defending that very order.

Political Realignment?

The third legacy of Brexit is that it brought about, in late 2019, the achievement of a decades-long goal of British Marxists, namely the collapse of the Labour Party and the partial revival of the political independence of the working class. Immediately experienced as a political "realignment"—with working-class support transitioning from Labour to the Conservatives well before the decisive election of 2019—the vote was in reality a decisive blow against the Labour Party over Brexit.[43] The next decade of British politics will be heavily influenced by the Conservatives' struggle to incorporate the working-class sections of their support base into a cohesive national project.[44] In this period, the logic of the British Left will be one of "moral minoritarianism," which looks to consultative (but nonbinding) measures such as citizens' assemblies or deliberative democracy to legitimate its favored policies, while demobilizing and delegitimizing working-class participation in politics.[45] If it is a classic trait of the petty bourgeoisie that they cannot have their own political project, but must speak on behalf of another, then this could well be taken as an accurate description of the British Left: moralizing and hypersensitive, they assert the working class as an object of politics, but never its subject. In this context, we can imagine the increased prominence of environmentalist ideas on the Left, as well as possibly a transfer of support of certain sections of the petty bourgeoisie from the Labour Party to the Greens. More importantly, the link between the working class and the Labour Party has been symbolically broken.

CONCLUSIONS: FROM BREXIT CULTURE WAR TO LOCKDOWNS AND THE "COVOID"

On January 31, 2020, Britain formally withdrew from the EU, finally enacting a decision taken in June 2016. But less than two months later, the country would enter its first lockdown, with a de facto state of emergency being announced on March 23: the British public was ordered to "stay at home" (apart from shopping for essential items, "absolutely necessary" travel to work, or carrying out one form of outdoor exercise each day) while all nonessential shops, libraries, places of worship, playgrounds, and outdoor gyms were closed. Although the "Mother of all Parliaments" had continued to meet throughout the Second World War and the threat of Nazi bombs, MPs declared their work to be inessential during the COVID-19 pandemic and decided to hide at home. The population was demobilized and associational life stopped, with the exception of essential workers who were expected to continue working. The 600,000-strong volunteer army for the NHS was little utilized.

The debate over COVID-19 picked up right where the Brexit culture war was threatening to leave off: defeated over the EU and humiliated by their inability to control society through their political "expertise," the petty bourgeois layers of British society very quickly rallied to strong support of the most punitive, risk-averse, and technocratic responses to COVID-19. Any contradiction between ostensibly "radical" antiestablishment politics and the support for a Conservative government's public policy was quickly overcome; the same people who denounced Boris Johnson's suspension of parliament in autumn 2019 now volunteered for house arrest, claiming to see a new form of freedom in the newly demobilized society.[46]

The Full Brexit analysis of COVID-19 lockdowns pointed to several key structural aspects of the situation that emerged from the member-state theory of the Brexit crisis. First, it was clear from the outset that no one was in control of the COVID-19 process, with all actors lacking the political authority to mobilize either resources or the citizenry toward a positive political response.[47] Medical expertise gradually filled this vacuum, but still lacked any sort of political project beyond the most basic preservation of human life. In this sense, the response to COVID-19 was, like the Brexit culture war, a symptom of the hollowed-out nature of all political forms. Moreover, COVID-19 accelerated this process to such an extent that we can now talk of the "Covoid": the hollow space ostensibly at the center of British politics. Second, Lee Jones, an International Relations specialist from Queen Mary, University of London, and a cofounder of the Full Brexit, developed along with colleagues an analysis of the state's response to COVID-19 that went beyond the standard explanations of Tory incompetence, austerity, or an unexpected disease that could never have been planned for, instead identifying how COVID-19 reveals the deep failure of the neoliberal regulatory state.[48]

Through both the Brexit culture wars and the period of the "Covoid," one of the key political questions raised by the Brexit culture wars concerns how we understand "the Left." Did the Left "fail" over Brexit, or did the extended process of political crisis in fact reveal with striking clarity the class composition, political strategy, and ultimate project of the British Left? This is for the reader to judge. For the Left to have "failed" over Brexit, in the sense of betraying its core principles, would have required forgetting decades of critique and ignoring basic democratic theory. Instead, we can understand the Brexit culture wars as probably the clearest illustration in the contemporary era of the class forces contending for power in the orbit of the EU today. Brexit, as a lightning strike, illuminated the position of the pieces on the board. If "the Left" in Britain has historically been understood as a coalition between left liberalism and socialism, then it is not clear that any of the latter remains in the ideological basis or political practice of the Left.

For those committed to working-class power (who for the sake of argument we can call "Marxists," though this term has lost almost all of its historical meaning), it is clear that the Left is an enemy. If Brexit revealed this much politically, it was just as illustrative theoretically. Above all others, the repudiation of the nation is the key strategy of the contemporary ruling class (and its ideological functionaries on the Left); characteristically, the rejection of the nation by the ruling class and its ideological supporters is on the grounds of conscience and the supposed racism, xenophobia, and incipient fascism of the domestic working class.[49] This matches perfectly with the ruling class' attempt to overcome the nation as a political unit that can constrain the free movement of capital; as Adam Smith recognized, the "proprietor of stock is necessarily a citizen of the world, and is not necessarily attached to any particular country," apt to abandon any specific nation if exposed to "vexatious inquisition."[50] We still face an old problem, namely that of how the working class can "constitute itself the nation" in Marx and Engels's words, being "itself national, though not in the bourgeois sense of the word."[51]

NOTES

1. Thank you to Philip Cunliffe, Lee Jones, Peter Ramsay, and Sally Turner for their comments. I would also like to thank the rest of the Full Brexit steering group for immensely stimulating conversations over a number of years, although it should be made clear that the argument of this chapter is attributable to the author alone and does not represent a shared Full Brexit position.

2. Costas Lapavitsas, a professor of economics at the School of Oriental and African Studies, University of London, was previously an MP for Syriza before joining the Popular Unity breakaway party in protest at Alexis Tsipras's decision to ignore the 2015 referendum on the EU bailout.

3. Dempsey continued, "Too many in the Labour Party have made a calculation that there's a certain section at the top end of the working class, in alliance with people, they calculate, from ethnic minorities and liberals, that's enough to get them into power." For more on the dispute, and the offer to further debate, see Hoare et al. 2019.

4. The central texts here are Heartfield 2007, 2013; Bickerton 2012; and Cunliffe 2020a.

5. See in particular Bickerton 2012 and Heartfield 2013.

6. For more on this, see Anderson 2020.

7. In particular, see Bickerton 2012 and Heartfield 2013.

8. Hobsbawm 1994.

9. See, for example, Hay 2007 and Stoker 2006 for analyses of this phenomenon.

10. See Mair 2013 for the full account of the "void" summarized here.

11. See Leys 2003 and Flinders and Buller 2006.

12. Hameiri and Jones 2016.

13. This point is taken from Anderson 2021.
14. See Bickerton 2016 for a good overview.
15. Benn 2016.
16. For a fuller account of the role of the idea of "Europe" and cosmopolitanism in the Brexit process, see Hoare 2022.
17. See for instance Lapavitsas 2018 for a good summary of these many valid criticisms of the EU as a political and economic institution.
18. See Anderson 2021 for a detailed account of the role of the ECJ in the workings of the EU and a partial history of some of its judgments.
19. Hochuli et al. 2021 put forward a view of the role of contextual political factors for conditioning the liberal establishment's response to the Brexit vote and the election of Trump understood as events that signaled the "end of the End of History."
20. It is worth remembering that the Remain campaign had included not just the vast majority of parliamentarians (with only 158 out of 650 declaring their intention to vote Leave) but also the pro-Remain state apparatus (which sent a pro-Remain leaflet to every household), as well as the majority of professionals, universities and academics, and even the then American President Barack Obama (BBC 2016).
21. Penny 2016.
22. See for example Virdee and McGeever 2018 or Norris and Inglehart 2019.
23. UK in a Changing Europe 2019.
24. For a fuller account, see Hoare 2022.
25. Streeck 2017.
26. That the Left still saw Brexit as a culture war even in 2019, overlooking the political stakes and any questions of popular sovereignty, can be seen from the journalist Ash Sarkar's tweet on December 12, 2019: "We couldn't overcome the Brexit culture war. I'm so sorry, to everyone who fought like lions til the close of polls. The movement continues, and we keep on keeping on tomorrow." See https://twitter.com/AyoCaesar/status/1205248597975031814. Accessed 6 July 2021.
27. Bickerton and Tuck 2018.
28. See Cerny 1997 and Jones and Hameiri 2021.
29. Jones 2018.
30. See Jones 2019 and Ramsay 2019 for a development of this argument.
31. See Cunliffe 2019 for a fuller analysis of the depoliticizing effects of the "Get Brexit Done" slogan.
32. See the analysis in Hoare 2020.
33. Bickerton and Jones 2018.
34. Tuck 2019.
35. Hoare 2020.
36. Full Brexit 2020.
37. In particular Jones 2015 and Mason 2016. Philip Cunliffe describes the position opposed to Lexit as a "Brexit Bolshevik" one, and although this term does not apply to the whole of the Full Brexit group, it is a relatively useful encapsulation of the broad position defended here. For more on this position, see Cunliffe 2018.
38. All quotes from Paul Mason in this section are taken from Mason 2016.

39. Lange and Pickett-Depaolis 2020. To extend the analysis given there, we might say that the specter of fascism is at its core the projection of petty bourgeois fear of the working class, which was a clear driver of the Brexit culture war.

40. Cited in Stewart 2017. See Davis 2008 for a critique of the idea that the EU has been a defender of workers' rights.

41. See Sloterdijk 1998. Here we might also discern the structure of a sort of "nihilist leftism" that responds to potential counterarguments by noting that they had already been assessed and rejected ("we've seen and heard it all, move on"), while showing a demonstrative disinterest in the opponent's motivations and views.

42. This is perhaps the British analogue of the American case: an ostensible critic of the Democratic Party who still impels people to "Vote Blue, No Matter Who," as the Republicans are worse.

43. Cunliffe 2019.

44. Hoare 2021b.

45. Hoare 2021a, 2021b.

46. For more on the new "freedoms" of lockdown see Milburn 2020, and for a critique of this tendency of the Left see Cunliffe 2020b.

47. Cunliffe et al. 2020.

48. For example, see McCormack and Jones 2020, Jones 2021, and Jones and Hameiri 2021.

49. See Crawford 2020.

50. Smith 1776, Book V, chapter 2. https://www.marxists.org/reference/archive/smith-adam/works/wealth-of-nations/book05/ch02b-2.htm. Accessed 6 July 2021.

51. Marx and Engels 1848.

Chapter 7

Dictatorship Contra Critique[1]

Samir Gandesha

We are confronted, today, by the prospect of the return of dictatorship.[1] This means the preponderance of the executive arm of the state unshackled by the rule of law, balanced and checked by neither judicial and legislative branches of government nor a free and independent press. Such a preeminence of executive authority once characterized the feudal order in which monarchs were taken to possess a "divine right to rule." The prospect of its return is becoming truly global in scope. From Eastern Europe through Turkey to India and beyond the possibility of the undisguised and unfettered assertion of sovereign power is unmistakable.[2]

In the United States, such an assertion took the form of an extraordinary legal brief in Donald J. Trump's impeachment trial in the U.S. Senate by none other than his Harvard-trained celebrity lawyer Alan Dershowitz. Dershowitz's argument boils down to the claim that Trump's withholding of funds to Ukraine in return for an investigation of his democratic opponent and successor Joe Biden (and his son Hunter) was not an impeachable act. The brief took the form of the following syllogism: Trump believed that his own reelection was in the public interest (major premise); the withholding of funds to the Ukraine would have served such reelection (minor premise); therefore, the withholding of funds to the Ukraine was in the public interest and not impeachable (conclusion).

In effect, Dershowitz was reprising, with the considerable chutzpah for which he is known, French sovereign Louis XIV's claim *"L'état, c'est moi"* (I am the state), only now it was *"L'état c'est Trump."*[3] The meaning was clear: Trump was above the law. Indeed, in an article in the *New York Magazine* rather early in the Trump presidency, Jonathan Chait, former senior editor at the *New Republic*, anticipated the forty-fifth president's relationship to the institutions of the U.S. Republic thus:

> Six months into his presidency, foundational republican concepts remain as foreign as ever to Trump. He believes the entire federal government owes its personal loyalty to him, and that the office of the presidency is properly a vehicle for personal and familial enrichment. If the rule of law survives this era intact, it will only be because the president is too inept to undermine it.[4]

The rule of law may well not survive the Trump presidency. The global trend toward dictatorship is a trend, it must be stated, that Trump simultaneously *reflected* and *enabled*. Trump reflected this trend toward what Viktor Orbán calls "illiberal democracy"[5] insofar as it has been set in motion prior to his presidency in the right-wing of the GOP, namely its populist, Tea Party faction. He enabled it by supporting autocracies such as those of Modi, Bolsonaro, Orbán, Putin, Erdogan, and Kim Jong-un, among others, across the globe.[6] Such an authoritarian trend is articulated against classical liberalism in general and the Enlightenment's bourgeois idea of "critique" or criticism, in particular. This idea of critique is, of course, central to Karl Marx's trifold, dialectical encounter, as Lenin noted, with the towering achievements of bourgeois philosophy, politics, and political economy.[7]

Yet, it could now be argued that, since Trump's loss of the 2020 election to Joe Biden, the threat has passed and the bourgeois order of the U.S. Republic has been restored. All is well with the world once more. One is tempted to retort with the following slogan invoking the medieval doctrine of the "King's two bodies":[8] "Trump is dead! Long live Trump." While he may have lost the election by over seven million votes, Donald J. Trump nonetheless garnered some 47% of the popular vote, astoundingly, during the COVID-19 pandemic that his administration handled catastrophically. Moreover, in contrast with its ostracization from the Republican Party in 2016 by the GOP's establishment, Trumpism has, today, fully captured the spirit of the party.[9] What is key in all of this is that the formal procedures of liberal democracy, inadequate as they are on their own from the standpoint of the Left, are under attack. So, too, are procedures such as rational argumentation, the provision of evidence and criticism. It must be said, here, though that Marx always insisted on a *dialectical* critique of bourgeois democracy, meaning that it be subjected not simply to *cancellation* but to an abolition which would at the same time *actualize* its emancipatory aspects, such as the vital idea of the free development of the individual which would finally no longer be understood in an antagonistic relation to the whole. As Marx and Engels insist,

> In place of the old bourgeois society, with its classes and class antagonisms, we shall have an association, in which the free development of each is the condition for the free development of all.[10]

The undialectical attack on liberal democracy is not, however, exclusive to the Right. It can also be discerned on the putatively "anti-fascist" Left. In a kind of pincer movement, liberal democracy is under simultaneous threat from the Right and from the Left.

I shall argue in the following that if the Left is suspicious of critique (and of reason more generally), and there is ample evidence that this is indeed the case, then its purported "anti-fascism" will ring increasingly hollow. As Nietzsche says in *Beyond Good and Evil*, "Whoever fights with monsters should see to it that he does not become one himself."[11] The reason for this is that fascism represents nothing less than the attempt to reverse the Enlightenment; it seeks to stand on its head Sigmund Freud's—that exemplary partisan of Enlightenment—famous slogan "Wo es war, soll ich werden" (Where id was, there ego shall be):[12] in place of reason, fascism seeks to install the powerful affects of anxiety and fear on which it bases a politics of safety and order. It is, in this sense, the inversion of psychoanalysis. An anti-fascism that mirrors core aspects of what it opposes perverts itself insofar as it becomes exactly what it opposes—fascistic. In the context of a creeping cancel culture, dialectical critique becomes impossible, insofar as it hinges on *Aufhebung* or a simultaneous cancellation *and* preservation of thought. As Michel Foucault writes in his preface to a book he describes as "an introduction to non-fascist living," Deleuze and Guattari's *Anti-Oedipus*:

> How does one keep from being fascist, even (especially) when one believes oneself to be a revolutionary militant? How do we rid our speech and our acts, our hearts and our pleasures, of fascism? How do we ferret out the fascism that is ingrained in our behavior?[13]

Adorno wrote about this logic in his exchange of letters with Marcuse on the Students' Movement shortly before his death in 1969: in their zeal to confront a lingering "fascism" in West German state and civil society, the students manifested some of those very authoritarian tendencies themselves.[14]

The Crown Jurist of the Nazi state, Carl Schmitt, argued in several books and articles that there exists an antinomy or irreconcilable opposition between "the political," properly understood in terms of the existential antagonism between "friend" and "enemy"—terms that he thoroughly aestheticizes—on the one hand, and liberal or parliamentary democracy on the other. While the former is the condition for the possibility of sovereign decision, the latter represents endless and interminable discussion, camouflaging the interests of social and economic elites. In *Dictatorship: From the Origin of the Modern Concept of Sovereignty to Proletarian Class Struggle*,[15] written in the immediate aftermath of the Russian Revolution, Schmitt seeks to explicate the concept of dictatorship (or emergency powers) as a valid constitutional principle traceable back to Roman law. The basic idea is that in times in which the institutions of the political order enter a deep structural crisis, extraordinary powers may be conferred on a figure empowered to address it. Schmitt distinguishes between two forms of dictatorship: the *commissarial* and the *sovereign*. The former is established with the aim of restoring the *status quo ante*, while the latter is oriented toward bringing into existence a new, revolutionary order.

The contemporary tendency toward dictatorship is poised somewhere, one could argue, between the commissary and sovereign forms in Schmitt's distinction. The authoritarian, or what has been called the "sado-populist"[16] challenge to the neoliberal order is oriented toward neither a purely commissary nor a purely sovereign dictatorship. Such a challenge today, despite its invocation of the past (i.e., the Trumpian slogan of MAGA), seeks neither to restore a previously existing order in crisis nor to establish a revolutionary new order but rather to maintain, despite appearances to the contrary, a crushing neoliberal stasis. It is perhaps best described by Antonio Gramsci's "The old world is dying and the new world struggles to be born. Now is the time of monsters."[17] This is indeed a time of monsters and, as I've suggested elsewhere, such monsters take the form of collective ethno-racial, gender, and other identities unalloyed by class. For authoritarian populism, social class is elided by the nebulous and amorphous concept of the people. For the identitarian Left, class is a category that is one of many identity markers with no specificity of its own. Such a position fails to notice that while other identity markers entail a politics of recognition and inclusion, and are therefore ultimately affirmative of the existing order, class understood critically is a thoroughgoing negative category. This means that proletarian identity cannot be properly included within a system based on the sale and purchase of labor power and the extraction of surplus value. Just as people with no place to live far from struggling for the recognition of their identity as "homeless" persons but rather for the abolition of their condition by the provision of housing, the proletariat struggles for the abolition of class society as such.[18]

An important corollary to the impending prospect of dictatorship is the eclipse of the very idea of critique and criticism, alluded to above. As Adorno argues, the institutional form of critique in bourgeois democracies is the idea that can be traced to Enlightenment political theorists John Locke and Charles-Louis de Secondat, Baron de La Brède et de Montesquieu, of the separation and balance of powers.[19] In other words, the sovereign power of the executive branch of the state would be offset by the other two arms—the judicial and legislative branches. Here, as in the Enlightenment idea of critique, the governing idea is the establishment of limits through rational self-reflection. The connection to cultural criticism ought to be clear: claims are confronted immanently by counterclaims oriented to exposing inner contradictions.

By insisting on the idea of critique, Adorno implicitly countered the Schmittian idea upon which dictatorship, the "political," and sovereignty were based, namely decisionism. Decisionism was based on an existential choice no longer oriented by limited (and limiting) rational criteria. Like the will of God itself, sovereign decision was released from every possible fetter on itself insofar as it evoked the will of the "people." It issued not from reason but from what Kierkegaard called, in connection with the Old Testament story of Abraham and Isaac, the "madness of decision." This is what he termed, in direct opposition to Hegel's rationalism, the "teleological suspension of the ethical."[20] The sovereign was always, as it were, the giver, though never the receiver of law; the sovereign, by definition, could therefore never be bound by it.

Historically, the rise of emergency powers was greeted by a revolutionary Left that sought to steadfastly maintain forms of critique while it sought, at the same time, in the words of Walter Benjamin, "to bring about the real state of emergency,"[21] by which, of course, he meant revolution. Now something quite different is afoot. Today, there are many signs that critique and criticism are themselves under attack by what presents itself as the "Left." Is it possible to discern the logic of dictatorship in the realm of art and culture more generally?

A MONSTROUS LEFT

Monsters can indeed be discerned in this realm and take the form of a drive by elements of the Left to seize extraordinary powers in the name of purportedly "authentic" identities. This is, of course, paradoxical, as the very idea of "Left" and "Right" emerge out of the French Revolution, but yet, the contemporary Left bids adieu to this revolutionary experience and its intellectual antecedent, the Enlightenment, as irredeemably "Eurocentric." The legacy of the twentieth-century Russian and Western European avant-gardes, with which Benjamin himself was in deep critical dialogue, continued on well into the 1970s and the 1980s in the work of artists such as Hans Haacke, Jeanne-Claude and Christo, Cindy Sherman, Martha Rosler, David Černý, and Tracey Emin, to name but a few. While it is in no way possible to reduce the works, practices, and gestures of these to a single theme, they all sought in their own idiosyncratic ways to take up what could only be called a radically negative, polemical posture to the world in general and the art world in particular. And the consequences were often serious, far-reaching, and enduring. For example, the controversies surrounding Haacke's "Shapolsky et al." (1971), Andres Serrano's *Piss Christ* (1987), and the ill-fated Robert Mapplethorpe exhibition "The Perfect Moment" in 1989 led to far-reaching and negative policy changes in the National Endowment for the Arts.[22]

Today, it seems that on questions of cultural representation, Left and Right have traded places. Now the Right invokes the anarchic, provocative spirit of Dada and surrealism, albeit as a form of what Marcuse would call "repressive desublimation," that is, to *tighten* rather than to *loosen* the grip of the present over the future. The Left, in contrast, articulates a moralistic neo-Zhdanovian line that insists that art must be *politically* correct for it to be *aesthetically* correct. An important part of the continuity is that both socialist realism and the woke mob identify "political correctness" as a position that *exposes* the governing contradiction of the society which art reflects—while, in fact, it *masks* it.[23] Effectively, it enables a form of dictatorship supposedly grounded in e.g. imagined "communities", constituted by an overarching "identity."[24]

But How Did We Get Here?

It is possible to argue that this situation finds its roots in three distinct developments originating in the late 1980s, developments in which a nascent authoritarianism can already be discerned. In fact, it is possible to suggest that a key moment in this reversal was the fall of the Berlin Wall and the fundamental disorientation of the Left that followed in its wake marked by an increasing turn toward vulgar anti-imperialism. By this I mean that the actual nature of the regime mattered less than its opposition to Western, in particular U.S. interests.

If the Left is motivated by two distinct, though overlapping approaches to justice from 1989 onward, those of *redistribution* on the one side and *recognition* on the other, there is a gradual shift toward the latter.[25] Struggles for redistribution become more fraught with the decline of the Soviet Bloc and the alternative to capitalist liberal democracy that it once represented. The so-called *trente glorieuses*, the postwar boom following the end of the Second World War, had to do not only with the process of reconstruction in much of Europe (the Federal Republic of Germany in particular), but also with the existence of the Soviet Union. The force field within which the postwar boom occurred was established between the two poles of the Marshall Plan established in 1947, on the one hand, and Comecon formed in response some two years later on the other. The existence of the Eastern Bloc kept Western liberal democracies honest insofar as they were forced to pay lip service to the principle of equality by way of a nominal commitment to redistribution, labor rights, workplace health, safety, and so forth.[26]

With the dissolution of the communist order and the onset of what has been called "capitalist realism,"[27] or the idea that, in the words of Margaret Thatcher, "there is no alternative" to capitalism, one sees a pronounced tendency toward a conception of justice grounded in recognition. We see this in the political philosophy of writers influenced by G. W. F. Hegel, including the work of Charles Taylor and Axel Honneth. In contrast to Thomas Hobbes, who argues that individuals manifest virtually inexhaustible desire for material goods, drawing on a tradition that stems from Rousseau and reaches back to the ancient idea of *thymos* (honor), Hegel argues that individuals desire *desire* itself. In other words, they desire not material goods but *recognition of the other's desire*. As Hegel put it in his *Philosophy of Right*, persons are recognized in the different "objective" structures constituting the social spheres of the family, civil society (economic life), and state citizenship.[28] The totality of these relationships creates the conditions in which individuals can manifest both particularity and universality. Recognition, for Hegel, was intrinsic to the meaningful exercise of freedom.

The reorientation of the Left also concerned the increasing awareness that not only was recognition key to personhood, but misrecognition could also be terribly damaging to it, in, for example, the form of racism. This was perhaps most acutely set forth by the Martiniquean psychiatrist, philosopher, and political activist Frantz Fanon. Fanon showed in *Black Skin, White Masks* the damage done by forms of racist misrecognition, which often amounted to the denial of humanity of e.g. the colonized.[29] These representations were taken to be of particular importance: representation through language and visual media in particular was seen to be potentially damaging.[30] Yet, Fanon's emphasis on the politics of recognition tended to be fetishized insofar as his subtle and vital analysis of the *role of class* in the liberation struggle set forth in *The Wretched of the Earth*[31] was increasingly ignored. If one reads Fanon carefully, questions of class take precedence over those of race, insofar as the task of building a genuinely postcolonial society entails a class struggle against the national bourgeoisie which simply seeks to replace the colonial powers, not to create a new egalitarian order. Racism follows from social class—not the other way around—insofar as this phenomenon amounts to what he calls the "epidermalization of (economic) inferiority."[32]

One of the most important statements of the damage done by representations fostering supposed "misrecognition" was the anti-pornography, and some might argue anti-sex position of feminist legal theorist Catharine A. MacKinnon. Her book *Only Words*[33] makes a powerful case for limiting free speech. She argues that certain forms of free speech and expression such as pornography are deeply damaging to women and therefore bring the First Amendment into deep conflict with the U.S. Constitution's commitment to equality. MacKinnon argued that, in their effects, there was little difference between the representation of an act of sexual violence and the actual act itself.[34]

All three of these developments—the post-1989 disorientation of the Left, the ensuing turn away from the politics of redistribution toward recognition (and misrecognition), and the emphasis on the potentially violent nature of representation—culminate in the reverberations felt in the wake of the fatwa issued by Tehran on Salman Rushdie for his depiction of the Prophet Mohammed in his novel *The Satanic Verses*.[35]

The Rushdie fatwa and its aftermath set the tone for a series of encounters that would expose some of the contradictions between, on the one hand, freedom of expression and the press and, on the other, religious freedom. It would be followed by the 2005 Danish Cartoon affair and then the massacre in the offices of the irreverent and provocative magazine *Charlie Hebdo* in 2015, which left twelve people dead and another eleven injured. The violence was justified, in part, by the idea that transgressive representations of Islam were harmful, which is to say that "retaliatory violence" could itself be justified if not enjoined by the faith.[36] The rationalism and anti-clericism that had theretofore been pillars of the Left dating back to the Italian Renaissance,[37] if not before, now come to be seen as potentially serving Eurocentrism, Orientalism, and a now discredited modernity and its literally *incredible* meta-narratives.[38]

Taken together, the turn toward an unmediated anti-imperialism in the wake of the Cold War which, in a sense, anticipates Samuel P. Huntington's "Clash of Civilizations" thesis[39] in inverted form, combined with a politics of recognition and an increased sensitivity to the power of representations in fostering negative depictions (misrecognition) of historically oppressed groups, culminates in an overinflation of the problem of harm. Recall that in the liberal defense of liberty, for example, in the work of J. S. Mill, freedom could be limited only based on *harm* to others.[40] The problem with this classical statement in *On Liberty* is that harm is not precisely defined. Today we witness the growing authoritarian propensity to limit freedom of speech and expression on the specious grounds that the latter opens the door to offense which is, itself, understood as synonymous with harm. If we follow this logic to its conclusion insofar as political speech acts are bound to offend one or more parties to any given dispute, and if we assume that offence is *by definition* harmful, then political speech acts and, indeed, politics itself is rendered impossible on the basis of *harm*. Liberalism, in the process, negates itself in a thoroughly depoliticized public sphere. While this logic might seem absurd, we can see its contours in the art world, to which I shall return.

DICTATORSHIP OF MORALITY

In a manner quite consistent with Schmitt's denigration of the liberal emphasis on discussion and debate, as well as the more politically engaged gesture of "critique" enabled by an open and contestatory public sphere, the identitarian Left increasingly seeks to impose a kind of dictatorship of its own which unilaterally defines the limits of the morally permissible. As with Schmitt, the terrain shifts from procedural categories to existential ones, from the argumentative articulation of truth claims and counterclaims grounded in logic and evidence to *ontological* ones grounded in proprietary claims to ownership of experience and highly questionable categories of "existence." In the sense, this is the reanimation of the deep-seated quarrel between categories of "consciousness" and "being." In the first, artworks are adjudicated in their truth and falsity; in the second, the language concerns a granting or denial of the right of bare existence to certain groups, epistemology or what can be known, on the one hand, and the *a priori* epistemic violence of speech acts, on the other.

If the Left has increasingly come to embrace a politics of recognition over that of redistribution, such a politics does not culminate in the Hegelian-Marxist theory of equal recognition corresponding to the triumph of the slave, which is to say, the historical possibility of the abolition of mastery, or the end of class society *per se*. Rather, it culminates in the triumph of what Nietzsche calls "slave morality." In his account, far from abolishing mastery, slave morality is premised precisely on the continued existence of masters. This is the case, argues Nietzsche, because the slaves define themselves via a negative relation to their masters—the identity of the slave is nothing other than a negative image of the master. The master, in contrast, is indifferent to the slave. The slaves first characterize the masters as *evil* and then themselves as their antithesis and therefore *good*. The utter abjection and powerlessness of the slave engenders what Nietzsche calls a "spirit of revenge." As Nietzsche argues in *Genealogy of Morals*, slave morality is based on an inversion of aristocratic values:

> [(good] = noble = powerful = beautiful = happy = beloved of God) and to hang on to this inversion with their teeth, the teeth of the most abysmal hatred (the hatred of impotence), saying "the wretched alone are the good; the poor, impotent, lowly alone are the good; the suffering, deprived, sick, ugly alone are pious, alone are blessed by God, blessedness is for them alone—and you, the powerful and noble, are on the contrary the evil, the cruel, the lustful, the insatiable, the godless to all eternity; and you shall be in all eternity the unblessed, accursed, and damned!"[41]

Whatever does not express itself outward turns inward. The powerlessness of the slave ensures that the lust for revenge also turns against himself. Such an internalization of revenge is nothing other than guilt itself.[42] It is this melancholy attachment to abjection and victimhood that has completely displaced the Hegelian slave's sensuous negativity, her ability to transform nature through her labor power, and ultimately therefore the possibility of challenging the master's position which was, itself, dependent upon nothing other than the precarious form of recognition that the slave, a lesser being, provided.

We can understand these tendencies in terms of the *Dialectic of Enlightenment*'s presentation of the formation of subjectivity. Drawing upon both Nietzsche's *Genealogy of Morals* and Freud's account of sexuality, the text sought to understand why, while it promised emancipation, enlightenment left only destruction in its wake. Horkheimer and Adorno show how the implosion of the enlightenment culminates in catastrophe. First, faced with a social world marked by a Hobbesian war of all against all, an apparent state of nature that is, in fact, the natural-historical reality of capitalism, the individual must divest himself of empathy and become cold and hard to be able to compete against others in the interest of self-preservation. He must subordinate himself to and therefore identify with the external imperatives of the prevailing performance principle of this order. At the same time, to be successful, such an adaptation to the outside must be introjected or internalized. This takes the form of an internalization of sacrifice or self-renunciation. The late bourgeois subject is, in its essence, self-sacrificial, constituted by guilt. The psychic cost of this dialectic of identification with and introjection of the external forces in the interest of self-preservation is a diminution of the capacity of the self to fully experience the world, think, and act within it. The self is reduced to a bundle of nonreflective, quasi-automatic reactions to external stimuli. And this entails dissociation. The life that is to be preserved at all costs turns, paradoxically, into mere existence; it becomes a kind of living death. "Every man his own speciality," declares Hamm to Clov in Beckett's *Endgame*, "I can't stand, you can't sit."[43] The accumulation of aggression that results from deepening repression and sublimation is unleashed on those groups and individuals that are taken to personify civilization itself.

DICTATORSHIP AND THE ART WORLD

Perhaps it is unfair to use the language of *dictatorship* here. But this concern, I think, can be allayed with the recognition that in these cases it is always a particular that presents itself as standing in for the whole by way of a forceful imposition. It is a small subsection of a given community or identity group that purports to be able to represent—without deliberation, consultation, or democratic will formation—the group in toto. But on what grounds, exactly? What dissenting voices from within the group are supposedly represented?

Surely, there are no actual democratic mechanisms of representation, no polling, no elections, and no votes cast—ultimately no *accountability*—to ensure the adequacy of such representation. The unmediated force of naked assertion suffices. It is simply an arrogation on the part of the community's self-selected representatives of the right to speak on its behalf. It is, indeed, tempting to call such representatives, after Nietzsche, the "priestly" caste—a caste that personifies the "spirit of revenge."[44]

In the literary world, there are no shortages of examples.[45] These dynamics, of course, have also shaken the art world to the core. The open letter written by the mixed-race artist Hannah Black to Dana Schutz (and signed by several others) declared that the painter apparently had "no right" to Black suffering and that her painting ought to be, by that token, not only withdrawn from the Whitney Biennale but in fact destroyed.[46] "That painting must go," declared Black's letter. Or perhaps this was its diktat meaning, according to the *OED*: "a decree, ruling, or directive; a categorical assertion or prescription."[47] Concerns over his depictions of the white hoods of the Ku Klux Klan in the wake of uprisings led by #BlackLivesMatter have led to numerous delays of a traveling exhibition of the work of Canadian-American self-identified "anti-racist" artist Philip Guston.

Perhaps the best example of such left-wing melancholy can be found in the furore surrounding the Russian American Communist painter Victor Arnautoff's mural at George Washington High School in San Francisco.[48] The mural dating back to the early 1930s was the first of its kind to depict this most iconic of founding fathers in a less than iconic light. It is a twelve-panel, meticulously researched work covering all the walls and stairwell of the entrance to the school. It is also an exemplary instance of a style of fresco that consists of applying paint directly into wet plaster—the so-called "buon" style. The mural took some ten months to complete. What's particularly interesting about the mural is the way it centers enslaved Africans, working-class revolutionaries, and Indigenous peoples, while at the same time displacing its putative subject, George Washington himself in a kind of inverted "great mantheory of history." One panel depicts Washington standing over the corpse of an Indigenous person and enslaved Africans, giving orders for the catastrophic westward expansion of the Republic. Criticism, here, would attend to the truth of the mural, its refusal to present a monumental, legitimating account of the U.S. as a "Shining City on a Hill." In contrast to such an account, Arnautoff brushes history against the grain to reveal the barbaric truth of the American civilizing mission. This is, by any account, exemplary of politically engaged art.

The cancellation of Arnautoff recalls that of an important work by his friend and comrade Diego Rivera. The work is the arresting 1934 mural "Man at a Crossroads" intended for the recently constructed Rockefeller Centre that presented the alternatives of capitalism and socialism. It was canceled for being offensive. Rivera later recreated the work now entitled "Man, Controller of the Universe" at the Palacio de Bellas Artes in Mexico City. The reason for the offense? Rivera had had the temerity to include the visage of Vladimir Ilyich Lenin and a depiction of a Soviet May Day parade.

Today, however, as in the case of Hannah Black's open letter, calls have been made for the destruction of Arnautoff's mural, because the work fails to depict these oppressed communities in a light that they consider appropriate. To be more precise, the work fails to depict these communities in ways that its self-appointed representatives might consider to be appropriate. As mentioned earlier, it does so in the complete absence of democratic mechanisms. Like the erasure of Lenin and May Day, Arnautoff's Washington mural was covered over. It is a version of the Bolshevik idea of democratic centralism, yet absent the *democracy*. Of course, one may reasonably agree that there is something about these representations that could be construed as having not aged particularly well, although this, in my opinion, is emphatically not applicable in the case of Arnautoff's George Washington Mural. Nonetheless, there will be those who reasonably disagree. The answer, as in the case of Dana Schutz's *Open Casket* (2017), therefore, is not to destroy the artworks themselves but, rather, to subject them to immanent criticism.

With Adorno, we might call this interrogating the work's dialectical falsity in light of its truth, and vice versa. Here the pertinent question would be, does the work subvert itself by intending solidarity with the oppressed, but presenting them as objects rather than as subjects of history, and therefore reifying them in the process? In other words, the work is marked by a historical wound that it opens forcefully but cannot, as it were, close or heal. (Of course, perhaps the artwork in late capitalist society can only open and never close wounds insofar as the latter is a matter of political *praxis* in any case.) This, it could be argued, is precisely the role of art criticism and political critique: understanding the fractured unity of the true and the false, the way in which a work's very success is dialectically dependent upon its own failure.[49] "Ever tried. Ever failed. No matter. Try again. Fail again. Fail better." Samuel Beckett's perhaps over-cited aperçu can be read as a commentary on the very activity of art making, in which failure is a key, irreducible moment: nothing that can be wished or airbrushed out of history.

In other words, an important premise of art criticism is that artworks are made in the spirit of experimentation, which means a spirit in which there are simply no *metaphysical* (much less *moral*) guarantees. Art presupposes an open-ended field that welcomes the experience of the new and the unexpected. Yet, today, as in the field of politics, the multiple crises of our times, economic, social, political, and above all ecological, lead to an increasing tendency to foreshorten the new and disavow unexpectedly by means of an imposed sovereign madness of decision. In a word: dictatorship.

NOTES

1. I would like to thank the editors, Elena Louisa Lange and Joshua Pickett-Depaolis, for their extremely helpful comments on a previous version of this chapter. A previous, shorter version was published as "Dictatorship Contra Critique," *L'Espace Art Actuel: Pratiques et Perspectives* 125 (Spring-Summer, 2020): 62–67.

2. It is perhaps for this reason that certain commentators speak of the return of a neofedual order. See, of example, Jodi Dean, "Neofeudalism: The End of Capitalism?" *Los Angeles Review of Books*, May 12, 2020. https://lareviewofbooks.org/article/neofeudalism-the-end-of-capitalism/. Accessed July 13, 2021.

3. Bump 2020.

4. Chait 2017.

5. https://www.economist.com/briefing/2019/08/29/how-viktor-orban-hollowed-out-hungarys-democracy. Accessed July 13, 2021.

6. This should hardly lead us to draw the inference that other Republican presidents such as the Bushes or Democratic ones such as Clinton and Obama were paragons of democratic virtue. Such is the nature of imperial power.

7. In a short text published in *Prosveshcheniye* No. 3, March 1913, dedicated to the thirtieth anniversary of Marx's death, Lenin stated that Marx's thought "is the legitimate successor to the best that man produced in the nineteenth century, as represented by German philosophy, English political economy and French socialism." https://www.marxists.org/archive/lenin/works/1913/mar/x01.htm. Accessed July 13, 2021.

8. Kantorowicz 1998.

9. This was made clear by the ousting of Liz Cheney, daughter of former vice president Dick Cheney, and third-ranking Republican in the House of Representatives, who is one of the very few high-ranking Republican figures to challenge Trump's claim that the election had been "stolen." Several conservative US states are now in the process of enacting legislation that would further restrict voting rights and gerrymander electoral districts to favor Republican candidates (see Gardner et al. 2021).

10. Marx and Engels 1970, 59. It should also be noted that the *Manifesto* showers praise on the technological innovations of the bourgeois world.

11. Nietzsche 2002 (1886), 69.

12. Freud 1981, 80.

13. Deleuze and Guattari 1983, xiii.

14. See Gandesha 2019. One of the most egregious of such events happened on the UC Berkeley campus, when an appearance by Breitbart journalist Milo Yiannopoulos's talk was shut down by force. The irony, of course, is that UC Berkeley was the birthplace of the Free Speech Movement. Such an irony was lost on no one. If the Alt-right's strategy is to back the left into the corner of betraying its own history and principles, it seems it may well be succeeding.

15. Schmitt 2014.
16. Snyder 2018.
17. Quoted in Muehlebach 2016.
18. Precisely because of this emphasis on social class, veteran African American activist and esteemed political scientist Adolph Reed Jr. has been canceled—by the DSA no less—as a "class reductionist." See https://www.nytimes.com/2020/08/14/us/adolph-reed-controversy.html. Accessed July 13, 2021.
19. T. W. Adorno 1998.
20. Kierkegaard 1986.
21. Benjamin 2003, 392.
22. See van Haaften-Schick 2012.
23. I thank Joshua Pickett-Depaolis for helping me clarify this point.
24. While there are no doubt profound countervailing tendencies, not least the grass roots movement crystallizing around Bernie Sanders's nomination bid for the Democratic Party's candidacy, the predominant response of the Left to its long-standing crisis has been a deepening sense of melancholy. If, according to Freud, mourning involves the gradual withdrawal of libido from the lost object, then melancholia entails a turning against itself of the subject who guiltily takes on blame for such object loss. What this has entailed is an endless self-destructive struggle of the Left against itself. What seems to elude those who drive this struggle is that the point of electoral politics is to *win* rather than to *lose* elections. A case in point is the demand from certain LGBTQ+ organizations that Bernie Sanders distance himself from the extremely valuable endorsement by former MMA fighter and comedian, Joe Rogan.
25. See Honneth and Fraser 2004.
26. See Piketty 2017.
27. Fisher 2009.
28. Hegel 1991. Of course, for Jacques Lacan, the successful acquisition of the desire of the other is an impossibility. This is the basis of Žižek's unique synthesis of Hegel and Lacan.
29. Fanon 2008.
30. Fanon's most famous example is that of a racist encounter with a young White French girl in the Paris metro when she says "Look mother a nigger."
31. Fanon 2005.
32. Fanon 1986, 4.
33. MacKinnon 1994.
34. Today, of course, MacKinnon and her colleague Andrea Dworkin's anti-porn feminism would be very much out of step with the times and might even be regarded as "SWERF" (sex worker exclusionary feminism).
35. Rushdie 1997. It is approximately at this point that Christopher Hitchens, for example, a close friend of Rushdie, turns away from the Left and toward neoconservatism.
36. See Smith 2015.
37. See Brecht 2008.
38. Lyotard 1984. Let's also remember that Islamophobia at this point in history took a clear back seat to Cold War sentiment and the Mujaheddin in Afghanistan

were regarded as close allies in the fight against the "Evil Empire," which is to say the Soviet Union.

39. Huntington 2011.

40. Mill 2015.

41. Nietzsche 1989, 34.

42. While I am unable to develop this here, such a subjective disposition to vengefulness and guilt can be located in the preponderance of finance and the pervasiveness of debt and indebtedness. See Lazzarato 2012 and Lazzarato 2013.

43. Beckett 2009.

44. Nietzsche 2003, 108.

45. *Inter alia.* Vanessa Place, Walter Kenneth Goldsmith, Sky Gilbert, and Robert Lepage.

46. See Greenberger 2017.

47. *Oxford University Press* https://www.oed.com/view/Entry/52722?redirectedFrom=Diktat&amp. Accessed July 13, 2021.

48. See Bogart 2019.

49. Significantly, van Haaften-Schick's catalogue entitled *Canceled* and presumably the exhibition it was produced for takes up the question of the meaning of failure. Moreover, perhaps it is because of this alliance between art and political criticism that Joseph Goebbels, as his first act as minister for propaganda, outlawed the former in order to annul the latter.

Chapter 8

Cultural Representation

The Backlash against Woke Aesthetics as Anti-*politics*

Maren Thom

The slogan "Go woke go broke" has been present on online platforms since 2018.[1] It describes the phenomenon of organizations and businesses subscribing to social justice principles and thereby alienating their customers. *Woke*, though, is bigger than that. Instead of simply meaning "awareness of social injustices," woke today indicates an almost religious zeal to uncover and pick at "systems of oppression";[2] it is a fully formed world view and system of criticism that informs cultural artifacts, their production, reception and goals.

But there is also a backlash against woke culture. The effects of woke have been blamed for box office flops such as *Ghostbusters* (2016) and *Charlie's Angels* (2019). Plummeting viewing figures for the Oscars and other self-promoting ceremonies within the industry, accompanied by a drastic fall in box office success and popularity of Oscar nominated films in the past 20 years, speak of a declining interest from the public in Hollywood—the *non plus ultra* of woke—and its ideas.[3] While "Twitter is not real life," the Twitter campaign to #DefundTheBBC, accusing the public corporation of political bias, has been gaining momentum since 2020. There is a sense that people feel disaffected by those that produce culture and the culture that is produced. Rather than seeing these reactions as expressions of a culture war between liberal and conservative values, I would suggest the culture war dynamic itself is evidence of a greater underlying process: the outright, if inarticulate, rejection of a managerial political class and the cultural theories that inform it. What is being rejected is the ideology-first, artistic-logic-second shoehorning of an ideological commitment to "representation"—and all that this entails—into cultural creation.

In this chapter I want to talk about how these populist revolts of *anti-politics* are accompanied by another rejection. There is a growing dissatisfaction with the annexation of culture by institutions staffed by an educated liberal class, or Professional Managerial Class, for the purpose of establishing, to paraphrase Frederic Jameson's famous essay, the cultural logic of neoliberal ideology—identity politics.[4] A culture war in which conservatives and liberals fight over different models of personal expression has become the battleground, with art itself the main casualty. The essence of art needs reasserting and defending, not only in itself but also in its role as making history.

HOW CULTURAL THEORY SERVES THE POST-POLITICAL

The emergence of postmodern theories of cultural meaning-making happened alongside a greater historical shift, which leaned on those theories for political legitimation. Termed by Francis Fukuyama as *The End of History*, he asserted (indirectly) that history in a Hegelian sense, as a dialectical progress toward freedom (*"Die Weltgeschichte ist der Fortschritt im Bewußtsein der Freiheit"*) had ended.[5] *The End of History* as the end of competing ideologies—usefully symbolized by the fall of the Berlin Wall in 1989—brought about a reorganizing of global political life around the principles of what has been termed neoliberal democracy. In general, this meant the depoliticization of institutions and the end of conflicting class interests, with the aim of freeing the market economy. In this context political struggle is dismissed as backward and extremist. Instead, the state and political agents see their mission as *management*—of market exchanges and of people. Their strategy is *post-politics*. The authors of the recent volume *The End of the End of History* (and equally the hosts of the *Aufhebunga Bunga* global politics podcast) explain this nicely: "Post-politics is a form of government that tries to foreclose political contestation by emphasizing consensus, eradicating ideology and ruling through managerial technocracy."[6] It is a populist acting out, rather than a coherent criticism, an expression of frustration at the lack of a sound ideological or practical opposition to third-way politics. "The experience of depoliticization . . . breeds an angry reaction: the institutions of formal politics come to be rejected by citizens."[7] This display of disobedience is often portrayed as a right-wing counter movement to the left-liberal consensus.[8] However, *anti-politics* is probably better understood as a general populist upheaval against neoliberal, centrist politics and the managerial state. While localized and different in many respects, anti-politics can be seen everywhere from leftist political outbursts like Podemos in Spain, to the anti-European Union politics of Brexit, the rejection of the political class with the Trump vote in 2016, and the French *Gilet Jaunes* protests in 2018. Neoliberal politics works to organize society without political discourse or competing visions, the consensus being that discourse is over. Inequalities between people, as well as the functions of daily life and its development, are a question of targeted well-intentioned regulation and empathetic management.

In this framework, class is demoted from a political category defining a group with a common relationship to material production to, at most, a category of identity, one of many groups which form the units of the new interest-management. People are encouraged to self-identify their interest groups according to their cultural roles, rather than their political interests, and in the absence of anything else also spontaneously do. The experience of class is substituted by the experience of the self as a cultural artifact—an entity shaped by language and structures.

The end of history turned people from political subjects—the active makers of history—to cultural subjects—the passive objects of social relations. If the making of history is foreclosed, yet inequalities persist, what seems natural are epistemological remedies that demand top-down policies and draconian management of social relations in the name of equality. For proponents of managerial politics, the fundamental principles that enable political discourse—such as freedom of speech and freedom of consciousness—have become anathematic and can be sacrificed as politics itself is redundant. At worst, these ideas are seen to threaten the managerial principles of post-politics itself. What is demanded instead is the safety of the body from harm, especially harm produced by cultural affect.

In this context, cultural theories of representation gained currency and theoretical weight as a way of ensuring social change without having to change the fundamental principles of capitalism.

THE REJECTION OF WOKE CULTURE IS ANTI-POLITICS—NOT A CULTURE WAR

The logic of woke as a cultural phenomenon could be called the woke aesthetic, the principles of representation and appreciation that guide the makers and consumers of woke conventions.

Representation is one of the main values and aesthetics of woke. Production decisions for film, TV, theatre, and so on, are made around identity and its representation. The artistic results are then either lauded or condemned by these metrics—the number of women or minorities, or lack thereof, in front of and behind the camera are typical indices. Critics of these policies are often painted as the conservative side of a culture war, protesting the liberal side, as those who want to persevere social conventions against those who want to change them. The debates over artistic products are framed and articulated this way. For example, there are ongoing arguments around historical dramas such as *Bridgerton* (2020) and *Anne Boleyn* (2021) in which historically White characters are played by Black actors. One side argues for a socially and artistically conservative value—the dramatic verisimilitude of historical accuracy—and the other for the necessity of normalizing Black actors in traditionally White narratives.

Posing this clash as a culture war is inadequate to the task of understanding and critiquing the content of the dispute. It fails to identify that both sides of this contestation, whether nominally conservative or liberal, demand limitations on and interventions into art and culture. Both sides instrumentalize art with demands that it should represent a social ideal. Neither allow for the possibility of art to transcend the framework of social demands placed upon it.

THE "WOKE" AESTHETIC AND THE FORECLOSURE OF ART

What is today experienced as a "woke" aesthetic has been around for longer than the term itself, which only gained traction around 2016, and encompasses a list of woke criteria, that is, identity-based mechanisms and rules born in academia as well as a "vernacular criticism"[9] that stories must be understood through and measured against. These mechanisms have been made concrete in concepts such as the Bechdel Test (how women are represented in films), or the Riz Test (how Muslims are represented) and others such as the DuVernay Test (race) or Landau test (a gender fail test). They are all geared toward the same end and function similarly, but simply switch out the identity group under investigation. These tests effectuate the criteria established by feminist and postcolonial film theory of cinematic composition as an apparatus, the mechanism through which human beings are subjectivized into hegemonic power structures. Every ambitious undergraduate can easily use these tests like a checklist to see if a cultural product is "woke." These criteria deal with and frequently prescribe matters of identity-based casting. Furthermore, they reduce cinematic devices such as camera angles, dialogue and blocking solely to the question of representations of power relations, typically assuming that more screen time or more lines means that a character has more power. Of course, it should go without saying that there are power dynamics between fictional characters within any narrative. Yet woke checklists deny ambiguities and alternative readings of on-screen relationships, prescribing a monolithic reading and, moreover, hold representations of on-screen power as constitutive to real social power relations and the real-life inequalities that come with it.

"Representation matters" as a slogan has only really found purchase with the rise of online platforms but has long been established in the academic discipline of postmodern cultural studies. This discipline emerged in the second half of the twentieth century, through the work of theorists such as Stuart Hall. He advanced the argument that where, what, and how things are represented in culture directly produces social life itself and, moreover, that it is through representation that subjects are understood—what things (including people) mean; "Representation," he says, "is the production of the meaning of the concepts in our minds through language."[10] Following Michel Foucault, power here becomes a dynamic, or *discourse*, that reproduces itself through psychological systems of control and punishment via its institutions. There is no real explanation how these systems emerged, in a historical sense, only that they sustain themselves through cultural patterns of subjectivation.

In this context, inequality is understood not as based in material reality, as something to be challenged and changed as such, but as a question of representation—a structural, ideological component of society to be negotiated. Here we can see how this methodology of postmodern cultural theory is one and the same as *post-politics*, with its praxis of bureaucratically managing inequalities through the legislation of representation, be it through quotas or screen time. In postmodern cultural theory, criticism is often expressed in epistemological models around race, gender and physicality, and is thus reduced to questions of interpreting which elements of society have been portrayed in a more "powerful" way. This approach is premised on the assumption that dictating how identities are represented on screen can actively help construct real-life relations between social groups. Narratives, it is believed, molded by the correct rules of representation, will have a trickle-down psychological effect to real-life relations between different identity groups. Representation has come to mean a specific way of seeing people not as individuals in and of themselves but, rather, as signifiers of social relations.

Ironically, this identity-based syllogism creates a situation in which people are no longer seen as of themselves, as self-determined individuals in all their contradictions—in all their diversity—but as defined through their identity group around the categories of sexuality, religion, race and culture.

This narrow approach to human subjectivity puts the onus on people to identify with what Kwame Anthony Appiah calls "life-scripts" that have been laid out for them.[11]

> Demanding respect for people as blacks and gays can go along with notably rigid strictures as to how one is to be an African American or a person with same-sex desires. . . . There will be proper modes of being black and gay: there will be demands that are made; expectations to be met; battle lines to be drawn.[12]

Kenan Malik goes further: "An identity is supposed to be an expression of an individual's authentic self but it can too often seem like the denial of individual agency in the name of cultural authenticity."[13]

When people are seen as cyphers for their identity group, it is easy to see how the inherent representative aspect of art is reduced to simply presenting people as signifiers of their identity. In its own terms, any identification with a representation of a person on screen must be shaped by their social experience of identity.

Taking this idea to its logical conclusion, the BBC diversity chief Miranda Wayland proclaimed in April 2021 that Idris Elba's character Luther in the BBC detective series of the same name is "not authentically black enough" because he did not do Black things like "eat jerk chicken" or have "black friends." Wayland's job at the BBC is to oversee programs and make sure they adhere to the dictates of the station's representation policies. This type of policy is similar to those in many other countries, and most companies in the UK are required to have in place since the "diversity act" of 2010.

Of representation, Wayland says, "It's about making sure that everything around them—their environment, their culture, the set—is absolutely reflective."[14] Wayland insists that these cultural markers would make the character feel more authentic, more real. What is interesting is not the truth or otherwise of this assumption, but that what is felt as giving verisimilitude to a character should come from assumptions around cultural identity. What is being put forward is not representation of what *is*, the truth of things in all its contradictions, but the representation of the appearance of things according to a very particular set of given parameters of identity-based signifiers. The threat of the reduction of *Luther* to these racialized gestures held the risk of alienating many fans. Rather than making him "more authentic" it would rob them of being "able to watch a show about a protagonist who happens to be black."[15] The experience of the show as a story in its own terms would have been compromised by the top-down corrective of racial representation.

REPRESENTATION

How effective, then, is representation as a tool for change? "Representation matters" has been entirely and easily co-opted by the managerial class. As a slogan, it can be found in almost every HR handbook. For employers, the politics of identity and representation are no threat. On the contrary, neoliberal capitalism is very much an advocate of identity politics. A conspicuous display of virtue does not hurt business, it panders to employees and, it is claimed, increases output through a diversity of experiences, with new perspectives on problems. These factors are a good indicator that representation does not materially affect social structures and that it cannot meaningfully challenge the domination of capital itself.

Representation, then, is not radical in any political sense. So why is it seen as such? It is because, as discussed before, academic theories of cultural representation said that the construction of meaning through culture, following Foucault, is also the construction of power; "Power relations permeate all levels of social existence and are therefore to be found operating at every site of social life,"[16] and because this explanation goes unchallenged by any truly radical materialist alternatives. Here, cultural representations imbue an individual with power or lack thereof. At first glance this would seem obvious. If someone is presented to us by an authoritative source as, for example, a king carrying all the symbols of power, we tend to think of them as a ruler. So, for thinkers like Hall, the way people are represented in culture is fundamental to the powers they are assigned in society. For Hall, representation matters because it empowers the disadvantaged. By deliberately creating a cultural depiction in which everyone is seen to belong and seen to succeed, reality will come to be constructed out of this depiction.

On closer inspection, however, the logic that production of authority, or power, is derived through the production of signs and signifiers does not hold water. There is no escaping that power has a materialist dimension. Power is having the means to act in one's interest—means, economic or political, that are real and can be taken away. If power is no longer understood as an expression of a material reality that can be acquired, any possibility of radically changing existing circumstances is foreclosed. The only option is to accept the parameters of the given circumstances.

Constrained by theories of representation and power, the only way people can imagine change is via the way society creates itself through culture. Cultural institutions and their cadre have become the gatekeepers of culture and art, adjudicating what it should *be* and *do* for society to progress. Almost without exception these positions are staffed with what Adolph Reed Jr. calls "left identitarians";[17] mostly represented in the Professional Managerial Class (PMC), people who are convinced that their understanding of how culture is to be produced, created, and consumed through tokenistic policies of diversity and representation is a political process of power redistribution.

Nothing illustrates this more clearly than Meghan Markle's interview with Oprah Winfrey in early 2021. The princess, who just beforehand had moved into an eleven million dollar mansion in California, talked about, when meeting her subjects in the Commonwealth, "how much it meant to them to be able to see someone who looks like them." For her, it was obvious that the main obstacle for many underprivileged people is that they did not see themselves represented in culture. "You have to see it to be it!"[18] she asserted. An affirmation seemingly straight out of a Hollywood yoga retreat perfectly demonstrates how equality is understood not in material terms of resources, or even formal legal terms, but in relation to cultural representation. In this version of events, as in a Disney movie, apparently everyone can be a princess given a diverse selection of princesses who look like them on TV.

Another example of how the role of representation is important for the stability of the status quo was brought up by the actor Riz Ahmed (as in the Riz Test), delivering Channel 4's annual diversity lecture in Parliament in 2017. Ahmed asserted that if people do not feel represented culturally, they do not feel like they belong to society. For young British Muslims like him that could mean that they would "switch off and retreat to fringe narratives, to bubbles online and sometimes even off to Syria."[19] Ahmed claimed that unless people's identities are represented, many will resort to anti-politics, in this case Islamic extremism. "If we fail to represent, we are in danger of losing people to extremism," he said.

> In the mind of the Isis recruit, he's the next James Bond, right? Have you seen some of those Isis propaganda videos, they are cut like action movies. Where is the counter narrative? Where are we telling these kids they can be heroes in our stories, that they are valued?[20]

In 2021, he presented a study that linked negative representations of Muslims with a rise in hate crimes and justifications for military interventions and asserted that these "toxic" portrayals literally "kill" Muslims.[21] This superficial appeal demands that those who make and commission culture follow a strict set of aesthetic narrativization guidelines to prevent the negative effects of stereotyping and the proliferation of far right ideas. Instead of seeing interventions into Muslim countries as first and foremost *politically* driven decisions, Ahmed interprets these as a logical conclusion of Western attitudes being shaped by negative depictions of Muslims.

In one sense Ahmed identified a real problem, albeit a narrow artistic one. During the height of the War on Terror, a countless number of movies and TV dramas were filmed from an American or British POV, in which Muslims played minor, caricatured roles as either victims or perpetrators. Showing a Muslim perspective, as did *Four Lions* (2007) in which Ahmed played the lead character, was rare.

But the problem here is not identified as an artistic one—that lame stereotypes are unsatisfying—nor even as a material problem—that minorities did not get their fair share of the production. Rather, it is seen as a problem of attitudes, of fantasies of empire, and patriarchal structures that have supposedly not caught up with reality. The problem of power structures standing in the way of the enforcement of cultural representations, in the name of progress toward equality, is exemplified in the idea of Old White Men. This trifecta of easily identified criteria can be employed by any halfwit as the basis for a particular kind of activism, one that serves to set its exponents apart from those are reluctant to embrace neoliberal capitalism, an activism Catherine Liu terms "virtue hoarding."[22]

THE GATEKEEPERS OF CULTURE

The category of PMC is much debated but has come to be shorthand for the liberal elite of the post-political era, "managers, 'specialists,' technocrats, technical intelligentsia" who exercise their dominance through cultural gatekeeping. These are "salaried mental workers"[23] and proponents of the neoliberal order, who do not themselves own capital but are fully committed to capitalist structures and would think of themselves as liberal and progressive. Liu describes the PMC as *Virtue Hoarders*, whose activism and political purpose consists of scouring cultural artifacts for "wrongthink" (wrongthink is a term that plays on Orwell's concept of Thoughtcrime and came to be associated with the alt-right[24]) from old movies and TV shows to adverts and exhibitions—but also to personal Tweets, WhatsApp conversations and other past personal transgressions. The values of the PMC prescribe what they see as necessary for the cause of social justice. They want equal representation of identities through targets, rules and quotas, not only in the industry but in the cultural products themselves.

In this ideological annexation of the meaning of art and performance, *Good Art*, art that is woke, is the only *good* art. Everything else is *problematic*. This appreciation of culture is not concerned with the artistic representation of the world in the work but is measured against the benchmarks and catechisms of easily verifiable numbers (who is seen how many times, who gets to say how many words) to see whether it passes the test—whether it can be accepted as part of the good cause or must be dismissed as an obstacle. These dismissals are usually formulated in terms of failing these identity representation tests. The film is too White, too male, too ableist, too *problematic*.

"Representation matters" is the watchword that this elite has written on its banner. To the PMC mindset, public institutions need to demonstrate visibly to people that they are valued members of society. Hence the demands for "inclusivity." The grim alternative, as Ahmed hints, is that people regress into barbarism.

THE LOGIC OF POLITICS IS ALSO THE LOGIC OF ART—BOTH ARE LOST IN THE POST-POLITICAL

Anti-politics emerged because of the foreclosure of politics after "the end of history." The cultural dimension of post-politics engendered a similar foreclosure of the experience of culture as culture in its own terms. The rejection of "woke aesthetics" is an expression of this. The potential of art to transcend given parameters of meaning is denied if it cannot be seen in and of itself. If art is pressed into service to fulfill a social role, it is limited by the ideological parameters of social engineering. Lately, the parameters are those of post-politics.

More than anything, post-politics is the impasse of the politics of the left. The left's abandonment of not only of class politics, but a theoretical foundation of societal development as dialectical, as a process of constant change through negation, has brought about a situation where not just politics but also art can only be understood as what Trotsky called "art with a tendency,"[25] that is, art that serves an ideological purpose, especially that of the ruling class. Art for its own sake is just as foreclosed as politics itself. Increasingly, the functions of film or TV shows as art or entertainment is secondary to their functions as ideological artifacts intended to shape society. Art is denied the possibility of meaning something in its own right, something outside the contemporary conventions of identity politics, to have value *as it is*. Concomitantly, we as spectator-consumers are denied the opportunity of experiencing art and entertainment to their full potential, of representing not just one monolithic idea but also the contradictions within it.

This represents a closing down of the potential of the individual to grow as a subject, a thwarting of subjectivity as an active process. Both art and politics depend on the possibility of the subject constituting itself through a check against social narratives. Through art, people have the potential to free themselves imaginatively, and through politics, people can make their own history. History is not "one damn thing after another" (as Henry Ford is alleged to have said), it is, in a Hegelian sense, a process of achieving a collective self-awareness within each individual. The subject as an individual is able, through dialectical experiences, to glean and appreciate ever greater notions of freedom, a *Weltgeist*, Hegel's term for collective self-awareness.[26] Every subject has the means—the ability to reason—to engage in history-making. To test their experiences through reason. However, this "check in" with reality is foreclosed in the woke aesthetic, in the tendential art of the post-political. The culture industry is firmly in the hands of ideological regulators; rules around representation are demanded from almost all sources of cultural production. The resulting shows, films, plays, and dramas are not genuine. The art *feels* inauthentic because *it is* inauthentic: it is prescribed. The logic of the piece does not come from the art itself but from external rules of representation. The internal logic of art, where the contradictions of real life are negotiated into a new form, is thwarted by the demands of the woke agenda.

Woke art is rejected not because it tells one truth over another, but because it is experienced as limited, much as the neoliberal deadlock of politics is experienced as unsatisfactory. The rejection of dialectics as a model to understand history has been paralleled by a rejection of dialectics as a means to make and enjoy culture.

THE EXPERIENCE OF REPRESENTATION

That art relies on phenomenal concepts of representation—how things appear to us—is self-evident. Phenomenologically, representation is the physical experience of what and how people encounter what is. How does it feel? The phenomenological experience, as described by one of the first thinkers of phenomenology, Edmund Husserl (1859–1938), relies on empathy (literally *Einfühlen*, feeling into) as the method of intersubjectivity—an appreciation of the other through one's own "lived body."[27] To communicate ideas through recounting the sensations of lived experience.[28] What is a filmic experience if not an absolute phenomenological experience, an experience of ourselves within our very own bodies, sometimes accompanied by physical reactions such as goose bumps, disgust, or chills? From the visceral thrills we experience watching *Alien* to the heartache experienced when listening to Puccini's *O Mio Babbino Caro*—through art at its best, be it popular or highbrow, we feel aroused, angry, enlivened, disturbed and joyous. We feel beauty and we feel alive.

This experience is the *sublime*. The sublime is the physical experience of what is greater than us. In his *Critique of Judgment*, Kant describes how the experience of the sublime is one of absolute truth, through which we can elevate ourselves over nature.[29] For Hegel, the absolute truth revealed through the sublime is the closest it is possible to experience the universal or *Weltgeist*.[30] It is a fleeting moment of universal connection to every other human being. For Schiller, it was through the sublime that we actually *feel* freedom: "Wir fühlen uns frei beim Erhabenen," roughly translated—through the sublime, we feel free.[31]

THE LIMITS OF CULTURAL THEORY

However, these liberating ideals have been replaced by other, arguably more anti-humanist approaches to the experience of art. Building on Husserl and Merleau-Ponty's arguments, that meaning is created by experiencing the world through one's body, cultural theorists such as Judith Butler see the phenomenological experience itself as deterministic, determining the self as a subject.[32] People are cast as subjects constructed through discourse but with no possibility of a dialectical or political counter narrative—in essence, either a victim or victor of circumstance, or just "bodies." In postcolonial and feminist film studies the representations of non-White people, women and non-straight people is often analyzed in the way these are presented as desirable objects. A deterministic gaze fetishizes and, in the spirit of postmodern culture theory, constructs these racist and sexist attitudes as all determining power structures.

Doubtless, women and non-White people have been portrayed in a fetishistic and stereotypical manner. Crucially, though, these portrayals lose their power through the progress of history. Few people today would deny that Mickey Rooney's character Mr. I. Y. Yunioshi in *Breakfast at Tiffany's* (1961) was not just insensitive but a crude, racist stereotype. Yet while it is perfectly possible to argue that the historically conditioned attitudes that underpin this stereotype and allowed it to function are no longer present in society, this possibility is denied by cultural theory; the character is not simply a relic but has the same racist affect as it did in 1961, when the Oscar-winning movie was screened.

From this perspective, an individual's self-determination is done through a culturally constructed identity, via socially correct or woke aesthetics. Images that are not woke are seen as dangerous, if not outright violent. Just like the real physical cruelties done to them in the past, women and minorities today must endure the pain caused by cultural effect on their bodies. The body, especially non-White, able, and female bodies, endure the phenomenological affects induced by insensitive representations in culture. This is often referred to as systemic or symbolic violence, Bourdieu's term for "the imposition on subordinated groups by the dominant class of an ideology which legitimates and naturalizes the status quo."[33] Moreover, seeing one's identity group humiliated induces real pain in the individual—even, or especially, if the event is not directly related to the individual. If racism is nothing more than a structural phenomenon even real-life princesses like Meghan Markle can be understood as victims of oppression. Culture thus serves as a tool of oppression and power. This is how "offensive" representations are seen as literally harmful by contemporary activists and trigger warnings need to be applied.

In one way, Bourdieu's concept of the cultural imposition of the dominant group makes sense. As Marx wrote, "The ideas of the ruling class are in every epoch the ruling ideas."[34] But where Marx describes how the *material* power the dominant class has expresses itself as the dominant *intellectual* force, cultural theorists, following Foucault, understand power as an entity in itself. Rather than material inequality, cultural theoreticians conclude that it is the symbolically loaded cultural structures that promote discrimination. Superficially, this analysis is seductive. If people can be nice as individuals, it must be society that makes them bigoted and biased. The idea of structures sustaining themselves through ahistorical systems, such as patriarchy and racism, perfectly and easily explains subjective experiences of marginalization. In this spirit, a goal of activism today is to trawl through the productions and producers of culture and "look for the power imbalances, bigotry, and biases that it assumes must be present and pick at them."[35] Contemporary activism concentrates on signs and signifiers, structures and systems of race and gender, and sees its aim as generating equal opportunities through means of diversity policies in all institutions. In this sense, cultural theory has become the ideological handmaiden of Third Way politics.

THE EMPTYING OUT OF ART

The most forceful critiques of cultural products today—the most vivid, with most purchase and cultural clout—are in terms of the politics of identity. These critiques are often expressed as a policing of both the content and production of culture. A small but obvious manifestation of this is the growing application of trigger warnings to even the most innocent TV or streaming shows, such as Disney's decision in 2021 to put a trigger warning on several episodes of *The Muppet Show* (1976–1981), or in more extreme cases their removal from public circulation altogether. Often these decisions are based on the depiction of obvious stereotypes, many of them clearly offensive, such as the singing Siamese cats in *Lady and the Tramp* (1955).

However, by deciding for the public a priori on the nature and content of what is offensive, the burden of interpretation no longer lies with the viewer. They are relieved of making moral choices, as they could get it "wrong." Moreover, they are freed from the possibility of experiencing contradiction—something that has profound artistic and subjective potential beyond feelings of righteousness. What if, for example, we are fully aware of the nasty stereotyping of Asian people by the two cats called Si and Am in *Lady and the Tramp* but we also, simultaneously, fully enjoy their Disney Villain nastiness and catchy musical number? As viewers we must test our own moral fiber to see where this contradiction could take us. Only if we are free to reach our own conclusions—if we experience cultural things in themselves—can we make truly moral choices.

The music of Richard Wagner is complex and meaningful, not despite his anti-Semitism, but because its magnificence makes us face our own contradictions as we listen to it. The traditional counterargument against moralistic condemnation of unpalatable artists, that of separating the art from the artist, is inadequate. Not only is it impossible to separate the art from the artist but also it is a denial of the contradiction between them, the phenomenological experience of art as experienced through our own consciousness, is part of the sublime experience of art.

The institutional employment of trigger warnings today is somewhat more sinister. Under the guise of public care, that which now constitutes social progress, and the right way to see social problems through the prism of identity is prescribed by those who have no problem with the neoliberal order itself.

The content of trigger warnings, beyond their immediate banality, is the bolstering of authority for an external self-selected arbiter of the meaning of cultural products, and the delineation of what is felt to be acceptable and unacceptable content. The targets of trigger warnings under question are precisely race, gender, and so on. The sum-total of these tendencies is a straightjacketing of cultural forms and themes.

Worse still, not only are there many unsolicited online critics proclaiming that they can't watch certain shows anymore, because they are "too problematic," many of the critics writing for the world's many prestigious magazines, such as Richard Brody from the New Yorker, frequently judges a film by the tropes of neoliberal identity politics, the film's lack of politically correct representation stopping his enjoyment. Here, Quentin Tarantino's movie *Once Upon a Time . . . in Hollywood* is reduced to "a ridiculously white movie" in which Tarantino, old White man that he is, fails to acknowledge the changing world outside his fantasy.[36]

In his own narrow worldview, Brody is right. When seen through a woke lens, *Once Upon a Time . . . in Hollywood* is "ridiculously white." But, freed from the obligations of woke, the film, with its contradictory elements of cinematic beauty and violence, visual languidness and provocations, provides a far greater experience of cinematic storytelling than is otherwise permitted. The film itself provokes the tumultuous and unnerving experience of being made to process one's own attraction to what is seen.

However, when what is seen as "the right way" to understand art is equated with what is seen as "the right way" to be in-the-world, aka *woke*, the concept of woke is an imposition on truth. If, in the case of *Once Upon a Time . . . in Hollywood*, it is not judged by its representation quota of minorities or with one of the feminist cinematic tests, it is a bad film. In this ideological annexation of meaning, only *Good* Art, art that is woke, is *good* art.

CONCLUSION

The popular rejection of woke culture is an expression of anti-politics and not merely a culture war over the specifics of cultural artifacts that can be taken at face value. This tendency is a development of the ways in which cultural theory both coincides with and expresses a Fukuyamaian *End of History*. The rejection of woke is the cultural version of what the creators of the political podcast *Aufhebunga Bunga* call *Anti*-politics: a public acting out when confronted with the deadlock of neoliberal consensus politics, or post-politics.

The populist rejection of the woke aesthetic is typically an acting out against impositions on the enjoyment of the art itself, pithily exemplified by YouTube Gamer AlphaOmegaSin: "They (SJWs) want fucking control over art and artist's creativity. I say fuck that and fuck them."[37] What is rejected is not the idea of equality but the censorious quality of woke aesthetics, its denial that art can be enjoyed and experienced in its own terms, that is to say, having the freedom of "grasping the point (the essential meaning) of an art object or art form."[38] The inability of critics of woke aesthetics to make a case for art in its own terms is an invitation for the advocates of woke to condemn these criticisms as "complainants denying their 'white privilege.'"[39]

The political arguments against the politics of diversity such as equal ops, with cultural representation as its chosen mechanism, have been made many times (see W.B. Michaels or A. Reed Jr.[40]). It does not work on its own terms, insofar as it does not facilitate greater equality. On the contrary, it limits people's freedoms, obscures real inequalities, and serves too easily as an ideological midwife to that which it is supposedly fighting, racism and sexism.

The artistic arguments against diversity as a mode of cultural production and critical consumption have been made less frequently. An obvious but frequently overlooked aspect of this broad phenomenon is that "woke culture" tends to produce bad, stunted art, and with it a jaded, cynical viewing public. Artist Franklin Einspruch says about the woke bureaucracy, "It positions art subordinately as a work-servant to democracy, justice, and communities. It characterizes art as a location where we—all of us—express ourselves, thus troping art as a toilet."[41]

The culture war encourages political readings of cultural objects at the expense of art itself. In one sense, the idea that people shape society through art and culture is not controversial. Art is both a mirror of social relations as well as, as Brecht describes it, a "hammer" with which to shape the world. People have always partaken of culture and enjoyed and produced art on these terms. But postmodern cultural theories reject history as human-made social change or progress. The failure of history to create a more inclusive world for women and non-White people is seen as a failure of the historical process itself. Thus, the adherence by contemporary leftists to post-politics. Cultural theory has provided a theoretical basis for the assumption that culture determines social relations.

In a narrow sense, this is not unreasonable. What things and people mean to one another is a social construction. But cultural theory also assumes that this happens to people as objects, via immaterial power systems. What is excluded in this assumption is that people are subjects, and have, potentially, a means to break these chains of meaning through their ability to imagine, question, think and ultimately bring about new ideas. In short, the process of history is what produces real structural change.

NOTES

1. See Chartered Institute of Marketing 2020.
2. For a useful evaluation, see Romano 2020.
3. I talk about the Oscars at Thom 2019.
4. Jameson 1992, 1.
5. Fukuyama, 1992; Hegel 1924 (*Einleitung*).
6. Hochuli et al. 2021, 45.
7. Ibid., 57.
8. As Anne Applebaum comments in the *Washington Post*, "The most energetic form of populism is 'right-wing.'" Applebaum 2016.
9. Gomez-Mejia 2020, 309.
10. Hall 1997, 17.
11. Appiah 2010, 110.
12. Ibid., 198.
13. Malik 2009, 176.
14. Moore 2021.
15. Bush 2021.
16. Hall 1997, 50.
17. Reed 2019.
18. The catchphrase "You have to see it to be it!" is attributed to the former tennis champion Billie Jean King talking about how girls are inspired by seeing women participate in sports.
19. Ahmed 2017.
20. Ibid.
21. See the BBC 2021.
22. See Liu 2021.
23. Ehrenreich and Ehrenreich 1979, 12.
24. Johnston 2017.
25. Trotsky 1923.
26. See Hegel 1807.
27. Smith and Smith 1995, 71.
28. Smith 2018.
29. Kant 1790.
30. Hegel 1807.
31. Schiller 1897.
32. Butler 2011, 176.
33. See Oxford Reference, *Symbolic violence*. https://www.oxfordreference.com/view/10.1093/oi/authority.20110803100546777 . Accessed June 4, 2021.
34. Marx 1845.

35. Pluckrose and Lindsay 2020, 128.
36. Brody 2019.
37. AlphaOmegaSin 2015.
38. Dutton 1974, 247.
39. O'Hagan 2020.
40. Michaels 2016 and Reed 2018.
41. Einspruch 2020.

Chapter 9

On What Art Is Not

Or Art as a Left-Wing Hobby

Haseeb Ahmed

It has become increasingly difficult to know how my artwork will be received or by whom. While solitude is often an important part of creation, artists do not live in or for isolation. The anticipation of the experience an artwork might induce is part of what gives it form. I find myself resorting to increasingly authoritarian means like creating large-scale installations which impose the place and time needed for thought and consideration. It is no coincidence that film is the dominant medium of our time. Through this chapter I draw on my experiences as an artist, an educator, and my experiences on the Left over the past fifteen years. Continuing to practice without returning to the question of reception has become increasingly difficult.

It is not that the form of subjectivity we share has been lost but rather it is our capacity to know it that has regressed. Eager for change in a truncated existence, many celebrate the proliferation of identities as evidence that a major social transformation has occurred. Ignoring all that reminds us that life in capitalism persists requires an exhaustive self- and social censorship. It is no surprise that "emotional labor" is added to the division. In this society, artists are ascribed the role of creating documents that fulfill these identities and validate the broader social vision. But when did this supposed transformation occur? Is it the fate of these artworks to be shredded to create confetti for the party? Perhaps yes, and moreover this is a justifiable or at least inevitable fate for artworks that will be forgotten for not attempting to transcend the form of prescriptions handed down.

The history of art can attest that there is no clear link between the political or even moral orientation of an artist and their ability to produce profound works of art. Unable to resolve this problem, those who would relegate artists to a representative role would rather prevent the work of questionable artists from being seen at all. At least Plato made a reasoned case for his ban of artists from the Republic. Today, artists only wish they could be honored with such regard. The difficulty for proponents of identity politics today arises in that art is not merely representation. A negation of what exists in favor of what could be lies at the core of each artwork, fulfilling its autonomy and indicating the possibility of a society that has redeemed its potential. In the following chapter I will show that the Left has reduced its concept of art to one of illustration which parrallels the dimished stakes of its ideology—whereas art once accessed freedom, universality, happiness, and emancipation for the Left.

In his 1934 essay "Artist as Producer," Walter Benjamin clearly explains how the political import of an artwork is derived from how an artist employs technique to reconfigure conventions of its time, rather than through the artist's political allegiances. A challenge I face in writing this chapter is that much of what the present demands as a response has already been said more clearly nearly a century ago by authors who benefited from clarifying their ideas through contemporary ideological struggles and their histories. In part this chapter reconstructs that political trajectory as I have partially received it. However, I also draw on my experiences as an artist today starting with this paradox: even the artist herself is subject to the effects of her own work as if it were made by another. This is how each artwork is implicitly social. Moreover, no artist can know exactly what they are doing as it has not been done before, if at least by virtue of the extreme particularity of their self-assigned task. It is in the capacity to make particularity universally relatable that the kernel of utopia lies.

For myself and those I know personally, becoming an artist often requires perseverance despite tremendous essential and existential uncertainty. Why do we put up with it? Many only do so for a time. Even those artists who are spared the essential uncertainty of generating income from their practice, being supported by generational wealth, are not spared the existential task implicit in creating meaning through material—as art. When speaking to my fellow artists I am reminded of the vortical form of a hurricane. Despite my own artistic preoccupation with the medium of air and wind, this figure holds. The center, the eye of the storm, remains seemingly empty while it is given form by the clouds revolving around it. Each artist sustains themselves on a vision of what truly fulfilling their concept would look and *feel* like. In a recent interview I conducted with the artist Latifa Echakhch she described it as such:

> The beginning of a love story is something that sounds so exceptional, so magical, but you are in the same state of mind as thousands of others. Everything sounds exceptional but it's not. I would love it if people recalled the first month of their love story when seeing my work. That would be a nice present for

them—do you remember these magical things? The materiality of the work is not exceptional, it's like a dry ruin of a memory. It could be seen as dramatic, but the potentiality of the moments is in the perception and not in the reality of the installation, which is just objects on a carpet tinted with black ink—it's actually quite dry and raw.[1]

The true fulfillment of an artwork would be the resolution of the antinomy of form and content in the minds of both the artist and the viewer. That which divides form and content also separates the conceptual object from the material thing, the subject from the object. Unable to overcome these fissures in reality, each artwork must be seen as an attempt to do so. Here art offers an analog to politics. These attempts are not unlike the Marxian drive to forge a society adequate to what we know are its potential capacities.

A NOTE ON MAKING ART

Artworks often do not turn out as anticipated. I am often surprised by the idiosyncratic logics exclusive to each work I make. The process of making art resembles a kind of schizophrenia. When making a painting, an artist steps back from the canvas to see it in full. However, in those steps a shift in subjectivity occurs. She looks at the painting as though through the eyes of another or any other person, as the anticipated viewer of the work, encountering it at some point in the future and some other place. She cannot know who that person is nor assume that they share the same gender, age, ethnicity, or education. With nothing being assured, a "universal subject" is constituted.

Walter Benjamin describes a similar occurrence when going out to dinner after having taken hashish. "I became my own most skillful, fond, shameless procurer, gratifying myself with the ambiguous assurance of one who knows from the profound study of the wishes of his employer."[2] A person having worked all day might say, "I deserve a break, to shop, or (in the case above) a nice meal." This split is an indication of how we can address ourselves as both subject and object. The ability to objectify oneself allows for the modulation between the employee and employer, self and other, and artist and the viewer. The ability of an artwork to mediate between the two gives the sense that maybe this seemingly intractable fissure can be commensurate.

Colloquially known as "audience" or "viewer," this universal subject is affirmed by being the anticipated audience of nearly every artwork. This founding of a "universal subject" is a utopian capacity on the verge of collapse. As a product of the European Enlightenment, it sits in contradiction with the racist policies enacted during colonialism. A dialectical method would seek what remains in this contradiction. This is a matter of necessity as the totalization caused by the latter has left little alternative. The anticipation of this universalized viewer is what holds the disparate art world together. It forms the premise of every artistic institution. This anonymous subject is continually actualized through an ever-varying group of people recorded in history. Is the specification of an audience through racial categories, as contemporary discourse suggests, an improvement? Museums are now ubiquitously referred to as "white institutions," but is this not an affirmation of the racialized world view that is presumed to be the object of critique? If we identify the bourgeois class with "old white men," how can we account for the many who are neither "white," nor old, nor men—as the composition of the boards of those museums can attest globally?

ART ACTING ON PERCEPTION, PERCEPTION ACTING ON REALITY

The most powerful experiences I have had with artworks hinge on their alteration of my perception of reality afterward. This notable shift throws into relief the otherwise unaddressed norms of perception. Suddenly the hues of light filtered through tinted glass appear strange and uncanny. A cool breeze no longer seems innocent or anonymous and is subject to suspicion. By creating a representation of a phenomenon, a divergence occurs between itself and an image of itself, and neither contains the whole. In response to a much-tortured question, this is the true political potential of art. The object of an artwork is fractured. It can no longer go on in identity with itself and is now open to become more or less than what it was.

The violence that the image enacts against the object is substantial. In this act of negation, a new space of creation is made. It's for this reason that contemporary artwork is implicitly secular. A contemporary artistic treatment of a religious subject would not leave it intact as an object faithfully manifesting a divine order. Even when an artist attempts to act in service of an identity, he either undermines it or produces a compromised work of art. Today even the liberal value of secularity is contested as a threat to the multiculturalism that liberalism itself has mobilized to preserve from the 1970s till the present.[3] Forms of liberalism recruit or even sacrifice artworks in their competition to define the inclusive society. In so doing, they erode the fundamental capacity for ambiguity that is the basis for which each artwork can attest its singularity. What is at stake is imagination, freed from what appears as necessary into what it can now become. Prescriptive artworks foreclose imagination, reducing it to an illustration of what already exists.

Much of the efforts of artists over the past 200 years have pushed against the boundaries of what can be considered art. This is what has made art an analog for the story of freedom. History is not necessarily linear nor humanity necessarily progressive. For example, the present situation compels me to define what cannot be considered an artwork. To be generous, we can say no *good* artwork is an illustration of prefigured ideas. I appeal to the faculty of aesthetic judgment to which all of humanity has a right, but which many political actors today would deny the artist in the name of humanity.

COLLAPSING HORIZONS OF ART CRITICISM, ART, AND IDEOLOGY

The shift in perception precipitated by the experience of an artwork is what Susan Buck-Morss calls a "critical moment."[4] Critical in that it induces a productive crisis as described earlier, but also in the sense of critical theory, which is a synonym for Marxian theory conceived during an era of political repression.[5] For Buck-Morss, this critical moment is sustained through art criticism and preserved in art history. An artwork's capacity for indeterminacy makes it unique among commodities. Once an artwork exists, anyone can form meaning from their experience of it. The meaning intended by the artist is only one among many possible outcomes and not necessarily privileged. Any viewer engages their faculty of judgment and hence criticism when they present their own experiences for judgment by, for instance, asking what one sees and why. How is this object meaningful, if at all?

One only needs to open any of the major art publications to see that art criticism has become marketing and advertisement. It appears an exhibition may not have happened at all if not solicited through the E-Flux mailing list at 2.000 Euros a go, or written up in *Art Review*. By consistently reading dedicated critics, their ideological orientation could be delineated. For instance, Susan Buck-Morss and the milieu around the journal *October* can be traced to a New Left attempting to distinguish itself from the supposed Marxist orthodoxy of Clement Greenberg who defined the stakes of artistic autonomy through his apologia for minimalism and abstract expressionism in the postwar period, whereas Jerry Saltz, senior art critic for *New York Magazine*, is the most vocal critic today and consistently presents Democratic Party positions as radical. The stakes of art criticism have greatly diminished or vanished altogether, and one can ask, if this is so, has the social capacity of art gone with it when this is left unaddressed?

In the absence of art criticism, artists have adapted or compromised to create artworks that receive themselves. This can take many forms, like placing increasing trust in a hyper-rationality where artworks demonstrate a foolproof internal logic.[6] A new degree of investment in the quintessential artistic gesture[7] leads back to the incontestable locus of creation, authorship, which was prematurely declared dead. As a research-based artist I often work collaboratively and anticipate the reception of my work by making this milieu the first audience for my work that is as broad as the disparate disciplines I mobilize in its production.

This is a vicissitude of a broader historical collapse of ideologies tasked with the overcoming of capital in favor of an emancipated society. For an artist, the political horizon is experienced as the possibility of what is communicable. The question "How is art political?" is no longer addressed in terms of how freedom can affect our perception and, hence, reality but rather in terms of how art can deliver a message. Whether given enthusiastically or under coercive pressure, artists today often offer their artistic license[8] to be used as a political instrument. The liquidation of the wide range of possibilities of art for its relatively narrow propagandistic function speaks to the desperation in politics today, especially when considering the bottom line that only a relatively small amount of people is even interested in art. The relationship between the political vanguards and artistic avant-gardes of the past had a radically different historical character, as I will explain here.

WHAT DOES ART HAVE TO DO WITH FREEDOM IN THE LEFT'S PERCEPTION?

After completing my Master's Thesis at the MIT Program in Art, Culture, and Technology, I went to the Jan van Eyck Academie in Maastricht, the Netherlands, for a two-year (2011–2013) research fellowship in fine art. Within six months of my arrival, I saw the newly empowered Dutch coalition government[9] approve devastating cuts to culture sector funding, together with cuts to education, mental health care, and immigration services. The cuts marked a sharp turn to the Right in Dutch politics, while the opposition revealed a deeply demobilized Left.

The largest opposition demonstration came on June 27, 2011, the eve of the debate that finalized the cuts to the culture sector. The demonstrations involved an estimated 10,000 people, many of whom had marched from Rotterdam in what was called the March of Civilization. Their slogans included "In Defense of Culture" and "No Culture No Future." The protests had no effect. The chosen path of defending culture per se led to a flattened ahistorical and even apolitical imagination. Its political content existed only insofar as one could equate culture to a supposed vanguard of civilization and art and civilization itself with progress. Its argument was that a cut to culture was a step backward toward barbarism. However, we know that culture too can be barbaric, especially when it portrays progress without acknowledging unfolding social catastrophes. Artists ought to know that the representation of barbarism too can be wielded strategically.

Geert Wilders, leader of the far-right PVV, expressed his support for the Secretary of Culture Halbe Zijlstra's measures when he said, "Art is a Leftwing hobby."[10] In fact, his statement has more nuanced political content than that of the would-be Left's attempt to claim stewardship over civilization itself.[11] There are a number of ways of interpreting it. Wilders recognizes the opportunism of the Left in its use of art to push multicultural identarian politics, which are in direct conflict to his monocultural identarian politics. I confess that my own provocation in conveying this statement comes from the desire to reconstitute the dialectical relationship between the Left and artistic production and to pose a critique of the apolitical character of the culture sector in the Netherlands and internationally.

To the would-be Left, Wilders and the PVV are clearly a far-right party. However, Wilders is more willing to call the Left by its name than the opposition of culture sector activists for fear that such a "label" may have reduced their public appeal. This is a role-reversal. Leszek Kołakowski expresses clearly that

> the Right, as a conservative force, needs no utopia; its essence is the affirmation of existing conditions—a fact and not a utopia—or else, the desire to revert to a state which was once an accomplished fact. The Right strives to idealize actual conditions, not to change them. What it needs is fraud, not utopia. The Left cannot give up utopia because it is a real force even when it is merely a utopia.[12]

If we do not want to make recourse to the Right to define the Left then we must appeal to history to recover the concept of the Left that is apparently lost today.

Marxian thinkers have consistently preoccupied themselves with art in the attempt to elaborate an emancipatory political project—but why? Kołakowski contends that the utopian is essential to the Left. The link between utopia, imagination, and art is an integral one. However, let us address this question without any preconceptions and begin by assuming nothing. Prehistorically giving thought a material form allowed for a correspondence between the two as magic. The Marxist art historian Ernst Fischer elaborates that

> this magic role of art has progressively given way to the role of illumination of social relationships, of enlightening men in societies becoming opaque, of helping men to recognize and change social reality. A highly complex society with its multiple relationship and social contradictions can no longer be represented in the manner of a myth. In such a society, which demands literal recognition and all-embracing consciousness, there is bound to be an overwhelming need

to break through the rigid forms of earlier ages where the magic element still operated, and to arrive at more open forms—at the freedom, say, of the novel.[13]

We may presume that the importance of the advent of the novel may now seem dramatically underwhelming to us, but the freedom that, for example, Trotsky offers to art is not. He states that

> our Marxist conception of the objective social dependence and social utility of art, when translated into the language of politics, does not at all mean a desire to dominate art by means of decrees and orders. It is not true that we regard only that art as new and revolutionary which speaks of the worker, and it is nonsense to say that we demand that the poets should describe inevitably a factory chimney, or the uprising against capital! Of course, the new art cannot but place the struggle of the proletariat in the center of its attention. But the plough of the new art is not limited to numbered strips. On the contrary, it must plough the entire field in all directions. Personal lyrics of the very smallest scope have an absolute right to exist within the new art. Moreover, the new man cannot be formed without a new lyric poetry. But to create it, the poet himself must feel the world in a new way.[14]

By contrast, influential contemporary art theory like *Relational Aesthetics*[15] would attempt to assert the social function of art by having artists wash dishes or prepare meals.[16] This is a greatly impoverished recognition of the artist's capacities. Today it is as though artists are recruited in service of an economy of representation, in which the frequency of appearance relates somehow to actual equality. We can draw upon Trotsky's conception of art from the history of the Left to track the degree of regression today.

The liberation of art from exclusive religious or aristocratic employment, to define its own being, was proclaimed as *l'art pour l'art* by many at the end of the nineteenth century. In the galleries or museums today, one might hear this statement uttered as an indictment of art's irrelevance to society by a viewer who is its self-appointed jurist—justifiably so, as explained above. Insofar as an artist can make whatever they can conceive of, it is the freest form of commodity production available to us today. What materializes can illuminate the social conditions of imagination. In this way art presents itself as an analog for the status of freedom within capital. Following Trotsky, the capacity for a political movement to recognize this function indicates the extent of its emancipatory character.

Within the context of extremely poor working conditions of the Industrial Revolution, the socialist and pioneering industrial designer William Morris (1834–1896) saw art as a model for the possibility of unalienated labor. His *Arts and Crafts Movement*'s slow hand production of medieval furniture would allow English workers to identify with their work, but this did not bring workers closer to freedom. Moreover, the movement itself was untenable and unprofitable. While an impressive undertaking, Morris failed to realize that freedom lies in alienated capitalist labor itself, as its novel contribution, which alienated labor in feudalism did not entail. If we do not identify with our labor, then we can become something other than what we do. Even today, the anxious and destructive character of modern life under capitalism sends some of us fleeing back to farm labor, tiny houses, and communes. The Marxist scholar Elena Louisa Lange (co-editor of the present volume) and myself created the artwork "Fetish/Non-Fetish" for the exhibition Transactions in 2016[17] to address that tendency. Marxian thought degenerated into the genre of culture criticism typically equates consumerism with fetishism without registering the dynamic by which a fetish itself is constituted. However,

> in his Critique of Political Economy, Marx intended to highlight the fetish-forms that come to dominate the people in the capitalist mode of production. To him, the commodity form, money, and capital were fundamental fetishes. Because, instead of being understood as categories of a particular social and historical production mode, they come to be reified as the "eternal natural forms of social production." Today, these classic fetishes have been joined by new forms that suggest capitalism can be organised more "justly" or "humanely"—think of "Fair Trade," "sustainability," the critique of "consumerism" or "distributive justice"—and thereby sure enough precluding the idea that *capitalism as such* can be abolished. FETISH/NON-FETISH contrasts these "new" fetishes of capitalism with innocuous and likeable non-fetishes, which in the topsy-turvy world of capital are however perceived as such. Yet, neither the spawns of pop culture, nor collector's crazes, nor sex utensils present the true fetishes of capitalist society.[18]

Money itself is commonly seen as the penultimate fetish. This attitude clearly manifests itself in the contemporary art world which, generally speaking, is composed of three different realms: institutions like museums, art academia, and commercial galleries. The latter is typically regarded by the former as corrupted, because it is financed through the sale of art, while state subsidy is regarded as "clean money." I have had the good fortune of being represented by Harlan Levey Projects since 2015.[19] During this time, I have the gallery cultivate artists' practices over the course of years while opening their doors to the general public without neither entry costs nor public funding. Artworks are commodities that attempt to demonstrate the possibility of the autonomy from this form. This negative bias against commercial galleries is delusional. It results from affirming the *attempt* while the rest of the world operates within the totality of capital. As a largely unregulated market, the art world can offer insight into how value is created from its moment of creation through its various transactions.

Capitalism brought both freedom and art into being as we know them today. Of both we may ask: What constrains the emancipation which we know to be possible? Paradoxically, by rupturing divine order maintained through ritual, modernity's most profound responsibility ascribed to art may be the introduction of the possibility of producing meaninglessness itself. Each artist oscillates between the extremes of producing meaning, something originally reserved for gods, or creating a thing that is even less valuable than the material and the time that went into making it.

This waste is an unforgivable failure for a society premised on the persistence of exchange value. Before condemning it, we can recognize each artwork as an attempt to overcome the meaninglessness that would otherwise prevail, just as society must create forms of organization adequate to its potential, beyond those seemingly ordained. Despite many attempts to escape, artists inevitably produce commodities because no artwork can change the fact that we still live within totalized capitalism where the inevitable commodity is people themselves, via the valuation of their time. Paradoxically, those artworks created to break the commodity form only demonstrate the commodity's flexibility.

Art history can be a record of this struggle to create both forms of meaning and unmask its objective constraints. For instance, the changing perception of a unique artwork over time can realize the deep historical contingency of subjectivity itself. To continue the analogy, the historically specific possibility for freedom must be redeemed through the transformation of the conditions of capital that make this endeavor possible.

DENIAL

To be the beneficiary of the history of the radical Left, one must read this history through its staggering failures, which as of yet provide no resolution that could fulfill the promise of a truly emancipated society. For this reason, thought taboos abound, and it is difficult to trace the origin of popular political ideas today. For instance, the furtive influence of Stalinism on contemporary Left thinking is yet to be accounted for. The artist, like the bourgeois intellectual, has no necessary social basis. Instead, the persistence of artists and intellectuals express what society can become if the supposedly necessary were to be revealed as mere presumption.

Making the point of this historical contingency can often only be done from the most contingent social positions themselves. This too is a perennial problem. In *Minima Moralia*, Adorno puts it this way:

That intellectuals are at once beneficiaries of a bad society, and yet those on whose socially useless work it largely depends whether a society emancipated from utility is achieved—this is not a contradiction acceptable once and for all and therefore irrelevant. It gnaws incessantly at the objective quality of their work. Whatever the intellectual does is wrong.[20]

AUTONOMY AND ART THEN AND NOW

In February 2021 I began teaching art to second-year bachelor students at a school in the Netherlands. Most of my students are no older than twenty-five. Individualized studio production lies at the core of what is called *Autonomous Art* (*Autonome Kunst*) education in the Netherlands. While this phrasing is unique to the Dutch-speaking context, the association of art and autonomy is a relic of Marxian thought. New Left activism embedded this thought figure in educational reform in the 1970s. While the term "autonomous art" may not be used in other educational systems, the sentiment is certainly shared.

Today the concept of autonomous art can be valuable if recalled as a question: Is it possible for art to be autonomous at all, and if so, autonomous of what? This is certainly the question of Trotsky and Adorno mentioned earlier, and many others. How can we see the struggle for the autonomy of art as a symptom engendered and constrained by modern capitalist society? Specific to my current art school's curriculum is that while theory and production are emphasized, art history has almost no place. This also conveys its origins in the New Left ethos committed to spontaneity at the expense of attention to historical circumstance, a tendency attributed to the old and failed Left.

We can start to rectify this by situating the concept of the autonomy of art as itself historically specific to the advent of capital. In *Sustaining Loss: Art and the Mournful Life*, Gregg Horowitz observes that "art, which ought to articulate the boundary between nature and culture, between the divinely ordered and the freely fabricated, instead makes that boundary impossible to stabilize, because art, set free from academic and aristocratic norms, appears now as asocial." This asocial character is a source of its potential autonomy—indicating that it just might be able to survive regardless of society.[21] In his essay "Modernist Painters," the Marxist art critic Clement Greenberg offers an apologia for abstract expressionism and minimalist sculpture, those artistic movements most often associated with autonomous art. These movements were a retreat into form to preserve something of itself from the barbaric regressions of the postwar period and its vicissitudes.[22] Their hermetic character is taken positively today as portraying the autonomy as art.

OBSERVATIONS ON AN ART STUDENT'S STRUGGLE, 2006–2021

This subtitle might suggest the significance of radical student organizing. However, that legacy is not the one of which I can speak yet. As a lecturer (or *docent* in Dutch) I enter students' studios for individual visits that often feel modeled on psychoanalysis sessions. In these moments, my contribution to their development is to ask questions about their work, their research, and their feelings toward both. My questions are often versions of the following: How do we give form to our desires and from where do these desires arise? Are these desires really, or only, our own? Considering an artwork, from its conception, as a form of wish-fulfillment brings to light its utopian character and its possible expression of a death drive. In either case, artworks today often appear as fragments that call for a forensic capacity to grasp their meaning.

In the wake of the killing of George Floyd in the summer of 2020, proclaimed *Black Lives Matter* protests rippled through Belgium and the Netherlands in solidarity with those of the United States. These protests adapted *Black Lives Matter* to regional concerns by calling for the end of Zwarte Piet, Saint Nicholas' Black servants' appearance in annual Christmas parades. A small number of my students are not White. While their ethnicities vary, they share an internal struggle resulting from a perceived demand that they invest their creative will into a response to their own supposed oppression as people of color. This is not something that the non-people of color students have had to concern themselves with.[23] Perhaps this is also how racial inequality manifests itself. The potency lies in the internal confusion created through identity, acutely felt as duty. It becomes difficult to situate the question from where or whom these concerns originate. Leveraging this link forged by identity can make an individual vulnerable to the politics of others who claim to be the same. I can speak to this from my own experience.

In 2006, I entered the second year of my bachelor's in fine art at the School of the Art Institute of Chicago. Like many, I had been politicized through the Palestinian Rights/Solidarity and Social Justice movements in my teenage years, growing up in a suburban Muslim community and attending Catholic Jesuit high school. Once in college, I followed this logic and founded a chapter of the Muslim Student Association (MSA). Islamophobia in the post-9/11 United States seemed to legitimate a politics based on countering it. However, my MSA chapter would prove to be short-lived and would disband, along with the Latin American Student Association founded by Pamela Nogales, the only other identity-based organization on campus. Already in an extremely liberal environment of an art school, neither Pam nor I saw the progressive possibility such an organization could offer. Instead, we discovered something new. Along with a handful of others, we would become the founding members of the Platypus Affiliated Society.[24]

Both students in Professor Christopher Cutrone's courses on Frankfurt School Critical Theory and the Philosophy of Modernism, we were compelled to learn of the underlying motives that could yield theoretical insights into the social and aesthetic experience that we had encountered. Led by Cutrone, we were joined by a few of his fellow PhD candidates studying under the important Marxist scholar Moishe Postone and his old comrade Richard Ruben. A figure of thought that Cutrone introduced distinguished between the "freedom to *be* and the freedom to *become*." As I explain this to my students now, the freedom to be is involved in expressing an identity which is already known. Cutrone offers Gandhi's famous dictum "Be the change you want to see in the world" as an example of prefigurative politics. Each case involves a preconception to be fulfilled. This mode favors a moral and often transhistorical principle, instead of the multiplicity within the potential of the individual, whereas "the freedom to become" is much more generous. Freedom is realized as a process in which there is no fixed object, only the subject, as it is now in relationship to its indeterminate future, to be clarified in a constant process of self-objectification. It is for this very reason that Marx did not describe what a fully socialist society would be like. Alienation, also called estrangement, is perhaps the most popularized term attributed to Marx and is almost always taken to be the source of misery in capitalist society. As a legacy of third-wave feminism, objectification too has been vulgarized to the extent that this essential process is itself seen as morally wrong. If we "think against the grain," like Benjamin, we can see that it is nonidentity, as alienation and estrangement, that holds the promise of freedom for an individual. Considering the limited imagination engendered by our social situation, becoming identical with our self-object would be suffocatingly tragic. Criticism is the process of objectification that liberates reality through a process of negation similar to the way art splits an object and its representation described earlier. If expanded to a social and historical process, the pursuit of nonidentity could shift in the structure of subjectivity itself. Georg Lukács explains that

> in this thought self-criticism is more than the self-criticism of its object, i.e. the self-criticism of bourgeois society. It is also a critical awareness of how much of its own practical nature has really become manifest, which stage of the genuinely practicable is objectively possible and how much of what is objectively possible has been made real. For it is evident that however clearly we may have grasped the fact that society consists of processes, however thoroughly we may have unmasked the fiction of its rigid reification, this does not mean that we are able to annul the "reality" of this fiction in capitalist society

in practice. The moments in which this insight *can* really be converted into practice are determined by developments in society. Thus proletarian thought is in the first place merely a *theory of praxis* which only gradually (and indeed often spasmodically) transforms itself into *a practical theory* that overturns the real world. The individual stages of this process cannot be sketched in here. They alone would be able to show how proletarian class consciousness evolves dialectically (i.e., how the proletariat becomes a class). Only then would it be possible to throw light on the intimate dialectical process of interaction between the socio-historical situation and the class consciousness of the proletariat. Only then would the statement that the proletariat is the identical subject-object of the history of society become truly concrete.[25]

The founding of Platypus coincided with the height of the Anti-War Movement, historically the largest protests in the world. We marched in the protests through downtown Chicago with banners that read "Long Live the Left, the Left is Dead!"; "You can't live a wrong life rightly," a translated quote from Adorno's *Minima Moralia*; and Max Horkheimer's "Humanity's interest lies in the Marxist clarification of the concept of freedom."[26] We tried to give voice to the lurking anxiety that even this impressive and monolithic mass would not be sufficient. Horkheimer's statement reminds us that the realization of hitherto unknown degrees of freedom for society is the goal of the Left. Today even the concept of freedom has been ceded to the Right, who are preoccupied with maintaining the status quo. Horkheimer reminds us that "[in] socialism, freedom is to become a reality. But because the present system is called 'free' and considered liberal, it is not terribly clear what this may mean."[27]

Affinity as a form of political organizing had become the norm since the 1999 WTO Seattle protests. Horizontal organizing and fervent belief in mass spontaneity became a political principle that allowed for groups as diverse as animal rights, migration rights, and abortion rights advocates to present a common front as the Anti-War Movement. Ideology tends to address totality, and for this reason is implicitly banned within these movements lest it reveal that there was no coherent political movement at all. Anarchists consistently organizing at the heart of these movements preserved the legacy of Platformism without identifying it or themselves as such. The extent to which the present rehearses the past, nothing new needs to be said to address it. In "Left-Wing Communism: An Infantile Disorder", Lenin reports that in his time, as in our own,

> driven to frenzy by the horrors of capitalism . . . anarchism is characteristic of all capitalist countries. The instability of such revolutionism, its barrenness, and its tendency to turn rapidly into submission, apathy, phantasms, and even a frenzied infatuation with one bourgeois fad or another—all this is common

knowledge. . . . Anarchism was not infrequently a kind of penalty for the opportunist sins of the working-class movement. The two monstrosities complemented each other.[28]

Following Carl Oglesby,[29] one of the primary functions of a political party for the Left is to maintain memory, a record of historical situations, and their responses to them. Since the popular milieu comprised of unions, activists, and parties like their own simply no longer existed, the surviving groups can now only be described as sectarian. Paradoxically, by engaging with these groups we in Platypus appeared to many on the Left as ultra-sectarian. Opposite to sectarianism was the broad and inevitable appeal that came at the end of every panel discussion asked in earnest "Ok, but what should we do?" These desperate voices of public concern too have become less frequent.

Insofar as the Left rehearses the past in which they were conceived, they offer access to otherwise obfuscated moments. We called them the "Zombie Left." In the case of the Spartacist League, these behaviors included boycotting our symposium "What Is Imperialism and Why Should We Be Against It?" As students hosting our first event, we almost felt honored. We did get the International Socialist Organization, the Revolutionary Communist Party, Marxist-Humanists, and the then recently refounded Students for Democratic Society to participate. At the time of writing, nearly all of the organizations above have collapsed completely or fallen into terminal decay, after nearly fifty or more years of existence.

Supporting the student movement, Herbert Marcuse broke with Adorno but still considered that "when the political reality as a whole is false, the unpolitical position may be the only political truth."[30] The collapse of these organizations ought not to be lamented on the basis of their (in)capacity to enact an emancipatory politics—but rather on the loss of the historical perspective they bring to bear on the present, as a record of the failures of the Left. This mass extinction corresponds directly to the return of identity politics as the primary form of mobilization today.

The enormous activist and radical energies of our millennial generation, mobilized in 2006 through the Anti-War, Occupy, and affiliated movements, inevitably revealed their political trajectory as attempts to leverage and reform the Democratic Party. This takes form first in Obama's two successful presidential bids built on the Anti-War Movement's organizing. Today the death of the Millennial Left is complete, and its funeral is attended by the Democratic Socialists of America, *Jacobin* magazine, the failed campaigns of Bernie Sanders, and later the glimmers of success with the election of Alexandria Ocasio-Cortez and the rest of "the Squad." The flames of anti-Trump fervor cauterized the imagination of the would-be Left in the United States.[31]

PRINCIPLES OVER THE PRESENT

A constant point of contention with the groups mentioned above during the Anti-War Movement had to do with the question whether you support the Islamic fundamentalists in the Iraqi insurgency against American and allied forces. The answer was often "yes, in principle we must support anyone who would deal a blow to American imperialism." Herein lies the problem. The regression of political consciousness to moral principle would lead leftists to support fascists, who would most likely not hesitate to kill the leftists in question, as they did in Iraq, if they were ever to meet them in person.

Even those who experienced the militant struggles of 1968 had succumbed to this regression of consciousness. In 2007, I organized an interview with Tariq Ali for Platypus. During the dinner that followed, Tariq ordered the most expensive bottle of wine that the Italian Village, a Chicago Landmark, had to offer. He did this just before provoking an argument expressing principled support of the fundamentalist insurgents in Iraq and then promptly left. We, broke young art students, were stuck with a bill far beyond what the student government had allotted. Following Walter Benjamin, experience does not equate to knowledge. Despicable as Ali's behavior was, it left me with what could be called receiving the quintessential experience of the leftist intellectual, whose opinions match his deeds in extraordinary fashion: both are vain and empty.

What remains of this time is the moral preoccupation of the would-be Left. "Solidarity" and "support" remain the primary political modus operandi and it becomes increasingly obscure to me what these words could possibly mean. Certainly "support" has almost no effect on those to whom we lend it, especially if overseas when no international Left exists to enact it. More likely is that this sentiment works only on those who proclaim it, demonstrating to themselves their virtue in "being on the right side of history." In a recent documentary, Taylor Swift came out in support of a democratic senator during the elections in a GOP state for the same reason. The "right side" is a moral category. Why not admit ambivalence instead? What would be lost? Certainly not one's soul.

At the height of the Occupy movement I interviewed Slavoj Žižek for *The Platypus Review*.[32] While a vocal figure within the movement, he offered this critique:

> The problem today is that we have a lot of "anti-capitalism," indeed an overload of anti-capitalism, but it is an ethical anti-capitalism.... All of these are moralistic critiques of distortions. This is not enough. The anti-capitalism of the popular media remains at the level of something to be resolved within the established structure: through investigative journalism, democratic reforms, and the like.

But I see in all of this the vague instinct that something more is at stake. The battle now, as for the capitalists themselves, is over who will appropriate it.[33]

The ethical anti-capitalist may now be a thing of the past, having given way to those who find the political in the personal as Jesus or Gandhi once led by example, especially in their inevitable martyrdom. I cannot imagine a more fatalistic form of politics. But perhaps time will reveal new horizons.

ART AND AMBIVALENCE

Art participates in the world as we know it and simultaneously preserves itself in maintaining an ambivalence toward it. In his essay "Poverty and Experience," Walter Benjamin shares Horowitz's thought that art's "asocial" and destabilizing character is a product of its freedom from preceding categorical order. The moral preoccupations of the political culture in which art is complicit today leaves little room for humanity to grow. Benjamin writes:

> In its buildings, pictures, and stories, mankind is preparing to outlive culture, if need be. And the main thing is that is does so with a laugh. This laughter may occasionally sound barbaric. Well and good. Let us hope that from time to time the individual will give a little humanity to the masses, who one day will repay him with compound interest.[34]

The artist, among others, takes on this responsibility to convey humanity to the masses, even while producing those images that are meant to outlive culture. The nuanced distinction between humanity, on the one side, and mass, art, and culture, on the other, is dialectical. What can we make of this ambivalence? Perhaps, only an endgame can be discerned. For instance, artists of the twentieth-century avant-garde constantly projected the end of art, most famously exemplified in Kazimir Malevich's painting *Black Square* (1915). In relation to it, Bret Schneider elegiacally explains that

> art wants to pass, it wants to finally die—it is not mere eccentricity that great artists once believed they were making the last artwork. If art finally died, this would signal that the "untransfigured suffering of man"[35] over the ages would finally be transfigured into something else. Simply pronouncing art dead, or irrelevant to the everyday is not enough to warrant its demise, as if it were so simple to eradicate the suffering of man. The culture industry—with its ceaseless thrusting of art in our faces—is the penance for failing to achieve socialism, but also the petrified reminder of its possibility. In this sense, art and culture are not the solution to, but rather the problem of, our own suffering, and the

crystallization of this problem also implies redemption. Does it not seem that, contrary to this, we want to *preserve* art, to restore the world through art, and wasn't this specifically a crucial element of fascism, or less dramatically, conservatism? In an era of where there are no historical tasks or clearly defined problems, any proposed solution is a false reconciliation. In Adorno's words, "that the world which, as Baudelaire wrote, has lost its fragrance and since then its color, could have them restored by art strikes only the artless as possible."[36]

Schneider's emphasis here is on total social transformation through which art could resolve its perennial antagonisms with the everyday. Its passing would signal the release of man's creative capacities to be transfigured into something hitherto unseen and adequate to this new form of society and subjectivity. I yearn for a social situation that would redeem this artistic martyrdom. Instead, paradoxically art participates in the reconstitution of the status quo by consistently proving its relevance to society as it is.

THE EMANCIPATION OF FORMS: MUQARNAS

If social emancipation is outside of the realm of current possibility, then I have tried to work on a smaller scale by attempting to liberate particular forms from the cultural and historical connotations that condition their existence. Perhaps a shift in the perception of the familiar catches the light and glimmers with broader possibility. At the moment in which I helped to found Platypus, I was preparing my first solo exhibition at the art space Around the Coyote in Chicago.[37] Entitled "The Common Sense," I decided I would throw into relief the underlying assumption of what constituted the aesthetic in modernity by objectifying my own past.

I decided to create a functional mosque inside of the gallery. The Kiblah niche that is always oriented toward the empty black cube in Mecca toward which all Muslims pray consisted of a black square in my exhibition. I wanted to see if this form could contain both the embodiment of the supposed oldest recorded interaction of God with humanity and the expression of absolute negation bound up in Malevich's *Black Square*, reinvested in throughout the history of minimalism. The question whether the gallery could contain the mosque was not one of goodwill on the part of curators but rather of contemporary art's necessarily secular orientation. For instance, would there be a prayer instead of a performance which no longer communicated to the divine but rather to an audience observing it?

The experiment was a failure. To the Muslim community I hoped to lure in as part of the object, I appeared as entirely other. And to the contemporary art community I appeared as a young Muslim artist—the farthest from what I had hoped. Marco Aurelio Torres, another founding member of Platypus, wrote a review of the exhibition in the inaugural issue of The Platypus Review clarifying what was at stake in the exhibition.[38]

This installation featured a sculpture made of Muqarnas pictured in figure 9.1. The process of making this sculpture continued to affect me. Muqarnas are an ancient form of ornament that is both structural and artifice. A family of modular blocks can be used to create a variety of architectural formations and domes in particular. While the history of Islamic architecture attests to the rapid expansion of empire through which regional styles were adapted, muqarnas are one of its most original forms. Muqarnas create a peculiar spatial experience between their two-dimensional geometric nets and three-dimensional spaces. It was this formal quality that I wanted to continue to elaborate. Would it be possible to see the forms I created beyond their cultural origins?

Fourteen years later I was presented with the context that might enable this. Nav Haq, senior curator and associate director of the Museum of Contemporary Art in Antwerp, Belgium, invited me to create an installation for his exhibition "Monocultures: A Recent History". I felt that he had created the context in which I could again try. In an accompanying text, Haq elaborates that

Figure 9.1 Detail: "Muqarnas" in "The Common Sense." *Source*: Haseeb Ahmed, 2007, Around the Coyote, Dimension: 150 cm × 90× 90.

166 *Haseeb Ahmed*

art is fundamentally ambiguous, and its ambiguity offers a negotiation of sorts. It pries open the rigid stimulus-response relationship, inviting us to experience and interpret these different characteristics and dimension in their simultaneity. The question is: is one willing to or fearful to undertake the challenge of exploring one's liberalisms? And if one is fearful, then it raises the subsequent question of how this negation might be mediated.[39]

The exhibition consisted of constellations of artworks and artifacts that expressed or addressed particular monocultures. Around the corner from my work hung a painting by Phillip Guston featuring his typical reductivism renderings of KKK Klansmen. Major international museums had announced the indefinite postponement of his retrospective during the show, bowing to identitarian pressure that to simply see a painting of a Klansmen, even a caricaturized one, may be potentially traumatic to some.[40] Seen together their monolithic character was relativized. I anticipated the opportunistic political Islamic imagination that would claim these forms by literally providing this tendency a "headquarters." The Ummah is an anachronism. The global community of believers that once existed is now used as a call for mobilization for factions that seek to instrumentalize people's personal beliefs.

The artwork pictured in figure 9.2 deploys a series of binary oppositions to create a resonance that shakes apart any monolithic concepts projected onto

Figure 9.2 **"Ummah HQ."** *Source*: Haseeb Ahmed, 2020, Museum of Contemporary Art, Antwerp, Belgium.

the artwork. The muqarnas dome is only partially complete. It appears to be in a state of ruin or under construction. The inscriptions around the perimeter are English transliterated into Arabic, to address the millions taught to read but not understand the Qur'an. The platform upon which the dome stands is painted in a specially formulated green, what at first glance appears as the symbolic green of Islam, but upon entering is revealed to be a green screen. A computer monitor reveals that underfoot is the interior view of the dome of Tomb of Zumurrud Khatun. Built in 1050 in Baghdad, Iraq, it is thought to be the first instance of muqarnas architecture. The digital effect of the green screen is rendered using security camera hardware dating to the 1980s. This feeble attempt to bridge the past and the present preserves the future. Each element is contradicted by another. There is no stable point within the artwork. In this way I hope I may have liberated the form of muqarnas to be seen in their formal qualities, free of their cultural origins.

In my recent research I have seen muqarnas appear in two unlikely places. The German expressionist architect Hans Poelzig's Großes Schauspielhaus built in Berlin in 1918–19, featured a central dome and pillar cornices covered in muqarnas. While he did not convey the structural principle of the ornament, the overall effect is undeniably similar. In 1933, the Nazis had deemed it a work of Degenerate Art ("entartete Kunst") and had its interior destroyed. David Lynch's film *Dune* sees muqarnas deployed in the set design of the desert planet's Arrakeen Palace, perhaps bringing the ornament back to their origins transfigured by their journey. Frank Herbert's book from which the film is adapted offers a strong criticism of religious identity and ends with the rise of a demagogue who launches an interplanetary *jihad*. Knowing this, can we replace muqarnas back into the context of the Iraqi desert from which they arose nearly a 1,000 years ago? As time goes on, forms accumulate the meanings projected onto them, each one claiming exclusive right to their capacity for signification. They become transient, unable to return to any one context. The form as such is liberated from the increasingly contradictory cultural association it supposedly bears. This is one way in which art gains autonomy today.

CONCLUSION

Throughout this chapter I have addressed the dialectical relationship of identity and nonidentity. This dynamic is at the core of the emancipatory potential seen in art throughout the history of the Left and in art. The ambitious proposal put forth in this chapter is to establish art's nuanced relationship to the Left through their mutual interest in freedom. However, judging by the contemporary attitudes on the Left, we may assume that art and artist's importance lies in their ability to create compelling representations that identify the artwork and artist with existing political positions. However, it is precisely art's capacity to create an experience that estranges our perception from reality that offers a glimpse of freedom from what we presume to be necessary. Traditionally, this capacity has been called art's autonomy by Trotsky, Adorno, Benjamin, and others referenced throughout this chapter. However, this too ought not to be taken affirmatively, as art expresses the situation of capital within which it is embedded. The autonomy of art is to be considered in the terms of an attempt to overcome conventions of the commodity form that bind the ability to produce meaning at present.

The artworks use technique to reconfigure genres and medium specificity to engender unlikely experiences. All artists, regardless of political orientation, have recourse to this lexicon and the license to create contradictions within it. As in the case of the Phillip Guston painting, many on the would-be Left would rather censor an artwork entirely than consider the merits of its political ambiguity. The significance of an artwork is felt in the way it shifts our perception of reality, rendering both perception and reality as something transformable. The conscious efforts to produce art can also result in meaninglessness, something that is historically specific to modernity.

Artists anticipate the reception of their own work in the collapse of art criticism. This collapse is part of a larger ideological collapse. Contemporary politics on the Left and Right now offer us the image of belonging to an identity as the freest form of social being possible. However, this prefigurative thinking is deeply limited. Instead, it is nonidentity, otherwise known as estrangement or alienation, that offers the freedom to become something which is not yet known. I have drawn on my own formative experiences within the Left to show the origins of today's "ethical Left" in the Anti-War Movement, Occupy movement, and inevitably in the legacy of the New Left's attempt to depart from the Old Left. By making recourse to the history of the Left, I could show that a shift has occurred that forecloses the imagination of both artists and the Left, drifting further from the horizon of an emancipatory politics.

NOTES

1. Ahmed, Haseeb, and Latifa Echakhch 2021.
2. Benjamin, Walter 1978, 140.
3. Since 2015 I have worked with curator Nav Haq. He consistently has organized exhibitions elaborating the role of identity today through a necessarily ambivalent experience with multiculturalism in his home country of the UK and its broad expressions in the art world. He seeks to redeem something of the strand of liberalism

that inspired it and which, for him, is becoming increasingly obscure due to the intolerance of emerging form of liberalism today like "cancel culture." In 2017, Daniel G. Baird and I produced the artwork "Has the World Already Been Made x10: Belfries" for the exhibition "WheredoIendandyoubegin—On Secularity," which explicitly addressed why art is secular today.

4. Buck-Morss et al. 1995.

5. Chris Cutrone's PhD Dissertation "Adorno's Marxism" elaborates the historical circumstances and transmission through which the term "critical theory" evolved. He situates the origins of critical theory as we know it today with the Frankfurt School as an immanent critique of existent theory of Marx. For instance, in his inaugural lecture of 1932 on "The Idea of Natural History," Adorno states that "it is not a question of completing one theory by another, but of the immanent interpretation of a theory. I submit myself, so to speak, to the authority of the materialist dialectic" (Cutrone 2013, 17).

6. The artworks of Forensic Architecture present the quintessential example of art's faith in rationality as a redemptive force. Utilizing architectural and criminal science techniques, they create installations that reconstruct the scenes of atrocities whose greatest triumph is being admitted in both galleries and courts of law alike. See https://forensic-architecture.org/investigation/the-murder-of-pavlos-fyssas. Accessed July 8, 2021.

7. The gesture is a term that commonly stands in for an action in art-making that is idiosyncratic. A broad and raw brushstroke that evokes the moment in which it was made is a common example. In the expanded visual language of contemporary art, a gesture can be the unusual placement of an object. It usually feels unresolved, making recourse to the artist and her intentions.

8. Artistic license is a term introduced to many in their first elementary school art classes. Teachers encourage students to use their artistic license when confronted with an aesthetic choice. Rather than rationalize the outcome one can attribute it to the freedom granted them as an artist creating her own work.

9. The coalition consisted of the Conservative People's Party for Freedom and Democracy (VVD) and the Christian Democrats (CDU), together with the far-right Freedom Party (PVV) of Geert Wilders.

10. Fogteloo, Margreet 2010.

11. For an extended discussion, see Ahmed 2011.

12. Kolakowski 1969, 144–58.

13. Fischer 1959, 14.

14. Trotsky 2005 (1924), 70–71. In Schneider 2017.

15. *Relational Aesthetics* is a term that epitomized a strain in art typically called social practice as it was understood until the 1990's when coined by the curator Nicolas Bourriaud. The artist Joseph Beuys may have given this tendency its impetus in his description of "social sculpture" as the real but immaterial outcome of an artwork existing in collective imagination of the audience. This is similar to Emil Durkheim's conception of the social power of fetish objects in aboriginal cultures as "mana," as described in his influential book "Elementary Forms of Religious Life" (1912). Social practice continues to develop today through its communitarian and collective preoccupations.

16. Bourriaud 2002 (1998).

17. The exhibition Transactions was curated by Michael Hiltbrunner as part of the Manifesta 11 parallel program at the University of Zurich.

18. Ahmed, Haseeb, and Elena Louisa Lange. "Fetish/Non-Fetish." *Universität Zürich*, May 25, 2016, www.manifesta11.uzh.ch/en/exhibition/happiness/fetish.html. Accessed July 12, 2021 (emphasis in original).

19. Harlan Levey Projects was founded in 2011 by Harlan Levey and his partner Wing Lam "Winnie" Kwok. They have continued to grow in Brussels where they now operate two gallery spaces and support artistic and community-based cultural projects.

20. Adorno 2020 (1951), 133.

21. Horowitz 2001, 4.

22. I owe this understanding the Ben Blumberg of the Platypus Affiliated Society who has read Greenberg extensively in light of his Marxism, and when he is regularly dismissed on the basis of being a supposedly the quintessential "cis-gendered white-male" art historian.

23. A recent exhibition by a former student at Het Research Atelier in Rotterdam is entitled "What does Diversity Mean if White Curators Are Still at the Center?"

24. The Platypus Affiliated Society continues to exist today and has chapters across the world. It publishes a monthly free publication that, like its symposia, brings together diverse perspectives on the Left to see what bearing the history of the radical Left of the twentieth century has on the present.

25. Lukács 1923 (emphasis in original).

26. Horkheimer 1978, 50–52.

27. Horkheimer 1978, 50–53.

28. Lenin, V.I. *Left-Wing Communism An Infantile Disorder* (Haymarket Books, 2014) found in Cutrone, Christopher "Adorno's Marxism." *The University of Chicago*, 2013, 27–27.

29. Oglesby, Carl. "The Idea of the New Left." *The New Left Reader* (Grove Press, 1978), 1–18.

30. Marcuse, Herbert. "Technology, War and Fascism Collected Papers of Herbert Marcuse, Volume 1." Translated by Douglas Kellner (Taylor and Francis, 2004), 217.

31. Chris Cutrone provides a concise yet nuanced account in the article "The Millennial Left Is Dead." *Platypus*, 31 Jan. 2018, platypus1917.org/2017/10/01/millennial-left-dead/.

32. Ahmed, Haseeb, and Chris Cutrone. "The Occupy Movement, a Renascent Left, and Marxism Today: An Interview with Slavoj Žižek." *The Platypus Review*, 5 Sept. 2017, platypus1917.org/2011/12/01/occupy-movement-interview-with-slavoj-zizek/.

33. Ahmed and Cutrone 2011.

34. Benjamin 1933.

35. Trotsky, Leon. "Literature and Revolution", trans. Rose Strunsky (Chicago: Haymarket Books, 2005 [1924]), 70–71.

36. Adorno 2004 (1970), 50. See Schneider 2017.

37. Founded in 1989, "Around the Coyote" was an important art space in Chicago. It offered the possibility for young and otherwise unexhibited artists to present their work. Paradoxically, for this reason it was also looked down upon by the rest of the contemporary art community in Chicago. It closed its doors in 2010. For more information see: https://fnewsmagazine.com/2010/05/around-the-coyote-bites-the-dust/. Accessed July 12, 2021.
38. Torres 2007.
39. Haq 2020, 36–48.
40. Jacobs and Farago 2020.

Part III

ECLIPSE OF EMANCIPATION—CONFRONTING STREAMS IN THE ACADEMIC AND ACTIVIST LEFT TODAY

Chapter 10

Racial Capitalism and Social Form

Nick Nesbitt

The development and deployment of racial ideologies necessarily occurs within a governing framework of economic relations. While racialist discourse is by no means limited to capitalism, nonetheless, in what Marx called the capitalist social form, race remains one—at times predominant—discourse among the various determinations of the general social compulsion to accumulate surplus value, a mode of ideology subject to a more general structure of social relations: commodification. Whether race or class is a more fundamental category of analysis is in this sense beside the point. Marx did not argue that class relations are the starting point for an analysis of capitalism, any more than race (though he certainly demonstrates that the sale and purchase of labor power, unlike racial difference, enables the production of surplus value, a crucial point I will return to later).

Instead, Marx begins his analysis from what he calls the "cell-form" of capitalism, "the commodity form of the product of labor."[1] In the crucial and conceptually difficult first section of chapter one of *Capital*, Marx analyses the essential nature of the commodity in the capitalist social form in terms of its dual nature as both use value and exchange value. Since Marx begins his analysis from neither the isolated commodity nor consumers' psychological motivations, but from a given, commodity-based social totality, it is exchange value that allows for the proportional, generalized equation of all commodities with one another. Marx then demonstrates that it is abstract labor— "human labor expended without regard to the form of its expenditure"—that provides, analytically, the common property or measure of the proportional equality allowing for their exchange.[2] "This quantity," Marx further specifies,

> is measured by its duration [in the form of] socially necessary labor time, ... the labor time required to produce any use value under the conditions of production

normal for a given society and with the average degree of skill and intensity of labor prevalent in that society.³

This temporal measure, in turn, requires the general equivalency of monetary form (price) to allow for the universal exchangeability of all commodities, which is Marx's starting point. Marx's crucial concept of *social form* (*gesellschaftliche Form*) indicates that social relationships under capitalism must be comprehended as functions of the essential governing element of that society, value, and its general form of appearance as commodities bearing a monetary price or exchange value.

Marx demonstrates in *Capital* that to be exchangeable in a commodity-based society, each commodity must necessarily possess a monetary price.⁴ He argues that money and the corresponding price form of commodities are no mere expedient aids to exchange, as classical and neoclassical economics, as well as traditional Marxism believed, but instead must be grasped as the necessary modes of appearance of value in the capitalist social form.⁵ Marx's unique contribution to the critique of capitalism was to analyze the (historically and analytically) specific social form governing the material-technical processes of production, as well as, inversely, the determination of capitalist social relations in general by the monetary form of value that labor assumes, in the form of a *monetary labor theory of value*. This admittedly complex theory of the capitalist social form is crucial for an analysis of the racialist dimensions of capitalism, since it is this monetary labor theory of value, rather than a (vulgar) theory of exploitation-as-personal oppression, that enables Marx to define concrete capitalist slave labor as a form of fixed, constant capital, such that it participates in the production of commodities (sugar, cotton) that can capture a profit upon market sale, but without that uncommodified labor having produced surplus value.⁶

By way of his critique of the classics, Marx introduced two far-reaching novelties into political-economic science: first, Marx was the first to ask and show why under capitalism labor must appear as what he called the "value-forms" (*Wertformen*, that is, the commodity, money, capital, wages, price, profit, rent, interest, etc.). Second, he demonstrated how the formal *equality* of commodity exchange—including the purchase and sale of wage (but not slave) labor—is nonetheless able to create *surplus value*.⁷ In his analysis, Marx explained why in a commodity society, to produce surplus value, labor must take the form of the commodity, and furthermore money, such that capitalist labor can assume a historically distinct form: abstract labor. Capitalist slave labor certainly produced use values (cotton and sugar) but did so as an unpaid means of production, in this no different from animal or steam power, and thus, as unpaid, uncommodified labor, remained incapable of creating surplus value.

Marx shows for the first time that it is the wage form that harbors "the secret of profit-making," in that the exchange of labor power for a monetary wage (equivalent or equal exchange) puts it to work for a whole working day, while its monetary "equivalent" (i.e., the wage) only pays for that part of the day by which the laborer reproduces her own means of subsistence.[8] Only the essential exchange of *nonequivalents* (between the wages and commodified capacity to work that Marx names labor power, which produces more value than it costs to the capitalist) based on the formal validity of *equivalent* exchange (the labor power-commodity is paid for with money at its actual market value) explains how capitalists can ultimately produce surplus value. An actual exchange of equivalents could never explain how more money evolves from the exchange process. And yet it must appear as such: the commodity labor power, like any other commodity on the capitalist market, must be sold for an equivalent at an equilibrium price. The essential relation between wage labor and capital, and therefore the exploitation of unpaid labor, is obscured.[9]

Though *individual* capitalist slaveowners could and did continue to produce profitable commodities (sugar, cotton) well into the nineteenth century without necessarily engaging wage labor, from the perspective of the total social economic system of relations that Marx interrogates,[10] slaves, like mule and waterpower, were tendentially displaced by wage labor and mechanized, scientific means of production.[11] In order to adequately construct his object of investigation (the capitalist social form), and to reproduce these complex and essential dynamics of the capitalist production of surplus value that Marx was the first to analyze, requires abstracting entirely from ideological questions of race, as it does from all other categories of the lived experience of the subjects of capitalism (gender, nationality, etc.). It requires the focus on the basic forms of social relations that allow for the production of surplus value, the sole object of capitalism. The three volumes of *Capital* that Marx drafted in his lifetime do not inquire into the racial origins of proletarian laborers, any more than they do their gender or national composition, not because Marx was unaware of such questions but because he rightly judged that such variables must be held in suspension at the level of abstraction his analysis constructs.

To demonstrate, in contrast to Marx's analytical abstraction from race, that racial ideology "produces the economy" or that it is "constitutive of the productive process and the social relations of production under capitalism," as various theorists of racial capital claim, would thus require proving that racialist discourse "produces" or "constitutes" some crucial dimension of this commodity-based social form of relations and/or produces surplus value.[12] Instead, the fact that, in the commodity-based form of social relations (capitalism), private labor must be socially valorized through market exchange remains a precritical given in this literature.[13] To take the example of what is otherwise a fascinating article on the deployment of debt foreclosure by North American colonists to capture and monetize native American lands, K-Sue Park's analysis never lives up to the author's initial grandiose promise to show how race "produces the economy." Instead, in a theoretical bait and switch, this case of racial discourse is subsequently claimed merely to "illustrate the dynamic relationship between race and economic growth" and to "shape the market" within a preexistent monetary, commodity-based social form.[14] Park notes that the Plymouth colonists arrived in seventeenth-century North America already laden "with debt burdens and a plan to engage in racial violence to satisfy them" in a violent instance of primitive accumulation used to "force an equivalence between money and land" in a pre-existing colonial market "structured by credit."[15] Park further emphasizes that, "in these English-Native transactions, there existed no mutual understanding of debt between lender and borrower." This remarkable case study of racially coded violence might have served to underscore the difference between the (English) capitalist and (Native American) precapitalist social forms. Instead, the author leaves this leaf unturned and merely rehearses the neoclassical assertion that "credit is commonly conceived as value extended," without pausing to notice that for social relations to be so powerfully determined by the monetary form of appearance of value as credit and debt, as her case study shows, requires a fundamental organization of social relations mediated by the commodity and its forms of appearance.[16]

Similarly, to focus on the racial disparity in wages within the capitalist social form, while no doubt necessary, is nonetheless to accept the organizing, racialist framework of one's oppressor and to miss the systematic analytical perspective of the social form that makes wages—whatever their level—a determinant category of historically conditioned existence. A case in point is the article "Under Capitalism, There's No Such Thing as a 'Fair Day's Wage for a Fair Day's Work'" by Hadas Thier.[17] Thier begins with a resonant summary of Marx's explanation of the nature of surplus value to which the title refers, rightly concluding that

> the capitalist pays you for the value of your labor-power, not for the value of the goods you produce. Thus your paycheck is worth the value of your labor-power. But your labor-power is set to work to produce commodities of greater value.

However, as soon as Thier digresses into an evocation of race-based wage inequality ("Black men are paid 70 cents and black women 61 cents in comparison to their white counterparts. Latina women earn 53 cents to a white man's dollar"), the principal point at issue is suddenly no longer the predominance of the wage form and its inherent, structural inequality, but the mere unequal treatment of diverse categories of laborers *within* the capitalist social form itself: "People of color . . . never enter a level playing field. . . . Inequality has long been built into the core fabric of the American business model." In other words, while Thier begins her analysis at the level of the capitalist social form ("Appropriating surpluses was a visible and obvious norm of previous class societies. In examining capitalist society however, we have to go beneath the surface appearance of a 'fair day's work' to uncover the inner essence of exploitation"), in suddenly moving to a discussion of racial injustice, she symptomatically and necessarily shifts the level and nature of her analysis to a criticism of inequality *within* the capitalist social form, the contingent nature of which necessarily remains unquestioned within this racialist framework.

Marx begins his critique of political economy in *Capital* with the analysis of the commodity, its historically specific form-determination, and the substance of its value, abstract labor. He does not begin with exploitation, the essential nature of which he only addresses in chapter 6. Racial difference, in contrast, is categorially and logically external to his analysis of the relation between wage labor and capital. The analysis of racialist ideology might only have found a logical place in subsequent projected volumes of *Capital*, for example, on the phenomenal dynamics of competition, volumes which Marx never drafted.[18] The first three chapters of *Capital* instead demonstrate that in the capitalist social form—historically unique in its dedication to the production and accumulation of neither concrete wealth nor human well-being, but instead to amassing surplus value—*only those objects that have an exchange value*, a monetary form of appearance, or, more simply, commodities, *can have value*. This is a proposition so simple it verges on tautology, yet one systematically ignored by generations of nominally "Marxist" thinkers. Though one may "value" the earth for its beauty, the dinner I cook for my family for its taste and nourishment, or the labor of the serf or slave for the concrete goods they provide the slave-owner or feudal lord to consume or sell for profit, none of these forms of "value" *count in the capitalist social form*, as none of them has an *exchange value* and monetary form of appearance.[19] This simple proposition, which Marx goes on to demonstrate in the enormous complexity of its implications, remains completely invisible to the field of racial capitalism studies, which sees in Marx only a historical examination of the industrial exploitation of labor.

THE LIMITS OF *BLACK MARXISM*

"There is much to be admired in those who have struggled under the inspiration of Marxism."[20] With unmistakable condescension, in the opening sentence of his Preface to the 2000 reedition of Cedric Robinson's *Black*

Marxism, the inventor of the concept of *racial capitalism* looks down on the misguided illusions of the secular Marxian commitment of the Black Atlantic intelligentsia from W. E. B. Dubois to C. L. R. James to Richard Wright. Such a view is readily understandable, for when one has presumptively dismissed an entire domain of thought, there is certainly no need to master the intricacies of Marx's critique of capitalism, his systematic demonstration across many thousands of pages, painstakingly researched, drafted, and reformulated, from the 1857 *Grundrisse* to the dense manuscripts that Engels refashioned into what we now know as the three volumes of *Capital*, to the notes and revisions Marx continued to draft up to his death in 1883. No need, certainly, to consult the sixty-five-plus volumes of the still-incomplete *Marx-Engels-Gesamtausgabe*, nor, truth be told, even to flip through the three published volumes of *Capital*, when a college anthology will do.[21]

None of this would matter, to be sure, had not Robinson chosen to write on Marxism to explicate the concept of racial capitalism. For while the book's three sections focus on, respectively, "The Emergence and Limitations of European Radicalism," "The Roots of Black Radicalism" in Atlantic slavery and "Black Radicalism and Marxist Theory"—that is to say, on nominally historiographic topics and Marxists rather than Marx's thought—as the latter title suggests, *Black Marxism* is intended also as a theoretical intervention going beyond its historicist prospectus. It serves as an intervention the keystone to which is precisely the concept of racial capitalism, namely the attempt at delegitimizing Marx's (ill-comprehended) critique.[22]

Given the blatant inadequacy of Robinson's theoretical references to Marx's critique of political economy, it may suffice briefly to note three interrelated dimensions of this inadequacy: first, Robinson's reduction of Marx's daunting theoretical accomplishments to a mere vulgar criticism of exploitation, a simplification Robinson further summarizes by the reduction of Marx's complex form-analytical method to the claims of historical materialism; second, the failure of *Black Marxism* to distinguish Marx's theoretical demonstration of the conceptual structure of capitalism from its empirical, historical development and forms; third, the culmination of this insufficiency in the theoretically hobbled concept of racial capitalism itself. This critique may then serve in what follows to indicate a more general inadequacy, of which *Black Marxism* stands as a mere, albeit influential, symptom: the repeated failure of Black Atlantic Studies since Eric Williams to construct a systematic notion of capitalism able to account for the necessary—as opposed to merely epiphenomenal and contingent—materialist logic governing categories such as slavery and race in their specific contribution to capitalism.

Black Marxism presents Marx's method as being exhausted in the doctrine of historical materialism, conceived in its most vulgar misrepresentation: "Marx's conceit was to presume that the theory of historical materialism explained history."²³ Such a woeful simplification allows Robinson to utterly ignore Marx's analysis of the capitalist social form as a complex dynamic governed by a plethora of both *tendential* and *counter-tendential* laws, an analytical framework, moreover, that allows for no possible prediction of historical development. Instead, having reduced Marx's analysis to a meager handful of paragraphs from the 1859 text "Forms which Precede Capitalist Production," Robinson can deflate the notion of a "structure" of capitalism to the claim that "the deepest structures of 'historical materialism,' the foreknowledge for its comprehension of historical movement, have tended to relieve European Marxists from the obligation of investigating the profound effects of culture and historical experience on their science."²⁴ The result of this simplification is a threadbare theory of the lived experience of exploitation in which Marx and Engels are claimed to have "characterized the capitalist mode of production as voraciously exploitative" and to have promulgated an "interpretation of history in terms of the dialectic of capitalist class struggles."²⁵

When Robinson does on occasion speak of Marxian analytic categories, such as primitive accumulation, his definitions bear little, if any, relation to Marx's actual analysis: "Marx had meant by primitive accumulation that the *piezas de Indias* had been produced, materially and intellectually, by the societies from which they were taken and not by those by which they were exploited."²⁶ This obscure comment completely misses the crucial historical significance of this phenomenon, that is, the historical production and reproduction of a class compelled to offer the sole commodity able to produce surplus value, its labor power, as a commodity to capital. The *historical* development of primitive accumulation is rightly relegated by Marx to his famous final chapters of the first volume of *Capital*.²⁷ In contrast, in the initial culmination of his categorial demonstration in Chapter 6 ("The Sale and Purchase of Labor Power"), the availability of this commodity to capital arguably constitutes the single most important demonstration of Marx's critique, his ingenious solution to the riddle that had confounded the entire field of thought of classical political economy: how the exchange of two commodities at their real and equivalent value could nonetheless produce a surplus value.²⁸

Robinson completely fails to distinguish between Marx's elaborately constructed thought-object (the book *Capital*) and the material, historical ordering of the social world, a facile conflation that allows him to dismiss as Eurocentric idealism the insights of Marx's materialist critique:

> Marx imagined a coherent ordering of things: congruous imperial sites from which cohorts of capitalists cultivated, directed, and dominated satellite societies. For Marx, capitalism consisted of a geometric whole whose elementary and

often hidden characteristics (price, value, accumulation, and profit) could be discovered with arithmetic means and certainty.[29]

Marx's critique is not primarily a historical study of nineteenth-century English or even North Atlantic capitalism but a *categorial* critique and analysis of any society whatsoever that is structured by the basic "cell-form" of the commodity relation.

RACIALIST EMPIRICISM

The study of the racialist dimensions of capitalism is necessarily limited to an empiricist description of the ideological forms of appearance of social relations. In the Introduction to *Reading Capital*, however, Louis Althusser articulates a comprehensive critique of empiricism to distinguish it from Marx's materialist methodology.[30] Not content to confront the familiar, and perhaps more vulnerable, concept of a sensualist empiricism, Althusser formulates his critique of "the empiricist conception of knowledge" in novel fashion, taking the term, he writes, "in its widest sense, since it can embrace a rationalist empiricism as well as a sensualist empiricism."[31]

Althusser's critical notion of empiricism is surprising, since one would expect Althusser, whose analyses in *Reading Capital* are decisively influenced by Spinoza, simply to have based his critique on the latter's familiar claim, in the Appendix to *Ethics* Book 1, for the radical inadequacy of all thought derived from sensory impressions, in its necessary movement from observed effects backward to their imaginary, ideological causes.[32] Instead, Althusser identifies an entirely different criterion that he will contrast with Marx's materialist method in *Capital*. Althusser proposes instead that "[the] whole empiricist process of knowledge lies in fact in an operation of the subject called abstraction. To know is to abstract from the real object its essence, the possession of which by the subject is then called knowledge."[33] This initial formulation already casts empiricism, in all its variants, as a dualist relation of subject to object, a conception of knowledge production that Althusser will then contrast with Marx's Spinozist "thought-concrete" that *reproduces* (as opposed to merely representing) the material, extensive "real" of the capitalist social form, that is, capitalism itself, in the attribute of thought.[34]

Althusser then takes a further step in this general critique of empiricism, to draw a necessary implication of the empiricist extraction of the essential truth from an object.[35] In all empiricist operations, Althusser asserts, encompassing both its sensualist and rationalist variants, the "sole function [of knowledge] is to separate, in the object, the two parts which exist in it, the essential and the inessential, [. . .] the gold [from the] the dross—by special procedures whose aim is *to eliminate the inessential real.*"[36]

Now, whatever we may make of these claims regarding the nature of all empiricism whatsoever, in the case of Marx's *Capital*, I believe Althusser makes a quite compelling claim indeed. For a real distinction should be drawn between the empiricist methods of Adam Smith, for example, and Marx's Spinozist materialism in *Capital*. In contrast to Cedric Robinson's simplistic equation of Marx's theoretical construction with the complexity of the social real, Marx's crucial 1857 methodological introduction to the *Grundrisse* notebooks flatly refuses such an empiricist model of representation. There, Marx rejects Adam Smith's empiricist method to assert instead a properly materialist, *productionist* epistemology. If Smith famously asserted the universally observable capitalistic nature of human economic comportment, such an assertion constitutes the abstract, merely conceptual *representation* and generalization of an empirically observable series. There exists, Smith writes in the first paragraph of *The Wealth of Nations*, "a certain propensity in human nature, [. . .] the propensity to truck, barter, and exchange one thing for another. [. . .] It is common to all men, and to be found in no other race of animals."[37] Transhistorically, these are said to constitute the basic anthropological features that need only, in this view, naturally come to flourish once the historical impediments to trade of previous social forms (agrarian, feudal, etc.) were lifted.

Against the inadequacy of Smith's method of mere empiricist representation, flawed in its derivation of general knowledge from immediate, sensuous impressions, Marx asserts the autonomy of conceptual production, the *reproduction* (as opposed to representation) of the real object as what Marx calls a "thought-concrete" (*Gedankenkonkretum*).[38] Althusser's point is well-taken, at least in the case of Smith and Marx, since not only does Smith appear to derive this universal notion from empirical abstraction, but he furthermore deploys it to discern an essential characteristic of human behavior from other inessential qualities common to human and other animal species ("passions," "acting in concert," etc.).

Marx, furthermore, does something significantly greater than merely demystify the illusory nature of the various phenomenal features of capitalism. These include concepts such as commodity fetishism, money, profit, the "freedom" of the labor contract, the illusion of a supposedly benevolent primitive accumulation and of the Trinity Formula of profit, land-rent, and wages, as well as many others. In every case, Marx does not simply dismiss these as inessential features of capitalism, in contrast to the more "essential" categories he discovers, such as abstract labor, labor power, or surplus value. Instead, in Spinozist fashion, he rigorously demonstrates in every case the systematic necessity that governs each category of the capitalist social form, *including its superficial forms of appearance.*[39] In addition to mere negative *critique*, *Capital* produces a positive *theory* of ideology and its forms of appearance.

Now, in the case of the critique of the racialist dimensions of capitalist ideology, one might make an identical critique of its necessarily empiricist limitations. Take, for example, the now familiar trope which claims that racism is "baked into the DNA" of American society.[40] The problem is not so much the functionalist metaphor of a society's "DNA" but rather that the claim itself is rhetorically suggestive but theoretically meaningless, in so far as this "DNA" (i.e., the structure of the capitalist social form in American society) remains entirely undefined. Instead, as with Smith's "propensity to truck and barter," one observes a general and common regularity of phenomena (the ubiquity of racist discourse and violence in American society) to then form a universal concept (racial capitalism).

In contrast to the empiricism of Adam Smith, Marx painstakingly derives his method, I argue, not from empirical observation of markets and factories, interviews with laborers, or debates within the First International. Marx developed his method by critically inquiring into the theoretical writings of political economy and of nascent socialism and did so sitting at his desk. There were no experimental, empiricist data for him to interpret, not even the famous parliamentary reports. These supplementary pages detail the mere quantitative fluctuations of the price of labor power amid the historical dynamic of class struggle; Engels did as much or more long before in his 1845 study of the working class. Instead, Marx asked a far more fundamental question in *Capital*: *What is the law of the tendency and the social form governing these empirical, quantitative fluctuations?* While his vast biographical experience with the world of nineteenth-century capitalism informed his critical orientation as a *condition* of his critique, and was decisive in his *political* writings, the empiricist dimension of the initial inquiries for *Capital* (the *Grundrisse*) and the decades of drafting and revision from 1859 to 1883 is arguably limited to scouring the markings across thousands of sheets of paper.

Capital must be read as a *logic*: not as a mere discursive, logical-positivist word game but as the apodictic demonstration of the necessary forms of appearance of human labor in the value forms, as well as the systematic critique of the process of its mystification.[41] This would mean, first, to discern in *Capital* a positive, synthetic mode of demonstration. In his recent book *Rationalist Empiricism*, Nathan Brown rightly distinguishes Hegel's *Logic* both from the psychologistic assertion of the "I think" as the subject of the experience of thought and from the Kantian transcendental unity of apperception, to show however that it remains an idealist logic, such that "being cannot be thought independently of thinking, or as external to thinking."[42] If then we are to think *Capital* as a logic, it cannot be one wedded to being in this sense; *Capital* is not only a materialist rejection of Hegelian idealism; it is, moreover, neither a metaphysics nor an ontology.

Instead, *Capital* reproduces as a thought-concrete, in apodictic, positive dialectical form, the structural logic governing the necessary *forms of appearance* of things in a historically specific social form, a social form axiomatically defined, in the first sentence of *Capital*, as characterized by the commodification of all social wealth. Logic has no power to induce the necessary existence of a world, with its particular ontological characteristics. When delinked in this fashion from its Hegelian suturing to ontology, as the general science of Being, logic must be taken to constitute, as Badiou says in his *Logics of Worlds, the science of appearance* (*la science de l'apparaître*), the necessary forms of appearance and relations of objects in a given world, precisely Marx's project in *Capital*.

Unlike both classical political economy and mainstream economic theory, Marx does not begin with individual commodities in isolation to then additively follow their total movement in sum (of prices, unit production, employment, GDP, etc.), but precisely the opposite.[43] Marx proceeds in materialist fashion from the total social fact and relational system that is capitalist society, from the total, given mass of commodities (a heap or "immense collection" [*ungeheure Warensammlung*] that defines it as a social form, as his opening phrase to *Capital* puts it) to then reproduce, step by step, in the form of a "thought-concrete" [*Gedankenkonkretum*], the real structure and tendential laws of this totality. In constructing his critique of political economy, Marx in this manner breaks completely with the classical theory of Smith, Ricardo, and their followers and critics alike, in his own Copernican Revolution. Since, as Patrick Murray observes, it was eminently clear to Marx that "the labour theory of value does not hold at the level of the individual commodity," Marx instead begins his analysis from a total aggregate mass, a relational, social perspective within which any individual commodity is understood to be an "aliquot part" or identical fraction of that totality.[44] He then proceeds to develop the analysis of the capitalist totality at two levels of abstraction, that of the production and distribution of surplus value as a total mass (Volumes I and II respectively), followed by the analysis of the distribution of that total surplus value among individual sectors and units of capital via competition, to then arrive finally at the analysis of the most familiar, but also most illusory and fetishized, forms of appearance of capital: commercial capital, rent, finance, and so on.

This complexity of Marx's thought-object is, however, completely lost in Robinson's *Black Marxism*, which flatly asserts that

> capitalists, as the architects of this system [as Marx conceives it], never achieved the coherence of structure and organization that had been the promise

of capitalism as an objective system. On the contrary, the history of capitalism has in no way distinguished itself from earlier eras with respect to wars, material crises, and social conflicts.[45]

While the latter may well be true, though even this is unlikely, it seems thoroughly absurd to imply that "capitalists" sought to implement capitalism as a historical project in the form of "the coherence of structure and organization" that Marx achieved in his critique of political economy. The key point in relation to the discourse of racial capitalism is that it is only by clearly conceiving the nature of capitalism as a historically specific social form, in which, for reasons Marx clearly demonstrates, labor power forms the only commodity capable of creating surplus value, that one can hope, for example, to grasp the essential place of slave labor in capitalism.[46]

THE CONCEPT OF CAPITALIST SLAVERY

Black Marxism suffers from a confusion between the labor and labor *power* of slaves. Throughout his study, Robinson moves indiscriminately between references to "the importance Black labor power possessed," on the one hand, and "African Labor as Capital," on the other.[47] "It was not as slaves," Robinson writes elsewhere, "that one could come to an understanding of the significance that these Black men, women, and children had for American development. It was as labor."[48]

One crucial point of Marx's critique of slavery is that without a monetary form of appearance it is not labor, but slaves themselves that constituted capital in the form of the means of production of profitable commodities. When Robinson writes that "the significance of African labor for the development and formation of the commercial and industrial capitalist systems can be only partially measured by numbers," he is not even half right, since that labor, lacking a monetary price, cannot be measured by numbers at all, yet nonetheless must contribute to capitalist production in some unspecified form.[49] Repeating this confusion, Robinson claims that "African labor power as slave labor was integrated into the organic composition of nineteenth-century manufacturing and industrial capitalism."[50] At issue in Robinson's confusion is simply the fact that, as should be obvious to even the most empiricist observer, it was not "African slave labor" that had a "market value" but *slaves themselves*; slaveowners purchased in the slave market the entire person of slaves, not their labor power. There was no commodity market for "slave labor"; even if we were to formulate this concept more accurately as "slave labor power," such a term is quite simply, as Marx clearly saw, a nonsensical contradiction, a "square circle." In this passage, Marx addresses the crucial differential characteristics between labor power, sold for a limited time (the working day), and slave labor, sold "once and for all":

> Labour-power can appear on the market as a commodity only if, and in so far as, its possessor, the individual whose labour-power it is, offers it for sale or sells it as a commodity. In order that its possessor may sell it as a commodity, he must have it at his disposal, he must be the free proprietor of his own labour-capacity, hence of his person. . . . For this relation to continue, the proprietor of labour-power must always sell it for a limited period only, for *if he were to sell it in a lump, once and for all, he would be selling himself, converting himself from a free man into a slave.*[51]

Marx memorably pilloried the muddled thinking of the Ricardians who tried to analyze what they called the "value of labour," and his observations hold into the present for all those like Robinson who continue to invoke a putative "value of [slave] labour."[52] It is only possible to "speak of the value of labour," Marx argues in his chapter on wages in *Capital* volume 1, from the fetishized perspective of "the surface of bourgeois society." Marx insists, in contrast, that "it is not labour which directly confronts the [capitalist] possessor of money on the commodity-market, but rather the worker. What the worker is selling is his labour-power."[53] The key point to be taken here is not simply that the slave cannot by definition sell this labor power to the capitalist, since she is juridically prevented from possessing her labor as property to sell or withhold. Even more fundamentally, Marx continues, "labour is the substance, and the immanent measure of value, but *it has no value itself.*" To speak of "the value of labor" makes no more sense than to speak of the "value" of any other unit of measure, such as the value of velocity or weight. With mocking irony, Marx drives his logical point home in the simplest terms imaginable: "In the expression 'value of labour,' the concept of value is not only completely extinguished, but inverted, so that it becomes its contrary. *It is an expression as imaginary as the value of the earth.*"[54]

Let us be clear what Marx is saying here, since it is at once a simple and straightforward point, and the key to determining one of the central problems at issue in racial capitalism studies, namely the relation of slave- and wage-labor in capitalist production. Marx says, "The value of labour . . . is an expression as imaginary as the value of earth." To claim that the value of the earth (or of labor) is a meaningless or "imaginary" statement cannot be a transhistorical, ontological affirmation on Marx's part: we can easily imagine and describe many forms of the "value" of the earth (or of labor *tout court*). The earth both supports and allows for human life, say, or it is a source of aesthetic wonder and beauty, and so on. We may well "value" these aspects of its being, but our personal feelings of "what is valuable" are irrelevant, or, more precisely, do not *count*, in a society in which the capitalist social form predominates.[55]

But as pointed out earlier, only a commodity can have value: "A thing can be useful, and a product of human labour, without being a commodity. He who satisfies his own need with the product of his own labour admittedly creates use-values, but not commodities."[56] To count as a value in the capitalist social form, a concrete object or service must, by definition, have an exchange value, a value that must be manifested in the form of a *price*. A commodity without a price is a logical impossibility. Capitalism is the social form in which, as the saying goes, everything has its price, or, more accurately, everything *of value* (from the perspective of capital) has its price, a value from which *surplus* value can potentially be realized.[57]

THE CONCEPT OF RACIAL CAPITALISM

Cedric Robinson's definitions of the concept of racial capitalism remain notably vague, never achieving the theoretical clarity of Marx's analysis of the capitalist social form.[58] In the Introduction to *Black Marxism*, Robinson summarizes his understanding of the concept:

> The development, organization, and expansion of capitalist society pursued essentially racial directions, so too did *social ideology*. As a material force, then, it could be expected that racialism would inevitably permeate the social structures emergent from capitalism. I have used the term "racial capitalism" to refer to this development.[59]

The concept of racial capitalism poses a distinct epistemological problem, one that Robinson's emphasis on ideology as a material social force suggests. This is to say that since race itself is not a scientific but rather ideological concept (the assertion that there are distinct human races is itself the basis of racist ideology), the critical purchase of the concept of racial capitalism is limited to a critique of the ideological construction of identity via racial discourses.[60] Such a critique, the vast scope of which is suggested by a volume such as Jenkins and Leroy's *Histories of Racial Capitalism*, can hope to address the ways these discourses and modes of representation enforce the incorporation of racially identified populations within capitalist production. Racialist discourse serves to enforce market dependency, with subjects' labor—whether commodified (wage labor) or directly forced (slavery)—and consumption variously exploited for the valorization of value, or excluded through imprisonment, impoverishment, and ghettoized marginalization.[61]

In fact, the editors of *Histories of Racial Capitalism* imply precisely such a limitation of the object of racial capitalism in the relatively precise and useful definition they give of the concept. After the ritual invocation of the historians' disavowal of any "insistence on a pithy definition" and the absurd, obscurantist claim that "to draw too sharp a distinction between capitalist and noncapitalist is usually to mystify how capitalism works,"[62] the editors actually proceed to offer an extremely suggestive definition of racial capitalism: "All capitalism, in *material profitability* and *ideological coherence*, is constitutive of racial capitalism. . . . Racial capitalism is the process by which the key dynamics of capitalism . . . become *articulated* through race."[63] While the "key dynamics" of capitalism are never analyzed in their Introduction (they offer only a schematic laundry list of contrasting pairs of debatable relevance such as credit/debt, accumulation/dispossession, and capitalist/worker), one might rephrase their definition to argue that racial capitalism is the study of the racially inflected forms of appearance of the substance of value, abstract labor, and the dynamics of its *telos*, the substance of capital that is the accumulation of surplus value. The problem with such a neat division of labor between categorial studies of the capitalist social form and the ideology of racial capitalism is that—absent an initial analysis of the categorial structure of capital—the study of race and racism in capitalism can do no more than describe the phenomenal forms of this ideology and moralistically critique its predominance. But it remains unable to account for its necessity in a *theory* of racial capitalism.

The conceptual object that Marx painstakingly constructs in its real material necessity is taken for granted in the descriptive historicist analyses of Cedric Robinson and the racial capitalism literature more generally. Robinson makes lavish claims for the centrality of race to the historical development of capitalism, but for these to bear analytical weight would require a clear articulation of their significance within the process of the accumulation of surplus value. Robinson states:

> The comprehension of the particular configuration of racist ideology and Western culture has to be pursued historically through successive eras of violent domination and social extraction that directly involved European peoples during the better part of two millennia. Racialism insinuated not only medieval, feudal, and capitalist social structures, forms of property, and modes of production, but as well the very values and traditions of consciousness through which the peoples of these ages came to understand their worlds and their experiences.[64]

While it is no doubt the case that various forms of racial discourse "insinuated . . . the very values and traditions of *consciousness* through which the peoples of these [medieval, feudal, and capitalist] ages came to understand their worlds and their experiences," such a claim is merely descriptive, calling only for a historicist narrative compiling and comparing the forms and modalities of racialist ideology across the broad arc of the historical record. But even the most scrupulous compilation of these "insinuations" can reveal nothing about the specific nature of capitalism absent a notion of the essential nature of the capitalist social form. Robinson's stronger—and in my view entirely unsupportable—claim is that this same racialism "insinuated . . . medieval, feudal, and capitalist social structures, forms of property, and modes of production."[65] Lacking a demonstration, or even a minimal definition, of the capitalist system's complex structure and of the nature, source, and modality of the production of surplus value in particular, it remains impossible to grasp *why* the empirical, historical development and persistence of what Robinson calls "racialism" would bear any crucial historical significance for capitalism.

THE RACIAL IMAGINARY

For Marx, no less than Aristotle—the inventor of logical formalization whom Marx unambiguously calls "the greatest thinker of Antiquity"—and thinkers such as Alfarabi or Spinoza, it is impossible to adequately understand an object (such as capitalism or racism) by moving from its phenomenal, sensuous forms of appearance backward to impute to it imaginary causes. At stake in the epistemological problem of racial capitalism is the very nature of materialist critique. Already in the 1845 *Theses on Feuerbach*, Marx decisively rejected all forms of vulgar, empiricist materialism that claim to derive knowledge from sense impressions and things in their physical materiality.[66] Instead, Marx's understanding of materialist critique seeks to demonstrate what he calls "the laws of the tendencies" of the capitalist social form as a system of tendential necessity: Marx's system cannot predict the empirical development of historical phenomena but rather identifies the lawlike structure governing any situation.

It was Spinoza who argued against Descartes that the synthetic method of presentation, moving from the essential nature or substance of a thing to its phenomenal, and equally necessary, forms of appearance is no mere heuristic method for the secondary, formal exposition and illustration of truths previously derived in an analytic passage from the known to the unknown. Rather, for Spinoza, the synthetic method finds its superiority in organizing the movement of thought from the adequate knowledge of causes to that of their effects.[67] In this manner, the thought-object (Spinoza's *Ethics*) does not merely conform to or accurately represent the real order of things (there is no ontological dualism between thought and extension for Spinoza as there is for Descartes); it literally *is* the real order of things, the order of things apprehended under the attribute of thought, rather than in their attribute of sensuous, material extension. This form of exposition gives Spinoza's text its critical, properly ethical force in a manner precisely analogous to the critical intent of *Capital*: in this view, if adequate understanding of Spinoza's *Ethics* should necessarily prove transformative to the reader's understanding, allowing her to grasp the radical inadequacy of illusory forms of thinking (thinking backward from perceived effects to imaginary causes), the same can be said of *Capital*, whose attentive reader is led to pierce the ideological illusions of "the fetishism of the commodity," and even more radically, to grasp the *necessity* of these illusory forms of appearance in the system of capital as a whole.

While race and identity more generally constitute the neo-Calvinist substance of Anglo-American social discourse, crucial moments in the millennial history of critical Black Atlantic thought have instead displaced race to a dependent position, arguing from essential, universal principals axiomatically to deduce the necessary consequences, in thought and political militancy, of this orientation. While elsewhere I have named this militant antislavery universalism "Black Jacobinism," it is a tradition that extends back centuries before Toussaint Louverture's world historical destruction of Atlantic slavery. It extends to what is arguably the world's first charter of the human right to be free from enslavement, composed in the twelfth-century Mande Charter of the Malian empire of Soundiata Keita.[68] In the wake of Louverture's Haitian Revolution, key moments in this tradition of militant, universalist antislavery include C. L. R. James's *The Black Jacobins* and Aimé Césaire's construction of the poetics and politics of Negritude.[69]

In contrast to the empiricist tendencies of racial capitalism studies, this tradition of thought proceeds from an axiomatic statement of the universal nature of the human—that, in the words of the Haitian Kreyol proverb, *tout moun se moun*: every human being is entirely and unalienably a human subject—to deduce the necessary implication of this nature in the absolute injunction against human slavery and, furthermore, in the political act. While such an axiomatic, deductive orientation of thought and politics avoids the empiricism that undercuts studies of racial capitalism, from the perspective of Marx's materialist critique, its idealist starting point (the idea of universal human equality) nonetheless imposes a blindness to the status of this subject of rights in relation to the capitalist social form. In other words, under the capitalist social form, the free subject of human rights is the unequivocally necessary and adequate subject of capitalism. This is a consequence of the Black Jacobin politics of human rights that remains unrecognized by these theorists. In a social form in which everything has its price, where everything can and must be monetized for profit under the imperative of accumulation, there can and *must* remain only one exception to this general rule: the free subject of human rights, the subject whose capacity for labor must be voluntarily offered as a commodity, labor power, the sole and unique commodity able to create surplus value, the lifeblood of capital. When a person is bought as a commodity, as a slave, Marx argued, they are not free to own their labor power as their property, and thus to sell it for a wage, but are instead debased to a mere means of production, a source of motive power no different, from the perspective of capital, than any donkey, steam engine, or robot. In contrast to the idealism of this Black Jacobin tradition, including political Marxists such as James and Césaire, Marx himself constructs a fully materialist critique that begins not from an idea but from the real governing social form of a society whose form of appearance, as the first sentence of *Capital* asserts, is that of an immense accumulation of commodities.[70]

Racialism is a *symptom* of the capitalist social form, one that can only be adequately critiqued and theorized in materialist fashion, which is to say, through *analysis* both of its general causes and its singular instantiations. The clinical resonance of the term analysis is in my view decisive for grasping the materialist nature of such a critique. If a *law* (such as Marx's analysis of the tendential laws governing capitalism) would constitute an abstract or general universal, the *constant* arising in a given instance (a recurrent symptom in the patient, or the recurrence of racist violence in society) calls for the adequate analysis and treatment of that case in its singularity: no universal treatment is proper for the singularity of each case, yet the analyst must construct an adequate knowledge of its causes and not be misled by mere surface impressions. In the case of racism, such a symptomatic, materialist critique would seek to construct in an "analysis" the causal mechanisms governing the specifically capitalist dimension of racial violence both in its generality and singular consistency.

Capital is a materialist analysis not because it conducts experiments, presents data, universalizes from sense impressions, or refers to a putative priority of being over thought, but because it refuses the inadequacy of backward reasoning from sense impressions to their imaginary causes. Instead, it seeks to grasp the necessary causes of the objects and social relations in capitalism as the science of demystifying the appearances of the various capitalist social forms, the value forms. For Marx, to write *Capital* under the materialist condition of the events of his age—1848, Napoléon III and the persistence of capitalism, the Paris Commune—required the development of an adequate theoretical syntax for this social form. It involves the construction of the critique of political economy in order to critique the inadequacy of concepts such as "labour" and to replace them with adequate concepts such as labor power, etc., to create a new universe of objects. The development of this theoretical model, remained strictly within the domain of thought and concepts, imaginary and symbolic. It seeked to replace ideology with adequate formalization and modeling, as an apodictic demonstration.[71] Marx's procedure is not an empiricism, measuring a theory against sensuous situations or "reality," but a conceptual intervention within the domains of political economy and socialism.

In this light, I would argue that any adequate critique of the racialist dimension of the capitalist social form must necessarily grasp the ideological manifestations and deployments of racial discourse and violence both in their generality and singularity. This would imply that within this historically specific social form, dedicated to the accumulation of surplus value, racist violence forms a general (though not universal) constant, the necessity of which is to produce and reproduce via market dependency proletarian subjects and their labor power, along with other forms of non-commodified labor (slavery, prison labor) that have historically served and continue to serve as means of production, though the latter do not produce surplus value. In addition to such general notions governing the racialist dimensions of the capitalist social form, a materialist study of racial capitalism would also attend to the singular cases of this general process, from the development of mortgage and other forms of debt as a means of creating market dependency and impoverishment to the recurrent instances of violence symptomatic of the compulsive nature of American capitalism. Whether the critique of the political economy of race in the form of racial capitalist studies can overcome the constitutive contradiction of its conception, however, remains a question, drawn as it is between two fundamentally incongruous levels of abstraction that threaten to "tear asunder," as Dubois famously wrote, the possibility of a scientific study of its object.

NOTES

1. Marx 1976, 90.
2. Marx 1976, 128.
3. Marx 1976, 129.
4. I. I. Rubin was the first to analyze the essential interdependency of Marx's theories of value and money in a single monetary theory of value in his 1928 "Essays on Marx's Theory of Money": "The theory of money not only results from the theory of value but, conversely, the theory of value cannot be constructed without the theory of money and is only completed in the latter. . . . For the starting point of his analysis Marx takes the fact of the generalized equation of all commodities for one another, which characterizes the money economy and is impossible without the mediation of money" (Rubin 2018, 626).

5. "Marx's theory of price in the first volume [of *Capital*]," Patrick Murray writes, "insists that the difference between value and price is not nominal. . . . The idea that social form reaches all the way down into a mode of production and, therefore, must be an element in the fundamental concepts of a mode of production, is Marx's watershed idea" (Murray 2017, 271 and 446).

6. I reconstruct Marx's analysis of capitalist slavery, the conclusions of which I here summarize, in the first two chapters of Nesbitt 2022. I discuss Marx's nonempiricist theory of exploitation later.

7. For abstract labor to serve capitalist ends—which is to say not simply producing exchangeable commodities but making ever more money in the form of profit and capital accumulation—requires that it itself take the form of a commodity: namely labor power, appearing as *wage labor* in its exchange with capital. This relation between the exchange of monetary equivalents (wages for labor power) *on the surface* of capitalist productive relations and the *essential* relation—namely the exploitation of unpaid labor, harbored in the wage form—necessarily implies *free labor* and therefore the tendential irrelevance of unfree forms of labor, such as slavery. See Lange 2019.

8. It is in this sense that the passage from chapter five to six ("The Sale and Purchase of Labour-Power") constitutes the crucial axis of Marx's critique, the moment in which he "solves" the mystery of the source of surplus value and its fetishistic forms of appearance. This is the mystery that the classical political economists whom he critiques not only were unable to solve but lacking the essential categorial distinctions Marx develops—concrete and abstract labor, use value, value, and exchange value, value and profit, necessary and surplus labor—they could only formulate them as an insoluble conundrum: "The money-owner . . . must buy his commodities at their value, sell them at their value, and yet at the end of the process withdraw more value from circulation than he threw into it at the beginning. . . . These are the conditions of the problem. *Hic Rhodus, hic salta!*" (Marx 1976, 269).

9. This is Marx's central insight into the operations of the capitalist mode of production and its obfuscation in the theories of classical and vulgar political economy: "All the notions of justice held by both the worker and the capitalist, all the mystifications of the capitalist mode of production, all capitalism's illusions about freedom, all the apologetic tricks of vulgar economics, have as their basis the form of appearance discussed above, which makes the actual relation invisible, and indeed presents to the eye the precise opposite of that relation" (Marx 1976, 680).

10. Marx's analysis takes as its object not specific individual commodities, as did classical economics, but the total mass of commodities, an undifferentiated, "immense heap" (*ungeheure Warensammlung*), in relation to which Marx will analyze individual commodities as identical subdivisions or "aliquot parts" as the general substance of capital. Marx initiates in this manner not a logical proof or representation of the structure of capitalism, but instead undertakes a demonstration of the essential nature of the real (commodified) social forms of relation in capitalism, to *construct*, under the aspect of thought (rather than sensuous material extension), actual capitalist social relations. See Rubin 2018; Moseley 2017.

11. Dale Tomich discusses from a Marxian perspective the enormously complex historical process of this tendential displacement in the case of Martinican sugar production from 1830 to 1848, in what is in my judgment the finest single study of the political economy of capitalist slave labor, *Slavery in the Circuit of Sugar* (Tomich 2018). There, Tomich analyzes the many factors by which Antillean slaveowners' cane sugar gradually became impossible to sell at profit in competition with more industrialized, wage labor–based European beet sugar. I discuss both the accomplishments and limitations of Tomich's book in Nesbitt 2022.

12. Park 2021, 27; Sweeney 2021, 58.
13. See Marx 1976, 151
14. Park 2021, 28.
15. Park 2021, 32.
16. Park 2021, 30 and 32.
17. Thier 2020.
18. Marx was of course not only eminently aware of the racism of his times, but via his journalism substantially contributed to the critique of American slavery and celebration of its abolition. See Anderson 2010.

19. "A thing can be useful, and a product of human labour, without being a commodity. He who satisfies his own need with the product of his own labour admittedly creates use-values, but not commodities." (Marx 1976, 131)

20. Robinson 2000 (1983), xxvii.

21. *Black Marxism* contains exactly one reference in its 436 pages to *Capital, Volume 1*, neatly tucked away in its footnotes (Robinson 2000 [1983], 347), and otherwise limits its two other references to *Capital* to selections gleaned from Robert Tucker's 1978 anthology.

22. I am far from the first to note the woefully inadequate interrogation of Marx's critique of political economy in *Black Marxism*. See Ralph and Singhal 2019, and in response, Burden-Stelly 2020.

23. Robinson 2000 (1983), xxix. "I have investigated the failed efforts to render the historical being of Black peoples into a construct of historical materialism, to signify our existence as merely an opposition to capitalist organization" (Robinson 2000 [1983], xxxv; see also 233). Marx's assertions in "Forms Which Precede Capitalist Production" have proven both influential and problematic. On the one hand, as analytical categories for historical investigation, their accuracy has not withstood subsequent historical and archaeological investigation. As Ellen Meiksins Wood summarizes, Marx's "account of all three major forms were, in varying ways and degrees, misleading, when not downright wrong" (Meiksins Wood 2008, 80). That said, as Marx delineates the parameters of each of these precapitalist modes of production, he underscores the dynamic and temporal nature of various social relations and configurations. Wood argues that in "Forms which Precede Capitalist Production," "each system of social property relations is driven by its own internal principles and not by some transhistorical law of technological improvement or commercial expansion" (Meiksins Wood 2008, 88). Against Robinson's misrepresentation of Marx's historical method, such an argument is precisely a *refutation* of transhistorical laws and technological determinism.

24. Robinson 2000 (1983), 2.
25. Robinson 2000 (1983), xxviii, 4.
26. Robinson 2000 (1983), 121.
27. In Chapter 6 of *Capital*, Marx simultaneously displaces historical considerations from his categorial analysis, while foreshadowing his discussion of primitive accumulation in Part 8. See Marx 1976, 273.
28. See Elena Louisa Lange 2018. On the question of the inseparability of the labor theory of value form the monetary theory of value, and vice versa, see Lange 2021b, 423–62.
29. Robinson 2000 (1983), xxviii–xxix. "History, for Marx, became the antagonistic play of the relations of living social categories whose existence was predicated on the particular characters of production and property that had been the basis of social life. . . . The materialist conception of history situated the objective and necessary forces of a society, distinguishing their significance from those categories of human activity that were the result of pure speculation (idealism) and ideology" (Robinson 2000 [1983], 52).
30. While *Reading Capital*, adapted from a series of 1964 seminar papers given by Althusser and his students, remains by Althusser's own express admission only a compilation of "incomplete texts, the mere beginnings of a *reading*," (Althusser 2017, 11, emphasis in original) these interventions, and in particular that of Pierre Macherey's long-overlooked analysis of the first five pages of *Capital*, initiate the reading of *Capital* as a categorial critique that informs my analysis here. See Nesbitt 2017.
31. Althusser 2017, 34.
32. Spinoza's critique of empiricism is absolute. See Spinoza 2018: 34–41.
33. Althusser 2017, 35.
34. Althusser 2017, 41.
35. Althusser 2017, 36.
36. Althusser 2017, 36.
37. Smith 1999 (1776). I take this example from the brilliant analysis of Marx's 1857 methodology by Juan Iñigo Carrera (see Carrera 2014).
38. "However far back we ascend, into the past of a branch of knowledge, we are never dealing with a 'pure' sensuous intuition or mere 'representation,' but with an *always-already* complex raw material, a structure of 'intuition' or 'representation' which combines together in a peculiar '*Verbindung*' sensuous, technical, and ideological elements; that therefore knowledge never, as empiricism desperately demands it should, confronts a *pure object* which is then identical to the *real object* of which knowledge aimed to produce precisely . . . the knowledge" (Althusser 2017, 43, emphasis in original).
39. Jacques Bidet develops this Althusserian argument in Bidet 2006 (1985).
40. For three highly visible deployments of this metaphor, see "Spike Lee calls us to recognize the racism baked into America's DNA," *Houston Chronicle*, February 29, 2019. https://www.houstonchronicle.com/opinion/outlook/article/Spike-Lee-calls-us-to-recognize-the-racism-baked-13647186.php. Accessed July 13, 2021. "Obama uses slur to make point on racism: Says history of slavery is part of nation's DNA,"

Boston Globe, June 22, 2015, https://www.bostonglobe.com/news/nation/2015/06/22/obama-says-racism-not-cured-makes-point-with-epithet/E2BprM8ffmtPJt37dp4wXP/story.html. Accessed July 13, 2021. "In order to understand the brutality of American capitalism, you have to start on the plantation," *The New York Times 1619 Project*, August 14, 2019, https://www.nytimes.com/interactive/2019/08/14/magazine/slavery-capitalism.html. Accessed July 13, 2021.

41. It was Althusser who first claimed (without demonstrating) that "in *Capital* we find a systematic presentation, an apodictic arrangement of the concepts in the form of that type of demonstrational discourse that Marx calls analysis" (Althusser 2015, 51).

42. Brown 2021, 78–79.

43. Marx clearly recognized that many of the unsurpassable contradictions and logical contortions of the classical labor theory of value arose from its focus on the various modes of algebraically combining individual commodity units. See Murray 2017, 16–28.

44. "Marx had to overthrow the individualistic classical labour theory of value in order to reconcile his [monetary, social] labour theory of value with the formation of a general rate of profit. Marx replaces the failed classical theory of value, which explains individual prices in terms of individual values and individual profits in terms of individual surplus values, with a labour theory of value that holds at the aggregate level (the level of total capital) and explains subordinate phenomena on that basis. . . . Marx revolutionizes the classical labour theory of value by making the aliquot or representative commodity the object of inquiry" (Murray 2017, 22–23).

45. Robinson 2000 (1983), 9.

46. I reconstruct Marx's analysis of capitalist slavery in precisely this fashion in Nesbitt 2022.

47. Robinson 2000 (1983), 4, 109.

48. Robinson 2000 (1983), 199.

49. Robinson 2000 (1983), 112.

50. Robinson 2000 (1983), 113.

51. Marx 1976, 271, emphasis mine.

52. In Nesbitt 2022, I analyze in greater detail other cases of this theoretical confusion beside that of Robinson, such as Robin Blackburn's *The Making of New World Slavery*, alongside Marx's critique of this indistinction, as well as his analysis of the essential nature of capitalist slavery.

53. Marx 1976, 677. Emphasis mine.

54. Marx 1976, 677. Emphasis mine.

55. It must always be recalled that the object of Marx's analysis is not human society as such but a historically specific social form: "What I have to examine in this work [*Capital*] is the capitalist mode of production and the relations of production and forms of intercourse that correspond to it." (Marx 1976, 91)

56. Marx 1976, 131.

57. In fact, the crucial exception to this general rule is the free wage laborer himself, as Patrick Murray notes, who cannot have a price lest he become a slave sold at market. Since capital depends upon the freedom of the worker to offer his labor power for sale to produce surplus value, this exception is in fact unsurpassable within the

capitalist social form. This also accounts for why domestic labor cannot be commodified (though the domestic worker can of course be oppressed in many other ways) to produce surplus value. If it were, the commodity she produces, by the definition of a commodity as someone's property to sell for a price, would be unfree "workers," in other words, slaves. See Murray 2017, 181.

58. Dustin Jenkins and Justin Leroy in the Introduction to their volume *Histories of Racial Capitalism* point out that the term "racial capitalism" does not in fact originate with Robinson's book, but in the anti-Apartheid struggle in South Africa in the 1970s, for example, in the founding 1983 manifesto of the National Forum drafted by Neville Alexander: "Our struggle for national liberation is directed against the system of racial capitalism that holds the people of Azania [South Africa] in bondage. . . . Apartheid will be eradicated with the system of racial capitalism" (Jenkins and Leroy 2021, 4). But as the editors to the present volume point out in the introduction, more than twenty years after the "peaceful" transition from White minority rule, South Africa remains one of the most unequal societies in the world (see Dessus and Hanusch 2018).

59. Robinson 2000 (1983), 2. Emphasis mine.

60. A classic summary of the ideological nature of the concept of race is found in Appiah 1986. Indeed, the essays in this founding volume of race studies focus almost entirely on race, racism, and their various forms and histories of representation. For more recent studies, see Wald Sussman 2014 and Golash-Boza 2017.

61. Jenkins and Leroy 2021, 3.

62. All scientific analysis must construct its object. Moreover, the practice of critique, even etymologically, is nothing but the adequate drawing of distinctions.

63. Jenkins and Leroy 2021, 1 and 3. Emphasis mine.

64. Robinson 2000 (1983), 66.

65. Robinson 2000 (1983), 66.

66. In *La philosophie de Marx*, Étienne Balibar observes in passing that, in the *Theses on Feuerbach*, "Marx's materialism has nothing to do with a reference to matter [but is instead] a strange 'materialism without matter'" (Balibar 2014 [1993], 98). Alberto Toscano has extrapolated on Balibar's suggestive comment in relation to Sohn-Rethel and I. I. Rubin's analysis of the value form, proposing that Marx's subsequent analysis of the capitalist social form of value precisely constitutes such a materialism, one in which, as Marx famously comments in *Capital*, "not an atom of matter enters into the objectivity of commodities as values" (Marx 1976, 138). See Toscano 2014.

67. The editors of I. I. Rubin's *Essays on Marx's Theory of Money* observe that Marx proceeds in analogous fashion, such that the critique of "political economy analytically determines its fundamental category [the commodity] and then synthetically reconstructs its subject matter in theory" (Rubin 2018, 621).

68. See Nesbitt 2013 and Nesbitt 2014, 11–20.

69. On James, see Nesbitt 2022; on Césaire, see Nesbitt 2015, 129–44.

70. As Marx affirms in his "Notes on Adolph Wagner," "I do not start out from 'concepts,' hence I do not start out from 'the concept of value.' . . . What I start out from is the simplest *social form* in which the labour-product is presented in

contemporary society, and this is the 'commodity.' I analyse it, and right from the beginning, *in the form in which it appears*. Here I find that it is, on the one hand, in its natural form, a useful thing, alias a 'use value,' on the other hand, it is a bearer of exchange value, and from this viewpoint, it is itself 'exchange value.' Further analysis of the latter shows me that exchange value is only a 'form of appearance,' the autonomous mode of presentation of the value contained in the commodity" (Marx 1996, 241–42, emphasis mine).

71. Feltham 2020, 37–56.

Chapter 11

Is Postcolonial Theory's Ethical Turn a Political Dead End?

Nivedita Majumdar

Postcolonial theory emerged with the claim of representing the subaltern subject where other theories had allegedly failed. While borrowing the idea of the "subaltern" from Gramsci, postcolonial theorists use it broadly to refer to groups and individuals who are in a relation of any kind of subordination. The theory marked a departure not just from colonialist, nationalist and bourgeois perspectives; those frameworks had been effectively challenged both through revolutionary struggles and through Marxist theories. The real claim to radical critique in postcolonialist theory is underpinned by its qualified rejection of Marxism. Like the older perspectives, postcolonial theory contends, Marxism, too, is unwittingly guilty of failing the subaltern. In its preoccupation with the economic realm, the claim goes, Marxism is unable to account for the every-day texture of exploitation and the lived experience of the subaltern. The charge against Marxist approaches expands into a broader ambivalence toward *all* collective politics and organized struggles. Postcolonial critiques contend that the experiential reality of the oppressed—in whose name such struggles are waged—is lost in the metanarratives of collective politics. It is the claim of deep solidarity, of being in tune with the subaltern subject where other theories had failed, that earned postcolonial theory its novelty and its radical mantle in academia.

A skepticism regarding organized political struggle and transformative social mobilization is a central feature of postcolonial theory; still, the theory defines itself as a political project centering on the subaltern subject. There is a deep contradiction here, which proponents of the theory resolve through a turn toward a specific kind of normative stance that underlies the "ethical turn." But is this strategy effective? By focusing on the works of a few key theorists, Gayatri Chakravorty Spivak, Homi Bhabha, Robert Young, Steven Morton, and Leela Gandhi, I try to show that it is not. In eschewing systemic critiques of capitalism and aligning with the poststructuralist suspicion of collective struggles, postcolonial theory, for all its radical pretensions, is left upholding a liberal politics of individual benevolence, which not only fails to advance its stated political mission, but actively undermines it.

Even though it emerged definitively in the 1980s, the genealogy of postcolonial theory can be traced back to the 1960s, when critical theory slowly pivoted to cultural and political matters away from textual inquiry. The intellectual shift was part of a political moment that witnessed flourishing social movements. Along with movements around racial and gender equity, it was also an epoch shaped by the Cuban revolution and the anti-war activism around Vietnam, as well as the decolonization of Africa. Between the end of the Second World War and the late 1960s, U.S. universities experienced phenomenal growth and expansion and their character was transformed from enclaves of elite culture to institutions of learning for the broader population as well as a credible ladder for upward mobility. Universities at this time became the most prominent sites of protests against wars and for campaigns on social justice issues. Broad social movements and a diverse student body led to fundamental shifts in the content of education away from canonical texts to a democratization of curriculum.

The liberal-Left milieu, however, was just as much shaped by a tacit acceptance of the defeat of a socialist vision. If labor unions and socialist organization of varied stripes had gained strength in a different political climate in the wake of the depression of the 1930s, by the late 1960s and, especially, after the economic downturn of the 1970s, the arc moved in the opposite direction, that of economic and political conservatism. The neoliberal doctrine with its deregulation of markets, free trade, and decimation of labor unions became the reigning doctrine in the 1970s and 1980s. The liberal-Left turn in universities in the same era offered no meaningful challenge to the neoliberal consensus. In fact, the rejection of Marxism in critical theory in general and postcolonial theory in particular bespeaks academia's accommodation to a larger political trend of defeat for progressive forces.

Postcolonial thought expresses the contradictory pulls of liberalism and conservatism by eschewing the centrality of class analysis and yet fashioning itself as a radical program. Drawing on the rapid decolonization of Africa, a developing ethos of Third-Worldism, as also, the robust affiliation of the Communist movement with the colonized world, the foundation of postcolonial critique was laid in terms of foregrounding the oppression of the global South. If the central preoccupation of the discipline speaks to its progressive credential, the scant engagement with capitalism exposes its accommodationist character. The discipline attempts to displace the study of capitalism with the assumption that the real culprit behind the predicament of the postcolonial world is colonialism. The move away from class analysis was strong enough to sideline any serious inquiry in the discipline regarding the relation between capital and colonialism.

Interestingly, the broader move in critical theory toward overtly political concerns of race, gender, sexuality, environment, and especially, the emergence of postcolonial discourse in the 1980s has been termed as the "ethical turn" in theory.

In a recent study, *The Ethics of Theory: Philosophy, History, Literature*, for instance, Robert Doran contends that critical theory has now "become synonymous with the ethical and political questions that agitate our times."[1] In attempting to locate the conditions that led to the putative ethical turn, Doran points to public disclosure of Heidegger's connections with Nazism in the 1930s and the discovery of early anti-Semitic writings by Paul de Man leading to a backlash against a kind of critical practice that was viewed as devoid of ethics. The death of the author was no longer an option, instead it heralded a resurrection of the ethical subject in the form of the author figure: "The fact that Derrida was a Jew born in (French) Algeria and the fact that Foucault was a homosexual, facts that were considered philosophically irrelevant in the 1960s and 1970s, suddenly became salient"[2] with the ethical turn.

While Doran's analysis certainly has its place, what is noteworthy is that in the discussion of the "ethical turn," the conservatism of critical theory in general and postcolonial theory in particular remains largely unacknowledged. Thus, critics view the work of foundational postcolonial theorists like Homi Bhabha and Gayatri Spivak as ethical practice. Maureen Moynagh, for instance, observes that the "increasing preoccupation with the ethical in postcolonial criticism betrays both an anxiety about the political efficacy of postcolonial theory and doubts about anti-imperialist projects of various kinds, including uncertainty about once cherished emancipatory categories such as the nation,"[3] and offers Bhabha's concern with migrant and diasporic populations, and Spivak's engagement with the location of the intellectual as central instances of such ethical practice. Similarly, for Rey Chow, Spivak's "final message is one of an ethical affirmation of the historical and social as the site for struggle against exploitation."[4]

ETHICAL DEAD ENDS

The "ethical" in postcolonial theory is typically realized in the context of an antipathy to systemic critiques of capital. In his Introduction to a new volume of *The Wretched of The Earth*, Bhabha, for instance, writes of the continuing relevance of Frantz Fanon to our contemporary context of global uneven development and "dual economies."[5] He acknowledges an urgent need to address inequality, especially, in light of the fact that, the debates on social equity have "perhaps focused too exclusively on the culture wars, the politics of identity and the politics of recognition."[6] The highlighting of structural inequalities might lead to the expectation that Bhabha would then turn to the role of capital. But consistent with postcolonial thought, he in fact makes the opposite move. He claims that Fanon's vision transcends binary divisions and posits that for the global South, the choice between capitalism and socialism is a false one because it's a cold war imposition. Instead, Fanon allegedly offered a non-universalist notion of historical agency that is "strategic, activist and aspirational" with struggles conducted on a terrain of local relevance. So how precisely does this reading of Fanon translate in the contemporary world? For Bhabha, this is accomplished through a politics that demands debt relief or forgiveness, health initiatives that work for the availability of generic drugs for HIV-AIDS as a matter of human right, and in work along these lines by NGOs, human rights organizations, legal and educational bodies. Such outfits, Bhabha claims, represent Fanon's opposition to the "*imposed* univocal choice of 'capitalism vs Socialism'."[7]

First, Bhabha's interpretation of Fanon's observation—that the real issue is not so much the confrontation between capitalism and socialism as it is the redistribution of wealth—is disingenuous and taken out of context.[8] The confrontation that Fanon is referring to is that of the cold war, a political conflict between superpowers that does not immediately address the question of structural inequality. Fanon is clear that it is not in the interests of the underdeveloped countries to get involved in the rivalries of the cold war, but he is equally clear that the global South must adopt the socialist path:

> We know, of course, that the capitalist way of life is incapable of allowing us to achieve our national and universal project. Capitalist exploitation, the cartels and monopolies, are the enemies of the underdeveloped countries. On the other hand, the choice of a socialist regime, of a regime entirely devoted to the people, based on the principle that man is the most precious asset, will allow us to progress faster in greater harmony, consequently ruling out the possibility of a caricature of a society where the privileged few hold the reins of political and economic power without a thought for the nation as a whole.[9]

In contrast to the homogenized and binary categories of postcolonial theory, Fanon did not subscribe to the idea of capitalism as a Western phenomenon, but recognized it to be a *global*, if uneven, system; and that its fundamental logic of exploitation produces resistance, often along socialist lines, in the global South as it does in the West. So, it is not Fanon, but Bhabha who insists on rejecting the centrality of both capitalism and socialism, but consistent with postcolonial preoccupations, he then also wishes to address structural inequities. This is the postcolonial dilemma—how to engage with issues of inequity and injustice under capitalism while rejecting a structural analysis of capital. Postcolonial theorists address the dilemma in the only possible way they can—by embracing a politics of liberal reformism but claim novelty by claiming it to be the "ethical turn." Thus, Bhabha steers clear of the systemic deconstruction of capitalism that only a socialist politics can offer, and instead embraces the palliative benefits of NGO like institutions as the only possible horizon for politics.

Spivak's theoretical engagements similarly exhibit a repudiation not just of class conflict, but an ambivalence toward all collective struggles, followed by an "ethical" agenda with little political impact. She embraces "subalterneity" while implicitly denying the validity of Gramsci and the larger Marxist tradition's structural analysis in which the concept is embedded. Her denial of class conflict in the context of the global South produces a rather peculiar analysis. One of the defining aspects of the proletariat in the South, Spivak contends, is that it is inserted into politics in a manner fundamentally different from that in the advanced West. In the West, the working class matures into class politics largely through "its training in consumerism," whereas "the urban proletariat in comprador countries must not be systematically trained in the ideology of consumerism (parading as the philosophy of a classless society) that, against all odds, prepares the ground for resistance."[10] In fact, in the sprawling export-processing zones and subcontracting arrangements typical of economic development in these parts of the world, she insists, the suppression of workers' wages means that "the training in consumerism is almost snapped." Hence, what makes a politics organized around class interests so unrealistic in the Global South is that the working class does not get properly trained in it, and what makes that training so rare is that its source is not available to them—an immersion in the ideology and practice of consumerism.

What we have here is a strange assertion of *consumerism* being a training ground for, or the fount of, class politics. Spivak assumes that the simple experience of work—the subordination to the employer's authority, long hours, brutal pace of labor, physical intimidation, exposure to injury, insecurity—that all of this is not what impels labor to organize. It is not the daily degradation and humiliation or the experience of grinding poverty that is behind class politics. It is, rather, the participation in consumerism. Spivak must know that there is a pivotal and venerable distinction between consumption and consumerism. Whereas the former refers to the quotidian act of physical reproduction by workers, the latter points to an ideological formation in which the internalization of goods is turned into an end for itself. The central importance of consumerism has been noted by many social theorists since Marx, most notably members of the Frankfurt School—but only as a development that impedes class consciousness and secures the working class ever more firmly to the mast of capitalism. In rebranding it as the training ground of class politics, Spivak obscures what is and has been the real source of working-class resistance in capitalism—the experience of impoverishment and degradation in the class relation—and at the same time sanctifies as the real source of such politics what is in fact one of the main obstacles to it. And by thus centering consumerism as the ground condition for class conflict, she forecloses any inquiry into organized workers' struggles in the global South.

But Spivak does not merely turn away from class struggle, she questions the efficacy of *all* collective politics. As in Bhabha, the rejection of organized struggles paves the path for a putative ethical agenda which amounts to little more than individual benevolence. So, repudiating organizing work necessary for collective struggles, Spivak insists that "no amount of raised consciousness field-work can ever approach the painstaking labor to establish ethical singularity with the subaltern."[11] By "ethical singularity" she means a deep empathetic relationship with the subaltern based on mutual recognition, for presumably only in such a relationship can the singularity of the subaltern subject be appreciated. Having raised an impossibly high bar for a meaningful relationship with the subaltern, Spivak acknowledges that it is indeed "impossible for all leaders (subaltern or otherwise) to engage every subaltern in this way."[12] The impossibility notwithstanding, Spivak holds that political movements are destined to fail unless they incorporate the "ethical singularity" of the subaltern. In other words, she first enumerates an impossible standard, and then signals the death knell of collective politics by declaring that the standard cannot be met.

While critiquing the politics of organized and collective action, Spivak still wishes to retain the radical element of such politics. Even as "ethical singularity" might be an impossible goal, Spivak attempts to acknowledge the value of political organizing by drawing on a romantic idea of a sincere and spontaneous relationship between the activist and the oppressed. She betrays an obliviousness to the fact that what she calls "free and fair exchange" between oppressed people and activists is never a spontaneous affair. Opening up to activists is never easy for the oppressed because it carries the formidable threat of retaliation by oppressors. And yet, the "free and fair exchange" does happen. But there is nothing spontaneous about it. It happens only because of the deep trust built through patient organizing work. Spivak speaks of the "impossibility" of deep individual connections between activists and members of oppressed groups. And yet, political actions, to the extent that they make an impact, are made possible precisely through building such long-term close relationships with members of oppressed groups. No doubt ground-level organizing in spite of patient, committed work often falter and fail because all the odds are stacked against such political activity. But Spivak's finger-wagging admonition to committed activists charging that their endeavors are doomed to failure because they do not rise to the level of appreciating the subaltern's "ethical singularity" is a little odd.

The massive influence of Spivak in the discipline has produced literary and social analyses that similarly repudiate the possibilities of collective politics and embrace an "ethical turn" signaling a return to a liberal politics of reformism and individual benevolence. Steven Morton's postcolonial reading of Arundhati Roy's *The God of Small Things*[13] offers a typical instance of such analyses. Morton discusses the significance in the novel of the murderous attack by the police on Velutha, an undercaste and an active member of the Indian Communist Party. The attack was also aided by Comrade Pillai, the local leader of the Communist Party. Velutha is punished for transgressing caste boundaries by having a sexual relationship with Ammu, an upper caste woman. Comrade Pillai indirectly colludes in this murder because he too subscribes to caste restrictions.

For Morton, the incident speaks to the inability of Comrade Pillai and the Communist Party to account for Velutha's transgression of caste boundaries within the collective political terms of the workers' movement. Evoking Spivak, he holds that the Party is not equipped to account for the "singularity of the subaltern" as evidenced in Velutha's transgressive act. Morton contends that "Comrade Pillai's reprehensible treatment of Velutha marks the ethical limitations of the Communist Party and the workers' movement vis-à-vis the singular position of the subaltern."[14] Expressing his clear hostility to class politics, he points to the necessity of "guard[ing] against the violence of political programs, which ignore the singularity of the subaltern." There is no interest here to integrate class struggle with other forms of resistance around gender or race. Instead, class politics is simply delineated as *intrinsically* exclusionary and violent. Velutha's class position, in this reading, unlike his caste and sexuality, is not a component of his "singularity."

Morton's reading is characterized by a constructed opposition between class on the hand and other identity markers on the other. Here, he echoes a general consensus of the "ethical turn" that while race, gender and sexuality speak to a subject's *lived* experience, class is experienced as an *abstracted* phenomenon. Bhabha, for instance, argues that it is the "peculiarity of regimes of racial oppression that they make immediately visible and vivid the more mediated and abstract practices of power such as class division, the exploitation of labor, and social hierarchies of status."[15] So class oppression supposedly only become "immediately visible" in colonial contexts which he terms as "regimes of racial oppression." Neither Bhabha nor Morton, or any other postcolonial theorist, explain exactly how class oppression is a "mediated" or "abstracted" phenomenon. Where is the *abstraction* in workers' experiences of chronic job insecurity, or frequent humiliation on the shop floor, or being forced to work under terribly unsafe conditions, or the debilitating inability to take care of loved ones in spite of routine backbreaking labor? Somehow none of this rise to the level of experiential immediacy for postcolonial theorists, and therefore, remain unworthy of an ethical stance.

Not surprisingly, when critics of the "ethical turn" venture into issues relating to the degradation of the environment, they choose to ignore the structural incompatibility between capitalism and ecological justice.[16] Robert Young,[17] for instance, highlights the well-publicized case of the Nigerian environmental activist, Ken Saro Wiwa's military execution in 1995 after he led a campaign against environmental degradation in the Niger Delta, an outcome of the operations of crude oil extraction perpetrated by the multinational petroleum industry, in particular, Shell. Young offers a detailed study shedding light on the close collusion between Shell and the Nigerian military regime where the latter actively aided the company's activities in the region that amounted to massive environmental wreckage and suffering for the local population. As an instance of Shell's active collusion with the dictatorship, the company even drew its own armed police from the Nigerian forces. Young produces archival evidence clarifying how the deaths of Ken Saro Wiwa and his compatriots, who were engaged in an effective organizing battle against Shell, was a desirable outcome for the company. In the conclusion to his study, Young points out that the issue of corporate degradation of environment and the wanton violation of human rights goes far beyond this one instance and is in fact progressively getting worse.

So what lessons does the eminent postcolonial critic draw from his own findings of this instance of egregious collusion between a state and a giant corporation which speaks to a general phenomenon? In his own words,

> Among the many lessons that have to be learned, the first is that all people in all countries in the world, whatever their standard of living or degree of "development," have a right to expect companies and governments to observe the same ethical standards that would be expected anywhere else. If companies are ethical, and individual governments not, then those companies should exert what power and influence they have to change them (just as governments also have a duty to ensure that companies operate ethically). . . . With the transition to civilian rule, Shell has now the opportunity to demonstrate definitively that its actions match up to its words. It has initiated a "debate" on "Profits and principles: is there a choice?"[18]

What we have here is essentially a call for the necessity of—and a faith in—ethical operation of corporations. It is as if Shell merely went astray and there are no structural reasons why the interests of such companies are fundamentally inconsistent with any responsibility toward the communities and environments where they operate. But it goes beyond that. Young would also want multinational companies to exert their "power and influence" over sovereign states to "change them." While corporate influence over governments signals a fundamental inversion of democratic principles in all instances, that Young would advance this view in the context of the operation of first world corporations in the global South is especially shocking. With Young, Spivak's call for ethical singularity has morphed into one for corporate ethics.

CULTURE AS ETHICS

The influence of the "ethical turn" is most pronounced in the culturalist underpinnings of the works of postcolonial critics. Culturalism does not just signal a shift in focus from underlying economic structures to culture but advances an analytical stance that holds culture to be the *primary source* of social phenomena. Once culture is ascribed causal primacy, it sidesteps political and economic conditions and produces analysis that tends to be both conservative and essentialist. Once again, Robert Young offers a telling instance of the phenomenon.[19] He rightly observes that postcolonial theory has not meaningfully engaged with the Israel-Palestine conflict, thereby implicitly acquiescing to the Western construction of radical Islam as an oppositional discourse whose terms are beyond engagement—an unbridgeable other. Othering, Young asserts, is what postcolonialists "should try to deconstruct."[20] And yet, the remedy proposed by Young only reinforces the stereotypical binaries of the secular West and of a region in the throes of radical Islam.

For Young, the corrective to the silence on Palestine in postcolonial theory would be to tear down the ideological veil of negativity surrounding Islam and instead foreground the laudatory aspects of the religion and its institutions. He complains that postcolonial theory has sidelined the political role of religion in general, and thus what needs to be foregrounded is how Islamic empires in fact offered alternatives modes of governmentality based on tolerance. Young's analysis is not surprising given that postcolonial critique rejects ascribing causality to underlying political and economic conditions. Therefore, the specificities of the oppression perpetrated by Israeli settler colonial policies on the Palestinian people is of little interest to him. And he remains oblivious to the actual causes fueling Palestinian resistance like the loss of political freedom and material deprivations.

Instead, Young insists that the conflict is fundamentally underpinned by religion, and that the religious resistance by the Palestinians might offer alternative modes of tolerance and coexistence, as in the Islamic empires of previous centuries. Young's analysis is disturbingly consistent with the premise of fundamental cultural differences between the West and the rest as instantiated in Samuel Huntington's thesis of "clash of civilizations."[21] Young maintains that the putative Islamic resistance by the Palestinians is indeed embedded in cultural difference, but only differs from the Huntingtonian model in holding that the resistance has something positive to offer. If Said highlighted the essentialization of the colonized's culture and the erasure of the colonized's actual history as the central characteristics of the constructed Other, then the task for the postcolonial critic would be to deconstruct the binary between the colonial and the colonized. In a curious twist, however, critics like Young reinstate the binary with the only difference that the non-West is cast in a positive light. The postcolonial critic's "ethical" analysis reverses oriental scholarship by turning the colonial subject into a repository of desirable characteristics while still subscribing to the orientalist premise of essentialized difference.

Leela Gandhi, another eminent theorist of the field, similarly builds on the foundation of postcolonial difference, but with a twist in the idea of the ethical. In *The Common Cause*,[22] Gandhi contends, first, that Western democracy evolved as a fundamentally illiberal concept, and second, that there are more meaningful and productive non-Western sources of democracy. She identifies an underlying principle in the development of the idea of democracy across the ideological spectrum in the West—the "ethicalization of the political." This "ethicalization" for Gandhi manifests in the putative "perfectionist bias" of Western political thought which while holding "disciplined self-fashioning" as the norm, excludes the ordinary and the unexceptional. In contrast, she upholds an ethic of "moral imperfectionism" in Indian history as evidenced by abnegation and inclusiveness in the anticolonial practices of spiritual leaders and in Mahatma Gandhi's politics. The ethic of "imperfectionism," located in non-Western spiritual and political traditions, is, for Leela Gandhi, akin to the core aspiration of inclusiveness in the concept of democracy.

Leela Gandhi repudiates the allegedly Western idea of the "*ethicalization* of politics," but much like other postcolonial theorists, asserts the desirability of an ethical politics—one that she firmly locates in the global South. Her work rehashes the core premises of the discipline on politics in general and on the relationship between the West and the periphery in particular but remains crippled by its fundamental analytical flaws. First, while the claim that the evolution of the democratic ideal in the West proceeds from the "ethicalization of the political," even if true, is ultimately uninteresting. Most political programs, regardless of place of origin, are underpinned by an ethical basis that determines their content. As an example of a politics that's supposedly not based on "ethicalization," Leela Gandhi offers Mahatma Gandhi's embrace of the oppressed and social rejects. But this is a strange contention. If "ethicalization" refers to the generalization or codification of political principles, then there is no reason to believe that Mahatma Gandhi would be opposed to that. Political campaigns, like ones led by Gandhi, are the products of generalization of political principles. And even though Gandhi did not play much of a role in the framing of the Indian constitution, he did have very specific prescriptions based on his politics that he would have liked India to follow. Mahatma Gandhi's politics, *in its formal structure*,[23] then is no different from the Western political practices of democracy that Leela Gandhi enumerates, in that they are both premised on ethical/political principles.

Leela Gandhi would have a more logical case if it was only built on contrasting the *content* of what she finds problematic in the Western instance and what she embraces from Indian history. On this register, her argument is that the "perfectionist" strain of Western thought excluded ordinary people from the democratic fold, while in the Indian case, the commitment to "imperfectionism" allowed for the inclusion of the wretched and the oppressed. Now, apart from cherry picking certain traditions of Western political thought in which Leela Gandhi reads this strain of so-called perfectionism, she is unable to establish how and why the democratic ideal in the West is built on marginalizing the already marginalized. How, one might ask, are the ideals that inspired the English and the French revolutions based on marginalizing the oppressed? One might also wonder what the role of "perfectionism" is in the development of socialist thought, aimed at struggling against a system that continually produces the kind of marginalized populations that Leela Gandhi purports to champion.

Finally, if Leela Gandhi's case was to be built only on the contrastive *practices* that emerge from political/ethical ideals in the West and the non-West, that too is unsustainable. One can readily agree that the West has mobilized ethical principles toward advancing inegalitarian and unjust agendas both at home and abroad. The converse, however, is true as well. Ruling classes in the non-West fare equally well when it comes to mobilizing progressive ideals toward furthering their class agenda. Since for Leela Gandhi, the central figure to enumerate the contrastive ideal of an inclusive democracy outside the West is Mahatma Gandhi, one might raise an issue on that score. It might be asked how Leela Gandhi squares Mahatma's Gandhi's defense of capitalism, of the caste system and of patriarchy with the democratic ideal of "endless inclusion." *The Common Cause* fails in establishing its postcolonial premise that the non-West offers a fundamentally different and superior political ethos.

In her earlier Work, *Affective Communities*,[24] Leela Gandhi starts out by adopting a somewhat different track and laments the homogenization of the West as imperialist in postcolonial theory. She then seeks to retrieve alternative Western political traditions of anti-colonialism that have not received due recognition. But the groups she chooses to elevate as the repertoire of Western anticolonial thought tethers her again to the orthodoxies of postcolonial thought. As the title of her book suggests, she chooses to focus on the politics of "friendship" as manifest in the ideas of marginal and marginalized groups and individuals—homosexuals, animal welfare workers, vegetarians, spiritualists, and aestheticists. Consistent with postcolonial wariness of collective politics, she only identifies groups which had negligible political impact, but whose ethical commitments rendered them "immune to the ubiquitous temptations of empire."[25] Even though "historical redressal" is one of Gandhi's stated objectives, she makes an ambitious theoretical claim positing the superiority of the kind of politics privileged by the theoreticians of the "ethical turn." Leela Gandhi is worth quoting in some detail where she compares postcolonial preferences to traditional political organizing work:

> Does a politics of relationality—the conjunctive modality that William James once described as the distinguishing feature of radical empiricism—ever change the world? Does it successfully dispatch imperial governments and occupying armies from native soil? Lead a disenfranchised people into the promise of self-determination? Mitigate in any way the burdens of colonial inheritance? Certainly not with anything like the speed and efficiency of those better organized and better focused (and more mature) revolutionary movements less inclined to found social change upon the painstaking labor of personal transformation. Yet precisely because of its inability to work its effects at industrial speed and scale, the politics that we have been pursuing in this discussion often alter the genetic structure of the societies in which they eventuate, subtly varying for future use their ethical, epistemic and political composition.[26]

First, it bears repetition that postcolonial theorists like Leela Gandhi are not merely engaged in expanding historical research to include underrepresented groups or subcultures; theirs is a political program, as Gandhi clarifies, aimed at demonstrating their superior engagement with the "genetic structure" of social transformation. And yet we're offered little to shed light on the possible blind spots of traditional organizing work, let alone a genuine comparison between that and what postcolonial theory has to offer demonstrating the relative strength of the latter. Instead there is simply an assertion that the politics championed by them, typically of small groups or individuals, is more profoundly transformative. The pejorative rhetoric here is worth noting in reference to social transformation undertaken by organized movements, they allegedly take place "at industrial speed and scale."

One might ask which movements Gandhi has in mind that supposedly effectuated transformation at "industrial speed." Is she thinking of the French or the Russian Revolution, or perhaps the Algerian or maybe the Indian independence movement? Regardless of where she might be casting her eye, the notion that any victory against systemic forces ever occurred at *industrial* speed, betrays an obliviousness to the basics of political struggles. It displays a remarkable unawareness of the long and "painstaking labor" of organizing work underlying any transformation. It is in line with Spivak's positing the notion of respecting the "ethical singularity" of the subaltern against that of traditional forms of political organizing. In both cases, the theorists remain profoundly out of touch with the nature of political work that builds resistance against systemic oppression. A recognition of the ground-level labor of organizing workers—the patience and the commitment that it demands of organizers—dismantles the basis of their fundamental opposition between political resistance against systemic oppression, and the putative *ethical* labor of small groups and individuals that they privilege.

CONCLUSION

Simon Gikandi, a postcolonial critic, makes an honest attempt at grappling with the contradictions of the field. He defines the dilemma of a theory which is produced by aligning with anti-humanism and yet remains intrinsically connected with the humanist project of decolonization:

> I think that's where the problem is; on the one hand, you want to argue that colonialism emerged out of a Western humanistic project. In that sense humanism was as much a problem as its categories. At the same time, however, the project of decolonization was very powerfully a humanistic project. Postcolonial theorists of one shade or another are no longer sure how to re-engage with that humanist project, partly because the imperative for the postcolonial paradigm has been an anti-humanistic project.... The dilemma, however, was that whichever way you looked at it, decolonization was an ethical project, and so how can you define it as an ethical project using a paradigm which premises itself on anti-humanism?[27]

After succinctly describing the postcolonial conundrum, Gikandi attempts to find a way out of it, but still from within the confines of the discipline. He believes that postcolonialists were too quick to reject decolonization by narrowly defining it as a project "imprisoned by nation and nationalism." While Gikandi agrees with the postcolonial critique of nationalism, he holds that decolonization has possibilities beyond both nationalism and globalization:

> If you see decolonization as that search for a new humanism, driven by powerful ethical concerns about the status of the human, and the status of culture, and the status of moral well-being, then perhaps we need to go back to that moment

and see how that ethical project could somehow politically and ethically be sustained and indeed, be debated. . . . I don't want to make a choice between colonialism and nation, because I don't want to see one as a reflection of the other, I've been calling attention to that middle space, and that's what I'm calling, perhaps for lack of a better word, decolonization.[28]

Gikandi is right in his reminder that progressive anticolonial thought carried within it the possibilities of a "new humanism" that goes beyond both the identitarian logic of nationalism and the false promise of freedom embedded in capitalist globalization. But what remains unaddressed by Gikandi is how it is possible to sustain the ethical and political project of "new humanism" from within the confines of an anti-humanist discipline. In fact, for all his insight into the foundational inconsistencies of the discipline, Gikandi positions himself within the field with the idea of occupying a "middle space" from which to wage the ethical battle for decolonization. But why use a nondescript phrase like "middle space" to name a position from where both colonialism and nationalism are subject to critique? The antipathy to Marx, endemic to the field, disallows Gikandi from even acknowledging that there is a robust Marxist critical tradition of critiquing both of those phenomena. The issue is certainly not that Gikandi does not align himself with Marxism, but that he evades even naming a school of thought that engages the very concerns and commitments which he elevates.

I have tried to highlight the contradictory impulse at the heart of a theory that rejects the possibility of systemic critiques and cultivates ambivalence not only toward class struggle but organized politics in general, while remaining committed to a vision of the political not just as critique but as transformative practice. Its only option then is to embrace a version of liberal politics in the name of "ethics." Leela Gandhi follows in Spivak's footsteps in privileging "affective communities" and the so-called ethic of "imperfectionism" practiced by some subcultures as the kind of politics that effectuate meaningful social transformation. If Bhabha's espousal of a politics of reformism is similarly aligned with the turn toward "ethical" change as opposed to radical transformation, Young's faith in *corporate ethics* signals the logical direction for a school of thought that has firmly turned its back on the possibility, if not desirability of systemic challenges. In a book-length eulogy to Spivak, Steven Morton's characterization of her position captures the spirit of the entire "ethical turn"; he upholds her "ethical commitment to achieving *one-on-one epistemic change* [that] is crucial for altering the structures of inequality, which underpin the contemporary global economic system."[29] Ironically, while postcoloniality was founded on challenging not just liberal humanism and its notion of the autonomous human, but also Marxism for its residual humanism, it ends up embracing the hoary liberal idea of effecting structural transformation by changing one person at a time. This is the price the discipline pays for eschewing systemic critiques of capitalism and aligning with the poststructuralist suspicion of collective struggles.

NOTES

1. Doran 2016.
2. Doran 2016, 13.
3. Moynagh 1999, 110.
4. Chow 1998, 53.
5. Bhabha 2004, xii.
6. Bhabha 2004, xviii.
7. Bhabha 2004, xvii (emphasis in original).
8. For an insightful discussion of Fanon's legacy and how it has been misappropriated by postcolonial theorists like Bhabha, See Bashir Abu-Manneh, "Who Owns Frantz Fanon's Legacy," *Catalyst: A Journal Of Theory and Strategy*, 5, no. 1 (Spring 2021): 11–38.
9. Fanon 2005, 55–56.
10. Spivak 1983, 42.
11. Spivak 1995, xxiv.
12. Spivak 1995, xxv.
13. See Morton 2007.
14. Morton 2007, 68.
15. Bhabha 2004, xx.
16. It is noteworthy that a branch of postcolonial critique marks a refreshing break from the culturalism endemic in the discipline – postcolonial ecocriticism. The field has been carved out by scholars who have centralized postcolonial concerns within the broader field of ecocriticism paying specific attention to issues like the distinction between Northern and Southern environmentalisms, the question of neo-colonialism and development and by highlighting ecofeminism and ecosocialism. See for instance, *Postcolonial Green: Environmental Politics and World Narratives*, Ed. Bonnie Roos, Alex Hunt; *Postcolonial Ecologies: Literatures of the Environment*, Ed. Elizabeth DeLoughrey, George B. Handley; and *Global Ecologies and the Environmental Humanities: Postcolonial Approaches*, Ed. Elizabeth DeLoughrey, Jill Didur, and Anthony Carrigan, Graham Huggan, Helen Tiffin in *Postcolonial Ecocriticism: Literature, Animals, Environment*, Upamanyu Mukherjee in *Postcolonial Environments: Nature, Culture and the Contemporary Indian Novel*.
17. See Young 1999.
18. Young 1999, 448.
19. See Young 2012.
20. Young 2012, 37.
21. Huntington 1993.
22. See Gandhi 2014.

23. For a perspective, which had the endorsement of Gandhi himself, on what a Gandhian constitution might have looked like, see Shriman Narayan, *Gandhian Constitution for Free India* (Allahabad, India: Kitabistan, 1946).
24. See Gandhi 2006.
25. Gandhi 2006, 2.
26. Gandhi 2006, 188.
27. Gikandi 2006.
28. Gikandi 2006.
29. Morton 2007, 173.

Chapter 12

Growth and the Appropriation of Nature

Left-Wing Misanthropy, the Rise of Authoritarianism, and the Pro-Capitalist Character of Environmental Discourse

Austin Williams

The expression "Industrial Revolution," used by Engels in 1844, was popularized forty years later by the historian and social reformer Arnold Toynbee in his book of the same name. It has since come to describe Britain's economic development from an agrarian and landowning economy to a mechanized society, predominantly spanning the end of the eighteenth century until the middle of the nineteenth century. The historian H. L. Beales, writing in 1929, suggested that the era may be deemed to extend from the accession of George III in 1760 to the accession of Queen Victoria in 1837. However ill-defined, it represents a dynamic period of British history that brought forward scientific advances, technical modernization, and social improvements to increase efficiency and improve productivity in order to support a growing population. The invention of, *inter alia*, the steam engine, the spinning jenny, the cotton gin, and the power-loom all played a role in socializing manufacture through industrial processes. A newly created division of labor compelled the remotest of regions "to make acquaintance with the outside world and accept the civilisation imposed upon them."[1] In other words, industrial capitalism imposed an order on society, and it imposed an order on nature.

Clearly, it created this order via the iniquitous social relations of capitalism and exacerbated the fundamentally exploitative relationship between the classes, but it was a political advance on what had gone before, leading to the emergence of the working class and the socialization of production. It provided the means by which collective identity and solidarity could be enacted. It is worth remembering, though, that one of the great benefits of the Industrial Revolution was that it presaged the decline of the rural in the form of backbreaking, tithed, manual labor and promised the emergence of the urban working class.

As Marx stated in *The Communist Manifesto*, capitalist social relations "put an end to all feudal, patriarchal, idyllic relations"; they had "torn asunder the motley feudal ties that bound man to his 'natural superiors.'"[2] The term "idyllic" is used sardonically, with Marx writing later that "the methods of primitive accumulation are anything but idyllic."[3] But the key part of the sentence is that the often brutal conditions in which feudal overlords asserted their right to rule in the time of primitive accumulation were deemed to be god-ordained and unassailable. The social order under feudalism was immutable; it was the law of nature writ large: the natural way of things.

But it was the transformative emergence of capitalism that provided an advancement on feudal relations and demonstrated that man could strive to overcome the limits provided by nature. Social order still manifested itself through exploitative relations, but capitalism at least created the productive capacity and secular conditions for rational thought to allow the possibility to push back against one's preordained place in the world. It created the possibility that humanity, including the laboring classes, could take control of its destiny. As Engels notes, "[in] the middle ages, it was not the expropriation of the people from the land, but on the contrary, their appropriation to the land which became the source of feudal oppression."[4]

This chapter explores how, through the prism of environmentalism, feudal thinking is making a comeback and how green ideologies are retro-restructuring society. In place of Marx's belief in humanity's universality and freedom,[5] environmentalism offers misanthropy and regulation, fragmentation, and authoritarianism: divide and rule. We'll explore these ideas throughout the chapter.

Admittedly, there is only marginal environmental support for a literal return to feudal relations, whereby manual labor would replace industrialization.[6] Clearly there is little appetite for modern developed economies to return to preindustrial means of production, but ours is an era in which environmental discourse tends explicitly to reject modernity. Anti-modernity has moved from a countercultural narrative to the mainstream.[7] It advocates variously for reduced consumption, minimal travel, and limits to growth. On the surface, it masquerades as anti-capitalist, challenging the prevailing methods of production, but it is not all that it seems. Leftist environmentalists seem all too keen to reinforce the capitalist framework. Indeed, they are often willing to accept the imposition of exploitative conditions on sections of society (as we shall explore in this chapter) and the enforcement of such strictures by governmental authority, the absolute authority of the judiciary, or even unelected supra-state institutions. For example, in a recent edition of the left-leaning *New Statesman* magazine, Labour MP and environmental campaigner Alex Sobel argued for a "Marshall Plan for the environment . . . to rebuild our economies."[8]

U.S. academic Joel Kotkin has labeled today's condition "neo-feudalism,"[9] in which a clerisy of experts determines the social organization and life-chances of the lower orders (those who have not yet got with the program). Similarly, Donald Gibson, professor of Sociology at the University of Pittsburgh, suggests that they believe that "the world is so complex and most people so inept that only a handful of experts, like biodiversity experts, can comprehend it. They must serve as our guides."[10] In this narrative, people are the problem, nature is our savior, and the Second Estate is the ultimate power broker.

The environmental discourse tends explicitly to reject or renounce the gains of modernity. The desire of human beings to overcome natural barriers is presented as the original sin against Mother Earth (as the world is termed in the Paris Accords[11]). While Bruno Latour's lectures on "natural religion" bemoan that there is no logical progression ("from God to Nature, then from Nature to Gaia"),[12] contemporary environmental discourse suggests that he spoke too soon. Mainstream environmentalism regularly accepts the notion that nature is sacrosanct and human dominion is exploitative, unsustainable, and wrong. The exploitation they speak of is that of humans over nature, not one class over another. Today, nature is king and humans merely its stewards. This seems to be the mantra of our age.

Among other things, contemporary environmentalism sanctifies limits, promotes restraint, and is formulated without significant democratic accountability. The acceptance that environmentalism is an unalloyed progressive position is drilled into young people globally today. A generation ago, an academic who favored "indoctrination" in schools could complain that "never has there been any real indication of acceptance that environmental education is an essential component of every student's and citizen's life."[13] What a difference forty-five years makes. In America, the Common Core science curriculum now aims to teach schoolkids "climate-change orthodoxy during their formative learning years."[14] And, of course, the preeminent recent examples are the global Climate Strikes in 2019, in which 1.5 million children around the world demanded centrality for environmental sustainability in their education.

This chapter will explore a number of these key foundations of contemporary environmental practice, although it will not deal with climate change *per se*. Instead, it hopes to challenge the negative perception of the human footprint.

THE MALTHUSIAN LEGACY IN THE LEFT

At the end of the eighteenth century, belief in the Enlightenment project and the "Age of Reason" had become jaundiced by disillusionment with the outcome of the French Revolution and the Terror. This was a time of hope and fear. In England at the time, the Enlightenment was viewed by many as an overly rational, soulless, and potentially barbarous moment of destructive disruption.

Worries such as these are evident in Reverend Thomas Malthus's (1766–1834) principal work *An Essay on the Principle of Population*, published in 1798. In it, he pursued a somewhat Enlightenment-inspired, rational analysis of the dangers inherent in an emergent urbanizing society. It was a critical commentary on social and economic progress. In his analysis, human populations increased exponentially, while crop yields could only increase arithmetically—thus resulting in an inevitable moment when the population would outstrip the resources available. At this crisis point there would not be enough food to feed everyone.

His mathematical approach suited the times: a critical assessment at the outset of the Industrial Revolution and the emergence of classical political economy. His solution was a mix of scientific reasoning and moral rectitude. For instance, for Malthus the population had to be restricted so that food supplies would suffice, and a logical means to achieve that was to restrict access to marriage to reduce the growth in legitimate family size. The calculus of Malthusianism was born.

A favorable reviewer might point out that for all his ugly misanthropy, his religious beliefs pointed to the possibility of change. He had, after all, observed developments from his own "contemplation of the great progress that (man) has already made from the savage state."[15] Hardly a ringing endorsement of human progress until compared to the misanthropy prevalent in much environmental discourse today, where humanity is frequently referred to as an irredeemable problem. Indeed, Malthus noted hopefully that insofar as there are barriers to improvement, "nothing would give me greater pleasure than to see them completely removed."[16] Today, barriers to progress are being confected almost every day with an unseemly delight. Writing in 2020, French philosopher Bruno Latour recommended that we "stop 'the progress train' with a shrill screech of the brakes."[17]

It is clear that Malthus's pessimistic view of humanity has led to his adaption by many in today's (so-called) progressive left as something of a "prophet" and an environmental "global brand."[18] Malthus's most enduring legacy, as far as latter-day environmentalists are concerned, is population restraint,[19] which Mark Wright, director of Science at WWF UK, simplifies down to "more people equals more consumption," which, for him, is a clear indication of more intractable problems.[20] Once you see humans and their inherent consumption patterns as a problem, then every issue will undoubtedly be interpreted through a misanthropic prism. It is little surprising that leading environmentalists such as Sara Parkin, the founding director of *Forum for the Future*, and Dame Jane Goodall are patrons of *Population Matters*, previously known as the *Optimum Population Trust*, an organization that considers population growth to be a major contributor to environmental degradation. "All our environmental problems become easier to solve with fewer people and harder—and ultimately impossible to solve—with ever more people," says *Population Matters* patron, Sir David Attenborough,[21] turning on its head the conception of humanity as a creative and progressive force of history. Few modern-day Malthusians explicitly argue that humans should be abolished, but ultimately their population-reduction narrative degrades the value of humanity.

Erstwhile left-wing commentators have dressed up the need for Malthusian restraint in various guises, but the advocacy of mechanisms to reduce population size still infuses the discourse. From Victorian-era restrictions on welfare to discourage the poor and feckless from procreating[22] to prewar eugenic policies and late twentieth-century medical interventions to force population restraint, nowadays we typically rely on restricting the "impact" of population. Regularly "impact" is a shorthand for "negative impact." This abstracts the discussion away from real people and focuses instead on their consumption habits, squaring the Malthusian circle by demanding that people do less and consume less. It also alleviates the pressure on capitalism to maximize productive outputs. Why competitively invest in the next round of accumulation, when you can condemn your competitors for irresponsibly producing too much and encouraging more profligate consumption? In this way, environmental activists are helping to stave off the capitalist crisis by emphasising the need for limits. The global pandemic has exacerbated this miserabilist trajectory with one commentator noting that "creative destruction is the silver lining of the COVID-19 crisis."[23] In reality, "creative" is a euphemism for the problems of "production atrophy."[24] In addition, under COVID-19 restrictions, the economic collapse of some sectors has been as arbitrary as the political and social decisions of governments.

In today's discussion, there are several ways to put the trajectory of Malthusianism and its manifestation over the twentieth and twenty-first century in perspective. The rise of eugenics forms an influential spin-off from classic Malthusianism in the twentieth century. From Sidney and Beatrice Webb to Harold Laski and H. G. Wells, various leading Socialist thinkers were central to the emerging eugenics movement.[25,26] For the left, in the early decades of the twentieth century, building a more equal society meant eradicating those that threatened it. So-called defectives were to be removed by contraception or forced sterilization. Fast-forward to today, and the "optics" of eugenics do not sit well with contemporary progressive leftists. But the essence of Malthusian environmentalism has allowed the same themes to be normalized. People are often treated as statistics; their selfhood sacrificed for a higher goal to save the planet. The anti-humanist agenda that situates people as the cause of planetary ills means that the erstwhile positive kernel of internationalism and human progress built up over the years has been turned on its head. No longer does history put human social, political, and cultural development at its core. To the contrary, humans are increasingly viewed as better eradicated from history: they are merely a hubristic destructive force to be "held back." As Irish commentator Fintan O'Toole writes, "The Earth has a toxic virus—us."[27]

The credo of Malthusianism still exercises the minds of luminaries such as Prince Charles, Sir Crispin Tickell (Chairman Emeritus of the *Climate Institute*), and Sir Jonathon Porritt (co-founder of *Forum for the Future*), carrying with them support from the radical left that might not otherwise have sided with such leading establishment figures. To provide an example from the opposite extreme, the Chinese Communist Party's thirty-five-year one-child policy, originating in 1978, was in part sponsored by the United Nations.[28] "The scientific rationale" for China's one-child policy, says Harvard professor Martin Whyte, "resulted from demographic projections produced by a small group of scientists headed by Song Jian, who were influenced by the Club of Rome's Limits to Growth and other Western doomsday writings in the 1970."[29]

The connection between environmentalism, misanthropy, and restraint is well-documented. The original United Nations' "Millennium Development Goals," for example, are a list of targets that act as indicators toward a sustainable future, and Goal 4 insists that "we must spare no effort to free all of humanity . . . from the threat of living on a planet irredeemably spoilt by human activities."[30] In this reading, the planet is the object to be saved, and humanity is the potentially destructive force to be condemned and contained.

No longer is social solidarity a concept of the oppressed united against an exploitative oppressor. Indeed, environmental finger-pointing breaches class politics and relies instead on contempt of one's fellow citizen for their profligacy and material ambitions. No matter, it seems, that Malthus has been disproved by centuries of advances in the productivity of the land, machine development, and scientific gains, from fertilizers to GM crops. No matter that the essence of mankind is to overcome natural barriers. Today's environmental movement has rejected the progressive project and instead tends to view "development" *per se* negatively and fellow human beings as potential threats. The starting point for modern environmental politics is that the mere act of human development is potentially destructive, and thus the solution is to encourage *sustainable* development. Logical fallacy or not, sustainable development implies that any action should ensure that we create and consume less today lest it cause harm to future generations. In the sustainability formulation, progress is often conflated with irresponsible hubris (in environmental literature). Sustainable restraint is deemed to be a moral good in itself. From minimizing energy use, travel, and construction, from foods to packaging to leisure, the perception is that there is too much unnecessary "stuff."[31] The orthodoxy of "reduce, re-use, recycle" stresses eating, traveling, heating, shopping, holidaying, and simply doing less. It is an assault on private citizens, often legitimated through the virtue-signaling of large corporations.[32] It is why there has been such contentment among environmentalists during the pandemic as society has shut down. Closing shops has thwarted consumption, job losses have minimized pollution, lockdowns have eliminated congestion, and so on. While workers' jobs have been decimated by the pandemic—or will be in the economic aftermath—influential commentators have spoken of their satisfaction with the situation. One academic writes of "the lockdown . . . induc(ing) numerous positive impacts on the environment and on energy consumption."[33] Another cites social media accounts claiming that the "Earth is recovering" as a result of COVID-19.[34] The medical journal *The Lancet* argued that the "second Great Depression" caused by the pandemic provides a "unique opportunity to . . . heal the planet."[35]

The concept of development itself becomes dangerous. Whereas once we looked to the future with anticipation, today we can only tremble with trepidation. Today, the future is regularly viewed with foreboding; experimentation is frequently discouraged as unnecessarily risky, and progress itself is often presented as a fallacy.[36] It is like the church's fear of the Enlightenment in Malthus's time. Retreating to a romantic notion of environmental sanctuary is reminiscent of the Utopian Socialists of the Victorian era hankering after a mythical past.

What has shifted significantly in the twenty-first century is that blame for the world's ills has tended to focus on excessive *consumption* and, in this way, on the individual rather than the state or the employer or the system. For example, the previously mentioned Sustainable Development Goals require "a shift to sustainable consumption and production in developed and developing countries."[37] These policies are designed to protect the environment and woe betide any developing nations getting ideas about industrializing their economies. Through a variety of green guises, sustainability and social justice have become vehicles for Western intervention into sovereign developing countries to better guide them in the ways of restraint in their consumption, production, and procreation. "Good governance" is the buzzword, alongside "responsible" or "sustainable" development. They semantically convey the notion that the protection and enhancement of the natural world is the primary concern. For humanity, it is "basic needs" only.

The Marxist geographer David Harvey has responded critically to this new shift in the reification of nature: "Control over the resources of others, in the name of planetary health, sustainability of preventing environmental degradation, is never too far from the surface of many western proposals for global environmental management."[38] In the latter decades of the twentieth century, global business and political interests, reflected in World Bank and International Monetary Fund interventions, would demand that so-called developing countries advance in a manner prescribed by those supra-state institutions in order to restore their balance of payments. The powerlessness of those countries would enable the international order to walk in and impose severe penalties under the guise of structural adjustment measures. In other words, they were paid only if they developed in the "right way." In recent years, that policy has shifted to one of providing financial assistance for underdeveloped countries precisely with the aim that they do *not* develop or at least that they rein in their unrealistic ambitions for development.

The central African country of Malawi is a case in point. Almost sixty years after gaining independence in 1964, the country remains one of the world's poorest in the world. According to the World Bank, 51.5% of the population live in poverty. Agriculture is the primary source of employment and only 11.4% of the population have access to electricity.[39] Even now, the country's manufacturing industry is virtually nonexistent. Unfortunately, the new buzzword "sustainable development" is premised on restraint and the precautionary principle, rather than on societal ambitions, significant investment, and development. Mechanisms to pull it out of poverty and enabling it to transcend its "basic needs"[40] are conspicuously absent, even judged by the standards of the usual lip service paid by "global environmental management." Consequently, a recent submission to the UK's International Development Committee that deals with Malawi's priorities condemned its development and population growth and lauded the country's "direct dependence on natural resources."[41] It resolved that Malawi "must conserve its valuable environmental resources," noting that the government "faces many challenges including . . . satisfying foreign donors that fiscal discipline is being tightened."[42] This shift in priorities from human to natural resources means that investment will be prioritized if it can be shown that the preservation of nature will be privileged. A modernization, industrialization, and urbanization strategy surely cannot be built on those flimsy foundations. This is eco-structural adjustment: loans will only be provided to ensure that the country doesn't develop too quickly. The carbon credits "saved" by not developing an energy-intensive industry can, of course, be sold to the West. We can safely call this neo-colonialism in the morally pure guise of preventing climate change.

Across the world, environmentalists decry industrial farming. This denunciation finds support in the United Nations (2021) who say that industrial farming "produces greenhouse gas emission, pollutes air and water, and destroys wildlife . . . (it) facilitate(s) the spread of viruses from animals to humans (. . . and) cause(s) epidemics of obesity and chronic disease."[43] When it comes to the non-industrialized world, it is much easier and cost-effective to get farmers back to the fields to grow produce by the sweat of their brow. What better way to impose developmental restraint than to imply that industrial farming will destroy the planet and threaten farmers' lives and livelihoods? To the rescue comes the United Nations in its campaign to legitimate exploitative relations which go hand in hand with small-scale, low-productivity human labor. All of this is ideologically backed by current environmental Malthusianism that finds its main cohort of supporters on the political left. The neo-colonialism of this situation—of reconstituting a feudal, patrician relationship with the underdeveloped world—and the simultaneous *disinterestedness* in this neocolonial reconstitution of the Global South by "progressives" is striking.[44]

David Harvey notes that "there is always an authoritarian edge somewhere in ecological politics."[45] The call for more emergency powers to deal with the "ecological crisis" is a case in point. Once an "emergency" is declared, emergency powers can be installed. Indian prime minister Indira Gandhi's (1917–1984) Emergency Rule in 1975 institutionalized military repression. At the time, a business leader said, "It's just wonderful. We used to have terrible problems with the unions. Now when they give us any troubles the Government just puts them in jail."[46] In the UK between 1973 and 1977, the Labour government's emergency powers allowed the police to detain Irish people for seven days without charge.[47] As we have seen throughout the pandemic, emergency powers tend to revoke civil liberties and increase the unaccountable power of the state. Fifty years after the concept of "ecocide" was initially mooted, there is now a legal definition that places an offence against the natural world as tantamount to a war crime.[48]

During the pandemic—and for those gazing into a post-pandemic world in crystal balls—there has been a tendency to advocate for social and economic restraint, and the curtailment of rights under the mantle of saving the planet. Caroline Lucas, leader of the Green Party in the UK, for example, said that "national emergencies in the past, whether pandemics or wars, have driven major social and economic change. Coronavirus must do the same."[49] As a result, environmentalist advocacy for anti-pollution measures, and restrictions on cars, flights, consumption, and various carbon-sourced activities have blossomed, referencing a "national emergency" to push through various measures that might otherwise have required public consultation, political debate, or democratic accountability. These policies can now be railroaded through, justified by their stated ambition to "save the planet"—whatever that means when humans are not part of the equation.

In a polemical report that argued for a return to a wartime economy a decade ago, the Green Party wrote (with the help of Andrew Simms of the *New Economics Foundation*) that "to deter people from using precious resources such as fuel . . . we should now start a national debate about whether some element of rationing or quotas would be a fairer approach."[50] Authoritarian policy-making, together with the assumption that any criticism is treacherous to a *faux* national war effort, has become tone-setting for politics on the left, and especially the radical left. It is testament to the success of environmental and public health orthodoxies that in some instances endorse and encourage state-led attacks on personal liberty. In place of left-wing challenges to state power and government assaults on hard-won freedoms, there has been a 180-degree shift to demand swifter and longer lockdowns (e.g., in the *Socialist Worker*[51]), in a bizarre renunciation of classically left-wing tropes such as self-determination, rejection of state power, and defense of working-class interests. The endorsement of state officials in exercising authority over human interactions, to restrict actions that are deemed "harmful" and environmentally "irresponsible," or to impose restraint in matters of global environmental health is shifting the poles of political engagement. Let's look at a few examples.

A GLIMPSE OF HOPE: THE *GILETS JAUNES*

In October 2018, the *Gilets Jaunes* protests were born in the rural and outer suburban areas around Paris. In just a few months, support for its aims quickly mobilized demonstrators in other major cities across France, all emanating from grievances people felt at a range of fuel price hikes. These were predominantly rural people who depended on their cars. One commentator notes that "many were people from small to middling rundown towns in the countryside where work, skills, traditions, thriving commerce and public funding have dried up. Others came from rustbelt communities in the north. . . . Few of them are unemployed"; they were "people in low-paid jobs on precarious contracts, exasperated pensioners, and small-scale entrepreneurs."[52] In other words, they fitted the model of *déplorables*,[53] the forgotten and left behind communities. The ensuing months have been described as a battle "between ultra-liberal capitalism and its self-described losers."[54]

The fuel increases had been brought on by world oil price increases, but anger had spilled over as a result of President Macron's environmentally motivated carbon tax policies. Similar unrest had occurred in Mexico and Canada. Some commentators fear the day when the American government pushes through Green plans to penalize drivers in a country where 95% of people do not use public transport to get to work.

But the force of feeling by ordinary working men and women in France was, to date, exceptional. The protests—comprising many tens of thousands of workers—mobilized in a variety of cities, from Paris to Marseilles, from Lyon to Bordeaux. Always on a Saturday, the marches continued, despite brutal treatment from the police, until the coronavirus curfews and lockdowns "naturally" eliminated the uprising in 2020. The insurrectionist atmosphere to the protests continued even after world oil prices fell and the carbon taxes were revoked, remaining as a symbol of the discontent felt by the dispossessed, from commuting workers to rural farmers and other economically disadvantaged groups. They all felt penalized by new financial-environmental penalties on their mobility.

There was an exciting, yet brief, moment in which it seemed that left-wing and internationalist solidarities could have been born in the fight against exploitative conditions and the iniquitous financial and social impact of obsessive carbon reduction targets on ordinary workers. One commentator described it as "a people's rebellion against the onerous consequences of climate-change policy, against the politics of environmentalism and its tendency to punish the little people for daring to live relatively modern, fossil-fuelled lives."[55] Long before coronavirus lockdowns were imposed, these taxes and fines were literally confining ordinary people to their locality and reducing wider travel opportunities. It was done by a president who had won an election with historically low turnout. It was done by a politician representing "an entire political class melting into a puddle of centrism."[56] It was done with little concern for the impact on workers' lives. And it was done without any consultation.

One socialist journal pointed out that "we cannot all drive cars. . . . It is a self-deception to believe we can,"[57] implying that driving would be a privilege for some and not for others. It was this kind of elitist environmental hauteur that generated the protests against "a Macron-esque 'climate' policy, rooted in neoliberal class warfare."[58] It spurred on the protest movement of ordinary, poor, nonurban, lower-middle-class, and working-class people to voice their anger at the decline in their spending power and their freedom to choose due to environmental policies made in the *Palais d'Élysée*.

More recently, in the UK, the Chancellor of the Exchequer boasted that there would be a £3000 subsidy for people switching to ecologically friendly electric cars (the cheapest hybrid at the time of writing is a Toyota Yaris Hybrid from £18,745). To most ordinary working people, this is replete with a *"Qu'ils mangent de la brioche!"* sentiment.

Admittedly, the *Gilets Jaunes*' manifesto did call for a ban on plastic bottles and GM crops, but these environmental extras (designed primarily to support the rural economy of French glass-production and regional farmers respectively) were overshadowed by the manifesto's progressive demand to reindustrialize the economy. The manifesto demanded that France engage in "massive construction projects to house 5 million homeless . . . and cancel debts accrued through usurious rates of interest."[59] As importantly, it demanded the authorities in France leave the European Union and exit NATO.[60] Aside from their distaste for drinking Perrier from a plastic bottle, there were remarkably few mentions of sustainability. The *Gilets Jaunes* were a radical, embryonic anti-state movement that saw environmentalism as an economic sanction and an establishment assault on their lives and livelihoods.

Nowadays, the belief that the human footprint—our travel, our consumption, and our numbers—is dangerous for the planet is mainstream. Greta Thunberg's famous two-week voyage to America on a £4 million racing yacht to attend a United Nations summit was the prime advertisement for how we need to minimize emissions although it was an inaccessible and remote example to many on their daily commute. Similarly, it is easier to restrict driving than to install the infrastructure for electric vehicles. Although the environmental message has percolated through society, many people realize that cars are essential and are resistant to curbs on their travel, transport, mobility, and foreign holiday needs—a vital part of working-class recreation, which ironically completely evades the reflections of those left-wing intellectuals who otherwise never fail to talk of "solidarity" and "kindness." In all, the pandemic seems to have provided a new mandate to impose and enforce immobility.

It does not require a giant leap of the imagination to translate the UK government's COVID-19 mantra "Stay Home, Save Lives" into blanket provision to ban cars, promote locality, and minimize travel opportunities. The environmental benefits of less pollution and clear skies have been promoted as further evidence of the need to restrict emissions and hence personal transport. Of course, it is a truism to say that *not* driving kills fewer people on the roads than would otherwise be the case, but as the lockdown has demonstrated, restrictions on mobility have effectively created ghost towns and destroyed jobs and livelihoods. Ordinary people across Europe have been under curfew or full lockdown and denied a social existence. They have suffered terrible hardship[61] and are now finding that they face other curbs on their mobility.[62] The response by environmental groups to such an unprecedented revocation of human rights and civil liberties by state authorities has generally been one of enthusiasm.

Restrictions on mobility are promoted less as an anti-congestion measure and more as an environmental benefit, but they are restrictions, nonetheless. Just like the government's Emergency Pandemic Legislation, restrictions on freedom of movement are being introduced by councils who have accepted that there is a "climate emergency." Sixty-seven percent of local authorities in the UK have declared a climate emergency, and both COVID-19 and climate emergencies are regularly conflated. Under COVID-19's "emergency powers," local authorities are entitled to close roads, section off-road space for cycle lanes, and form low-traffic neighborhoods with no public consultation or prior notification. It has nothing to do with COVID-19. This is an exercise in willful contempt of the people by those democratically elected to act on their behalf. Here are just two responses from an area-wide survey conducted by the Horrendous Hackney Road Closures campaign group (HHRC):

> I'm a single mum, self-employed as a cleaner and I have to drive to my clients, due to all the necessary equipment I use. I also care for my disabled granddad who lives in another borough. I take him for medical appointments and take care of him. Without a car I simply would not be able to work.

> We underestimate the usefulness of our cars as a community resource.... Many in our neighbourhood are held together by informal networks of helpers, carers, companions and shoppers. So often the car is an essential part of that equation.[63]

Democratic mobilization against environmental impositions on working people's lives is growing but struggling to be heard. Meanwhile, an explicitly antidemocratic institution is building support among the establishment and politicos eager to impose more restrictions on everyday freedoms: Extinction Rebellion (XR).

A MISANTHROPIC MANIFESTATION IN THE REALM OF ACTIVISM: XR

Founded in May 2018 by two UK academics, Roger Hallam and Gail Bradbrook, XR has become one of the leading environmental organizations in the UK. Its left-wing credentials stem from its rhetorical challenges to "the third world war—profit versus life . . . a pathological obsession with money and profit,"[64] and its fame has been garnered from a variety of stunts that have shut down businesses, infrastructural services, and government departments. The inspiration for XRs initial iteration came from Bradbrook's brief foray into her own subconscious. Years ago, she says that she flew to a retreat in Costa Rica and "prayed in a deep way" with some psychedelic medicine, poisonous tree frog secretions, and other psychotropic substances.[65] During one hallucinogenic episode, "she offered up a prayer calling on the universe to show her the 'codes for social change.'"[66] From this emerged the mission statement that "Indigenous cultures . . . have long evoked an Earth manifesto, saying we are the land: as earth-guardians, we are nature defending itself."[67]

What this statement shows, to the contrary, is that we are a long way from the practicalities of building a democratic movement reflecting class interests and antagonisms that might challenge capitalist social relations. In XR's formulation, humans are merely "earth guardians"—serfs tied to, and protecting, the natural estate.

It has been suggested that democratic debate with, and criticism of, these issues undermines a more noble cause. By claiming that "the debate is over" one merely asserts that climate change counterarguments are fallacious or malign and tantamount to heresy.[68] It posits democratic debate as a nicety that we cannot afford because the outcome is so important, and there is a fear among the establishment that, like the Brexit referendum, a free and open discussion might not lead to the desired outcome.

The conclusion often drawn by XR activists is that democratic change is too risky, and disruption is the only way to force change. Rather than pledging to improve the democratic process, to hold people more firmly to account, they campaign to work around it. Indeed, it is the democratic process that they seek to overturn, not capitalism. A decade ago, the militant Occupy movement's slogan "We are the 99 per cent" had the gloss of democratic representation (even though, of course, no one had asked the 99%). XR, on the other hand, have dispensed with the merest hint of democratic pretensions. They say that they only need "the involvement of 3.5 per cent of the population to succeed," that is, to pressure governments to change tack and shift from business-as-usual to carbon neutrality. This contention has been calculated through academic research on social movements worldwide. It concludes that no government has withstood a challenge from 3.5% of their population mobilized against it. This figure has become entrenched in XR folklore, even though the original researcher has recently written a "cautionary update" in 2020 to point out that "the 3.5% figure is . . . not necessarily a prescriptive one, and no one can see the future."[69] Votes, elections, referenda, representation, and plebiscites are discarded in the fight for social and political change in favor of a technocratic mobilization of a politically amorphous groupuscule. In this way, the general public are treated as either stage extras or mere datasets rather than active subjects of history.

In the early days of English suffrage, Marx placed great stock on the power vested in the right to participate in civil society and to vote in democratic elections. "The vote is the immediate, the direct, the existing and not simply imagined relation of civil society to the political state," he said. "In unrestricted suffrage, both active and passive, civil society has actually raised itself for the first time to an abstraction of itself, to political existence as its true universal and essential existence."[70] While understanding that this was a critique by a young Marx against Hegel's defense of monarchical authority, we can fast-forward to today and XR's magisterial approach to accountability, by contrast, to see that this defense of democracy has become even more timely. XR's "Declaration of Rebellion" contends that "we, in alignment with our consciences and our reasoning, declare ourselves in rebellion against our Government."[71] No mass mobilization, politicization, or explanation needed. But is XR rebelling against the government or simply pushing the government to run society and encourage business in different ways?

XR seeks (rather than proposes)

> an economy that maximises happiness and minimises harm; that restores soil health and the honourable harvest, taking only what is freely given from the wind, sun and tides. In a decarbonised and relocalised system, it embraces frugality for the sake of fairness.[72]

Frugality, or thrift, was once a symbol of Thatcherite "Victorian values", but also reflected the belief that there was not enough to go around. Frugality was a way of minimizing our consumption to eke out a little more from limited resources. Once again, we find Malthusianism rearing its head.

In retrospect, Thatcher was suggesting that thrift—reining in public spending and calling on the nation to tighten its belt—was, at the time, an economic survival mechanism as well as an incentive toward creating a more productive economy in the future. "Less is more," said engineer Buckminster Fuller, speaking of the efficacy of efficiencies in engineering. But he, like Thatcher, intended such efficiency to be a springboard for yet more, not a permanent state of less.[73] History shows that Thatcherite thrift was hoisted by its own petard, with government spending far exceeding what had gone before, year on year.[74] But XR's frugality is permanent. Thrift is a mere starter course for a lifetime of dieting.

THE GREEN OATH OF FEALTY

Greta Thunberg's assertion in 2019 that "there are no 'solutions' within our current systems" sounds positively revolutionary and a radical frame of reference for a new generation.[75] Whatever countercultural narrative that environmentalists have constructed to justify their "rebellious" tag, there is a growing realization that the state has fully absorbed the environmental mantra. Boris Johnson has metamorphosed from a bitter critic of environmentalism to its chief cheerleader. Environmental issues are being reconfigured to give the establishment a glimmer of ideological clarity for the forthcoming post-pandemic recession. Marx's 1846 statement that "the ideas of the ruling class are in every epoch the ruling ideas"[76] is as timely as ever, and in some respects, the foot soldiers of environmental fundamentalism, having done their work, are being sidelined.

From Davos to the Confederation of British Industry, from Bill Gates to Harry and Meghan, environmental business attitudes have captured the moral high ground. The Damascene conversion of erstwhile gas-guzzling business leaders and political elites to the cause of Gaia is not a conspiracy or a con but a conscious strategy to reboot the economy and to give a renewed sense of purpose (and profit) to a beleaguered establishment. Environmentalism poses as a radical alternative but simply represents the continuation of the existing system by other means. The ability of capitalism to morph into Green Capitalism will be orchestrated through the power of the state: through its authority to suspend democracy. Environmental activists are the useful idiots necessary to create the conditions of legitimacy.

Bill Gates, in his book *How to Avoid a Climate Disaster* (2021), concurs that "This is a huge economic opportunity: The countries that build great zero-carbon companies and industries will be the ones that lead the global economy in the coming decades."[77] Those that cannot, presumably, will be condemned to the back seat of history for a little while longer. The "left" interprets environmentalism (or the rhetoric of sustainability) as quintessentially anti-capitalist, whereas, in fact, it is merely new capitalists battling it out with older forms of capital through a period of economic stagnation, deflation, and rising unemployment.[78]

However, there is a battle of sorts being fought out among the elites. On the one hand, there are old school technofixers who are happy to counter the concerns about carbon reduction, restrictions, and natural limits with massively subsidized carbon capture, bioengineering, and a cheap, pliant, labor-intensive workforce. For its own reasons, it needs to downplay the fearful, precautionary vision of a world teetering toward extinction. They have to undo the damage of an alienated generation of children attending the global Climate Strike protests, who cry, "How can we do exams if there's no world to live on once we've done them?"[79] On the other hand, those who are fully invested in the Malthusian precautionary principle believe that productive decay is the solution. These proponents of "degrowth" believe that the problem was not too little but *too much* growth.

Meanwhile, across the world, around 790 million people do not have basic electricity, and nearly 3 billion lack access to clean cooking fuels. And yet, the UN Sustainable Development Goals 2030 insist that people maintain their lifestyles in "harmony with nature", while removing their access to efficient fuel. It is the same argument used by XR: instead of raising living standards, interventions are aimed at slowing or sidestepping development to protect the environment. Prioritizing the environment, encouraging a suspicion of development, creating antagonism toward human population, and mandating the defense of nature condemn millions to poverty, misery, sickness, and death.

Development, once seen as a long-range target for underdeveloped countries, is now beyond the pale. The UN Department of Economic and Social Affairs is promoting the Green agenda on the basis that nations must move beyond GDP as a measure of wealth and instead use the concept of "natural capital" to benchmark their developmental status. As such, the amount of forestry that a country has, or coastline, unspoiled landscape, wildlife, or ecosystems must be factored in a nation's economic accounts. In this way, peasant economies can be world-beating. Forget vaccines: the World Bank even says that protecting nature can act as "a buffer between humans and pathogens."[80]

Whether the hard or soft Greens win the argument, workers in the developed world will see living standards drop and hard-won rights eroded. Many in the developing world will find that they are still denied a flourishing economy but will be expected to steward the land—unhindered by energy-intensive modern farming, technologically-advanced industry, progress, or material development—and hand over their unused carbon credits to their Green overlords.

NOTES

1. Engels 1844.
2. Marx 2017 (1848), 53.
3. Marx 1887 (1867), 507.
4. Engels 1887.
5. See Chitty and McIvor 2009.
6. See de Decker and Smets 2017.
7. See Eder 1990.
8. Sobel 2019.
9. Kotkin 2020.
10. Gibson 2002, 128.
11. United Nations 2015.
12. Latour 2017, 281.
13. Linke 1976, 125–29.
14. Tice 2015.
15. Malthus 1798, 4.
16. Malthus 1798, 3.
17. In Watts 2020.
18. Mayhew 2014, 154.
19. Hardaway 1997.
20. Wright 2019.
21. Attenborough 2018.

22. Kreager 2014.
23. Foroohar 2021.
24. Mullan 2020.
25. Redvaldsen 2017.
26. Paul 1984.
27. O'Toole 2020.
28. Greenhalgh and Winckler 2005.
29. Whyte et al. 2015, 154.
30. United Nations. n.d.
31. Leonard 2010.
32. Kotkin, 2017.
33. Mousazadeh et al. 2021, 1.
34. Allison 2020, 4.2.
35. Landrigan et al. 2020, 447–48.
36. Williams 2008.
37. García 2020, 2.
38. Harvey 1993, 25.
39. World Bank 2019, 8.
40. Earth Charter Commission 2000.
41. HC 2012.
42. HC 2012.
43. United Nations Environment Programme. n.d.
44. Williams 2021.
45. Harvey 1993, 21.
46. Frank 1977, 465.
47. Smyth 2017.
48. Siddique 2021.
49. Lucas 2020.
50. Simms 2011, 36.
51. Socialist Worker 2021.
52. Harding 2019.
53. Moutet 2021.
54. Harding, 2019.
55. O'Neill 2018.
56. Bristow 2017.
57. Haynes 2019.
58. Saltmarsh 2021.
59. Gilets Jaunes n.d.
60. International Times 2019.
61. British Academy 2021.
62. Borkowska and Laurence 2020.
63. HHRC 2021.
64. Griffiths et al n.d.
65. Mackintosh 2019.
66. Abbit 2019.
67. Extinction Rebellion, n.d.

68. Ridley 2021.
69. Chenoweth 2020, 1.
70. Marx 1844, 191.
71. Extinction Rebellion, n.d.
72. Griffiths et al. n.d.
73. Williams 2001.
74. Samuel 1978.
75. Thunberg 2019.
76. Marx 1968.
77. Gates 2021, 35.
78. Mullan 2017.
79. McNeice 2019.
80. The World Bank. n.d.

Chapter 13

Outside(r) Fetishisms
Pathologies of Displaced Critique
Raji C. Steineck

In his analysis of value in *Capital*, Marx pointed right at the heart of the capitalism's mode of exploitation and its order of appearances. Instead of developing this critique, the left has largely turned to fetishes of hope and disdain within that order. The current trend to embrace outsiders and outsides to capital, from nature to remnants of precapitalist societies to all sorts of social rebellions, exacerbates the need to reflect on unfinished business of critique in Marx, and on the ongoing, but mostly unacknowledged, religious elements in leftist thought: its eschatology, moralism, and infatuation with saints and villains.

"WE WERE SO IN LOVE WITH REVOLUTION"— DANIEL COHN-BENDIT

When unified Germany's mobs first laid arson to the homes of migrant workers and refugees in the early 1990s, the then-home secretary Rudolf Seiters, in a familiar rhetorical move, placed responsibility at the feet of immigrants.[1,2] Some years and quite a number of casualties later, the ruling parties (conservatives and liberal democrats) together with the social democrats agreed to a revision of the *Grundgesetz*. The new Article 4.a made it impossible for anyone who had arrived in Germany by sea or land to successfully request political asylum. Even to the eyes of liberal critics, "semblance" had been instituted as "a principle of the constitution."[3] From that point onward, anyone publicly acting to protect the safety and rights of the immigrant population and their descendants was, almost automatically, a radical—which, at that time, was synonymous with also being a leftist. Having landed in that crowd, what never ceased to amaze me was the fervor with which major parts of it claimed to be revolutionary. Ongoing struggles between anarchist and communist factions notwithstanding, this was the common denominator. It was also the main criterion by which they distinguished themselves from the reformist left, basically considered to be traitors to the cause. At a time when our demonstrations regularly drew a crowd of 100–150 people in a city of 300,000, I remember looking up at the windows behind which ordinary folks were going about their business, wondering what "revolutionary" meant under such circumstances. In the beginning I thought of it as being merely a peculiar, perhaps romantic, exaggeration, but over time and with experience I learned how this peculiarity was connected to other, and by no means innocent, traits of what identified itself as the radical left. One was the fetishism of militancy, another the endless search for revolutionary subjects, and groups that might represent them. Then there was a vicious factionalism, based on a vague conviction that the revolution was mainly a question of "getting it right" in terms of ideology. I once overheard a member of the communist wing saying to an anarchist Antifa comrade "We will take care of you later, after the revolution." That was thought to be funny, at least among the self-professed communists. There were the contradictions between revolutionary claims and a strict in-group code of behavior, between egalitarian procedures—oh, the discipline of endless meetings where everyone adhered to the protocol of speaking strictly in turn!—and a steep informal hierarchy, between politically correct speech and entrenched patriarchal and often also racist practices.

Over the years, it became increasingly clear that these were not contradictions of a small group in a fairly small German town. In fact, compared to larger cities like Hamburg or Berlin, things seemed more relaxed where I was. The problems were also not new, and neither have they been resolved since. There is the long-standing alignment of left "anti-capitalist" or "anti-imperialist" rhetoric and action with anti-Semitism, most egregiously epitomized in Germany by members of the "Revolutionären Zellen" selecting Jewish passengers from the hijacked Air France flight 139 in Entebbe (and claiming, ironically in light of the radical left's self-avowed Marxism, "idealism" as a justification).[4] Anti-Semitism has also proven a conveyor belt bringing radical leftists to the extreme right—with Horst Mahler, erstwhile member of the RAF, perhaps the most prominent German example. The fact that another faction of the German left has embraced unquestioning support for even the most oppressive policies of the Israeli government is only the flipside of that coin; witness Jürgen Elsässer, previous editor of the *doyen* of leftist journals in Germany, *konkret,* and now editor of the right-wing magazine *Compact.*[5]

There is the search for a mass base and idolization of the common people that has led the left to tie up with reactionaries and racists, for example, in environmental protests. In the late 1990s leftists choose to demonstrate against Nuclear Power with German farmers reminiscing about the Second World War in rural Gorleben, celebrating the long-lost unity with the common people.[6]

Japanese leftists giving up proletarian internationalism and antiauthoritarianism in favor of "national ethics," reverence for the emperor, and imperialist expansionism in the 1930s,[7] or looking toward "innocent" rural communities in the 1960s and 1970s,[8] or the current love of "climate rebels" for local production and their willingness to go together with reactionaries as in current Swiss campaigns against the "CO2 Law" are all reiterations of this deeply entrenched tendency. This love of ethnic community, the instinct to sort people by their ethnic origin or religion rather than class, ties in well with the way the "radical" left in the wealthier capitalist zones of the globe has conducted its search for revolutionary subjects in far away places. Instead of assessing the situation they are in and tackling the thorny issues of class struggles in front of them, revolutionist leftists have turned to support causes in rural peripheries or far away from home, as long as they represented an imagined *outside* to capitalism. A truly internationalist spirit and support for working-class struggles in other countries around the globe would have been one thing—but for several decades, the revolutionist left has not cared about, say, strikes by Korean factory workers, or the struggle to improve conditions in Chinese sweatshops, not to speak of the situation of migrant workers in local meat factories at home, unless they could be turned into a semblance of revolutionary action.

REVOLUTION VERSUS VALUE CRITIQUE

There are probably many reasons for this madness. At its intellectual core, or so I argue, is what I will here call "revolutionism," a misunderstanding or displacement of the essence of the radical critique of capitalism. Instead of squarely facing and working from Marx's analysis of value, which points right at the heart of capitalism's central mode of exploitation, the left operated from a truncated understanding of this analysis and mainly clung to his much less substantiated anticipation of the next revolution. It has replaced the true core of critical analysis by a focus on "making the revolution."

Marx in the pertinent chapters of *Capital*'s vol. 1 explains how relations of production in capitalism force everyone to function as part of a machinery that, under the veil of freedom and justice, automatically distributes resources away from those who live by selling their labor power to those who live off revenue from capital—and continue to do so by maximizing the appropriation of surplus value. Production of use values is subordinate to the same ends:

use values are not produced to fulfill human needs, but as a means to enable the accumulation of capital.[9]

Marx and Engels were convinced that the internal logic of this mechanism would swiftly create a situation where social reproduction could be achieved without the mediation of value, by way of conscious and rational social decision-making. Once production was entirely run and organized by hired labor, capitalists would cease to have a productive function. A proletarian revolution could then do away with this class of oppressors, who would have become as obsolete as French aristocrats in 1789. The revolution would move on to install a new, class-less society, or in short: communism. In communism, goods would be produced and distributed according to human needs, and without the intercession of value.[10]

The claim of the revolutionist left has always been that this revolution is close at hand. We only must find the right way to make it happen. But in truth, the communist revolution has never been in sight. Not really. This much should have been clear at least by the mid-twentieth century, when the Soviet experiment had created new class divisions and failed to introduce relations of production independent from the value form.[11] The vision of imminent revolution and the hope of the soon-to-come advent of socialism was, however, apparently too good to let it go. By sticking to this promise, instead of a sober analysis of present conditions, the left has squandered the relentless critique of everything there is in violent support of one *fata morgana* after the other. Marxist slogans, militant iconography, materialist philosophy were mixed with red stars, flags, and icons of "revolutionary leaders" to project the imagery of an imminent revolution on a reality that was, and continues to be, capitalist to the core. As reality defied such anticipation time and again, the revolutionist left has replaced analysis and critique with belief, the veneration of leaders and martyrs, moral rigorism, and an obsession with true faith. Leftist ideology became an opium like any other religion, albeit one that is increasingly not for the masses, but for select members of the educated petty bourgeois youth. Therefore, a sober assessment of the notion of revolution, in its relation to Marx's critique of value, is an essential starting point to achieve a realistic standpoint on which to base the political fight for emancipation, and against capitalist exploitation.

REVOLUTION: ITS CHARACTER AND ITS CONDITIONS

There are competing definitions of what constitutes a revolution. The historical-materialist one put forth by Marx understands revolution to be the final phase of a fundamental shift in relations of production. It is a violent upheaval that seeks to remedy a situation where the political order and the social hierarchies no longer represent the realities of the social reproduction of human life, where the class that has the real power and competence to organize such reproduction is excluded from decision-making or severely under-represented in the corridors of power. This class may align itself with other disenfranchised parts of society in order to wrest power from the hands of the old elite, and it will present itself as acting for the common good to that end. But that does not mean that it will seek to realize this lofty aim once the real goal, power, has been achieved. The revolution will result in a political structure that is better aligned with the relations of production, and probably more efficient for that matter, but that does not necessarily mean that the general population stands to profit from this. The French Revolution is a case in point: the bourgeoisie first aligned itself with farmers and workers, only to subjugate them once again after achieving its "proper place" at the table of those in power. The French Revolution was also the prototypical revolution everyone writing in nineteenth-century Europe had in mind—including Marx and Engels when they wrote about the communist revolution.

Put in these sober, but abstract terms, a revolution is not necessarily something invoking hope for the common people. The revolution is made by, and for the sake of, the competent, and not for the destitute. That is, its driving force and ultimate winners are those who stand at the center of the new relations of production, and those most strongly oppressed within the old system. The link between the revolution and emancipation/the common good—a link made by Marx and Engels in their *Communist Manifesto* and never questioned by the revolutionist left—is based on two further premises: first, the ultimately Hegelian belief (which accommodated the ideas of Christian mysticism into philosophy) that there is a progressive realization of reason, and therefore, freedom in history; and second, the "materialist" conviction that this progress toward reason and freedom is the outcome of the processing of class conflicts, where a currently oppressed class, by its revolutionary actions, propels society forward onto the next stage of freedom.

This second idea is again based on a Hegelian notion, that of the dialectics of master and servant. In the pertinent sub-chapter of his *Phenomenology of the Spirit*, Hegel had argued that in the master-servant relationship, the servant is forced to work, and thereby, to *deal with reality*. In doing so, he will gain a higher stage of reason and competence than the idling master.[12] In a left Hegelian reading, that makes the servant the next revolutionary subject. Note the implicit link between oppression, revolution, and progress to freedom and the common good.

Unfortunately for traditional Marxism and its identification of the proletariat as the revolutionary subject, it is a link with only a partial basis in reality. The master-servant dialectics may work in the way described by Hegel in those cases where the masters are idle, a "leisure class" that lives entirely off the efforts of other people. *Active* masters, however, that is, in Marxist terms, members of the ruling class who organize and re-organize production, scout for and introduce new technologies and so forth, are obviously not part of that picture. Awareness of such limitations to the Hegelian master-servant dialectics was, however, hampered in traditional Marxism by the popular idea that as a dialectic relation, the antagonism between master and servant was moving in and of itself toward a tipping point, where a new level may be reached.[13]

To sum up, the argument for communist revolution put forth in the *Communist Manifesto* is that the subject of this revolution is to be not a class in possession of the means of production, but precisely the class of those who do not privately possess their own means of production: the proletariat. This class, for this very reason, represents humanity as such. And its victory, again for the same reason, would ensure the end of class antagonisms, and the end of all oppression. Or so the story goes.

When writing the *Communist Manifesto*, Marx and Engels believed that capitalism had already reached a stage where its inherent tendency to monopolization had inadvertently resulted in a socialization of production, and that this in turn had left the real competence to organize production in the hands of those who had to sell their labor power to survive: the proletariat. The obvious next step was for the proletariat to nurture awareness of that fact and, as a consequence, to struggle to overcome an economic and political system which prevented it from fully exerting its competence to rationally organize production for the common good. The few pages Marx wrote in the first volume of *Capital* about the historical tendency inherent to capitalist accumulation still carry forward that hope.[14]

However, the decisive critical core of *Capital*, the critique of value, if taken seriously and put in proper conjunction with the historical-materialist concept of revolution, places that hope in a much more precarious position. Capitalism, according to *Capital*, is that social form where the reproduction of human life is mediated (and driven) by the appropriation of surplus value. Surplus value's basic category, value, appears in various forms (money, commodity, rent, capital, etc.), which obscure its relation to human labor, beginning with its realization in monetized commodity exchange. The measure of value is the expenditure of socially necessary labor time. Value is realized by monetized commodity exchange, and commodities are produced with specific use values in order to motivate that exchange. The core exchange in this whole process is that of labor power for money. It involves a decisive asymmetry: the purveyor of labor power (the capitalist) unilaterally appropriates the surplus value created through labor (the difference between the labor time necessary to reproduce that labor power and the labor time expended during the contracted time). Because of this asymmetry, even under social and political conditions where labor power is bought and sold at a "just" price (a monetary price commensurate to its value), social resources accumulate disproportionately in the hands of the purveyors of labor power. Capital can therefore always outcompete labor in the race to appropriate scarce resources, economic and otherwise (e.g., land, clean water, public attention). This opens roads to manifestly "unjust" forms of exploitation through coercion, usury, abuse of the law, political favoritism, and so forth. Two questions remain, however: first, how the "just" price for labor power is defined, which depends on socially accepted standards of living. Second, to what extent conditions for a "just" exchange may be maintained. Both points ultimately depend on the power dynamics between the classes, with working-class unity being the pre-eminent condition for success on this side.

If value is, as *Capital* has it, the pivot of capitalist relations of production, the necessary condition for a revolution to end capitalism is that new relations of production have developed that function *without* the mediation of value. This is different from simply giving up private property of the means of production, or free markets as the forum for monetized commodity exchange; it means to give up the whole principle of production for equivalent exchange, whatever its modes of realization. A side note is required here on the question of use value. According to the value analysis in *Capital*, use value is a moment (in the Hegelian sense) of the value relation; to understand use value as separate from value and its expression in the money form is to overlook how money is already implied in simple commodity exchange. The revolution is not about liberating the production of use values from the fetters of monetized commodity exchange; it must build on entirely new relations of production that are independent of the notion of producing or exchanging equivalents—although to this day, there is not even a good fictional account of what such relations might look like.

Moreover, such relations of production must not only be *possible* (imaginable)—imaginary socialism is the hallmark of petty bourgeois utopianism—, but they must already exist: a sizeable class of goods, and most importantly, the larger part of daily necessities, must already be produced and distributed outside of the sphere of value. A great number of people must experience capitalist social relations as an impediment to their actual mode of survival in their daily lives, not to speak of their joys of life, instead of the mode they have to submit to, however grudgingly, in order to survive at all, attain basic creature comforts, and participate in the social and cultural exchanges within their society. Then, and only then, can the class chiefly responsible for this new mode of production, claim the title of a possible "revolutionary subject," because it can plausibly claim to stand for a new order that promises a better life for all of society. And if their mode and relations of production can live up to the standard established by the term communism, they may be called the subject of the communist revolution.

Now, the conundrum is that if communism is to be brought about by the proletariat because they do not privately own the means of production: how is the proletariat to become the carrier of that new mode of production? How does it gain access to those means outside of the sphere of value, when in fact it is condemned to live its life within its confines? Where would it be able to create the space for itself to develop new relations of production? The traditional Marxists' hope and promise was that, once capitalism's relations of production were fully and completely realized, their inherent antagonisms would also place the proletarians in a position from where they could organize the production and allocation of goods in a new fashion. From Engels to Lenin, the idea was that, after the "expropriation of the expropriators," the proletariat would initiate a process of rational planning, diligent accounting and administrative control to avoid private profiteering and realize production and distribution for the benefit of all.[15] As it turned out, this scheme went horribly wrong. The mere appropriation of capitalist means of production and the transition of control from representatives of capital to representatives of the proletariat does not change the core engine of the relations of production: the value relation. It also does not change the submission of laborers to the factory machine and its organization. (Lenin's appreciation of Taylorist methods is a case in point, as is his willingness to experiment with piece rate pay.[16]) To assume otherwise, that is, to believe that it is possible to appropriate capitalist means of production, to adapt a capitalist organization of production, and then create socialist relations of production *from these*, leads to a denial of reality. Even the collective wisdom of Soviet philosophers could not come up with one single reason why the socialist revolution could be successful when starting before non-capitalist relations of production had been built. They simply stated that it would be so.[17]

Forcing the denial of reality upon society requires an apparatus of terror; and the readiness with which traditional Marxists have developed and used that apparatus not only against those acting to reinstate the old order, but against their very own has belied their own good faith.

It would be just another variant of bourgeois idealism to speculate on how capitalist relations of production may one day be overturned. For the time being, it is sufficient to state that neither the proletariat nor any other social group has formed extensive relations of production that substantially operate outside the sphere of value and could replace the social forms of capitalism without condemning larger parts of society to destitution, if not death. There is, therefore, no replacement of value and no revolution in sight. Consequently, the forces of emancipation must work from within capitalist social relations, with no illusions about a way out in the foreseeable future. This is not reformism, which is based on the false promise that capitalism may be converted, by intelligently modeling its rules of operation, into a well-calibrated system of harmonious social relations, offering freedom and well-being to all. The antagonisms inherent to capitalism cannot be resolved. The point is that, when there is no way out in sight, an emancipatory politics must accept, and concentrate on, the struggle within; and a mode of struggle that does not count on having overcome capitalism two steps ahead. But this must come without submitting to capitalism's self-representation as a natural, inevitable state of things, without buying the illusions that come with capitalist ideology, and with a clear consciousness of the priority of class antagonisms and the function of social divisions that paper over this division and weaken the position of the proletariat. A critical, and sober, analysis of current developments and of dominant ideologies and their impact on emancipatory struggles, as well as public interventions against ideologies that divide and weaken the side of the proletariat is what intellectuals can contribute, apart from taking part in the struggles necessary where they stand. In a situation where intellectual work has become increasingly proletarianized, this also coincides more strongly with their own self-interest. The temptation to self-aggrandize and pose as prophets, let alone leaders of revolution will, however, continue to exist.

PATHOLOGIES OF REVOLUTIONISM

With no real revolution in sight, the revolutionist left has turned to fabricating semblances that legitimize its view of itself, its opponents, and its role in the world. In doing so, it reproduces patterns of thought and behavior that properly belong to the domain of religion. The linguist Algirdas Greimas already pointed out in the 1960s that the story of communist revolution conforms to a common mythological type—that of heroic quest. In its classical version, the proletariat would act as the hero who is charged by history to bring about a classless society, and therefore, freedom for all humanity. Its opponent is obviously the capitalist class, and communists are its main supporters.[18]

Conformance with a mythical pattern by itself would not make the idea of revolution irrational. If the conditions for the proletarian revolution were fulfilled, this story of revolution would provide for an intuitive grasp of given situations and help to incite the vigor and tenacity necessary to sustain the hardships involved in revolutionary action. This is the function of myth, and something that is indispensable to navigate a complicated and often opaque reality and to create a collective sense of purpose.

Even then, an emancipatory politics must remain careful not to get trapped in the confines of a storyline and the roles it defines. One of the decisive strengths of Marx's critique of political economy is that it moves beyond a moralistic account of heroes and villains to explain the anonymous dynamics that shape the behavior of individuals and groups. Emphasizing the story of revolution over and against the analysis of objective forces and dynamics was already a step toward irrationalizing the left. When myth becomes the prime driving force, the freedom of judgment and the ability to adjust to new knowledge concerning the situation at hand get lost.

Moreover, when it turned out that there was no situation that placed the proletariat in the role of the revolutionary subject, the myth of revolution lost its rational function altogether. It should have been replaced by another story, one more in line with the prospects of entrenched and even expanding capitalist relations of production.

If sticking to an obsolete myth was already a problem, it was exacerbated decisively when the proletariat was replaced with other stand-in heroes. When capital's antagonist from within had failed to fulfill its supposed duty of making the revolution, the left turned its hopes toward all sorts of (imagined) outsides to the capitalist realm. With this turn to the margins, left mythology lost its senses altogether, and entered the realm of mere wishful thinking—defended, however, with all the zeal and vitriol that comes with religious beliefs.

The argument, if there is one, is based on a half-truth: as stated above, the communist revolution must be carried by a subject that is not tied up with capitalist relations of production, one that has already realized the new (socialist/communist) mode of reproducing the needs of human life. Only that, taking this truth in the abstract (as bourgeois thinking is wont to do), the hopeful gaze of the left turned to groups which supposedly lived by precapitalist, communitarian modes of production. With a truncated view of Marx's critique of value in mind, such groups were associated with the "pure" production of use values, untainted by the money form and commodity exchange. In turning to these groups, the revolutionist left conveniently forgot that these modes of life offer even less freedom than capitalism, and that they cannot be projected on a modern, industrialized society. The experiment has been made, and it ended in the Cambodian killing fields.

Only that in the intellectual clouds of a cuckoo land of post-proletarian revolutionism, historical evidence does not count. Instead, the clouds are filled with romantic illusions about communitarian modes of life that have, mysteriously, been left intact and were only "formally subsumed" into the capitalist realm. The idea is that these form examples of "successful resistances" to capital.[19] They must, therefore, be welcomed as models, and supported by the left, which by now has a venerable record of aligning itself with most violently reactionary groups, from the PLO and the IRA to Hizbullah.[20] When joining a demonstration of the non-reformist left, one is consistently forced to a steeplechase routine if wanting to avoid association with symbols and images celebrating authoritarianism, anti-Semitism, nationalism and other reactionary ideologies. That may help to separate true believers, who place revolution above all, from lukewarm rationalists, who insist on ground rules of emancipatory practice and a basic sense of both reality and decency. But it has done a disservice to the political prospects associated with the left. In a kind of desperate jouissance, the revolutionist left accordingly embraces one fashionable symbol of resistance after the other. The only content requirements are that the resistance come with some anti-capitalist rhetoric and that it addresses the right devils: the figureheads of capitalism, the USA, major US and multinational companies, the finance industry, and, of course, Israel. A further, procedural requirement is that it must be violent, as spectacular militancy is another token of true revolutionary spirit the left will demand.

Violence is part and parcel of capitalist relations of production. The police and private security protect the property rights of capital, and history is replete with examples of their doing so even where these stand against the survival of massive parts of the population. They simply execute by force what the founding father of liberal economy, Adam Smith, had demanded of those who could not find a way to support their lives through the market: that they go out of existence, and quietly if you please.[21] For those who starve surrounded by riches beyond their grasp, as for those facing forceful evictions from their home and land—think of farmers in the Amazon rain forests driven off their land by corporate militias—violence is not a choice to make; it is a reality they must confront and resist as best as they can. The same holds, on various levels, for groups and individuals subject to violence instigated by one of the many bourgeois ideologies (the bourgeoisie is pluralist, after all—they can be racist, nationalist, ethnicist, sexist, bigots all in one or separately, in groups of a kind). A dogmatic politics of non-violence—ironically also a region of the leftist cloud cuckoo land, although not of its revolutionist parts—is a fantasy, not least because capitalist regimes will re-define violence at will to cover everything but meek subservience to their orders. German penal law, for example, defines and prohibits the means of protection against police violence as "passive armament."[22] You are armed and violent if you refuse to receive the force of police clubs with an unprotected body, or their pepper spray with unprotected eyes.[23] That can easily make non-violent street protests an option for martyrs only.

That said, emancipatory politics needs to reasonably control decisions about violent means in two ways: first, by their relation to the ends to be achieved and second, by a strategic assessment of the situation at hand. Spectacular violence regularly arrives at the opposite of what it purports to achieve. Examples from Germany include the hapless terrorism of the RAF and its impact on civil rights and the politics of internal security, or the more recent militant exploits during the G20 summit in Hamburg 2017.[24]

Nonetheless, such violence is a favorite of the revolutionist left, to the extent that it is eulogized even where it has nothing to do with emancipatory ends, or where, as in the case of Hamburg 2017, it cannot achieve anything but exciting images, media attention, and a number of injured people. But that may in fact have been the actual goal.

If there is an overarching strategy to such actions, it is to expose the violent character of the state, incite it to act in an ever more repressive fashion, and in that way to fan anger and resentment against it—the old logic that things must get much worse before they can get better. Again, this is a logic that is by now well repudiated by historical evidence, and also a favorite with the neoliberal crowd. But we have already seen that the left revolutionism is in a state of constitutive denial.

A further symptom of their bad faith consists in revolutionists' love of crises. There is the general leftist *schadenfreude*: we told you capitalism is bad and dysfunctional, and there you have it. But there is also an ever-renewed hope. With each crisis, whenever one bubble collapses, the left sees capitalism's doomsday coming. Climate change and the visibility of concomitant disasters is only the current iteration. A decade ago, it was the financial crisis, and before that, the internet bubble. On this subject, as on that of revolutionary subjects, the revolutionist left operates on short-term memory. In truth, capitalist crises do not weaken capitalism, and not even capital as a whole. They re-distribute capital between different groups of capitalists, and from the proletariat to capital. The one thing that is sure is that those who need to sell their labor power will pay, and not profit. Rejoicing in catastrophes is thus a luxury good, to be enjoyed only by those who imagine themselves at a distance. It is another sign that revolutionism is a fashion for the sheltered but disenfranchised middle class.

CONCLUSION

Ever since Marx and Engels wrote the *Communist Manifesto*, capitalism has been expanding, and not on the retreat. The mediation of goods through value-exchange has integrated ever new domains; witness the current rise of care work, the commodification of science, or the commercial exploitation of private communication by way of social networks and messenger apps. In this situation, the proclamation of the communist revolution as a political option was and is illusory at best. Making it into a doctrine has transformed radical left thought into a kind of religion. Capitalism can manage revolutionist violence, an outlet for discontent and rage or the simple joy of destruction, like it manages hooliganism, and use it as a pretense to tighten security regimes. At the same time, the concomitant fetishism of various outsides diverts attention from the conflicts and prospects at hand: a new form of escapism. As such, it is again entirely compatible with capitalism. The obsessions with fetishized outsides can be readily commodified and integrated as so many fashions, alongside with others. The religion's priests serve a useful function as they deflect attention to peripheral issues, absorb energy into scholastic debates, or provide intellectual credibility to positions that peddle vain hopes and serve to divide, rather than unite, different segments of the labor force.

To reiterate: in the absence of a revolutionary situation, emancipatory politics needs to concentrate on the struggles within capitalism, working to strengthen the position of those who depend on the sale of labor power to survive. The office of critical theory is to reflect the twists and turns of capitalism's development, and to expose and debunk the ideologies that legitimize exploitation, division, and oppression, or poison the minds with vain hopes and illusion. Everything else, red flags, kowtowing to revolutionary saints and Marxist terminology notwithstanding, is reactionary ideology.

NOTES

1. Cohn-Bendit 2001.
2. Bereicherung 2008.
3. Schuettauf/Marx 1996.
4. Tinnin 1977.
5. Lang 2016.
6. Café Morgenland 1997.
7. Hoston 1983, 96–118.
8. Iida 2002, 114–63.
9. Marx/Engels 2008 (1867), 49–98.
10. Marx/Engels 1987, 36–41, 48.
11. Camus' *L'homme révolté* may be full of petit bourgeois obfuscations, but his critique of contemporary Marxism was correct in this regard. See Camus, 1951.
12. Hegel 1970 (1807), 145–55.
13. Konstatinow, 1961, 315–18.
14. Marx/Engels 2008 (1867), 789–91.
15. Engels 1847.
16. Lenin 1972 (1918).
17. Konstatinow 1961, 561–64.
18. Greimas posits humanity as the hero, and the proletariat as its main supporter. Greimas 1966, 18.
19. Harootunian 2015, 19; see also my review at Steineck 2018, 1339–53.
20. Evans 2006.
21. Montag 2005, 7–17.
22. Helmrich 1987, 108–10.
23. Perspektive online 2019.
24. Malthaner, Teune, and Ullrich 2018.

Bibliography

Abbit, Beth. 2019. "Extinction Rebellion Was Started by a Group of 12 at a House in the Suburbs After the Co-Founder Took 'Psychedelic Medicines'." *Manchester Evening News*, September 1, 2019. https://www.manchestereveningnews.co.uk/news/greater-manchester-news/extinction-rebellion-started-group-12-16845727. Accessed June 19, 2021.
Abu-Manneh, Bashir. 2021. "Who Owns Frantz Fanon's Legacy." *Catalyst: A Journal of Theory and Strategy* 5, no. 1 (Spring 2021): 11–38.
Adorno, Theodor W. 1998. "Critique." In *Critical Models: Interventions and Catchwords*. New York: Columbia University Press, pp. 281–288.
Adorno, Theodor W. 2004 [1970]. *Aesthetic Theory*. Translated by Robert Hullot-Kentor. New York: Continuum.
Adorno, Theodor W. 2019. "Remarks on *The Authoritarian Personality*." In *The Authoritarian Personality*, edited by Else Frenkel-Brunswik Adorno, Daniel J. Levinson, and R. Nevitt Sanford. New York: Verso, pp. xli–lxvi.
Adorno, Theodor W. 2020 [1951]. *Minima Moralia: Reflections From Damaged Life*. London: Verso.
Ahmed, Haseeb. 2011. "News From the Netherlands." *FUSE Magazine*, Winter 2011/12, pp. 35–37.
Ahmed, Haseeb, and Chris Cutrone. 2011. "The Occupy Movement, a Renascent Left, and Marxism Today: An Interview with Slavoj Žižek." http://platypus1917.org/2011/12/01/occupy-movement-interview-with-slavoj-zizek/. Accessed July 5, 2021.
Ahmed, Haseeb, and Latifa Echakhch. 2021. "Latifa Echakhch and Seeing Things as If They're Vibrating (an Interview): CFA." *Conceptual Fine Arts*, July 5, 2021. www.conceptualfinearts.com/cfa/2021/07/05/latifa-echakhch-and-seeing-things-as-though-theyre-vibrating/. Accessed July 10, 2021.
Ahmed, Riz. 2017. "Riz Ahmed – Channel4 Diversity Speech 2017 @ House of Commons." Riz Ahmed, *Facebook*, March 3, 2017. https://www.facebook.com/watch/?v=10154393155118997. Accessed June 5, 2021.

Allison, Marcia. 2020. "'So Long, and Thanks For All the Fish!': Urban Dolphins as Ecofascist Fake News During COVID-19." *Journal of Environmental Media* 1, suppl. 1 (August): 4.1–4.8.

AlphaOmegaSin. 2015. "SJWs Need to Leave the Entertainment Industry Alone & Fuck Off." *YouTube*. https://www.youtube.com/watch?v=UygWA8kgUtk. Last Modified July 21, 2015. Accessed July 5, 2021.

Althusser, Louis. 1997. "The Only Materialist Tradition, Part I: Spinoza." In *The New Spinoza*, edited by Warren Montag and Ted Stolze. Minneapolis: University of Minnesota Press.

Althusser, Louis. 2014 [1971]. *On the Reproduction of Capitalism. Ideology and Ideological State Apparatuses (Notes Towards an Investigation)*. Translated by Ben Brewster. London/New York: Verso.

Althusser, Louis. 2017. *Reading Capital: The Complete Edition*. New York: Verso.

Anderson, Kevin B. 2010. *Marx at the Margins: On Nationalism, Ethnicity, and Non-Western Societies*. Chicago: University of Chicago Press.

Anderson, Perry. 2020. "The European Coup." *London Review of Books*, December 17, 2020. https://www.lrb.co.uk/the-paper/v42/n24/perry-anderson/the-european-coup. Accessed May 30, 2021.

Anderson, Perry. 2021. "Ever Closer Union?" *London Review of Books*, January 7, 2021. https://www.lrb.co.uk/the-paper/v43/n01/perry-anderson/ever-closer-union. Accessed June 1, 2021.

Andreas, Michael, and Natascha Frankenberg (eds). 2013. *Im Netz der Eindeutigkeiten. Unbestimmte Figuren und die Irritation von Identität (In the Web of Unambiguousness. Indeterminate Figures and the Irritation of Identity)*. Bielefeld: Transkript Verlag.

Appiah, Kwame Anthony. 1986. "The Uncompleted Argument: Du Bois and the Illusion of Race." In *Race, Writing and Difference*, edited by Henry Louis Gates Jr. Chicago: University of Chicago Press, pp. 21–37.

Appiah, Kwame Anthony. 2010. *The Ethics of Identity*. Princeton, NJ: Princeton University Press.

Applebaum, Anne. 2016. "The Dangerous Promise of Populism: Free Money." *The Washington Post*, September 23, 2016. https://www.washingtonpost.com/opinions/global-opinions/the-dangerous-promise-of-populism-free-money/2016/09/23/1c6595d2-81b6-11e6-8327-f141a7beb626_story.html. Accessed June 5, 2021.

Aristotle. 1960. *Posterior Analytics*. Cambridge, MA: Harvard University Press.

Assmann, Jan. 2003. *Die Mosaische Unterscheidung oder Der Preis des Monotheismus (The Mosaic Differentiation or The Price of Monotheism)*. Hanser Akzente: München.

Astarian, Bruno, and Gilles Dauvé. 2015. *Everything Must Go! The Abolition of Value*. Berkeley: LBC Books.

Attenborough, David. 2018. "Sir David Attenborough: We Must Act on Population." Interview by Evan Davis. *BBC Newsnight*, October 8, 2018. https://populationmatters.org/news/2018/10/sir-david-attenborough-we-must-act-population/. Accessed June 10, 2021.

Badiou, Alain. 2008 [2006]. *Logics of Worlds*. London: Continuum.

Balibar, Etienne. 2011. "Is there a 'Neo-Racism'?" In *Race, Nation, Class: Ambiguous Identities*, 2nd edition, edited by Etienne Balibar and Immanuel Wallerstein. London/New York: Verso, pp. 17–28.
Balibar, Etienne. 2014 [1993]. *La philosophie de Marx*. Paris: La Découverte.
BBC. 2016. "EU Vote: Where the Cabinet and Other MPs Stand." *BBC News*, June 22, 2016. https://www.bbc.co.uk/news/uk-politics-eu-referendum-35616946. Accessed May 23, 2021.
BBC. 2021. "Actor Riz Ahmed Wants to Stop Hollywood's 'Toxic Portrayals' of Muslims." https://www.bbc.co.uk/news/entertainment-arts-57438750. Accessed June 12, 2021.
Beales, H. L. 1929. "The Industrial Revolution." *The Journal of Historical Association* 14, no. 54 (July): 125–129.
Beckett, Samuel. 1964. *Endgame and Act Without Words*. London: Faber and Faber.
Beckett, Samuel. 1983. "Worstward Ho." http://www.samuel-beckett.net/w_ho.html. Accessed July 5, 2021.
Behrens, Diethard (ed.). 1993. *Gesellschaft und Erkenntnis. Zur materialistischen Erkenntnis- und Ökonomiekritik (Society and Cognition. Contributions to a Materialist Epistemological and Social Critique)*. Freiburg: Ça ira.
Bell, Daniel. 1964. "Interpretations of American Politics (1955)." In *The Radical Right*, edited by Daniel Bell. Garden City, NY: Doubleday, pp. 47–73.
Benjamin, Jesse. 2020. "Racial Capital from Pan-Africanism and Coloniality to Epistemic Rupture: New Directions in a Life with Marxism." *Monthly Review* 72, no. 3 (July 2020): 74–92.
Benjamin, Walter. 1933. "Experience and Poverty." In *Die Welt im Wort* (Prague), December 1933. Translated by Rodney Livingstone. In *Gesammelte Schriften* II. Frankfurt: Suhrkamp, pp. 213–219. https://www.atlasofplaces.com/essays/experience-and-poverty/. Accessed July 5, 2021.
Benjamin, Walter. 1978. "Hashish in Marseilles." In *Reflections*. New York: Schocken Books, pp. 137–145.
Benjamin, Walter. 2003. "On the Concept of History." In *Selected Writings Volume 4: 1938–40*. Cambridge, MA: Harvard University Press, pp. 389–400.
Benn, Hilary. 2016. "We Are in the Fight of Our Lives to Avoid the Damage Brexit Would Cause." *Guardian*, June 22, 2016. https://www.theguardian.com/commentisfree/2016/jun/22/fight-of-our-lives-avoid-damage-brexit-would-cause. Accessed June 15, 2021.
Bereicherung. 2008. "Zitate: Rudolf Seiters." *Youtube*. Filmed 1992 in Rostock, DE, uploaded March 12, 2008. https://www.youtube.com/watch?v=n7PB6-gmDfw. Accessed June 12, 2021.
Bhabha, Homi K. 2004. "Foreword: Framing Fanon." In *The Wretched of the Earth*, edited by Frantz Fanon, translated by Richard Philcox. New York: Grove Press.
Bickerton, Chistopher. 2012. *European Integration: From Nation-States to Member States*. Oxford: Oxford University Press.
Bickerton, Christopher. 2016. *The European Union: A Citizen's Guide*. London: Penguin.

Bickerton, Christopher, and Lee Jones. 2018. "The EU's Democratic Deficit: Why Brexit is Essential for Restoring Popular Sovereignty." *The Full Brexit*, June 11, 2018. https://www.thefullbrexit.com/the-eu-s-democratic-deficit. Accessed May 19, 2021.

Bickerton, Christopher, and Richard Tuck. 2018. "Why is Brexit Proving so Difficult to Implement?" *The Full Brexit*, June 11, 2018. https://www.thefullbrexit.com/why-implementing-brexit-difficult. Accessed May 13, 2021.

Bidet, Jacques. 2006 [1985]. *Exploring Marx's Capital*. Chicago: Haymarket.

Blackburn, Robin. 1998. *The Making of New World Slavery 1492–1800*. New York: Verso.

Bogart, Michele H. 2019. "The Problem with Canceling the Arnautoff Murals." *The New York Review of Books*, September 16, 2019. https://www.nybooks.com/daily/2019/09/16/the-problem-with-canceling-the-arnautoff-murals/. Accessed July 5, 2021.

Böhm, Steffen, Campbell Jones, Chris Land, and Mat Paterson. 2006. "Introduction: Impossibilities of Automobility." *The Sociological Review* 54, no. 1 suppl (2006): 3–16.

Borkowska, Magda, and James Laurence. 2020. "Coming Together or Coming Apart? Changes in Social Cohesion During the Covid-19 Pandemic in England." *European Societies* 23: 618–636.

Bourriaud, Nicolas. 2002 [1998]. *Relational Aesthetics*. Translated by Simon Pleasance and Fronza Woods, with the participation of Mathieu Copeland. Paris: Les Presses Du Réel.

Brecht, Bertolt. 2008. *Life of Galileo*. London: Penguin.

Brick, Howard. 2006. *Transcending Capitalism: Visions of a New Society in Modern American Thought*. New York: Cornell University Press.

Bristow, Gabriel. 2017. "Macron's Victory is Skin-Deep – The Abstentions Tell a Different Story." *The Guardian*, June 20, 2017. https://www.theguardian.com/commentisfree/2017/jun/20/macron-victory-abstention-french-president-legislative. Accessed June 1, 2021.

British Academy. 2021. *The COVID Decade: Understanding the Long-Term Societal Impacts of COVID-19*. London: The British Academy.

Brody, Richard. 2019. "Review: Quentin Tarantino's Obscenely Regressive Vision of the Sixties in 'Once Upon a Time . . . in Hollywood'." *The New Yorker*, July 27, 2019. https://www.newyorker.com/culture/the-front-row/review-quentin-tarantinos-obscenely-regressive-vision-of-the-sixties-in-once-upon-a-time-in-hollywood. Accessed June 12, 2021.

Brown, Nathan. 2021. *Rationalist Empiricism: A Theory of Speculative Critique*. New York: Fordham University Press.

Buck-Morss, Susan. 1995. "Visual Culture Questionnaire." *October* 77: 25–70.

Bukharin, Nikolai, and Yevgeni Preobrazhensky. 1922 [1920]. *The ABC of Communism: A Popular Explanation of the Program of the Communist Party of Russia*. Translated by Eden and Cedar Paul. London: The Communist Party of Great Britain.

Bump, Phillip. 2020. "Trump's Impeachment Team Argues That Anything He Does to Win Re-election isn't Impeachable." *Washington Post*, January 29, 2020. https://

www.washingtonpost.com/politics/2020/01/29/trumps-impeachment-team-offers-trumpiest-possible-argument-his-defense/. Accessed July 5, 2021.
Burden-Stelly, Charisse. 2020. "Modern U.S. Racial Capitalism." *Monthly Review* 72, no. 3 (2020): 8–20.
Bush, Stephen. 2021. "Of Course Idris Elba's Luther Has No Black Friends. He's a Police Officer." *New Statesman*, April 16, 2021. https://www.newstatesman.com/culture/2021/04/course-idris-elbas-luther-has-no-black-friends-hes-police-officer. Accessed June 12, 2021.
Butler, Judith. 1990. *Gender Trouble: Feminism and the Subversion of Identity*. London/New York: Routledge.
Butler, Judith. 2011. *Gender Trouble: Feminism and the Subversion of Identity*. United Kingdom: Taylor & Francis.
Café Morgenland. 1997. "Völkische Gesellschaft." *Aneignung. Material für Wissenschaft und Widerstand* 2 (1997): 13–17.
Camatte, Jacques. 1988 [1976]. *Capital and Community: The Results of the Immediate Process of Production*. Translated by David Brown. London: Unpopular Books.
Campbell, Bradley, and Jason Manning. 2018. *The Rise of Victimhood Culture: Microaggressions, Safe Spaces, and the new Culture Wars*. New York: Palgrave Macmillan.
Camus, Albert. 1951. *L'homme révolté*. Collection Idées. Paris: Gallimard.
Carlebach, Efraim. 2019. "Forgetting Mark Fisher." *The Platypus Review* 115 (April 2019). https://platypus1917.org/2019/04/01/forgetting-mark-fisher/. Accessed July 1, 2021.
Cerny, Philip G. 1997. "Paradoxes of the Competition State: The Dynamics of Political Globalization." *Government and Opposition* 32, no. 2: 251–274.
Chait, Jonathan. 2017. "Donald Trump: L'etat, C'est Moi." *New York Magazine*, July 20, 2017. https://nymag.com/intelligencer/2017/07/donald-trump-ltat-cest-moi.html. Accessed July 5, 2021.
Chartered Institute of Marketing. 2020. "When Brands Go Woke, Do They Go Broke?" February 3, 2020. https://www.cim.co.uk/exchange/editorial/when-brands-go-woke-do-they-go-broke/. Accessed July 5, 2021.
Chenoweth, Erica. 2020. "Questions, Answers, and Some Cautionary Updates Regarding the 3.5% Rule." *Carr Center Discussion Paper Series* 20, no. 5.
Chesterton, G. K. 1927. *The Return of Don Quixote*. Leipzig: Bernhard Tauchnitz.
Chitty, Andrew, and Martin McIvor. 2009. *Karl Marx and Contemporary Philosophy*. Houndmills: Palgrave Macmillan.
Chow, Rey. 1998. *Ethics After Idealism: Theory-Culture-Ethnicity-Reading*. Bloomington and Indianapolis: Indiana University Press.
Cohn-Bendit, Daniel. 2001. *Wir haben sie so geliebt, die Revolution* (*We Were So in Love With Revolution*). Berlin: Philo.
Collomp, Catherine. 2011. "'Anti-Semitism among American Labor': A Study by the Refugee Scholars of the Frankfurt School of Sociology at the End of World War II." *Labor History* 52, no. 4 (November): 417–439.
Colquhoun, Patrick. 1797. *A Treatise on the Police of the Metropolis: Containing a Detail of the Various Crimes and Misdemeanors by which Public and Private*

Property and Security Are, at Present, Injured and Endangered: and Suggesting Remedies for Their Prevention, the fourth edition, revised and enlarged. London: H Fry.

Combahee River Collective. 2019 [1977]. "A Black Feminist Statement." *Monthly Review*, January 1. https://monthlyreview.org/2019/01/01/a-black-feminist-statement/. Accessed July 12, 2021.

Cox, Oliver Cromwell. 1948. *Caste, Class, and Race: A Study in Social Dynamics*. Garden City, New York: Doubleday.

Cox, Oliver Cromwell. 1987. *Race, Class, and the World System: The Sociology of Oliver C. Cox*. Edited by Herbert M. Hunter and Sameer Y. Abraham. New York: Monthly Review Press.

Crawford, Matthew. 2020. "How Race Politics Liberated the Elites." *Unherd*, December 14, 2020. https://unherd.com/2020/12/how-race-politics-liberated-the-elites/. Accessed June 1, 2021.

Cunliffe, Philip. 2018. "I May Be a Brexit Bolshevik, But I'm No Lexiter." *Medium*, December 18, 2018. https://medium.com/@thephilippics/i-may-be-a-brexit-bolshevik-but-im-no-lexiter-6d20560a56c1. Accessed May 30, 2021.

Cunliffe, Philip. 2019. "The Workers' Revolt Against Labour." *The Full Brexit*, December 18, 2019. https://www.thefullbrexit.com/workers-revolt-against-labour. Accessed May 20, 2021.

Cunliffe, Philip. 2020a. *The New Twenty Years' Crisis: A Critique of International Relations, 1999–2019*. London: McGill-Queens' University Press.

Cunliffe, Philip. 2020b. "The Resistance Volunteers for House Arrest." *The Full Brexit*, March 31, 2020. https://www.thefullbrexit.com/volunteers-for-house-arrest. Accessed June 1, 2021.

Cunliffe, Philip. 2020c. "Are We All Covid Communists Now?" *Medium*, March 23, 2020. https://medium.com/@thephilippics/are-we-all-covid-communists-now-9825a2067d51. Accessed July 1, 2021.

Cunliffe, Philip, George Hoare, Lee Jones, and Peter Ramsay. 2020. "Covid-19: 'We're Not in Control'." *The Full Brexit*, March 28, 2020. https://www.thefullbrexit.com/not-in-control. Accessed June 1, 2021.

Cutrone, Chris. 2013. *Adorno's Marxism* (PhD Dissertation, unpublished). https://www.academia.edu/3085199/Adornos_Marxism_2013_?auto=download. Accessed July 5, 2021.

Cutrone, Chris. 2017. "The Millennial Left is Dead." http://platypus1917.org/2017/10/01/millennial-left-dead/. Accessed July 5, 2021.

Daum, Meghan. 2019. *The Problem with Everything. My Journey Through the New Culture Wars*. New York: Gallery Books.

Davis, Mary. 2018. "The Chimera of Workers' Rights in the EU." *The Full Brexit*, July 15, 2018. https://www.thefullbrexit.com/labour-rights-eu. Accessed May 12, 2021.

De Decker, Kris, and Melle Smets. 2017. "Could We Run Modern Society on Human Power Alone?" *Low-Tech Magazine*, May 28, 2017. https://www.lowtechmagazine.com/2017/05/could-we-run-modern-society-on-human-power-alone.html. Accessed June 11, 2021.

Deleuze, Gilles. 1983. *Nietzsche and Philosophy*. New York: Columbia University Press.
Deleuze, Gilles, and Félix Guattari. 1983. *Anti-Oedipus, Capitalism and Schizophrenia*. Minneapolis: University of Minnesota Press.
DeLoughrey, Elizabeth, and George B. Handley (eds). 2011. *Postcolonial Ecologies: Literatures of the Environment*. New York: Oxford University Press.
Dessus, Sebastien C., and Marek Hanusch. 2018. *South Africa Economic Update: Jobs and Inequality (English)*. South Africa Economic Update; No. 11. Washington, D.C.: World Bank Group.
Donovan, Jack. 2016. *Becoming a Barbarian*. Milwaukie: Dissonant Hum.
Doran, Robert. 2016. *The Ethics of Theory: Philosophy, History, Literature*. London: Bloomsbury Academic.
Dubois, W. E. B. [1935] 2017. *Black Reconstruction in America*. Oxford: Oxford University Press.
Dutton, Dennis. 1974. "To Understand It on Its Own Terms." *Philosophy and Phenomenological Research* 35 (1974): 246–256.
Earth Charter Commission. 2000. "The Earth Charter." https://earthcharter.org/read-the-earth-charter/preamble/. Accessed June 21, 2021.
Eder, Klaus. 1990. "The Rise of Counter-Culture Movements Against Modernity: Nature as a New Field of Class Struggle." *Theory, Culture & Society* 7, no. 4 (November): 21–47.
Ehrenreich, John, and Barbara Ehrenreich. 1979. "The Professional-Managerial Class." In *Between Labor and Capital*, edited by Pat Walker. Boston: South End Press, pp. 5–45.
Einspruch, Franklin. 2020. "Bureaucracy, Tyranny, and Woke Aesthetics." *Artblog.net*, July 9, 2020. http://www.artblog.net/post/2020/07/woke-aesthetics/. Accessed July 5, 2021.
Endnotes. 2008. *Endnotes 1: Preliminary Materials for a Balance Sheet of the 20th Century*. London/Oakland.
Engels, Friedrich. 1844. "The Condition of England." *Vorwärts!* 72 (September). http://marxism.halkcephesi.net/M&E/1844/condition-england/ch01.html. Accessed June 20, 2021.
Engels, Friedrich. 1847. "Grundsätze des Kommunismus" ("Foundations of Communism"). http://www.zeno.org/Philosophie/M/Engels,+Friedrich/Grunds%C3%A4tze+des+Kommunismus. Accessed June 12, 2021.
Engels, Friedrich. 1887. "Preface to the American Edition." *The Condition of the Working Class in England*. http://marxengels.public-archive.net/en/ME1746en.html. Accessed June 20, 2021.
Engels, Friedrich. 1952 [1882]. "Nationalism, Internationalism and the Polish Question (1882)." In *The Russian Menace to Europe: A Collection of Articles, Speeches, Letters, and News Dispatches*, edited by Karl Marx, Friedrich Engels, Paul W. Blackstock, and Bert F. Hoselitz. Glencoe, IL: The Free Press, pp. 116–120.
Engels Friedrich. 1976 [1847]. "Principles of Communism." In *Karl Marx and Friedrich Engels, Selected Works in Three Volumes: Volume One*. Moscow. Progress Publishers, pp. 81–98.

Engels, Friedrich. 1990 [1891]. "A Critique of the Draft Social Democratic Program of 1891" in *Engels: 1890–95.*" In *Marx Engels Collected Works*, Vol. 27. London: Lawrence & Wishart, pp. 217–232.

Engels, Friedrich. 2010 [1884]. *The Origin of the Family, Private Property and the State*. Introduced by Tristram Hunt. London: Penguin.

Engels Friedrich. 2010 [1892]. "Engels to Paul Lafargue, 12 November 1892." In *Letters 1892–1895: Marx Engels Collected Works*, Vol. 50. London: Lawrence & Wishart, pp. 29–30.

Engels, Friedrich, and Karl Kautsky. 1977 [1887]. "Juridical Socialism." *Politics and Society* 7, no. 2 (1977): 203–220.

Epictetus, Arrian. 2018. "Chapter 17." In *Enchiridion & The Discourses of Epictetus Including the Fragments*. Translated by W. A. Oldfather. e-artnow.

Evans, Harold. 2006. "'We Are All Hizbullah Now.' Really?" *The Guardian*, August 8, 2006. http://www.theguardian.com/commentisfree/2006/aug/08/weareallhizbullahnowreall. Accessed June 12, 2021.

Extinction Rebellion. n.d. "Declaration of Rebellion." https://extinctionrebellion.uk/declaration/. Accessed June 20, 2021.

Fanon, Frantz. 1986. *Black Skin, White Masks*. London: Pluto Press.

Fanon, Frantz. 2005 [1961]. *The Wretched of the Earth*. Translated by Richard Philcox. New York, Grove Press.

Feltham, Oliver. 2020. "One or Many Ontologies? Badiou's Arguments for His Thesis 'Mathematics is Ontology'." *Filozofski vestnik* XLI, no. 2 (2020): 37–56.

Fields, Karen E., and Barbara J. Fields. 2012. *Racecraft: The Soul of Inequality in American Life*. New York: Verso.

Fife, Benjamin, and Taylor Hines. 2020. "I Can't Relate." *Damage Magazine*, March 9, 2020. https://damagemag.com/2020/03/09/i-cant-relate. Accessed July 1, 2021.

Fischer, Ernst. 1959. *The Necessity of Art: A Marxist Approach*. Translated by Anna Bostock. London: Penguin Books.

Fischer-Lichte, Erika. 2008. *The Transformative Power of Performance: A New Aesthetics*, London/New York: Routledge.

Fisher, Mark. 2009. *Capitalist Realism: Is There No Alternative?* Bognor Regis, UK: Zero Books.

Fisher, Mark. 2014. "For Now, Our Desire is Nameless." *The European*, May 19, 2014. https://www.theeuropean.de/en/mark-fisher--2/8480-is-there-an-alternative-to-capitalism. Accessed July 1, 2021.

Flinders, Matthew V., and Jim Buller. 2006. "Depoliticisation: Principles, Tactics and Tools." *British Politics* I, no. 3: 293–318.

Fogteloo, Margreet. 2010. "Dag Linkse Hobby's." *De Groene Amsterdammer*, October 6, 2010. www.groene.nl/artikel/dag-linkse-hobby-s. Accessed July 12, 2021.

Foreman, Dave (ed.). 1980. "EARTH FIRST Statement of Principles and Membership Brochure ("Draft Platform")." http://www.environmentandsociety.org/mml/earth-first-statement-principles-and-membership-brochure-memo. Accessed June 19, 2021.

Foroohar, Rana. 2021. "Creative Destruction is the Silver Lining of the Covid-19 Crisis." *The Financial Times*, May 9, 2021. https://www.ft.com/content/91ecc4b6-4baa-4b6f-b86b-15cecf0401fe. Accessed June 12, 2021.

Frank, Andre Gunder. 1977. "Emergence of Permanent Emergency in India." *Economic and Political Weekly* 12, no. 11 (March): 463–465, 467–475.

Fraser, Nancy, and Axel Honneth. 2004. *Redistribution or Recognition? A Political-Philosophical Exchange*. London: Verso.

Freud, Sigmund. 1953 [1905]. "Three Essays on the Theory of Sexuality." In *The Standard Edition of the Complete Psychological Works of Sigmund Freud, Volume VII (1901–1905): A Case of Hysteria, Three Essays on Sexuality and Other Works*. London: Hogarth Press, pp. 123–246.

Freud, Sigmund. 1961 [1920]. *Beyond the Pleasure Principle*. Translated and edited by James Strachey. London/New York: Norton.

Freud, Sigmund. 1981. *Standard Edition of the Complete Psychological Works of Sigmund Freud: New Introductory Lectures in Psychoanalysis and Other Works (Volume XXXII)*. Toronto: Hogarth.

Freud, Sigmund. 2012 [1921]. *Group Psychology and the Analysis of the Ego*. Las Vegas: Empire Books.

Fromm, Erich. 1941. *Escape From Freedom*. New York: Holt, Rinehart and Winston.

Fukuyama, Francis. 1992. *The End of History and the Last Man*. New York: Free Press.

Full Brexit. 2020. "The UK-EU Trade and Cooperation Agreement: Minimum Brexit." *The Full Brexit*, December 30, 2020. https://www.thefullbrexit.com/uk-eu-deal. Accessed May 18, 2021.

Gandesha, Samir. 2019. "The Authoritarian Personality Reconsidered: Adorno, Marcuse and the Phantom of 'Left Fascism'." *The American Journal of Psychoanalysis* 79 (2019): 601–624.

Gandesha, Samir. 2020. "A Composite of King Kong and a Suburban Barber: Revisiting Adorno's 'Freudian Theory and the Pattern of Fascist Propaganda'." In *Spectres of Fascism: History and Theory in International Perspective*, edited by Samir Gandesha. London: Pluto Press, pp. 120–141.

Gandhi, Leela. 2006. *Affective Communities: Politics, History, Culture*. Durham, NC: Duke University Press.

Gandhi, Leela. 2014. *The Common Cause, Postcolonial Ethics and the Practice of Democracy, 1900–1955*. Chicago: Chicago University Press.

García, Álvaro Castaño. 2020. "High Consumers: A Literature Review." https://www4.shu.ac.uk/research/cresr/sites/shu.ac.uk/files/high-consumers-a-literature-review_0.pdf. Accessed May 22, 2021.

Gardner, Amy, Kate Rabinowitz, and Harry Stevens. 2021. "How GOP-Backed Voting Measures Could Create Hurdles for Tens of Millions of Voters." *Washington Post*, March 11, 2021. https://www.washingtonpost.com/politics/interactive/2021/voting-restrictions-republicans-states/. Accessed July 5, 2021.

Gates, Bill. 2021. *How to Avoid a Climate Disaster*. New York: Penguin Random House.

Gibson, Donald. 2002. *Environmentalism: Ideology and Power*. Hauppauge: Nova Science.

Gikandi, Simon. 2006. "Postcolonialisms Ethical (Re)Turn: An Interview with Simon Gikandi by David Jefferess." *Postcolonial Text* 2, no. 1 (2006). https://www.postcolonial.org/index.php/pct/article/view/464/845. Accessed July 6, 2021.

Gilets Jaunes. n.d. "25 Demands for a Free France." http://internationaltimes.it/yellow-vest-manifesto-25-demands-for-a-free-france. Accessed June 1, 2021.

Golash-Boza, Tanya Maria. 2017. *Race and Racisms: A Critical Approach*. Oxford: Oxford University Press.

Goldmann, Lucien. 1969. "Criticism and Dogmatism in Literature." In *To Free a Generation: The Dialectics of Liberation*, translated by Ilona Halberstadt and edited by David Cooper. New York: Collier, pp. 128–149.

Gomez-Mejia, Gustavo. 2020. ""Fail, Clickbait, Cringe, Cancel, Woke": Vernacular Criticisms of Digital Advertising in Social Media Platforms." In *Social Computing and Social Media: Participation, User Experience, Consumer Experience, and Applications of Social Computing*, edited by G. Meiselwitz. HCII 2020. *Lecture Notes in Computer Science*, Vol. 12195. Berlin: Springer, pp. 309–324.

Gonzalez, Maya. 2013. "The Gendered Circuit: Reading the Arcane of Reproduction." *Viewpoint Magazine*, September 28, 2013. https://viewpointmag.com/2013/09/28/the-gendered-circuit-reading-the-arcane-of-reproduction/. Accessed July 12, 2021.

Greenberger, Alex. 2017. "'The Painting Must Go': Hannah Black Pens Open Letter to the Whitney About Controversial Biennial Work." *ARTNews*, March 21, 2017. https://www.artnews.com/artnews/news/the-painting-must-go-hannah-black-pens-open-letter-to-the-whitney-about-controversial-biennial-work-7992/. Accessed July 5, 2021.

Greenhalgh, Susan, and Edwin A. Winckler. 2005. *Governing China's Population: From Leninist to Neoliberal Biopolitics*. Stanford: Stanford University Press.

Greimas, Algirdas Julien. 1966. *Sémantique Structurale: Recherche De Méthode*. Paris: Larousse.

Griffiths, Jay (ed.). n.d. "About Us: Why We Rebel." *Extinction Rebellion*. https://extinctionrebellion.uk/the-truth/about-us/. Accessed June 18, 2021.

Grunberger, Béla, and Pierre Dessuant. 2000. *Narzissmus, Christentum, Antisemitismus. Eine psychoanalytische Untersuchung (Narcissism, Christianity, Anti-Semitism. A Psychoanalytical Study)*. Stuttgart: Klett-Cotta.

Guénon, René. 2001 [1945]. *The Reign of Quantity and the Sign of the Times*. Translated by Lord Northbourne. Hillsdale, NY: Sophia Perennis.

Hafner, Kornelia. 1993. "Gebrauchswertfetischismus" ("Use Value Fetishism"). In *Gesellschaft und Erkenntnis. Zur materialistischen Erkenntnis- und Ökonomiekritik (Society and Cognition. Contributions to a Materialist Epistemological and Social Critique)*, edited by D. Behrens. Freiburg: Ça ira.

Hall, Stuart. 1997. *Representation: Cultural Representations and Signifying Practices*. London: Sage (in association with the Open University).

Hameiri, Shahar, and Lee Jones. 2016. "Global Governance as State Transformation." *Political Studies* 64, no. 4 (2016): 793–810.

Hammond, Simon. 2019. "K-punk At Large." *New Left Review* 118 (July–August 2019): 37–67.
Haq, Nav. 2020. "Ambiguity and Liberalisms: Artistic and Institutional Practices as a Sphere of Cultural Influence." In *The Aesthetics of Ambiguity: Understanding and Addressing Monoculture*, edited by Nav Haq and Pascal Gielen. Amsterdam: Valiz, pp. 36–48.
Haraszti, Miklós. 1981. *A Worker in a Worker's State: Piece-Rates in Hungary*. Harmondsworth: Penguin in Association with New Left Review.
Hardaway, Robert M. 1997. "Environmental Malthusianism: Integrating Population and Environmental Policy." *Environmental Law* 27, no. 4 (Winter): 1209–1242.
Harding, Jeremy. 2019. "Among the Gilets Jaunes." *London Review of Books*, March 21, 2019. https://www.lrb.co.uk/the-paper/v41/n06/jeremy-harding/among-the-gilets-jaunes. Accessed July 1, 2021.
Harootunian, Harry D. 2015. *Marx After Marx: History and Time in the Expansion of Capitalism*. New York: Columbia University Press.
Harrabin, Roger. 2020. "Coronavirus: Banning Cars Made Easier to Aid Social Distancing." *BBC News*, April 20, 2020. https://www.bbc.co.uk/news/science-environment-52353942. Accessed June 1, 2021.
Harrison, Mark. 1983. "N.A. Voznesensky (1 December 1903–30 September 1950). A Soviet Commander of the Economic Front." *Warwick Economic Research Papers*, no. 242.
Harvey, David. 1993. "The Nature of Environment: Dialectics of Social and Environmental Change." In *Real Problems, False Solutions. A Special Issue of the Socialist Register*, edited by R. Miliband and L. Panitch. London: The Merlin Press.
Hay, Colin. 2007. *Why We Hate Politics*. Cambridge: Polity.
Haynes, Mike. 2019. "Socialism With a Bit of Greenwash Can't Save the Planet Either." *RS21*, September 14, 2019. https://www.rs21.org.uk/2019/09/14/socialism-with-a-bit-of-greenwash-cant-save-the-planet-either/. Accessed June 17, 2021.
Hazard, Anthony Q, Jr. 2011. "A Racialized Deconstruction? Ashley Montagu and the 1950 UNESCO Statement on Race." *Transforming Anthropology: Journal of the Association of Black Anthropologists* 19, no. 2 (2011): 174–186.
Heartfield, James. 2007. "European Union: A Process Without a Subject." In *Politics Without Sovereignty: A Critique of Contemporary International Relations*, edited by C. Bickerton, P. Cunliffe, and A. Gourevitch. London: Routledge, pp. 131–149.
Heartfield, James. 2013. *The European Union and the End of Politics*. Winchester: Zero.
Heartfield, James. 2014. "The Failure of the Capitalist Class and the Retreat from Production." *The Platypus Review* 70 (October 2014). https://platypus1917.org/2014/10/26/the-failure-of-the-capitalist-class-and-the-retreat-from-production/. Accessed July 1, 2021.
Hegel, Georg Wilhelm Friedrich. 1807. *Phänomenologie des Geistes*. Projekt Gutenberg. Posted November 9, 2012. https://www.gutenberg.org/cache/epub/6698/pg6698.html. Accessed July 5, 2021.

Hegel, Georg Wilhelm Friedrich. 1970 [1807]. *Phänomenologie des Geistes*. Werke 3. Frankfurt am Main: Suhrkamp.
Hegel, Georg Wilhelm Friedrich. 1924. *Vorlesungen über die Philosophie der Geschichte I*. Verlag von Philipp Reclam jun. Leipzig, 1924, Projekt Gutenberg. https://www.projekt-gutenberg.org/hegel/vorphilo/vorphilo.html. Accessed July 5, 2021.
Hegel, Georg Wilhelm Friedrich. 1973 [1818–1819]. "II. Naturrecht und Staatwissenschaft: Vorlesung 1818/19 nach der Nachschrift Carl Gustav Homeyers." In *Vorlesungen über Rechtsphilosophie (1818–1831), Band 1*, edited by Karl-Heinz Ilting. Stuttgart-Bad Cannstatt: Friedrich Frommann Verlag, pp. 217–352.
Hegel, Georg Wilhelm Friedrich. 1991. *Elements of the Philosophy of Right*. Edited by Alan Wood. Translated by H. B. Nisbet. Cambridge: Cambridge University Press.
Hegel, Georg Wilhelm Fiedrich. 2010. *The Science of Logic*. Cambridge: Cambridge University Press.
Helmrich, Herbert. 1987. "Recht Sichert die Freiheit: Bilanz der Rechtspolitik der CDU in der 10. Legislaturperiode/Ausblick auf die 11. Legislaturperiode" ("The Law Safeguards Freedom: The CDU's Legal Policy in the 10th Legislative Period/Outlook on the 11th Legislative Period"). *Zeitschrift Für Rechtspolitik* 20, no. 4 (1987): 108–110.
Hoare, George. 2020. "Brexit Britain Still Acts Like a Member State of the EU." *The Full Brexit*, December 17, 2020. https://www.thefullbrexit.com/post/brexit-britain-still-acts-like-a-member-state-of-the-eu. Accessed May 21, 2021.
Hoare, George. 2021a. "Moral Minoritarianism from the Ashes of Left Populism." *Damage Magazine*, January 13, 2021. https://damagemag.com/2021/01/13/moral-minoritarianism-from-the-ashes-of-left-populism/. Accessed May 21, 2021.
Hoare, George. 2021b. "After Left Populism, Part Two: Pro-Worker Conservatism in the UK." *Damage Magazine*, February 3, 2021. https://damagemag.com/2021/02/03/after-left-populism-part-two-pro-worker-conservatism-in-the-uk/. Accessed May 7, 2021.
Hoare, George. forthcoming. "On Brexit, Cosmopolitanism, Sovereignty, and the Question of 'Europe'." In *Contesting Cosmopolitan Europe: Euroscepticism, Crisis, and Borders*, edited by J. Foley and U. Korkut. Amsterdam: Amsterdam University Press.
Hoare, George, Peter Ramsay, and Lee Jones. 2019. "Transforming Britain After Brexit: Eddie Dempsey and the Divided Left." *The Full Brexit*, April 4. https://www.thefullbrexit.com/post/2019/04/04/transforming-britain-after-brexit-eddie-dempsey-and-the-divided-left. Accessed June 1, 2021.
Hobsbawm, Eric. 1994. *The Age of Extremes: The Short Twentieth Century, 1994–1991*. London: Michael Joseph.
Hochuli, Alex, George Hoare, and Phillip Cunliffe. 2021. *The End of the End of History. Politics for the 21st Century*. Winchester and Washington: Zero Books.
Hofstadter, Richard. 1964. "The Pseudo-Conservative Revolt" [1955] and "Pseudo-Conservatism Revisited" [1962]. In *The Radical Right*, edited by Daniel Bell. Garden City, NY: Doubleday, pp. 75–95, 97–103.

Honneth, Axel, and Nancy Fraser. 2004. *Redistribution or Recognition? A Political-Philosophical Exchange*. London: Verso.

Horkheimer, Max. 1978. *Dawn and Decline, Notes 1926–1931 and 1950–1969*. Translated by Michael Shaw. New York: Continuum.

Horkheimer, Max. 1982. "The Authoritarian State." In *The Essential Frankfurt School Reader*, edited by Andrew Arato and Eike Gerhardt. New York: Continuum, pp. 95–117.

Horkheimer, Max, and Theodor W. Adorno. 2007 [1944]. *Dialectic of Enlightenment*. Translated by Edmund Jephcott. Stanford, CA: Stanford University Press.

Horowitz, Gregg M. 2001. *Sustaining Loss: Art and the Mournful Life*. Stanford: Stanford University Press.

Horrendous Hackney Road Closures. 2021. "LTN Road Closures Hitting Women Hardest." http://freeourstreets.uk/ltn-road-closures-hitting-women-hardest. Accessed June 1, 2021.

Hoston, Germaine A. 1983. "Tenkō: Marxism & the National Question in Prewar Japan." *Polity* 16, no. 1 (1983): 96–118.

House of Commons International Development Committee. 2012. "The Development Situation in Malawi: Third Report of Session 2010–12." Vol. 2: 30. https://publications.parliament.uk/pa/cm201213/cmselect/cmintdev/118/118vw.pdf. Accessed June 1, 2021.

Huggan, Graham, and Helen Tiffin. 2015. *Postcolonial Ecocriticism: Literature, Animals, Environment*. New York: Routledge.

Huntington, Samuel P. 1993. "The Clash of Civilizations?" *Foreign Affairs* 72, no. 3 (1993): 22–49.

Huntington, Samuel P. 2011. *The Clash of Civilizations and the Remaking of World Order*. New York: Simon & Schuster.

Iñigo Carrera, J. 2014. "Method: From *Grundrisse* to *Capital*." In *In Marx's Laboratory: Critical Interpretations of the Grundrisse*, edited by Riccardo Bellofiore, Guido Starosta, and Peter D. Thomas. Chicago: Haymarket, pp. 43–70.

Iida, Yumiko. 2002. *Rethinking Identity in Modern Japan: Nationalism as Aesthetics*. Hove: Psychology Press.

International Labour Office. 2021. *World Employment and Social Outlook: Trends 2021*.

Jacobs, Jack. 2015. *The Frankfurt School, Jewish Lives, and Antisemitism*. Cambridge: Cambridge University Press.

International Times. 2019. "Yellow Vest Manifesto: 25 Demands for a Free France." http://internationaltimes.it/yellow-vest-manifesto-25-demands-for-a-free-france/. Accessed June 19, 2021.

Jacobs, Julia, and Jason Farago. 2020. "Delay of Philip Guston Retrospective Divides the Art World." *The New York Times*, September 25, 2020. www.nytimes.com/2020/09/25/arts/design/philip-guston-exhibition-delayed-criticism.html. Accessed July 12, 2021.

James, C. L. R. 1963. *The Black Jacobins: Toussaint Louverture and the San Domingo Revolution*. New York: Vintage.

Jameson, Fredric. 1992. "Postmodernism, or the Cultural Logic of Late Capitalism." In *Post-Contemporary Interventions*. Durham, NC: Duke University Press.

Jenkins, Destin, and Justin Leroy. 2021. *Histories of Racial Capitalism*. New York: Columbia University Press.
Johnston, Neil. 2017. "Alt-Right Has a Word for Its Own Ideology: Wrongthink." *The Times*, November 1, 2017. https://www.thetimes.co.uk/article/alt-right-has-a-word-for-its-own-ideology-wrongthink-2msd66frw. Accessed July 5, 2021.
Jones, Lee. 2018. "The Brexit Party: Creature of the Void." *The Full Brexit*, May 13, 2018. https://www.thefullbrexit.com/brexit-party-creature-of-the-void. Accessed May 5, 2021.
Jones, Lee. 2019. "British Politics in Chaos: Brexit and the Crisis of Representative Democracy." *The Full Brexit*, December 12, 2019. https://www.thefullbrexit.com/british-politics-chaos. Accessed May 8, 2021.
Jones, Lee. 2021. "From Rolls Royce to Skoda: How the Pandemic Has Exposed Britain's Failed 'Regulatory State'." *The Telegraph*, January 26, 2021. https://www.telegraph.co.uk/global-health/science-and-disease/rolls-royce-skoda-pandemic-has-exposed-britains-failed-regulatory/. Accessed June 1, 2021.
Jones, Lee, and Shahar Hameiri. 2021. "Covid-19 and the Failure of the Neoliberal Regulatory State." *Review of International Political Economy*. DOI: 10.1080/09692290.2021.1892798.
Jones, Owen. 2015. "The Left Must Put Britain's EU Withdrawal on the Agenda." *Guardian*, July 14, 2015. https://www.theguardian.com/commentisfree/2015/jul/14/left-reject-eu-greece-eurosceptic. Accessed June 15, 2021.
Kantorowicz, Ernst H. 1998. *The King's Two Bodies: A Study in Mediaeval Theology*. Princeton, NJ: Princeton University Press.
Kautsky, Karl. 1902. *The Social Revolution*. Translated by A. M. Simons and Mary Wood Simons. Chicago: Charles H. Kerr & Company.
Kautsky, Karl. 1910 [1907]. *The Class Struggle (Erfurt Program)*. Translated by William E. Bohn. Chicago: Charles H.Kerr.
Kant, Immanuel. 1790. *Kant's Gesammelte Schriften, Band V. Kritik der Urtheilskraft* (1790). Posted November 9, 2017. Projekt Gutenberg. https://www.gutenberg.org/files/55925/55925-h/55925-h.htm. Accessed July 5, 2021.
Kazan, Elia (dir.). 1947. *Gentleman's Agreement*. Beverly Hills, CA: Twentieth Century Home Entertainment, 2002. DVD.
Kazan, Elia (dir.). 1954. *On the Waterfront*. Culver City, CA: Columbia Tristar, 2001. DVD.
Kazan, Elia (dir.). 1957. *A Face in the Crowd*. Burbank, CA: Warner Home Video, 2005. DVD.
Kendi, Ibram X. 2019. *How to be an Antiracist*. New York: One World.
Kierkegaard, Søren. 1986. *Fear and Trembling*. London: Penguin.
Kołakowski, Leszek. 1969. "The Concept of the Left." In *The New Left Reader*, edited by Carl Oglesby. New York: Grove Press, pp. 144–158.
Konstatinow, Fjodor Wassiljewitsch. 1961. *Grundlagen der marxistischen Philosophie (Foundations of Marxist Philosophy)*. Berlin: Dietz Verlag.
Kotkin, Joel. 2017. "Why The Greens Lost, and Trump Won." *New Geography*, July 22, 2017. https://www.newgeography.com/content/005695-why-greens-lost-and-trump-won. Accessed June 29, 2021.

Kotkin, Joel. 2020. *The Coming of Neo-Feudalism: A Warning to the Global Middle Class*. New York City: Encounter Books.
Kreager, Philip. 2014. "On the History of Malthusian Thought: A Review Essay." *Population and Development Review* 40, no. 4 (2014): 731–742.
Lacan, Jacques. 1999. *The Seminar of Jacques Lacan VII: The Ethics of Psychoanalysis, 1959–60*. Edited by Jacques-Alain Miller. London/New York: Routledge.
Landrigan, Philip. 2020. "COVID-19 and Clean Air: An Opportunity for Radical Change." *The Lancet* 4, no. 10 (October): 447–449.
Lang, Jürgen P. 2016. "Biographisches Porträt: Jürgen Elsässer." ("Biographical Portrait: Jürgen Elsässer"). In *Jahrbuch Extremismus & Demokratie (E & D)*, edited by Uwe Backes, Alexander Gallus, and Eckhard Jesse. Baden-Baden: Nomos Verlagsgesellschaft, pp. 225–240.
Lange, Elena Louisa. 2018. "Capital." In *The Bloomsbury Companion to Marx*, edited by Jeff Diamanti, Andrew Pendakis, and Imre Szeman. London: Bloomsbury, pp. 273–280.
Lange, Elena Louisa. 2019. "Form Analysis and Critique: Marx's Social Labour Theory of Value." In *Capitalism: Concept, Idea, Image: Aspects of Marx's Capital Today*, edited by Peter Osborne, Eric Alliez, and Eric-John Russell. London: CRMEP Books.
Lange, Elena Louisa, and Joshua Pickett-Depaolis. 2020. "The Middle-Class Leviathan. Corona, the 'Fascism' Blackmail, and the Defeat of the Working Class." *Crisis and Critique* 7, no. 3 (2020): 145–158.
Lange, Elena Louisa. 2021a. "Gendercraft: Marxism-Feminism, Reproduction, and the Blind Spot of Money." *Science & Society* 85, no. 1 (2021): 38–65.
Lange, Elena Louisa. 2021b. *Value Without Fetish. Uno Kōzō's Theory of 'Pure Capitalism' in Light of Marx's Critique of Political Economy*. Leiden: Brill.
Lapavitsas, Costas. 2018. *The Left Case Against the EU*. London: Polity.
Latour, Bruno. 2017. *Facing Gaia: Eight Lectures on the New Climatic Regime*. Cambridge: Polity Press.
Lazerus, Sylvain. 2015 [1996]. *Anthropology of the Name*. Translated by Gila Walker. Calcutta: Seagull Books.
Lazzarato, Maurizio. 2012. *The Making of Indebted Man*. Cambridge, MA: MIT Press.
Lazzarato, Maurizio. 2013. *Governing by Debt*. Cambridge, MA: MIT Press.
Lenin, Vladimir Ilyich. 1939. *Imperialism, The Highest Stage of Capitalism: A Popular Outline*, Revised Trans. New York: International Publishers.
Lenin, Vladimir Ilyich. 1962 [1905]. "Two Tactics of Social-Democracy in the Democratic Revolution." In *V. I. Lenin, Collected Works Volume 9 June–November 1905*, edited by George Hanna and translated by Abraham Fineberg and Julius Katzer. Moscow: Progress Publishers, pp. 15–140.
Lenin, Vladimir Ilyich. 1967 [1899]. *The Development of Capitalism in Russia*. Moscow: Progress Publishers.
Lenin, Vladimir Ilyitch. 1970 [1918]. "The Immediate Tasks of the Soviet Government." https://www.marxists.org/archive/lenin/works/1918/mar/x03.htm. Accessed June 12, 2021.

Lenin, Vladimir Ilyich. 1972. *Marxism on the State: Preparatory Material for the Book the State and Revolution*. Moscow: Progress Publishers.

Lenin, Vladimir Ilyich. 1973 [1921]. "The Tax in Kind (The Significance of the New Policy and its Conditions)." In *V.I. Lenin Collected Works Volume 32 December 1920–August 1921*, edited by Yuri Sdobnikov. Moscow: Progress Publishers, pp. 329–365.

Lenin, Vladimir Ilyich. 1974 [1919]. "Greetings to the Hungarian Workers." In *V.I. Lenin Collected Works Volume 29 March–August 1919*, edited by George Hanna. Moscow: Progress Publishers, pp. 387–391.

Lenin, Vladimir Ilyich. 1977 [1894]. "What the 'Friends of the People' Are and How They Help the Social Democrats." In *V.I. Lenin Collected Works Volume 1 1893–1894*. Moscow: Progress Publishers, pp. 129–332.

Lenin, Vladimir Ilyich. 2014 [1920]. *Left-Wing Communism: An Infantile Disorder*. Chicago: Haymarket Books.

Leonard, Annie. 2010. *The Story of Stuff: How Our Obsession with Stuff is Trashing the Planet, Our Communities, and Our Health - And a Vision for Change*. London: Constable.

Leys, Colin. 2003. *Market-Driven Politics: Neoliberal Democracy and the Public Interest*. London: Verso.

Linke, Russel D. 1976. "A Case for Indoctrination in Environmental Education." *South Pacific Journal of Teacher Education* 4, no. 2 (1976): 125–129.

Linkola, Pentti. 2009. *Can Life Prevail? A Radical Approach to the Ecological Crisis*. Budapest: Arktos.

Lipset, Seymour Martin. 1964 [1955]. "The Sources of the 'Radical Right'." In *The Radical Right*, edited by Daniel Bell. Garden City, NY: Doubleday, pp. 307–371.

Liu, Catherine. 2021. *Virtue Hoarders: The Case Against the Professional Managerial Class*. United States: University of Minnesota Press.

Lucas, Caroline. 2020. "Clean Air And Clear Skies Must Become the New Normal When Lockdown Lifts." *Huffington Post*, April 29, 2020. https://www.huffingtonpost.co.uk/entry/coronavirus-climate-change_uk_5ea9352ac5b6106b8ecfa3aa. Accessed June 20, 2021.

Lukács, Georg. 1923. "The Standpoint of the Proletariat." In *History and Class Consciousness*. www.marxists.org/archive/lukacs/works/history/hcc07_5.htm. Accessed July 12, 2021.

Lukács, Georg. 1980. *The Destruction of Reason*. London: Merlin Press.

Lyotard, Jean-François. 1984. *The Post-Modern Condition: A Report on Knowledge*. Minneapolis : University of Minnesota Press.

Macherey, Pierre. 2001. *Introduction à l'Ethique de Spinoza: La première partie, la nature des choses*. Paris: PUF.

MacKinnon, Catharine, A. 1994. *Only Words*. Cambridge, MA: Harvard University Press.

Mackintosh, Eliza. 2019. "A Psychedelic Journey, a Radical Strategy and Perfect Timing. How the World's Fastest-Growing Climate Movement Was Made." *CNN*, December 25, 2019. https://edition.cnn.com/2019/12/25/uk/extinction-rebellion-gail-bradbrook-gbr-intl/index.html. Accessed June 1, 2021.

Macnair, Mike. 2018. "Intersectionalism, the Highest Stage of Western Stalinism?" *Critique: Journal of Socialist Theory* 46, no. 4 (2018): 541–558.
Mair, Peter. 2013. *Ruling the Void: The Hollowing of Western Democracy*. London: Verso.
Malik, Kenan. 2009. *Strange Fruit: Why Both Sides Are Wrong in the Race Debate*. London: Oneworld Publications.
Malthaner, Stefan, Simon Teune, and Peter Ullrich. 2018. *Eskalation: Dynamiken der Gewalt im Kontext der G20-Proteste in Hamburg 2017* [Report] (*Escalation: Dynamics of Violence in the Context of the G20 Protests in Hamburg 2017*). Berlin: Zentrum Technik und Gesellschaft der TU.
Malthus, Thomas. 1798. *An Essay on the Principle of Population*. London: J. Johnson.
Marcuse, Herbert. 1969. "Liberation from the Affluent Society." In *To Free a Generation: The Dialectics of Liberation*, edited by David Cooper. New York: Collier, pp. 175–192.
Marcuse, Herbert. 1978. "Theory and Politics: A Discussion with Herbert Marcuse, Juergen Habermas, Heinz Lubasz and Telman Spengler." Translated by Leslie Adelson, Susan Hegger, Betty Sun, and Herbert Weinryb. *Telos* 38 (December): 124–153.
Marcuse, Herbert. 2004. *Technology, War and Fascism. Collected Papers of Herbert Marcuse vol. 1*. Translated by Douglas Kellner. London: Routledge.
Marcuse, Herbert. 2014. *Marxism, Revolution and Utopia: Collected Papers of Herbert Marcuse vol. 6*. Edited by Douglas Kellner and Clayton Pierce. London and New York: Routledge.
Marcuse, Herbert. 2015. *Herbert Marcuse's 1974 Paris Lectures at Vincennes University: Global Capitalism and Radical Opposition*. Edited and published by Peter-Erwin Jansen and Charles Reitz. Kansas City, MI: Frankfurt a. M.
Marx, Karl. 1845. "The German Ideology." https://www.marxists.org/archive/marx/works/1845/german-ideology/ch01b.htm. Accessed May 2, 2021.
Marx, Karl. 1887 [1867]. *Capital*. Translated by Samuel Moore and Edward Aveling. Moscow: Progress Publishers. https://www.marxists.org/archive/marx/works/download/pdf/Capital-Volume-I.pdf. Accessed June 7, 2021.
Marx, Karl. 1897 [1853–56]. *The Eastern Question: A Reprint of Letters Written 1853–56 Dealing with the Events of the Crimean War*. Edited by Eleanor Marx Aveling and Edward Aveling. London: S. Sonnenschein & Co.
Marx, Karl. 1965 [1874–5]. "Konspekt von Bakunins Buch *Staatlichkeit und Anarchie*." In *Karl Marx-Friedrich Engels: Werke Band 18*. Berlin: Dietz Verlag.
Marx, Karl. 1968. *The German Ideology*. Translated by S. Ryazanskaya. Moscow: Progress Publishers. https://www.marxists.org/archive/marx/works/download/Marx_The_German_Ideology.pdf. Accessed May 22, 2021.
Marx, Karl. 1973 [1857]. *Grundrisse: Foundations of the Critique of Political Economy (Rough Draft)*. Translated by Martin Nicolaus. London: Penguin Books.
Marx, Karl. 1975. *Early Writings*. Translated by Rodney Livingstone and Gregor Benton. London: Penguin Books.
Marx, Karl. 1976 [1867]. *Capital: A Critique of Political Economy, Volume 1*. Translated by Ben Fowkes. Harmondsworth: Penguin Books.

Marx, Karl. 1978 [1885]. *Capital. A Critique of Political Economy, Volume 2*. Translated by David Fernbach. Harmondsworth: Penguin Books.
Marx, Karl. 1979 [1853]. "The British Rule in India." In *Marx and Engels Collected Works, Volume 12. 1853–54*. Moscow. Progress Publishers, pp. 125–133.
Marx, Karl. 1981 [1894]. *Capital: A Critique of Political Economy, Volume 3*. Translated by David Fernbach. Harmondsworth: Penguin Books.
Marx, Karl. 1994 [1861–1864]. "Economic Works 1861–1864." In *Marx-Engels Collected Works Vol. 34*. London: Lawrence and Wishart.
Marx, Karl. 1995. *Capital: A New Abridgement*. Translated by Samuel Moore and Edward Aveling and edited by David McLellan. Oxford and New York: Oxford University Press.
Marx, Karl. 1996. *Later Political Writings*. Translated by Terrell Carver. Cambridge: Cambridge University Press.
Marx, Karl, and Friedrich Engels. 1848. "The Communist Manifesto." https://www.marxists.org/archive/marx/works/1848/communist-manifesto/index.htm. Accessed June 1, 2021.
Marx, Karl, and Friedrich Engels. 1970 [1848]. *Manifesto of the Communist Party*. Peking: Foreign Languages Press.
Marx, Karl, and Friedrich Engels. 2008 [1867]. *Werke - Das Kapital I*. Marx-Engels-Werke Band 23. Berlin: Dietz, 2008.
Marx, Karl, and Friedrich Engels. 2017. *The Communist Manifesto*. Translated by Samuel Moore. London: Pluto Press.
Mason, Paul. 2016. "The Leftwing Case for Brexit (One Day)." *The Guardian*, May 16, 2016. https://www.theguardian.com/commentisfree/2016/may/16/brexit-eu-referendum-boris-johnson-greece-tory. Accessed June 15, 2021.
Mayhew, Robert. 2014. *Malthus: The Life and Legacies of an Untimely Prophet*. Cambridge: Harvard University Press.
McCormack, Tara, and Lee Jones. 2020. "Covid-19 and the Failed Post-Political State." *The Full Brexit*, April 17, 2020. https://www.thefullbrexit.com/covid19-state-failure. Accessed June 1, 2021.
McLennan, Rebecca. 2009. *The Crisis of Imprisonment: Protest, Politics and the Making of the American Penal State (1776–1941)*. Cambridge: Cambridge University Press.
McNeice, Stephen. 2019. "Students in Ireland and Around the World Take Part in Latest Climate Strikes." *Newstalk*, May 24, 2019. https://www.newstalk.com/news/climate-strikes-students-ireland-863232. Accessed June 1, 2021.
Meyer, Thomas. 2001. *Identity Mania: Fundamentalism and the Politicization of Cultural Differences*. New York: Zed Books.
Michaels, Walter Benn. 2016. *The Trouble With Diversity: How We Learned to Love Identity and Ignore Inequality*. United States: Picador.
Milburn, Keir. 2020. "The Pandemic is Changing How It Feels to Be Free." *Novara Media*, June 1, 2020. https://novaramedia.com/2020/06/01/the-pandemic-is-changing-how-it-feels-to-be-free/. Accessed June 1, 2021.
Mill, John Stewart. 2015. *On Liberty, Utilitarianism and Other Essays*. Oxford: Oxford University Press.

Montag, Warren. 2005. "Necro-Economics: Adam Smith and Death in the Life of the Universal." *Radical Philosophy* 134 (2005): 7–17.
Montagu, M. F. Ashley. 1945. *Man's Most Dangerous Myth: The Fallacy of Race*, 2nd edition. New York: Columbia University Press.
Moore, Jason W. 2015. *Capitalism in the Web of Life. Ecology and the Accumulation of Capital.* London and New York: Verso.
Moore, Jason W. (ed.). 2016. *Anthropocene or Capitalocene? Nature, History, and the Crisis of Capitalism.* Oakland: PM Press.
Moore, Matthew. 2021. "Idris Elba's Luther 'Isn't Black Enough to be Real', Says BBC Diversity Chief." *The Times*, April 14, 2021. https://www.thetimes.co.uk/article/idris-elba-luther-black-drama-crime-bbc-diversity-chief-8dgzjkx7v. Accessed July 5, 2021.
Morton, Stephen. 2007. *Gayatri Spivak: Ethics, Subalterneity and the Critique of Postcolonial Reason.* Malden, MA: Polity Press.
Moseley, Fred. 2017. *Money and Totality: A Macro-Monetary Interpretation of Marx's Logic in Capital and the End of the "Transformation Problem."* Chicago: Haymarket.
Mousazadeh, Milad. 2021. "Positive Environmental Effects of the Coronavirus 2020 Episode: A Review." *Environment, Development and Sustainability* (February): 1–23.
Moutet, Anne-Elisabeth. 2018. "Macron Faces Up to France's Déplorables." *CapX*, December 13, 2018. https://capx.co/macron-faces-up-to-frances-deplorables. Accessed June 17, 2021.
Moynagh, Maureen. 1999. "The Ethical Turn in Postcolonial Theory and Narrative: Michelle Cliff's No Telephone to Heaven." *ARIEL: A Review of International English Literature* 30, no. 4 (1999): 109–133.
Muehlebach, Andrea. 2016. "Time of Monsters." *Society for Cultural Anthropology*, October 27. https://culanth.org/fieldsights/time-of-monsters. Accessed July 5, 2021.
Mukherjee, Upamanyu. 2010. *Postcolonial Environments: Nature, Culture and the Contemporary Indian Novel.* UK: Palgrave Macmillan.
Mullan, Phil. 2017. *Creative Destruction: How to Start an Economic Renaissance.* Bristol: Policy Press.
Mullan, Phil. 2020. "It's Time to Transform the UK Economy." *Spiked*, May 15, 2020. https://www.spiked-online.com/2020/05/15/its-time-to-transform-the-uk-economy. Accessed June 21, 2021.
Murray, Patrick. 2017. *The Mismeasure of Wealth: Essays on Marx and Social Form.* Chicago: Haymarket.
Nesbitt, Nick. 2008. *Universal Emancipation: The Haitian Revolution and the Radical Enlightenment.* Charlottesville: University of Virginia Press.
Nesbitt, Nick. 2013. *Caribbean Critique: Antillean Critical Theory from Toussaint to Glissant.* Liverpool: Liverpool University Press.
Nesbitt, Nick. 2014. "Resolutely Modern: Politics and Human Rights in the Mande Charter." *Savannah Review* 4 (2014): 11–20.
Nesbitt, Nick. 2015. "From Louverture to Lenin: Aimé Césaire and Anticolonial Marxism." *Smallaxe* 48 (2015): 129–144.

Nesbitt, Nick (ed.). 2017. *The Concept in Crisis: Reading Capital Today.* Durham: Duke University Press.
Nesbitt, Nick. 2022. *The Price of Slavery: Capitalism and Revolution in the Caribbean.* Charlottesville: University of Virginia Press.
Nietzsche, Friedrich. 1989. *Genealogy of Morals and Ecce Homo.* New York: Vintage.
Nietzsche, Friedrich. 2002 [1886]. *Beyond Good and Evil: Prelude to a Philosophy of the Future.* Edited by R.-P. Horstmann and J. Norman. Translated by J. Norman. New York: Cambridge University Press.
Nietzsche, Friedrich. 2003. *Thus Spake Zarathustra: A Book For All and None.* Translated by Thomas Wayne. New York: Algora Publishing.
Norris, Pippa, and Ronald Inglehart. 2019. *Cultural Backlash: Trump, Brexit, and Authoritarian Populism.* Cambridge: Cambridge University Press.
Oglesby, Carl. 1978. "The Idea of the New Left." In *The New Left Reader*, edited by Carl Oglesby. New York: Grove Press, pp. 1–18.
O'Hagan, Ellie Mae. 2020. "The 'Anti-Woke' Backlash Is No Joke – And Progressives Are Going to Lose If They Don't Wise Up." *The Guardian*, January 30, 2020. https://www.theguardian.com/commentisfree/2020/jan/30/anti-woke-backlash-liberalism-laurence-fox. Accessed July 5, 2021.
O'Neill, Brendan. 2018. "In Praise of the Gilets Jaunes." *Spectator*, December 3, 2018.
O'Toole, Fintan. 2020. "Earth Has a Toxic Virus – Us." *Irish Times*, April 4, 2020. https://www.irishtimes.com/opinion/fintan-o-toole-earth-has-a-toxic-virus-us-1.4217850. Accessed June 29, 2021.
Oxford Reference. "Symbolic violence." https://www.oxfordreference.com/view/10.1093/oi/authority.20110803100546777. Accessed June 4, 2021.
Park, K-Sue. 2021. "Race, Innovation, and Financial Growth: The Example of Foreclosure." In *Histories of Racial Capitalism*, edited by D. Jenkins and J. Leroy. New York: Columbia University Press. pp. 27–52.
Paul, Diane. 1984. "Eugenics and the Left." *Journal of the History of Ideas* 45, no. 4 (Winter): 567–590.
Penny, Laurie. 2016. "I Want My Country Back." *New Statesman*, June 24, 20216. https://www.newstatesman.com/politics/uk/2016/06/i-want-my-country-back. Accessed May 20, 2021.
Perspektive Online. 2019. "Verfassungsklage: Ist Plastikfolie eine Passiv-Bewaffnung?" ("Complaint of Unconstitutionality: Is plastic film a passive armament?"). In *Perspektive* (blog), September 22, 2019. https://perspektive-online.net/2019/09/verfassungsklage-ist-plastikfolie-eine-passiv-bewaffnung/. Accessed June 12, 2021.
Pfaller, Robert. 2012. *Zweite Welten - und andere Lebenselixiere* (*Second Worlds - and Other Elixiers*). Frankfurt: S. Fischer Verlag.
Pfaller, Robert. 2014. *On the Pleasure Principle in Culture: Illusions Without Owners.* London/New York: Verso.
Piketty, Thomas. 2017. *Capital in the Twenty-First Century.* Cambridge, MA: Belknap Press.

Plekhanov, Georgi. 1977 [1883]. "Socialism and the Political Struggle." In *Selected Philosophical Works in Five Volumes: Volume One*. London: Lawrence and Wishart, pp. 49–107.

Plekhanov, Georgi. 1977 [1884]. "Our Differences." In *Selected Philosophical Works in Five Volumes: Volume One*. London: Lawrence and Wishart, pp. 107–359.

Pluckrose, Helen, and James Lindsay. 2020. *Cynical Theories: How Activist Scholarship Made Everything About Race, Gender, and Identity – And Why This Harms Everybody*. United States: Pitchstone Publishing.

Post, Charlie. 2020. "Beyond 'Racial Capitalism': Toward a Unified Theory of Capitalism and Racial Oppression." *Brooklyn Rail*, October. https://brooklynrail.org/2020/10/field-notes/Beyond-Racial-Capitalism-Toward-A-Unified-Theory-of-Capitalism-and-Racial-Oppression. Accessed July 12, 2021.

Postone, Moishe. 1993. *Time, Labor and Social Domination*. Cambridge: Cambridge University Press.

Ralph, Michael, and Maya Singhal. 2019. "Racial Capitalism." *Theory and Society* 48, no. 6 (2019): 851–881.

Ramsay, Peter. 2018. "The Brexit Party: Vital Stop-Gap, But No Solution." *The Full Brexit*, May 13, 2018. https://www.thefullbrexit.com/brexit-party-stopgap. Accessed May 2, 2021.

Redvaldsen, David. 2017. *Eugenics, Socialists and the Labour Movement in Britain, 1865–1940*. Oxford: Oxford University Press.

Reed, Adolph, Jr. 2018. *Without Justice For All: The New Liberalism And Our Retreat From Racial Equality*. United Kingdom: Taylor & Francis.

Reed, Adolph, Jr. 2019. "The Myth of Class Reductionism." *The New Republic*, September 25, 2019. https://newrepublic.com/article/154996/myth-class-reductionism. Accessed July 5, 2021.

Ridley, Matt. 2011. "Scientific Heresy." *Lecture, Royal Society of the Arts, Edinburgh*, October 31, 2011. https://bit.ly/3wJRhWX. Accessed June 27, 2021.

Riesman, David. 1954 [1951]. "Some Observations Concerning Marginality." In *Individuality Reconsidered*. New York: Free Press, pp. 153–165.

Riesman, David, and Nathan Glazer. 1964 [1955]. "Intellectuals and Discontented Classes." In *The Radical Right*, edited by Daniel Bell. Garden City, NY: Doubleday, pp. 105–135.

Riesman, David, Nathan Glazer, and Reuel Denney. 1953. *The Lonely Crowd: A Study of the Changing American Character*, abridged edition. Garden City, NY: Doubleday.

Robinson, Cedric. 1983. *Black Marxism: The Making of the Black Radical Tradition*. London and Chapel Hill: The University of North Carolina Press.

Romano, Aja. 2020. "What Is Woke: How a Black Movement Watchword Got Co-Opted in a Culture War." *Vox*, October 9, 2020. https://www.vox.com/culture/21437879/stay-woke-wokeness-history-origin-evolution-controversy. Accessed July 5, 2021.

Roos, Bonnie and Alex Hunt (eds). 2010. *Postcolonial Green: Environmental Politics and World Narratives*. Charlottsville: University of Virginia Press.

Roufos, Pavlos. 2018. "The Aggressiveness of Vulnerability." *Brooklyn Rail*, July–August 2018. https://brooklynrail.org/2018/07/field-notes/The-Aggressiveness-of-Vulnerability. Accessed July 1, 2021.

Rubin, Isaak Illich. 2018. "Essays on Marx's Theory of Money (1926–28)." In *Responses to Marx's Capital: From Rudolf Hilferding to Isaak Illich Rubin*, edited by Richard B. Day and Daniel F Gaido. Chicago: Haymarket Books, pp. 619–727.

Rushdie, Salman. 1997. *The Satanic Verses*. Toronto: Vintage Books.

Saltmarsh, Chris. 2018. "Taking to the Streets." *Fabian Society*, December 19, 2018. https://fabians.org.uk/taking-to-the-streets/. Accessed June 3, 2021.

Samuel, Raphael. 1978. "Margaret Thatcher's Return to Victorian Values." *Proceedings of the British Academy* 78 (1978): 9–29.

Sartre, Jean-Paul. 1988. "Black Orpheus (1948), Translated by John MacCombie." In *What is Literature? and Other Essays*. Cambridge, MA: Harvard University Press, pp. 289–330.

Sartre, Jean-Paul. 1995. *Anti-Semite and Jew*. Translated by George J. Becker. New York: Schocken.

Schiller, Friedrich. 1879. "Ueber das Erhabene." *Schillers Sämtliche Werke, Vierter Band*, pp. 726–738. Projekt Gutenberg. https://www.projekt-gutenberg.org/schiller/erhaben/erhaben.html. Accessed May 13, 2021.

Schmidt, Alfred. 1968. "On the Concept of Cognition in the Critique of Political Economy." In *The Critique of Political Economy Today. 100 Years of Capital*, edited by W. Euchner and A. Schmidt. Europäische Verlagsanstalt, pp. 30–43.

Schmitt, Carl. 2014. *Dictatorship: From the Origin of the Modern Concept of Sovereignty to Proletarian Class Struggle*. Cambridge, UK: Polity.

Schenwar, Maya, Joe Macaré, and Alana Yu-lan Price. 2016. *Who Do You Serve, Who Do You Protect?: Police Violence and Resistance in the United States*. Chicago: Haymarket.

Schneider, Bret. 2017. "Trotsky's Theory of Art." *The Platypus Affiliated Society*, September 6, 2017. http://platypus1917.org/2011/07/01/trotskys-theory-of-art/#_edn1. Accessed July 5, 2021.

Schuettauf, Konrad, and Wolfgang Marx. 1996. "Wird Scheinhaftigkeit zum Verfassungsprinzip?" *Die Zeit*, April 5, 1996. https://www.zeit.de/1996/15/Wird_Scheinhaftigkeit_zum_Verfassungsprinzip_/seite-3?utm_referrer=https%3A%2F%2Fswisscows.com%2F. Accessed June 12, 2021.

Sennett, Richard. 1977. *The Fall of Public Man*. New York: Knop.

Siddique, Haroon. 2021. "Legal Experts Worldwide Draw Up 'Historic' Definition of Ecocide." *The Guardian*, June 22, 2021. https://www.theguardian.com/environment/2021/jun/22/legal-experts-worldwide-draw-up-historic-definition-of-ecocide. Accessed June 22, 2021.

Simms, Andrew. 2011. "The New Home Front." *The Green Party UK*. https://www.greenparty.org.uk/assets/files/reports/the_new_home_front_FINAL.pdf. Accessed May 17, 2021.

Singh, Nikhil Pal. 2016. "On Race, Violence, and So-Called Primitive Accumulation." *Social Text* 128, no. 34:3 (2016): 27–50.

Sloterdijk, Peter. 1988. *Critique of Cynical Reason*. London: Verso.

Sloterdijk, Peter. 2014. *You Must Change Your Life*. London: John Wiley & Sons.
Smith, Adam. 1776. *An Inquiry into the Nature and Causes of the Wealth of Nations*. London: Strahan and Cadell. https://www.marxists.org/reference/archive/smith-adam/works/wealth-of-nations/book05/ch02b-2.htm. Accessed July 6, 2021.
Smith, Adam. 1846 [1776]. *An Inquiry Into The Nature and Causes of the Wealth of Nations, With a Life of the Author, and Introductory Discourse, Notes, and Supplementary Dissertations by J.R. McCulloch Esq.* Edinburgh: Adam and Charles Black and William Tate.
Smith, Adam. 1999 [1776]. *The Wealth of Nations*. London: Penguin.
Smith, Barry, and David Woodruff Smith (eds). 1995. *The Cambridge Companion to Husserl*. Cambridge Companions to Philosophy. Cambridge: Cambridge University Press
Smith, David Woodruff. 2018. "Phenomenology." In *The Stanford Encyclopedia of Philosophy*, Summer 2018 edition, edited by Edward N. Zalta. https://plato.stanford.edu/archives/sum2018/entries/phenomenology. Accessed July 5, 2021.
Smith, John. 2015. "The British Left's desperate Confusion Over Charlie Hebdo." *openDemocracy*, January 9. https://www.opendemocracy.net/en/opendemocracyuk/british-lefts-desperate-confusion-over-charlie-hebdo/. Accessed July 5, 2021.
Smyth, Robbie. 2017. "We Need to Talk About Liam." *An Phoblacht*, November 22, 2017. https://www.anphoblacht.com/contents/27221. Accessed June 17, 2021.
Sobel, Alex. 2019. "Britain Needs a Marshall Plan for the Environment." *New Statesman*, March 4, 2019. https://www.newstatesman.com/politics/staggers/2019/03/britain-needs-marshall-plan-environment. Accessed June 21, 2021.
Socialist Worker. 2021. "New Wave Forced Tories to Keep Lockdown." *Socialist Worker*, June 14, 2021. https://socialistworker.co.uk/art/51953/New+wave+forced+Tories+to+keep+lockdown. Accessed June 28, 2021.
Spinoza, Benedictus de. 1954 [1677]. *Ethics*. New York: Hafner.
Spinoza, Benedictus de. 2002. *Complete Works*. Translated by Samuel Shirley. Indianapolis: Hackett Publishing.
Spinoza, Benedictus de. 2018. *Ethics: Proved in Geometrical Order*. Edited by Matthew J. Kisner and Michael Silverthorne. Translated by Mathew J. Kisner. Cambridge: Cambridge University Press.
Spivak, Gayatri Chakravorty. 1983. "Can the Subaltern Speak?" In *Reflections on the History of an Idea: Can the Subaltern Speak?* edited by Rosalind C. Morris. New York: Columbia University Press, pp. 21–80.
Spivak, Gayatri Chakravorty. 1995. *Imaginary Maps: Three stories by Mahashweta Devi*. New York: Routledge.
Steineck, Raji C. 2018. "Time Subsumed or Time Sublated?" *Asiatische Studien-Études Asiatiques* 71, no. 4 (2018): 1339–1353.
Stephan, Cora. 1993. *Der Betroffenheitskult. Eine politische Sittengeschichte (The Cult of Concernment. A Political History of Mores)*. Berlin: Rowohlt.
Stewart, Heather. 2017. "Brexit: Workers' Rights Best Secured by Staying in Single Market, Says TUC Chief." *Guardian*, September 11, 2017. https://www.theguardian.com/politics/2017/sep/11/brexit-workers-rights-best-secured-by-staying-in-single-market-says-tuc-chief. Accessed June 15, 2021.

Stoker, Gerry. 2006. *Why Politics Matters: Making Democracy Work*. London: Palgrave Macmillan.
Streeck, Wolfgang. 2017. "Caution: European Narrative. Handle with Care!" In *European Union and Disunion: Reflections on European Identity*, edited by A. Amin and P. Lewis. London: British Academy, pp. 14–22.
Sundermeier, Theo. 1999. *Was ist Religion? Religionswissenschaft im theologischen Kontext (What Is Religion? Religious Science in Theological Context)*. Gütersloh: Kaiser.
Sweeney, Shauna J. 2021. "Gendering Racial Capitalism and the Black Heretical Tradition." In *Histories of Racial Capitalism*, edited by D. Jenkins and J. Leroy. New York: Columbia University Press, pp. 53–83.
Táíwò, Olúfẹ́mi O., and Liam Kofi Bright. 2020. "A Response to Michael Walzer." *Dissent Magazine*, August 7, 2020. https://www.dissentmagazine.org/online_articles/a-response-to-michael-walzer. Accessed July 12, 2021.
Taylor, Keeanga-Yamahtta. 2019. "Black Feminism and the Combahee River Collective Statement." *Monthly Review*, January 1, 2019. https://monthlyreview.org/2019/01/01/black-feminism-and-the-combahee-river-collective/. Accessed July 12, 2021.
Thier, Hadas. 2020. "Under Capitalism, There's No Such Thing as a 'Fair Day's Wage for a Fair Day's Work.'" *Jacobin*, July 9, 2020. https://jacobinmag.com/2020/09/capitalism-marxism-economics-hadas-thier-book-excerpt. Accessed July 5, 2021.
Thom, Maren. 2019. ""How the Oscars Became Irrelevant." *Spiked*, February 27, 2019. https://www.spiked-online.com/2019/02/27/how-the-oscars-became-irrelevant/. Accessed July 5, 2021.
Thunberg, Greta. 2019. "On Friday March 15th, 2019, Well Over 1.5 Million Students School (sic) Striked for the Climate in 2083 Places in 125 Countries on All Continents." *Facebook*, March 17, 2019. https://www.facebook.com/732846497083173/posts/793441724356983. Accessed June 12, 2021.
Tice, Paul H. 2015. "Schoolroom Climate Change Indoctrination." *Wall Street Journal*, May 27, 2015. https://www.wsj.com/articles/schoolroom-climate-change-indoctrination-1432767611. Accessed June 12, 2021.
Tinnin, David. 1977. "Books: Like Father." *Time*, August 8, 1977. http://content.time.com/time/subscriber/article/0,33009,915234-2,00.html. Accessed June 12, 2021.
Tomich, Dale. 2018. *Slavery in the Circuit of Sugar, Second Edition: Martinique and the World Economy, 1830–1848*. Albany: State University of New York Press.
Torres, Marco Aurelio. 2007. "Review: 'The Common Sense.'" http://platypus1917.org/2007/11/01/review-the-common-sense/. Accessed July 5, 2021.
Toscano, Alberto. 2014. "Materialism Without Matter: Abstraction, Absence, and Social Form." *Textual Practice* 28, no. 7 (2014): 1221–1240.
Toynbee, Arnold. 2011. *Lectures on the Industrial Revolution in England: Popular Addresses, Notes and Other Fragments*. Cambridge: Cambridge University Press.
Trotsky, Leon. 1923. "The Social Roots and the Social Function of Literature." https://www.marxists.org/archive/trotsky/1923/art/tia23b.htm. Accessed May 1, 2021.

Trotsky, Leon. 2005 [1924]. *Literature and Revolution*. Translated by Rose Strunsky. Chicago: Haymarket Books.
Tuck, Richard. 2019. "Parliament has No Sovereignty Higher Than a Popular Mandate." *The Full Brexit*, September 3, 2019. https://www.thefullbrexit.com/parliamentary-sovereignty. Accessed 22 May 2021.
Tucker, Robert C. (ed.). 1978. *The Marx-Engels Reader*. New York: Norton.
UK in a Changing Europe. 2019. "Brexit and Public Opinion 2019." http://ukandeu.ac.uk/wp-content/uploads/2019/01/Public-Opinion-2019-report.pdf. Accessed May 9, 2021.
UNESCO and its Programme. 1950. *The Race Question*. Paris: UNESCO.
United Nations. 2015. "Paris Agreement." https://unfccc.int/sites/default/files/english_paris_agreement.pdf. Accessed June 15, 2021.
United Nations. n.d. "United Nations Millennium Declaration." https://www.ohchr.org/EN/ProfessionalInterest/Pages/Millennium.aspx. Accessed June 21, 2021.
United Nations Environment Programme. n.d. "10 Things You Should Know About Industrial Farming." https://www.unep.org/news-and-stories/story/10-things-you-should-know-about-industrial-farming. Accessed June 20, 2021.
van Haaften-Schick, Lauren. 2012. "Canceled: Alternative Manifestations & Productive Failures." *Introduction to Exhibition Catalogue*. https://www.laurenvhs.com/writing-publications/canceled-alternative-manifestations-productive-failures-exhibition-catalogue-introduction/. Accessed July 14, 2021.
Viereck, Peter. 1964 [1955]. "The Revolt Against the Elite." In *The Radical Right*, edited by Daniel Bell. Garden City, NY: Doubleday, pp. 161–183.
Virdee, Satnam, and Brendan McGeever. 2018. "Racism, Crisis, Brexit." *Ethnic and Racial Studies* 41, no. 10 (2018): 1802–1819.
Waldenburg, Marek. 1980. *Il papa rosso: Karl Kautsky*. Translated by Maria Di Salvo. Rome: Editori Riuniti.
Wald Sussman, Robert. 2014. *The Myth of Race*. Cambridge: Harvard University Press.
Walzer, Michael. 2020. "A Note on Racial Capitalism." *Dissent Magazine*, July 29, 2020. https://www.dissentmagazine.org/online_articles/a-note-on-racial-capitalism. Accessed July 12, 2021.
Watts, Jonathan. 2020. "Climate Crisis: In Coronavirus Lockdown, Nature Bounces Back – But For How Long?" *The Guardian*, April 9, 2020. https://www.theguardian.com/world/2020/apr/09/climate-crisis-amid-coronavirus-lockdown-nature-bounces-back-but-for-how-long. Accessed June 14, 2021.
Weber, Max. 2004. "Science as a Vocation." In *The Vocation Lectures*, edited by David Owen and Tracy B. Strong and translated by R. Livingstone. Indianapolis/Cambridge: Hackett, pp. 1–31.
Whyte, M. K., F. Wang, and C. Yong. 2015. "Challenging Myths About China's One-Child Policy." *The China Journal* 74 (July): 144–159.
Williams, Austin. 2001. "Zen and the Art of Life-Cycle Maintenance." In *Sustaining Architecture in the Anti-Machine Age*, edited by Ian Abley and James Heartfield. Chichester: Wiley-Academy, pp. 42–52.
Williams, Austin. 2008. *The Enemies of Progress: The Dangers of Sustainability*. Exeter: Societas-Imprint Academic.

Williams, Austin. 2021. *Greens: the New Neo-Colonialists* (*Letters on Liberty*). London: Institute of Ideas.
Williams, Eric. [1944] 1994. *Capitalism and Slavery.* Chapel Hill: University of North Carolina Press.
Wood, Ellen Meiksins. 2002 [1999]. *The Origin of Capitalism: A Longer View.* London and New York: Verso.
Wood, Ellen Meiksins. 2008. "Historical Materialism in 'Forms Which Precede Capitalist Production'." In *Karl Marx's Grundrisse: Foundations of the Critique of Political Economy 150 Years Later*, edited by Marcello Musto. London: Routledge, pp. 79–92.
World Bank. 2019. "Charting a New Course." *Malawi Economic Monitor.* https://openknowledge.worldbank.org/handle/10986/31929. Accessed February 5, 2021.
World Bank. n.d. "Understanding Poverty." www.worldbank.org/en/topic/natural-capital#1. Accessed June 20, 2021.
Wright, Mark. 2019. "The Last Elephant in the Room: Human Population and the Sixth Mass Extinction." *Population Matters.* YouTube Video. https://www.youtube.com/watch?v=uzeEWfVBaro. Accessed June 10, 2021.
Young, Robert. 1999. "'Dangerous and Wrong': Shell, Intervention and the Politics of Transnational Companies." *Interventions* 1, no. 3 (1999): 439–464.
Young, Robert. 2012. "Postcolonial Remains." *New Literary History* 43, no. 1 (Winter): 19–42.
Žižek, Slavoj. 1993. *Tarrying With the Negative: Kant, Hegel, and the Critique of Ideology.* Durham: Duke University Press.
Žižek, Slavoj. 2008. *Violence.* New York: Picador.

Index

abolition: of class society, 121; of politics, xii; of wage labor, xiii; of the working class, 81
abstraction: as applied to worker experience, 207; as empiricist operation, 182, 183; performed by social reality, xx, xxi; from race, 177; required to identify the capital relation, xvii
abstract labour, 80, 175–76, 179, 183, 189
accounting, 76, 244
Adorno, Theodor W., 3, 6, 9, 59, 115–117, 124, 156
affirmation: of bourgeois society, xvi, xxv; of the proletariat, 76–77
Ahmed, Riz, 136
Ali, Tariq, 162
Althusser, Louis, xviii, 33, 182–83
Anthropocene, xx
anti-capitalism, 61, 73, 74, 162–63
anti-imperialism, 118, 120, 203, 238
antinomy: between form and content in art, 149; between the political and liberalism according to Schmitt, 115
anti-politics, xi, 129, 130, 136, 137, 142, 143
anti-racism, xviii, xix, 9–10

anti-Semitism, 7, 9–10, 15, 37, 141, 238, 246
anti-war movement, 161–62
Arendt, Hannah, 35
Aristotle, 190
Arnautoff, Victor, 123–24
Arruzza, Cinzia, 45
Attenborough, Sir David, 221
austerity, 60, 106, 109
authoritarianism, 118, 218, 246

Badiou, Alain, 185
Bakunin, Michail, 83
Baron Cohen, Sacha, 35
Bastiat, Frédéric, xxi–xxii
Bechdel Test, 132
Beckett, Samuel, 122, 124
Bell, Daniel, 10, 11
Benjamin, Walter, 117, 148, 149, 159, 163, 168
Bhabha, Homi, 201, 203–7, 214
Bhattacharya, Tithi, 45
Biden, Joseph, xxx, 69, 113, 114
Black, Hannah, 123, 124
Black Lives Matter, 123, 158
Bohrer, Ashley, xvii–xviii
Bolshevism: and democratic centralism, 124
book bloc, 59

bourgeois: democracy, xxvi–xxviii; political economy, xiv, xv; socialists, 107; worker's parties, 81
Bradbrook, Gail, 229
Brecht, Bertolt, 143
Brexit, 97–113, 130, 230
Brody, Richard, 142
Buck-Morss, Susan, 151
Butler, Judith, 33, 44, 139

Cambodia: killing fields in, 246
cancel culture, 65, 115
carbon credits, 224, 233
carbon tax, 226, 227
Carlyle, Thomas, 74
Catholic Church, 57
Césaire, Aimé, 191, 192
Charlie Hebdo, 120
civil society, 46, 47, 115, 119, 230
class, xii–xxxv, 3–25, 44–47, 49–52, 55, 56, 61–62, 64–67, 69, 75, 80, 82, 92n37, 99, 101, 110, 116, 126n18, 130–31, 138, 140, 160, 175, 202, 205–7, 230, 232, 239–42; capitalist, the, 81, 84, 245; composition/decomposition, 73–75, 86; educated middle, the, xi. *See also* Professional Managerial Class (PMC) professional middle, the, xiii, 134.; (PMC) sex-based, 44, 48, 53–54; struggle, 76, 82–84, 86, 89, 181, 207, 214, 239; working, the, xxvii, 3, 5–6, 45, 50–51, 54–56, 62–63, 66, 77, 80–81, 84–87, 97, 101–2, 105, 108, 110, 205, 217–18, 227
climate change, xi, 219, 224, 230, 248; emergency, 229; strike, 219, 232
Club of Rome: influence on PRC one child policy of, 222
CO_2 Law: opposition in Switzerland to, 239
Cohn-Bendit, Daniel, 237
Cold War: consensus in sociology, 10; period in articulation of class relation, 83

Combahee River Collective, xxii–xxv, 46
Comintern: Seventh Congress of, xxiv
Common Core: and climate change, 219
common good, 241–42
communism: acid, 64, 65, 67; as non-Marxist concept, 73–95, 246; removal from post-war US sociology, 11
communization, 73–95
competition, xx, 179, 185
concrete, the: against the abstract, xxi; forms of power, xiv
Confederation of British Industry, the, 232
conformist rebellion, xiii, xxv, xxvi, 74, 97, 105, 107
Conservative Party, 101, 103, 107
consumerism, 61, 99, 155, 205–6
Corbyn, Jeremy, 60, 61, 65, 68, 106
Corona, 68, 69, 71, 225, 227
corporate ethics: in postcolonial theory, 209, 214
COVID-19, xi, xxix, 66, 69, 70, 98, 104, 108, 109, 114, 223, 228, 229
Cox, Oliver Cromwell, 16
Crenshaw, Kimberlé Williams, xxii
Cuban revolution, 202
cultural studies, 38, 133
culture war, 45, 56, 97, 100, 102, 105, 108, 109, 129–32, 143, 204
Cutrone, Christopher, 159

debt foreclosure, 178
decisionism, 117
decolonization, 84, 202, 213–14
Deleuze, Gilles, 39, 59, 61, 115
democracy: absence in Brexit Party, 102; as characterised by inclusion in postcolonial theory, 210; crisis of, 102; illiberal form of, 114; Marxist critique of, xxvi–xxviii; neoliberal limitation of, 66; suspension of in Green transition, 232
Democratic Party, 161
Dempsey, Eddie, 98
Dershowitz, Alan, 113

Descartes, René, 32, 190–91
dialectic, 48, 64, 67, 74, 77, 114, 115, 122, 124, 130, 138, 139, 153, 160, 163, 167, 181, 185; between master and slave, 7, 121, 241–42; as thought-praxis, xxvi
dictatorship, 73–95, 113–29, 208
discrimination, xiii, xiv, xxiv, 3–25, 29, 52
diversity, xiv, xviii, 13, 133–36, 141, 143
domination, xi, xii, xiii, xiv, xv, xxii, xxiv, xxvii, 16, 46, 57, 75, 79, 135, 189
Dubois, W.E.B, 12, 180, 193

Eastern Bloc, 118
ecocide, 225
economy, the, xiv, xvi, xix, xxx, 13, 34, 54, 70, 106, 114, 130, 154, 155, 177–81, 184–86, 192, 193, 217, 220, 226, 228, 231–33, 245, 247
Elba, Idris, 134
Elsässer, Jürgen, 238
emancipation, xii, xvi, xxv, xxviii, 6, 46, 47, 49–51, 56–58, 74, 75, 80, 87, 88, 122, 148, 156, 164, 240, 241, 244
emergency powers, 115, 117, 225, 229
empiricism, xxv, 182–84, 191, 193, 212
Endnotes, 75
Engels, Friedrich, xxvi, 39, 48, 78, 110, 114, 180, 181, 184, 217, 218, 240–42, 244, 248
Enlightenment, the, xxviii, 7, 32, 82, 114–17, 122, 149, 220, 223
environmentalism, 218, 219, 222, 227, 228, 231, 232
Epictetus, 36
equality, xv, xviii, xxvii, xxviii, 20, 26, 46–47, 50, 54, 58, 118, 131, 136, 143, 154, 175, 176, 191
eschatology: of leftist thought, 237
estates: Habsburg, 63; in precapitalist society, 56
ethical turn, in postcolonial theory, 201–17
eugenics, 221–22

Eurocentrism, xxi, 117, 120, 181
European Union, 97, 228
Eurozone, 60
exchange value, xxvi, 82, 88, 89, 156, 175, 176, 179, 188
exploitation, xii, xiv, xv, xvii, xviii, xix, xxi, xxii, xxiii, xxiv, xxvii, xxviii, xxx, 21, 44, 46, 48–51, 53, 54, 56, 57, 176, 177, 179–81, 201, 203, 204, 207, 219, 237, 239, 240, 243, 248, 249
expropriation of the expropriators, 244
Extinction Rebellion (XR), 229–31

family, 30, 39, 45, 48, 50, 119, 165, 179, 220
Fanon, Frantz, 119, 203–4
fascism, xiii, xxiv, xxvi, 12, 27, 105, 106, 110, 115, 164
Federici, Silvia, 45
feminism, xvii, xxii, 43–59, 159
fetishism: of the commodity, xiv, xvii, 155, 183, 191; of the "outside" to capital, 246, 248; of use value, xx–xxii
feudalism, 58, 155, 218, 219
Fischer, Ernst, 153
Fisher, Mark, 59–71
Ford, Henry: on history, 138
Fordism, 45, 62, 63
form determination, xii, xxi, 179
Foucault, Michel, 35, 115, 133, 135, 140, 203
Frankfurt School, xx, 3–11, 205
freedom, xv, xxvi, xxviii, xxix, 47, 57–58, 62, 75, 80, 82, 109, 120, 130, 131, 143, 152, 154–56, 159, 160, 163, 167, 209, 213, 227, 229, 239, 241, 245, 246
French Revolution, 35, 117, 211, 220, 241
Freud, Sigmund, 32, 36–38, 71, 115, 122, 248
Fromm, Erich, 11, 15
frugality, 231
Fukuyama, Francis, 90, 130, 142

Full Brexit, the, 97–98

Gandhi, Leela, 201, 210–13
Gandhi, Mahatma, 210–11
Gates, Bill, 232
gender, xiii, xiv, xxii, xxiii, 43–58, 62, 63, 116, 132, 133, 141, 142, 149, 177, 202, 203, 207
Gilets Jaunes, 226–28
globalization, 65, 66, 68, 99, 213
Gorleben: anti-nuclear protests in, 239
Gramsci, Antonio, 61, 116, 201, 205
grand narratives, 30
Greenberg, Clement, 151, 157
Green Party, the, 225, 226
Greimas, Algirdas Julien, 245
Grundgesetz (of the Federal Republic of Germany), 237
Grundrisse, the, 180, 183, 184
G20, 2017 protests at, 247
Guénon, René, 88

Haider, Asad, xviii–xix, 64
Hall, Stuart, 133, 135
Hallam, Roger, 229
Haraway, Donna, 70
harm: according to J.S.Mill, 120; to cultural subjects, 131, 140
Harvey, David, 224, 225
Heartfield, James, 66, 98
Hegel, G.W.F, xxvi, 7, 26, 117, 119, 121, 122, 130, 138, 139, 184–85, 231, 241–43
Heidegger, Martin, 68, 203
heteronomity, xvii
heteronormativity, 29
heterosexuality, xxi, xxiii, 38, 39
historical materialism, 180–81
Hizbullah, 246
Hofstadter, Richard, 11
homosexuality, 38, 39, 203, 212
Horkheimer, Max, 3–6, 122, 160
Horrendous Hackney Road Closures, 229
Houellebecq, Michel, 69
Hrdlicka, Alfred, 27

humanism, 63
human rights, 47, 104, 191–92, 204, 208, 228
Huntington, Samuel P., 120, 209
Husserl, Edmund, 139

idealism, xviii, xxi, 44, 48–49, 181, 185, 192, 238, 244
ideology, xii, xiii, xviii–xix, 10, 13, 16, 30–37, 130, 160, 175, 177, 179, 184, 188–90, 192, 193, 205, 238, 240, 245, 249
idiots: in ancient Greece and in postmodernity, 35
Iglesias, Pablo, 61
immediacy, xxvi, 76, 85, 208
indeterminacy, 30–39, 151, 159
Indignados, 60, 64
individualism, 12, 21
industrial farming, 225
Industrial Revolution, 154, 217–18, 220
integration: of Europe, 98, 100; of the workers movement, xi, 5–6, 63, 75, 85
International Monetary Fund (IMF), 224
intersectionality, xvi, xvii, xxii–xxv, 46
Irigaray, Luce, 53
Irish Republican Army (IRA), 246
Islamism: left support for, 120, 162, 209–10, 246

Jacobinism, xv, 58, 191–92
James, C.L.R, 180, 191–92
James, Selma, 45
James, William, 212
Jameson, Frederic, 130
Johnson, Boris, 102–3, 106, 109, 231
Jones, Lee, 109

Kant, Immanuel, 139, 184
Kautsky, Karl, 4
Kazan, Elia, 15–21
Keita, Soundiata, 191
Kelley, Robin, xvii
Kendi, Ibram X., xxxi
Kierkegaard, Søren, 117

Kofi Bright, Liam, xvii
Kołakowski, Leszek, 153

Labor: abstract, xvii, 79–80, 175–76, 179, 183, 189, 194n7; African, 186; aristocracy, 4; human, xvi–xvii, 175, 184, 242; power, xvi, 45, 50–52, 54, 77, 83, 92n37, 175–78, 184–87, 192–93, 194n7, 242–43; reproductive, 44, 54; unpaid, xx, 176–77, 194; of women. *See* women, labor
Labour Party, 60, 103, 107–8
Landau Test, 132
language, 121, 131, 133; codes, 65; dehumanizing, 53; gender-inclusive, 52
Latin American Student Association, 158
Latour, Bruno, 219–20
left: academic, xii, 43, 59; activist, xii–xiii, 60, 107; identitarian, xxvii, 116, 135; millennial, xxviii, 59–71, 161; monstruous, 117–18; romantic, 61, 73, 238, 246
Lenin, Vladimir Ilich, xxvii, 4, 114, 124, 160, 244
Lexit, 105–7
LGBT, 57, 126n24
liberal: democracy, 104, 114–15, 118; economy, 247
liberalism, xxvi, 150, 202; left, 97–127; lockdown, 70
liberation, xxvi–xxviii, xxix, 5, 56, 78, 80, 87, 154; national, xxvii, xxxivn57, 45, 74; struggles, xxvii, 5, 119
literary psychology, 10
Liu, Catherine, 137
lived experience, xi, 45, 139, 177, 181, 207
lockdown, 69–70, 104, 108–9, 223, 226–28
logic, xiv, xxvi, 115, 117, 121, 130, 137–39, 149, 151, 184–88, 248; identitarian, 213; internal, 240;

of market expansion, 56; materialist, 180; structural, 185
Lumpenproletariat, 4–5
Luxemburg, Rosa, 46, 51

Macron, Emanuel, 226–27
Malthusianism, 220–26, 231–33
manifesto: Black Feminist Statement, xxii; Communist, 218, 241–42, 248; *Gilets Jaunes*, 227–28
Marcuse, Herbert, 5–6, 59, 61, 115, 118, 161
marginality, 12–14, 65
marginalization, 14, 188; representational, 44, 47
market, xxi, xxvi, 31, 51, 56, 61, 66–69, 156, 177–78, 184, 202, 243; commodity, xxxiin17, 186–87; dependency, xxii, 188, 193; economy, 130; participation, xv
Marshall Plan, 118, 219
Marx, Karl, 110, 114, 121, 140, 176–77, 183–85
Marxism, 51, 74–75, 79, 176, 201–2, 241–42; black, 179–82
Marxism-feminism, xxii, 43, 45–46, 51
Marxist: analysis, 74, 179, 181, 192, 205; culture, 62; democracy, 66, 102; mass, 163; theory, xxi, xxv, 201; thought, xx, 155, 157; tradition, xi, 73–74, 80, 214, 244
material: interests, 48–49, 105; power, 140; profitability, 189
materialism, 198n66; empiricist, 190; historical, 180–81; Spinozist, 183; vulgar, 190
materialist analysis, xviii, 47, 54, 192
May Day, 27, 124
means of subsistence, xiv, 177
mechanism of capitalist society, xvi, 132, 192
mediation, xxi, 70, 74–76, 85–86, 240; social, xiv, xxv
medieval (middle) ages, 32, 114, 189–90, 218
Meiksins Wood, Ellen, 46, 195n23

member-state theory, 98–101, 109
metanarrative. *See* narratives
method, xxi, 16, 180, 184, 190; dialectical, 149; empiricist, 183; historical, 195n23; of intersubjectivity, 139; of production, 218, 244
methodology, xv; materialist, 182; of postmodern theory, 133
microaggression, xiv, xxxin12, 35
middle class, xi–xiii, xviii, 7–8, 13–14, 45, 66, 70, 248. *See also* Professional Managerial Class (PMC)
militancy, 60, 62, 67, 191, 238, 247
Minima Moralia, 156, 160
minority (groups), 5–6, 38, 105, 131, 136, 140
misanthropy, xxix, 218, 220–22, 229–31
mobilization, 66, 69, 161, 166, 229–31; social, 201
modernism, 62, 159
modernity, 40n9, 73–74, 90n4, 98, 120, 156, 165, 168, 218–19
monetary: dimension of the law of value, xiv, 176; form of social mediation, xxv; theory of value, 176, 193n4, 196n28, 197n44
money, xiv, xx–xxii, 9, 155, 176–78, 183, 187, 229, 242–43
monopoly, 78, 105, 204, 242
Moore, Jason, xx–xxi
moralism, xiii, xiv, xxi, 51, 65, 99, 101, 120–22, 141, 189, 220, 237, 240
movement: social, 57, 158, 202, 230; student, xiii, 5–60, 115; worker's, xi–xii, 63, 75–81, 84–90, 207
multiculturalism, 150, 153, 169n3
muqarnas, 164–67
Muslim Student Association, 158
Muslim workers, 27
mystification, xiv, xix, 47, 184; bourgeois, xv–xvii; of the wage relation, xvii, xxv

mythology, 245–46

narcissism, 35–40, 107
narratives, 28, 120–21, 132–33, 136, 190, 201, 218–19; grand, 30, 32; social, 138
nation, xii, xvi, 62, 97–102, 110
nationalism, xxiii, 101, 213–14, 247
national liberation, xxvii, xxxivn57, 45, 74
naturalization, xvii, xxv, 140; essentialist, 44; of gender, 55; of labor, xx, 45; of the wage relation, xviii
nature, xx, 139, 157, 217–35, 237; nature as essence. *See* naturalization, essentialist subordination of, xxi
Nazism, 7, 27, 108, 115, 167, 203
negation, 77, 89–91, 138, 148, 150, 159
Negritude, 191
neoclassical: economy, 176, 178; marginalism, xvii
neo-feudalism, 219
neo-leftism, 61
neoliberal: class warfare, 227; counterculture, 60, 64; counterrevolution, 62; governance, 99; ideology, xii, xiii, 34, 58, 130; order, xi–xiii, 62, 67, 116, 137, 142; pseudo-policies, 25; restructuring, 84; state, 62, 66, 71; turn, 62–66
neoliberalism, xv, 28, 56, 62–64, 68–69
neoracialism, xx–xxii, xxiv
New Left, the, xiii, 59–71, 151, 168; activism, 157
nihilism, xxvi, 82, 112n41
normalization, 13, 30, 132, 222
normativity, gendered, 29, 44
North Atlantic Treaty Organization (NATO), 228
nuclear power, 239

objectivity, social, xix
Occupy, 60, 64, 67, 161, 168, 230
October Revolution. *See* Revolution

Old Left, 59–71, 168
Old White Men, 136, 142, 150
On Liberty, 120
opportunism, 62, 153, 166
opposition, 62, 82, 152, 207
oppressed, 140
oppression, xv, xxvi–xxviii, 37, 67, 129, 213; class, xxiii, 207; feudal, 218; horizontal, xiv; material, 44, 47; personal, xv, 176; racial, xviii, xxiii–xxiv, 207; of women, 44, 50–52, 54
oppressor, xv, xxiii, 178, 206, 222, 240
order: capitalist, xiii, xxiv, 63; neoliberal. *See* neoliberal, order
orientalism, 120, 210
Origins of the Family, 39, 48
outside to capital, 82, 237–49
outsourcing of household tasks, 45–46
overcoming: of bourgeois society, xvi, xxx, 77; of capitalism, xviii, 57, 64, 74, 79, 82, 152, 245

Palestine, 68, 158, 209–210
Palestine Liberation Organization (PLO), 246
pandemic, xxix, 108, 114, 221, 223, 225
Paris Commune, 192
participation, xv, 34, 46, 99, 102
particularities, historical, 86
party, 85, 88, 98, 101; communist, 64, 78, 161, 207, 222; democratic, 151; Green, 225–26; Labour. *See* Labour Party mass, 66
patriarchy, xiv, 46–52, 54, 140, 211
People of Color, 140, 158, 179
perception, 150–51, 168
personal: domination, xiii, xv, xxvii, 46, 56–57; freedom, 57; oppression, xv, 176
petty bourgeoisie, xxvi–xxviii, 108–9, 240, 243
phenomenology, 139
Phenomenology of Spirit, the, 241

philosophy, 241; bourgeois, 114; materialist, 32, 240; political, xi, 119; Soviet, 244
Philosophy of Right, 119
Plato, 43, 59, 147
Platypus Affiliated Society, the, 159–62, 164
The Platypus Review, 64, 162, 165
police, xxvii, xxix, 59, 227, 247
political: antagonism, xiii; autonomy, 85; categories, 26, 131; class, 99, 101, 104, 129–30, 227; correctness, xxiii, 118, 142, 238; discourse, 130; economy, xiv, xvi–xvii, xix, 13, 114, 155, 179–81, 184–86, 192–93, 245; framework, 81; question, 203
politics: of emancipation, 103, 153, 161, 168, 240, 245, 247, 249; of friendship, 212; identity, xiii, xxii–xxiii, xxv, 12, 26, 28, 46–52, 56, 130, 134, 138, 141–42, 148, 161, 204; of recognition, 44, 116, 119–21, 204; of resentment, 51
popular sovereignty, 97–112
populism, 74; authoritarian, 116; left-wing, 60–68, 70; right-wing, 11
positivism, xiv, xxv, 184
postcolonialism, 119, 132, 201–15
postmodernism, 25–37
Postone, Moishe, 91n11, 159
post-politics, xi, 130–33, 137–38, 143
post-sexual, 37–38
poststructuralism, 202, 214
postwar period, 10, 18, 69, 84, 104, 118, 151, 157
poverty, xi, 5, 163, 205, 224, 233
power: imperial, xx, 125n6; impersonal, xiv; relations, 132, 135; structures, 52, 132, 136, 140
precapitalist: class society, 56; modes of production, 195n23, 246; social form, 178
prejudice, xix, 14
price, xvi, xxi, 176, 194n5, 243

primitive: accumulation, xxii, 178, 181, 183, 218; immediacy, xxvi
privatization of public sphere, 34
privilege, 30, 44, 47, 50, 143
privileged, the, 19, 38, 204
production: of art, 131, 148, 157; material, 131, 176; mode of, 80–81, 85–87, 155, 189–90, 243–44, 246; process, 55, 84–85, 88, 176–77; of relative surplus value, 45, 50, 86; social, xii, xvii
productive forces, 75, 78, 84, 88
Professional Managerial Class (PMC), the, 130, 135, 137
profit, 52, 176–77; margins, xviii; source of, xvi–xvii
programmatism, 75–80, 85–86
progressivism, xiii, 56
project: class, 56, 81; European, the, 99; socialist, the, xxiii; state, xii, 82–83, 86, 89, 92n36
proletarian: action, 87; culture, 63; identity, 116; politics, 77, 80–81, 85; revolution, the, 77, 88, 240; state, the, 83–84, 88–89, 92n34; thought, 160
proletariat, the, xxiv, 3–11, 51, 63, 76–77, 80–88, 91n10, 116, 205, 242, 244–46, 248
public: debt, 60; sphere, the, 120–21; transportation, 227

quantification, 76, 86–89
quantified time: as money, xx
queer theory, xiii, 47, 53
quietism, 76, 89–90
Qur'an, 167

racial: capitalism, xvii–xix, xxii, 175–95; imaginary, 190–93; inequality, 158; paternalism, xxiii; segregation. *See* segregation, racial unity, 13
racialism, xix, 188–90, 192. *See also* neoracialism
racism, xix, 8–9, 16, 101, 105, 110, 119, 140–41, 189; postmodern, 35

radical Islam, 209
radicalism, xvii, 180
radicals, xiv, 61
RAF. *See* Red Army Fraction
rationalism, 117, 120
rationality, 32; capitalist, xx
reactionary, xxvii, 5, 246; anti-capitalism, 73–74; ideology, 247, 249
Reading Capital, 182, 196n30
real: abstraction, xx–xxi, 182; contradiction, xix, xxvii, 138; subsumption, 46, 78–79
realignment, political, 108
realism, capitalist, xii, 59–61, 66, 68
reality, xxvi, 150–51, 159, 168; material, xix, 135; social, xx, xxiv, 22n14, 46
realization of communism, 74
reason, xxviii, 9, 138, 220
rebellion, xiii, xxv, 74, 97, 105, 227, 229, 231, 237. *See also* conformist rebellion
recognition, 26, 44, 48, 116, 118–22, 204, 206
Red Army Fraction (RAF), 238, 247
redistribution, xviii, 6, 44, 102, 118, 120–21, 135, 204
reductionism: class, xvi–xx, 50; race, 9
Reformation, the, 58
reformism, 214, 238, 244
regression, xviii, 88–89; as liberation, 82
reification, 155, 159, 224; transactivist, 44
relations: capitalist, xii–xiv, xvii, xxiv, 51–52, 80–81, 88, 176, 243–44, 246–47; of exploitation, xviii, xxiv, 49–50, 218, 225; material, xix, 48; of oppression, xviii; of production, xi, xiv, xxiv, xxvii, 54, 80–81, 88–89, 177, 194, 240–41, 243–46; social, xii, xiv, xvii, xxi, 49, 80, 131, 133, 143, 175–78, 218
religion, 7, 31, 133; of identity, 25, 27, 167

rent, 176, 185
representation, 120, 123, 129–45, 150; cultural, 118, 129–45; empiricist, 183
repression, xxvii
reproduction: of capital, xviii, 74–75, 81; of life, 48; social. *See* social, reproduction of the wage relation, xiv
Republican Party, 69, 114, 162
resentment, xvii, 11, 51, 248
resistance, 204–5, 207, 209; worker, xv
restriction of rights, xxx
revenue, xvi–xvii, 239
revolution, xxx, 4–6, 76, 79–81, 85, 89, 117, 237–45; agricultural, 49; Bourgeois, 58, 88; Copernican, 185; Cuban, 202; French. *See* French Revolution Haitian, 191; Industrial. *See* Industrial Revolution October, 75, 83–84, 86, 115, 212; proletarian, 77, 88, 240; Socialist, xxiii, 63; world. *See* world, revolution
revolutionary: force, 4–5; leaders, 240, 245; potential, 5–6, 11; situation, 246, 249; vision of emancipation, 6
revolutionism, 160, 239, 245–48
Ricardians, 187
Ricardo, David, xvi, xvii, 185
Rights, xxx, 34n58, 47, 51, 56, 58, 160, 191, 225, 233, 237, 247; civil, xxiii, 247; democratic, xxx, 47, 58; human, xxviii, 47, 104, 191–92, 208, 228; workers', 107, 112n40, 118
Riz Test, 132

safe spaces, xxv, 54
Said, Edward, 209
sanction, 54, 62, 228
Schmidt, Alfred, xx
The Science of Logic, 184
scientific (proletarian) consciousness, 81, 85–86
Second World War. *See* World, War II
sectarianism, 60, 161
secularity, 60, 150, 165, 169n3, 180, 218

segregation, racial, xiv, 16
self-care, xxiii
self-censorship, xxv, 147
self-determination, xxvii–xxviii, 69, 133, 140, 212, 226
self-identification, 32, 45, 55, 57, 131
self-objectification, 149, 159
self-organization, 76, 85–86
semifeudal, xxvii, xxxvn62
sensitivity, xiv, 25, 108, 120
sex industry, 45
sexism, xiii–xix, xxiii, xxvi, 140, 143, 247
sexual: division of labor, 44; identity, 25, 37, 39; orientation, 38; preference, 44; violence, 119
sexuality, 29, 35, 39, 57, 122, 133, 203, 207
silencing, xiii
singularity, 192–93, 206–9, 213
slave, xv, xx, 123, 179, 192; economy, xxxv; labor, 176–77; market, 176, 186; morality, 121; states, xxvii
slaveowner, 177, 179, 186, 195n11
slavery, 186–88, 193; Atlantic, 180, 191; chattel, xxvii
Smith, Adam, xvi–xvii, 110, 183–85, 247
social: consciousness, xi–xii, 51, 85; construct, xix, 17, 43–51, 143; emancipation, xii, xxv–xxvi, 156, 165; forces, xii, 77, 99, 129; injustice, xiv, 29; reproduction, xvii, 44, 54, 240–41; transformation, 49, 147, 165, 201, 212, 214
socialism, 5, 70, 160, 184, 204; utopian, 223
socialization of labor, xxv, xxvi, 82
Social Justice Warrior (SJW), 143
Social Reproduction Theory, xvii
society: bourgeois, xi, xv–xvi, xxvi, 47, 77; class, xiv–xv, 49–50, 116, 179; feudal, xiv, 88; modern, xiv, 57; precapitalist, 237; traditional, 46

solidarity, xvi, xxii–xxv, 4, 30, 65, 124, 162, 222, 227–28; negative, xxiii, xxxiiin43
sovereignty, 66, 69, 116–17; popular, 97–112
Soviet: Bloc, the, 118; experiment, the, 240; philosophers, 244; Union, the, 78, 88, 118, 127n38
Spartacist League, the, 161
Spinoza, Baruch, 33, 182, 190–91
Spivak, Gayatri Chakravorty, 201–14
stagnation, xi, xiii, xxviii, 62, 89, 232
Stalin, Josef, 63, 91n34, 92n43
Stalinism, xxv, 64–65, 88, 156
state, 28, 56, 62, 66, 69, 81, 89, 98–101, 106; capitalism, 61, 91n34; citizenship, 119; proletarian. *See* proletarian, state; neoliberal, state
state of emergency, xiii, 108, 117
status quo, xiii, 68, 97, 100, 105–7, 116, 136, 140, 160, 164
stay-at-home-order, 108
"Stay Home, Save Lives", 228
stereotype, 136, 141, 209; gender, 45; racist, 9, 140
structural inequality, 133, 178, 204, 214
struggles: for identity, 26, 30; proletarian, 81, 84, 116
student movement, xiii, 5–60, 115
subaltern, the, 201, 206–7, 213. *See also* Spivak, Gayatri Chakravorty
subject, 33–34, 69, 76, 138; cultural, 131; female, 53; historical, 230; neoliberal, 55; political, 101–2, 131; postmodern, 33; revolutionary, 5, 238–39, 241–44, 246, 248; universal, 149
subjectivity, 48, 159–60, 164; class, 75, 85; human, 133; political, 80, 89
subject-object-relation, xxi, 131, 149, 160, 182
subsumption, 76–85, 88; formal, 86, 91n18; real. *See* real, subsumption
suffrage, xxxivn56, 63, 230

supremacy: impersonal capitalist, xiv; moral, xxi
surplus value, xix, 56, 175–79, 181, 185–86, 188–89, 192–93, 239, 242; relative, 45, 86
syndicalism, 79

tautology, xix, 43, 179
Tea Party, 114
technocracy, xiii, 109, 130, 137
Théorie Communiste, 75–93
theory, xviii, 77; Cold War, 3–24; critical, xxi, xxv, 151, 159, 169, 202–3, 249; cultural, 130–31, 133, 139–43; gender, 39; intersectional, xii–xiii, xvi–xvii, xxii–xxv, 46; leftist, xiii, 202; postcolonial, 132, 201–15; of representation, 131, 133, 135
Theses on Feuerbach, 190, 198n66
third wave feminism, 159
Third Way, the, 60, 130, 141
Third-Worldism, 202
thought-concrete (*Gedankenkonkretum*), 182–83, 185
tolerance, 13–14, 35, 39, 209; postmodern, 35
Tory, 11, 99, 101, 109; Brexit, 106–7
totality, xi–xii, xiv, 119, 160, 185; of capital, 156; social, xxv–xxvi, 74, 76, 80, 82, 87–88, 175
toxic masculinity, 45, 48
trade union, 66, 92n37, 107
trans activism, 44, 47, 53
transgender ideology, 43, 52–54
transhistoricity, xiv, 159, 183, 187, 195n23
transnational policy networks, 99
transphobia, xi, xiii
trigger warning, 140–42
Trinity Formula: of bourgeois economy, xvi–xx, 183; leftist of race, class and gender, xv, xix, xxv–xxvi
Trump, Donald, 113–14, 130
Trumpism, 114, 116

Twitter, 65, 129

unemployment, 3–4, 232
UNESCO, 16–17
unitary structure, xxiv
United Kingdom, 25, 60, 97–112
United Nations (UN), 51–52, 222–25, 228, 232–33
United States, xviii, xxvii, 25, 57, 60, 113, 158, 161
universal: community, xxvi; emancipation, xvi, 51, 75; exchange, xxv–xxvi, 176; freedom, 75; health care, 65
universalism, 30, 191
universality, xviii, 119, 148, 218; of the individual, 56
urbanization, 220, 224
use value, xxxiin28, 69, 175–76, 188, 194n8, 199n70, 239, 242–43: fetishism, xx–xxii
use-values (*Gebrauchswerte*), 188, 195n19
utopia, 148, 153; capital's, xiii
utopianism, bourgeois, 243

valorization, 47, 79, 84, 188; capitalist, xiii, 56; reactionary, 44, 48
value, 176–78, 242–43; critique of, xvi–xvii, 176, 194n8, 239–40, 242, 246; exchange, xxvi, xxxivn50, xxxv63, 74, 82, 88–89, 156, 175–79, 181, 194n8, 199n70; of labor, 45, 187; law of, xiv, 56; measure of, 187, 242; monetary, xx, 176; relation, 77, 80, 82, 243–44
value-form, xvii, xxii, 176–79, 184, 192, 198n66, 240, 242
vanguard, political, 152
victimhood, 121
victims: of oppression, xv, 140; of racism, 8, 140
violence, 10, 50, 120, 140, 178, 192–93, 247; domestic, 47; police, xxvii, 247; sexual. *See* sexual, violence

virtualization, 50
Virtue Hoarders, 137
void, socio-political, 66–67, 69, 97, 101–2, 108–10
vulgar economists, xvii, xxi, 194n9
vulnerable, the, 35, 99, 158

wage, the, xv, xx, 176–78, 192, 205; dependency, xx–xxi, 80, 92n37; as a form of value, xiv, xvii, xxii, 176–79, 187, 194n8; labor, xii–xviii, xx–xxii, 74, 87, 91n10, 176–79, 187, 194n7; monetary, xv, xx, 177, 194n7; relation, *xiv–xviii*, xxi, xxv, 85–86, 177, 194; slavery, xxxiiin36, 48; struggles, 52, 85, 201; worker, xxxvn63, 4, 81
War, 27, 69, 225–26; Cold, 10–18, 83, 120, 204; culture. *See* culture war: on Terror, 136. *See also* World, War I; World, War II
The Wealth of Nations, xvi–xvii, 183
welfare, 63, 64, 102, 211, 221
Weltgeist (World spirit), 138–39
West, the, 57, 63, 69, 204–5, 209–11, 224
Western society, 34
West Germany, 115
White: people, xxi, 16, 27, 55, 140, 158; privilege, 143
woke, 49, 54, 129–45
woman question, the, 51
women, xxi, xxiii, 44, 46, 50–58, 131–32, 140; labor, xx–xxi, 28, 49–51, 53–54, 178; as a separate social class, 46, 50–52, 54
worker, xi, xviii, xxvii, 4, 8, 45–46, 51–52, 61, 63, 86, 155, 223, 227; consciousness, 4–5, 51, 85; essential, xviii, 108; movement, xi–xii, 63, 75–81, 84–90, 207
workerism, xviii, 65, 85
work force, xiii, 51, 54, 232
world: revolution, 63, 75, 84, 89; social, 122; war I, 75, 81, 82, 86; war II, 108, 118, 202, 239; war III, 229

World Bank, 224, 233
World Economic Forum (WEF), 51
World Trade Organization (WTO), 160
World Wide Fund for Nature (WWF), 220
The Wretched of the Earth, 119, 203

xenophobia, xix, 101, 105, 110

Yugoslavia, xxviii

Zetkin, Clara, 51–52
Zionism, 13

Author Biographies

Elena Louisa Lange is a philosopher and Senior Research Fellow and Lecturer at the University of Zurich. Her research on Marx's critique of political economy has been widely published. Her latest monograph is *Value without Fetish: Uno Kōzō's Theory of "Pure Capitalism" in Light of Marx's Critique of Political Economy* (2021).

Joshua Pickett-Depaolis is an independent researcher and an editor of the political theory journal *Counter Attack*. His interests include Marxist strategic thought and the Clausewitzian tradition of political realism.

Todd Cronan is associate professor of Modern Art at Emory University. He is the author of *Against Affective Formalism: Matisse, Bergson, Modernism* (2013) and *Red Aesthetics: Rodchenko, Brecht, Eisenstein* (2021). He is also the editor in chief of *nonsite.org*.

Robert Pfaller, philosopher, teaches at the University of Art and Industrial Design in Linz, Austria, and is a founding member of the Viennese psychoanalytic research group "stuzzicadenti." He is the author of award-winning books and publications.

Jane Clare Jones is a feminist philosopher and editor in chief of *The Radical Notion—A Feminist Quarterly*. She lives and teaches in the UK.

Anton Jäger is a postdoctoral researcher at the Universities of Cambridge and Brussels, working on the history of populism in the United States. Together with Daniel Zamora, he is currently working on an intellectual history of basic income for University of Chicago Press.

George Hoare is a researcher and writer based in London. He is on the steering group of *The Full Brexit* and is one of the hosts of the global politics podcast *Aufhebunga Bunga*. He is the coauthor of *The End of the End of History: Politics in the 21st Century* (2021).

Samir Gandesha is associate professor of Humanities at Simon Fraser University. He is the coeditor of works on Adorno and Critical Theory. His most recent work is *Spectre of Fascism: Historical, Theoretical and Contemporary Perspectives* (2020).

Maren Thom is a London-based writer and film expert. She is adjunct professor at the University of Southern California and teaches at the Centre for Education and Teaching Innovation, University of Westminster, UK. Her writings have appeared in magazines in the UK.

Haseeb Ahmed is an American research-based artist based in Brussels. His work has been exhibited, among others, at the Museum of Contemporary Art Chicago (United States), The Gothenburg International Biennial of Contemporary Art (Sweden), the Museum Barengasse Zurich (Switzerland), and De Appel in Amsterdam (The Netherlands). He is represented by Harlan Levey Projects in Brussels.

Nick Nesbitt is a professor of French Literature at Princeton University and senior researcher in philosophy at the Czech Academy of Sciences. Most recently, he is the author of *The Price of Slavery: Capitalism and Revolution in the Caribbean* (2021).

Nivedita Majumdar is associate professor of English at John Jay College, City University of New York, and is author of *The World in a Grain of Sand: Postcolonial Literature and Radical Universalism* (2021).

Austin Williams is the director of the Future Cities Project and author of *China's Urban Revolution: Understanding Chinese Eco-Cities* (2017).

Raji C. Steineck is professor of Japanese Studies at University of Zurich and visiting professor at the Research Institute for Time Studies in Yamaguchi, Japan. He is the author of *Kritik der symbolischen Formen* (*Critique of Symbolic Forms*, 2014 ff.) and senior editor of *Concepts of Philosophy in Asia and the Islamic World, Vol. 1: China and Japan* (2018).

www.ingramcontent.com/pod-product-compliance
Lightning Source LLC
Chambersburg PA
CBHW022009300426
44117CB00005B/100